DISPOSED OF
BY LIBRARY
HOUSE OF LORDS

STUDIES IN LABOUR AND SOCIAL LAW

GENERAL EDITORS

BOB HEPPLE

Master of Clare College, Cambridge; Visiting Professor of Law, University College London; Barrister of Gray's Inn; Advocate of the Supreme Court of South Africa

PAUL O'HIGGINS

Vice-Master, Christ's College, Cambridge; Member of the Royal Irish Academy; Emeritus Professor in the University of London at King's College; Honorary Professor of Law, Trinity College, Dublin; Visiting Professor of Law, City University, London; Barrister of the King's Inns and of Lincoln's Inn

Paul O'Higgins © Eaden Lilley Photography

Human Rights and Labour Law

Essays for Paul O'Higgins

Edited by
K.D. EWING, C.A. GEARTY
AND B.A. HEPPLE

MANSELL

First published 1994 by
Mansell Publishing Limited, *A Cassell imprint*
Villiers House, 41/47 Strand, London WC2N 5JE, England
387 Park Avenue South, New York, New York 10016-8810, USA

British Library Cataloguing in Publication Data
A catalogue record for this book is available from the British Library.
ISBN 0-7201-2148-5

Library of Congress Cataloging-in-Publication Data
Human rights and labour law: essays for Paul O'Higgins/edited by
K. D. Ewing, C. A. Gearty and B. A. Hepple.
p. cm. — (Studies in labour and social law)
'A Bibliography of the writings of Paul O'Higgins': p.
Includes index.
ISBN 0-7201-2148-5
1. Labor laws and legislation. 2. Freedom of association.
3. Human rights. 4. O'Higgins, Paul. I. O'Higgins, Paul.
II. Ewing. K. D. (Keith D.) III. Gearty, C. A. IV. Hepple, B. A.
V. Series.
K1705.6.H86 1994
342'.085—dc20
[342.285] 93-30797
CIP

Set in 11/12 pt Compugraphic Baskerville
by Colset Private Limited, Singapore
Printed and bound in Great Britain by
Biddles Ltd, Guildford and King's Lynn

CONTENTS

The Contributors

Brian Bercusson, Professor of European Social and Labour Law, European University Institute, Florence; Professor of Law (Elect), University of Manchester

Breen Creighton, Professor of Legal Studies, La Trobe University, Victoria, Australia

Patrick Elias, QC, Inner Temple, Barrister

Keith Ewing, Professor of Public Law, King's College, London

Michael Forde, Barrister; Lecturer in Law, University College, Dublin

Julian Fulbrook, Department of Law, London School of Economics

Conor Gearty, Reader in Law and Director of the Civil Liberties Research Unit, King's College, London

Bob Hepple, Master of Clare College, Cambridge

John McEldowney, Senior Lecturer in Law, University of Warwick

Sonia McKay, Labour Research Department

Gillian S. Morris, Professor of Law, Brunel University

Brian Napier, Digital Professor of Information Technology Law, Queen Mary and Westfield College, London

Martin Partington, Professor of Law, University of Bristol

Philippa Watson, Barrister, England and Wales, and Ireland

Introduction

This volume of essays is dedicated to our teacher and friend, Paul O'Higgins, who has retired from his Chair of Law at King's College London – but not from his active involvement in human rights and labour law.

Paul O'Higgins was born on 5 October 1927 and spent his early formative years in Ireland. He studied medicine for several years in Trinity College, Dublin, and then switched to law, graduating in 1957. He was called to the Irish Bar in the same year and two years later was called to the English Bar. His great concern with international human rights led him to the University of Cambridge, where, under the supervision of Professor (later Sir) Robert Jennings, he wrote a brilliant PhD thesis on the subject of political asylum. Although many of his early writings drew heavily on the thesis, it was never published, though it still repays careful reading in the Cambridge University library.

Paul was a research student at Clare College, where Bill (later Lord) Wedderburn was a Fellow. Unsurprisingly, in view of this influence and his own strong commitment to the labour and trade union movement, Paul became involved in a course entitled 'Industrial Law', which Bill Wedderburn persuaded a reluctant faculty to introduce in 1962. When Wedderburn left in 1964 to take up a chair at the London School of Economics, Paul took over the Industrial Law course, later renamed Labour Law despite the fears of those who thought this too subversive.

Paul had become a Fellow of Christ's College in 1959 and subsequently became a University Assistant Lecturer and later Lecturer. He was promoted to the first Readership in Labour Law in Cambridge's history in 1979. In addition to Labour Law, he taught Constitutional and Administrative Law, Civil Liberties and Public International Law. He was one of the first to recognize the importance of the academic study of social security law, surmounting the resistance of those distinguished professors who thought that old age pensions and Commissioners' Decisions should not be studied because they were not 'law'.

In 1984 Paul returned to Trinity College, Dublin, to the prestigious Regius Chair of Laws. While Cambridge was his adopted home, it was Ireland where his heart remained. Throughout the Cambridge years he had kept close connections in Dublin, in particular working on his mammoth bibliographies and on Irish legal history. His contributions to Irish legal scholarship were recognized by his LLD degree from Trinity (he also holds a Cambridge LLD) and his election to the Royal Irish Academy in 1986. Sadly, for health and personal reasons, he had to give up residence in Ireland in 1987. King's College London seized the opportunity to offer him a Chair, which he held for five years until retirement. He is currently Vice-Master of Christ's College.

Through his teaching Paul O'Higgins developed ideas that have made a major contribution to the future shape of the law. Topics we now take for granted, such as the international and European dimensions of labour law, were pioneered by him. His interest in and commitment to human rights and labour law are both unique and inspirational, as is his capacity to see the subjects in all of their aspects. One of the students auditing Paul's courses in 1964 was Bob Hepple, whose research on racial discrimination in employment was supervised by Paul. Hepple recalls that the reaction of other potential supervisors whom he approached was 'But there's no law on that!' However, Paul immediately and enthusiastically recognized that it was precisely because of the absence of legislation at the time that the subject was immensely important.

Like the many dozens of other research students who passed through Paul's hands, Hepple encountered a supervisor enthusiastic in his support and encouragement, bubbling with ideas. It is unsurprising that Paul should thus have built up a remarkable community of graduate students and teachers in the fields of labour and social security law, and human rights. As a result partly of Paul's leadership Cambridge became a centre of excellence in these subjects, the pre-eminent place for supervised graduate research. Indeed, a large part of the scholarly output in these fields since the late 1960s (some of them in the series on Labour and Social Law in which this volume appears, and of which he is joint Editor) has come from those who were supervised or taught by Paul at Cambridge.

This volume is a modest tribute to Paul by many of those who studied in Cambridge. It begins with three essays on international and comparative labour law. In Chapter 1 Breen Creighton examines Britain's record in relation to the freedom of association Conventions of the ILO. This is followed by the account by Gillian Morris in Chapter 2 of the protection of freedom of association under a number of international instruments, which draws out difficulties caused by the different standards adopted in the different instruments. The third essay on this theme, by Bob Hepple in Chapter 3, deals with the problems of labour law in transitional societies, comparing particularly the different experiences of Russia and South Africa.

Chapters 4, 5 and 6 consider contemporary problems of EC labour law. In chapter 4 Philippa Watson gives a full account of the role of the ECJ in the development of EC social policy. Brian Bercusson considers in Chapter 5 the extent to which labour standards at the European level can be protected by collective bargaining and examines some of the recent EC Directives with this in mind. Brian Napier concludes the treatment of EC issues by examining in Chapter 6 the role of EC law as a source of protection of workers' rights and concentrates mainly on the Acquired Rights Directive of 1977 and the Transfer of Undertakings Regulations of 1981. This is followed by three chapters which address the general question of the constitutional protection of human rights.

In Chapter 7 Keith Ewing considers the question of whether this can be appropriately done by means of a judicially enforceable Bill of Rights, asking the question whether such arrangements are consistent with democratic principle. Conor Gearty examines in Chapter 8 the implications of such a document for social and economic rights, having regard in particular to the experience in Ireland, where a Bill of Rights has operated since 1937. The constitutional dimension is concluded in Chapter 9 by Michael Forde, who examines the extent to which constitutional guarantees can be enforced against parties other than the State. This wide-ranging treatment is set in the context of the recent abortion controversy in Ireland.

In the remaining chapters we move from the constitutional protection of human rights to the protection of social rights in domestic law. Two essays by Sonia McKay (Chapter 10) and Patrick Elias (Chapter 11) consider issues relating to the right to strike, examining respectively the legal sanctions that may be visited upon those who take industrial action generally and, more specifically, whether industrial action must always be regarded as a breach of contract. In Chapter 12 John McEldowney considers the development of labour law in Ireland. The two concluding essays by Julian Fulbrook (Chapter 13) and Martin Partington (Chapter 14) examine current issues relating to social security law, highlighting Paul's concern for human rights in its widest sense. The first of these essays examines current social security policy by drawing important historical parallels, while the second considers difficult questions of administration and adjudication.

Paul's own contribution to published legal scholarship appears in the form of a bibliography of his writings, which concludes this volume.

What is perhaps not apparent from this, and helps to explain our attachment to him, is the warmth of his personality and his devotion to friends and students. Martin Partington's experience is not untypical. When he could not raise a grant for graduate study, Paul suggested that he could come and live with his family for a year for nothing. He negotiated with the College to waive the tuition fees, and gave Martin the confidence to achieve a first class degree. Paul's generosity of spirit as Tutor for Advanced Students at Christ's (1970–9) is legendary. The high regard in which he is held by students is shown by his appointment as Patron of the Cambridge University Graduate Union and Trustee of the Cambridge Union Society (1973–84).

Paul is a man of strongly held political views. He is a Vice-President of the Haldane Society of Socialist Lawyers and also of the Institute of Employment Rights, and a Governor of the British Institute of Human Rights. He is a committed trade unionist, having been President of his local Association of University Teachers, a member of the Staff Side Panel of the Civil Service Arbitration Tribunal, and Vice-President of the Institute of Safety and Public Protection. His lectures have shocked and inspired generations of students because of the directness of his language and his challenge to orthodox assumptions. Yet in his scholarly output he has always remained scrupulously objective: passion and commitment are the characteristics of the man, deep scholarship is the hallmark of his work. There is also a lighter side. 'At homes' with Paul and his wife Rachel are long remembered for the pleasures of their food, wine and, greatest of all, conversation. The contributors to this volume offer them both our gratitude and affection.

1

The ILO and Protection of Freedom of Association in the United Kingdom

Breen Creighton

THE CONTEXT

The ILO and Freedom of Association

The original Constitution of the International Labour Organisation (ILO), which was adopted in 1919, bears clear witness to the importance of respect for the principles of freedom of association, not only for the functioning of the Organisation, but for its very *raison d'être*. The primary purpose of the Organisation, then as now, was to ensure and maintain peace through the promotion of social justice. One of the 'methods and principles' through which these objectives were to be achieved was respect for 'the right of association for all lawful purposes by the employed as well as by the employers'.[1] Article I of the Declaration of Philadelphia was to like effect:[2]

> The Conference reaffirms the fundamental principles on which the Organisation is based and, in particular, that
>
> (a) labour is not a commodity;
>
> (b) freedom of expression and of association are essential to sustained progress;
>
> (c) poverty anywhere constitutes a danger to prosperity everywhere;
>
> (d) the war against want requires to be carried out with unrelenting vigour within each nation, and by continuous and concerted international effort in which the representatives of workers and employers, enjoying equal status with those of governments, join with them in free discussion and democratic decision with a view to the promotion of the common welfare.

This affirmation serves to emphasize not only that the right to associate is an important value in itself, but also that respect for the principle of freedom of association is an essential precondition of the effectiveness of the ILO as a tripartite organization. Meaningful tripartism necessarily depends upon the existence of free and effective organizations of employers and workers. Self-evidently, such organizations can develop and function only in an environment where there is proper respect for the right of employers and workers freely to associate, and to organize their activities.

These imperatives are reflected in the fact that the International Labour Conference has adopted no fewer than eight Conventions which seek to ensure respect for the principles of freedom of association:

Right of Association (Agriculture), 1921 (No. 11)

Right of Association (Non-Metropolitan Territories), 1947 (No. 84)

Freedom of Association and Protection of the Right to Organise, 1948 (No. 87)

Right to Organise and Collective Bargaining, 1949 (No. 98)

Workers' Representatives, 1971 (No. 135)

Rural Workers' Organisations, 1975 (No. 141)

Labour Relations (Public Service), 1978 (No. 151)

Collective Bargaining, 1981 (No. 154)[3]

Of these, by far the most important are Convention Nos 87 and 98. Between them, these instruments embody all the core ILO principles on freedom of association. Their special status can be gauged from the fact that they are frequently used as a point of reference in other international instruments in the field of human rights,[4] and from the fact that they are among the most highly ratified of all ILO Conventions.[5]

The significance of respect for the principles of freedom of association for the effective functioning of the ILO is also reflected in the special procedures that have been developed to deal with alleged failure to do so: the Fact-Finding and Conciliation Commission on Freedom of Association (FFCC) and the Governing Body's Committee on Freedom of Association (CFA). The distinctiveness of these procedures resides in the fact that they can be invoked even in relation to governments which have not ratified any or all of the freedom of association Conventions.[6] This is possible because it is assumed that the very fact of membership of the Organisation carries with it a constitutional obligation to respect the principles.[7] Arguably, it is also an obligation that derives from customary international law.[8]

The United Kingdom and ILO Standards on Freedom of Association

The British Government played a crucial role in the establishment of the ILO in 1919,[9] and in its development and consolidation in the inter-war years. In the period after the Second World War, the British approach to freedom of association issues, as expressed by government, employer and worker representatives on the Governing Body and at the International Labour Conference, exerted a profound influence upon the form and content of the two pivotal Conventions of 1948 and 1949. It also helped to influence the decision to establish the FFCC and the CFA in the early 1950s.[10]

The strength of British commitment to the principles of freedom of association is further evidenced by the fact that the United Kingdom was the first country to ratify Conventions No. 87 and No. 98 (on 27 June 1949 and 30 June 1950 respectively). It has also ratified all the other freedom of association Conventions, with the exception of the most recent, No. 154.[11]

It is clear, therefore, that the United Kingdom has a long-standing commitment to the international recognition and protection of freedom of association, and that this commitment has had a major influence upon the activities of the ILO in this area. However, as will appear presently, the nature and extent of that commitment has increasingly been called into question in recent years.

THE UNITED KINGDOM AND THE SUPERVISORY BODIES IN RELATION TO FREEDOM OF ASSOCIATION ISSUES

Basis for Compliance

Long-standing British policy has required that ILO Conventions be ratified only when law and practice complied with the standards laid down therein. In the case of Conventions Nos 87 and 98 it was assumed that this could be demonstrated through a combination of common law and statutory rules,[12] together with the fact that 'the trade union movement here is sufficiently strong to make legislation on these matters unnecessary'.[13] This view appears to have been shared by both employer and worker organizations, and by governments of all political persuasions right up to the early 1980s.

Although Conventions Nos 87 and 98 are framed in such a manner that compliance can be demonstrated without specific legislative provision, both Jenks and Kahn-Freund[14] warned against too ready a preparedness to accept this approach to implementation. Their caution appears to be fully vindicated by events since 1979.

While there was a broad social and political consensus as to the role of trade unions and the conduct of industrial relations, the lack of legislative measures giving effect to these Conventions did not appear to be any cause for concern at either the domestic or the international level. However, the advent in 1979 of a government which rejected the traditional consensus on industrial regulation quickly showed just how fragile the basis for compliance really was.

It is true that without entrenchment of basic human rights in a formal constitutional instrument, there would have been no legal reason why 'freedom of association legislation', had it existed, could not have been repealed by an ordinary Act of Parliament. Indeed, to some extent that is what has happened: for example, in relation to the narrowing of legislative protection against liability for industrial action. But these protections were not embodied in provisions that were directly related to the implementation of international standards on human rights, and indeed the Thatcher amendments could readily be presented in terms of removing unacceptable 'privileges', rather than eroding internationally recognized human rights.[15]

It can be only a matter for speculation whether the situation would have been radically different had there been 'freedom of association' legislation in place in 1979. After all, the Thatcher Governments had no compunction in denouncing, and then legislating in a manner that was inconsistent with, other ratified Conventions.[16] Whether they would or could have behaved in quite such a cavalier manner in relation to freedom of association standards is more problematic. For example, the fact that they did not (publicly at least) canvass the possibility of denunciation of Conventions Nos 87 and 98 suggests that there was perhaps more sensitivity in this area than in relation to 'labour clauses' in public contracts or to truck legislation.[17] Be that as it may, the fact remains that the freedom of association Conventions were not denounced,[18] the Government introduced legislation that was inconsistent with their requirements, and in consequence has been subjected to unprecedented levels of criticism by both the CFA and the Committee of Experts.

The Governing Body's Committee on Freedom of Association

Between 1950 and 1970 the United Kingdom was respondent to more complaints to the CFA than any other member of the Organisation.

However, all but three of these cases related to dependent territories, and as such fall outside the scope of this study.[19] There was just one complaint in relation to the United Kingdom proper during the 1970s, while a further nine have been lodged since 1980.

RECOGNITION AND TRADE UNION SECURITY

The first three metropolitan cases all concerned complaints by small unions which considered that they had been unfairly disadvantaged by the operation of union security and/or recognition arrangements. In all three cases the complainants were unsuccessful.

In *Case No. 96* in 1954[20] a small union of aeronautical engineers alleged: (a) that its members were being denied the right to belong to the union of their choice; (b) that certain of its members had been subjected to adverse treatment in order to pressurize them to join another union; and (c) that the refusal of the employers to recognize the union for collective bargaining purposes, and its exclusion from national bargaining arrangements, constituted a breach of Article 4 of Convention No. 98.

Each of these allegations was rejected by the CFA. First, it took the view that while it was true that workers had to join a union by virtue of the closed shop arrangement, they could choose for themselves the *particular* union to which they wished to belong. Second, it restated the view endorsed by the Conference when Convention No. 98 was adopted, to the effect that 'the Convention could in no way be interpreted as authorising or prohibiting union security arrangements, such questions being matters for regulation in accordance with national practice'.[21] This led the Committee to conclude that there was no breach of Article 1 in the circumstances of the present case.[22]

As concerned the union recognition issue:

> The Committee considers, especially having regard to the interpretation given by the International Labour Conference to Article 1 of the Convention in relation to union security arrangements, that nothing in Article 4 of the Convention places a duty on the Government to enforce collective bargaining, by compulsory means, with a given organisation, an intervention which, as the Committee has already stated in a previous case . . . 'would clearly alter the nature of such bargaining'.[23]

Both the complainant and the issues in *Case No. 162* (1957) were the same as in *Case No. 96*, and the Committee simply restated the position it had adopted three years previously.[24] The complainant in *Case*

No. 182 (1958) was another small union which alleged that its rights and those of its members were being infringed by the operation of closed shop arrangements in the engineering industry. This complaint was rejected on essentially the same grounds as in *Cases Nos 96* and *162*.[25]

COLLECTIVE BARGAINING IN THE BANKING INDUSTRY

In 1962 the TUC and the National Union of Bank Employees (NUBE) lodged a complaint which raised a number of complex issues relating to: recognition for purposes of collective bargaining in the banking sector; employer domination of staff associations; and the implementation of Article 4 of Convention No. 98.[26]

With regard to the recognition issue, the Committee restated its earlier position to the effect that 'a government, having given legal recognition to trade unions as competent to regulate employment conditions is not under a duty to enforce collective bargaining by compulsory means which would clearly alter the nature of such bargaining.'[27] It did, however, note that *Case No. 96* (and by inference *Nos 162* and *182*) was decided against a background of union security arrangements, with the consequence that 'the factual circumstances are not comparable with those in the present case'. This raised the possibility that 'if . . . NUBE were to establish that no bona fide independent trade union is recognised at all by those banks, the Committee would be faced with a situation which, in fact, it has never been called upon to examine hitherto'.[28]

Given the complexity of the issues, the Committee decided that it required more detailed and reliable factual information before reaching any conclusions. It suggested that this could be done by means of either a national or an international procedure, and expressed a strong preference for the former.[29] The Government responded by appointing a Scottish judge, Lord Cameron, to conduct an extra-statutory inquiry into the TUC/NUBE allegations.

Lord Cameron's report was forwarded to the Committee in December 1963. In his Lordship's opinion the 'complainers' had not established any breach of either Conventions Nos 87 or 98, although he did go on to make several recommendations for improving industrial relations in the banking sector. In transmitting the report to the Committee the Government indicated that it accepted the findings in their entirety. At its meeting in July 1964 the Committee signified its acceptance of the findings as to the factual situation, but rather pointedly observed that 'any decision as to whether there is or has been any violation of the Convention on the basis of the facts submitted, if it should at any time become necessary to decide the question, is a matter for determination by the appropriate international procedures'.[30] The Committee also emphasized that its decision in *Case No. 96* had turned upon the particular facts of that case - especially the operation of closed shop arrangements.[31] This clearly suggests that at that stage the Committee had not reached any decided view as to whether compliance with Convention No. 98 might require the adoption of some form of compulsory recognition procedures in certain circumstances.

Despite this affirmation of its jurisdictional competence, and the express reservation of the 'compulsory recognition' issue, the Committee never actually made any formal finding on the merits of the NUBE complaint. Instead, having noted Lord Cameron's findings, it 'invited' the Government 'to consider possible means of encouraging appropriate arrangements for determining the representative character of workers' organisations where necessary'.[32]

At intervals over the next four years the Committee took note of various communications from the Government describing a number of unsuccessful attempts to establish satisfactory bargaining arrangements in the banking industry. Eventually, in November 1968, the Committee referred to communications from the Government, which indicated that following strike action in December 1967, and subsequent Government intervention, national negotiating machinery had been established for the industry and was 'already functioning'. The Committee responded by recommending 'the Governing Body to note with satisfaction the information . . . and to decide that the case does not call for further examination'.[33]

PUBLIC SECTOR COLLECTIVE BARGAINING

It was not until 1981 that the Committee was again called upon to examine a substantive complaint against the British Government.[34] The complaint in *Case No. 1038* was presented by the TUC, the International Confederation of Free Trade Unions (ICFTU) and the Public Services International. It related to the unilateral suspension by the Government in late 1980 of existing arrangements for the negotiation of civil service pay, and to the denial of access to certain information on pay movements in the private sector, on which public sector settlements were based. The complainants alleged that the Government's behaviour was in breach of Conventions Nos 87 and 98, and of Articles 7 and 8 of Convention No. 151.

The Government argued that Conventions Nos 87 and 98 were not relevant to the dispute and had not been infringed. The Committee accepted that 'since a large proportion of the employees involved in the dispute are employed in the administration of the State and are thus excluded under Article 6 from the terms of Convention No. 98, this Convention cannot be invoked in discussion of the whole dispute'.[35] It also found that there had been no breach of Convention No. 87. This was because there had in fact been high-level negotiations that had eventually led to the resolution of the dispute. However, in reaching this conclusion the Committee acknowledged that Article 3 of the Convention had potential application in this situation because it 'provides for the right to [*sic*] trade unions to organise their activities and formulate their programmes, a right that has always been considered by the Committee to embrace the right of trade unions to engage in collective bargaining on behalf of their members'.[36] Despite the generalized character of the Committee's comments, this is one of the few occasions when it has expressly stated that Article 3 protects the right to engage in collective bargaining, although as a matter of logic that would indeed appear to be the case.[37]

Having determined that there had been no breach of either Convention No. 87 or No. 98, the Committee went on to find that the Government had contravened Article 7 of Convention No. 151 through its unilateral suspension of existing negotiating arrangements and its denial of access to the data relating to levels of pay. This latter placed the union side 'in a weaker position than they would have normally been during the negotiation of the terms and conditions of employment of civil servants'.[38] The Committee did not consider that the Government had breached Article 8, although it noted that the method of negotiation selected by the Government 'did not have the confidence of the trade unions, a situation which might have been avoided had the Government accepted recourse to arbitration as it has agreed to do in the event of disagreement in the 1982 pay negotiations'.[39]

The unilateral suspension of established bargaining arrangements in the public service was again at issue in *Case No. 1619*.[40] This complaint arose out of the Government's refusal to refer a dispute relating to London weighting for civil servants to arbitration and its subsequent decision, without consultation with the relevant unions, to terminate the Civil Service Arbitration Agreement with effect from 31 March 1992. The Committee determined that the Government's actions were not inconsistent with Convention No. 151, but at the same time expressed its 'regret' at the fact that the Government had not only breached the Arbitration Agreement but had also unilaterally decided to terminate it. On the other hand, the Committee also noted 'with interest' the fact that the parties had subsequently agreed upon new procedures and 'trusted' that these new arrangements would provide a suitable framework for the resolution of disputes.[41]

Quite apart from its intrinsic importance, *Case No. 1038* is significant as the first occasion on which the Committee made an adverse finding against the British Government in a complaint relating to its metropolitan territory. With the partial exception of *Case No. 1619*, it has done so in every subsequent case in which it has reached definitive conclusions!

THE GCHQ CASE

Beyond question, the most highly publicized British CFA complaint to date is *No. 1261*, the '*GCHQ case*'.[42] The background to, and decision in, this case have been examined in detail by several commentators.[43] For present purposes it suffices to note: (a) that the Committee unequivocally determined that the Government's unilateral action in depriving workers at GCHQ of their right to belong to the unions of their choice was not in conformity with Article 2 of Convention No. 87; (b) that the Committee rejected the Government's argument that Convention No. 151 'enables a government to exclude a particular category of public servants (viz those in highly confidential positions) from the basic right of association that is guaranteed to them under Convention No. 87';[44] and (c) that the Committee called upon the Government 'to pursue negotiations with the civil servants' unions involved' and to make 'a genuine effort . . . to reach an agreement which would ensure not only the Government's wish as regards continuity of operations at GCHQ but also its full application of the freedom of association Conventions which it has ratified'.[45] Not only has the Government consistently refused to enter into negotiations as advocated by the Committee, it has also resolutely refused to accept either that its actions were in breach of its international obligations, or the Committee's view as to the relationship between Conventions Nos 87 and 98 on the one hand, and No. 151 on the other.[46]

THE TEACHERS' CASES

The relationship between Convention No. 151 and other freedom of association Conventions was also at issue in *Case No. 1391*.[47] This complaint was presented by the World Confederation of Organisations of the Teaching Profession (WCOTP), the National Union of Teachers (NUT), the Association of Metropolitan Authorities, the TUC and the Association of County Councils. It related to the Government's dismantling of the Burnham machinery for pay determination for schoolteachers in England and Wales, and its replacement by a statutory mechanism which would deny those teachers the right, through their unions, to engage in collective bargaining.

In its response to these allegations the Government raised essentially the same argument as to the relationship between Conventions Nos 87, 98 and 151 that had been rejected in the *GCHQ case*. The Committee again rejected the Government's arguments on this issue. It was reinforced in this decision by an observation by the Committee of Experts to the same effect.[48] The Committee also found that the system for the determination of the terms and conditions of employment of teachers which was put in place by the Teachers' Pay and Conditions Act 1987 was not in conformity with Article 4 of Convention No. 98, and expressed the hope that then-current consultations 'will give the Government the opportunity to make the necessary legislative amendments to give effect to the fundamental principle of the voluntary negotiation of collective agreements, as contained in Convention No. 98'.[49]

The Committee was to be disappointed! The operation of the 1987 Act was subsequently extended until April 1991, and in December 1989 the NUT and the WCOTP presented a further complaint against the United Kingdom: *Case No. 1518*.[50] This complaint resulted in a further finding not only that the operation of the 1987 Act should not be continued beyond April 1992 (the Government having announced yet another extension while the complaint was before the Committee), but also that certain aspects of the *new* arrangements that the Government proposed to put in its place appeared to be incompatible with Article 4.

TRADE UNION AUTONOMY AND THE RIGHT TO STRIKE

In between the two *Teachers' cases* the Committee was presented with a highly complex complaint, which mounted a comprehensive challenge to the Government's labour legislation between 1980 and 1988. *Case No. 1439* started life as a narrowly based complaint by the TUC in relation to what eventually became s. 3 of the Employment Act 1988.[51] However, in the later part of 1988 the National Union of Mineworkers (NUM) and the International Miners' Organisation made a series of submissions which called into question virtually every change effected by the Employment Acts of 1980, 1982 and 1988, and by the Trade Union Act 1984.

The Committee first discussed the complaint in February 1989, but decided to adjourn its consideration of the case until its next meeting, 'pending examination of the relevant legislation by the Committee of Experts . . . at its March 1989 Session'.[52] In May 1989 the Committee had before it a working paper which took account of the observations of the Committee of Experts two months previously. The Committee did not, however, reach any conclusions on the basis of this paper. Instead, it 'decided that in view of the complexity of the issues involved it would be appropriate to defer consideration of this case until its next [i.e. November 1989] meeting'.[53]

In the interval between the May and November meetings all three complainants decided to withdraw their complaints. In its letter of withdrawal the TUC indicated that 'following careful consideration of the clear and unequivocal observations' of the Committee of Experts it had decided that 'no useful purpose would be served by requesting the Committee on Freedom of Association to examine the same complex and wide-ranging questions upon which the Committee of Experts had already expressed its opinion'. Having noted the contents of the complainants' communications, the CFA determined that the case did not require further action on its part.[54]

The decision to withdraw the complaint in this case was somewhat unusual.[55] Conceivably, the complainants genuinely felt that it would be pointless to proceed with the matter before the CFA in light of the observations of the Committee of Experts. It seems more likely, however, that the decision to withdraw reflected a perception that the CFA, which after all is not a technical committee, was not the most suitable body to deal with a complex complaint relating to abstract issues of statutory interpretation and common law doctrine, and that the more appropriate course would be to lodge complaints with the CFA relating to specific instances of the operation of the legislative changes that had been impugned by the Committee of Experts. More prosaically, the complainants' decision may have reflected a desire to 'get out while the going was good'!

Whatever the reason for, and in spite of, the withdrawal, the fact remains that the complaint in *Case No. 1439* served to trigger important findings by the Committee of Experts as to the application of the principles of freedom of association in the United Kingdom - especially in relation to trade union autonomy and the right to strike.

VICTIMIZATION ON GROUNDS OF UNION MEMBERSHIP OR ACTIVITIES

As will appear presently, the Committee of Experts' review of post-1979 industrial legislation, which was prompted by the complaint in *Case No. 1439*, highlighted the continuing absence of adequate protection for workers in Britain who were dismissed in the course of, or in consequence of, industrial action. This issue was also central to

Case No. 1540, in which the National Union of Seamen (as it then was) complained about the dismissal of some 2000 of its members in the course of a dispute with P & O European Ferries in 1988, and its subsequent inability to pursue claims for unfair dismissal on behalf of 1200 of those workers who refused to accept re-engagement on less advantageous terms than those which had operated before the dispute.[56]

Both the complainant and the Government presented elaborate arguments in relation to the requirements of Conventions Nos 87 and 98, and of the associated jurisprudence. However, as the Committee itself pointed out, the issue was essentially a simple one.[57] The Committee has consistently taken the view that 'the use of extremely serious measures, such as dismissal of workers for having participated in a strike and refusal to re-employ them, implies a serious risk of abuse and constitutes a violation of freedom of association'.[58] The Government accepted this statement of principle, but argued that it applied only to dismissals *after* the conclusion of a strike, and not to dismissals *during* the course of a strike, as had occurred in this instance. This somewhat arcane distinction did not commend itself to the Committee:

> The Committee considers that this view cannot be sustained. Respect for the principles of freedom of association requires that workers should not be dismissed or refused re-employment on account of their having participated in a strike or other industrial action. It is irrelevant for these purposes whether the dismissal occurs during or after the strike. Logically, it should also be irrelevant that the dismissal takes place in advance of a strike, if the purpose of the dismissal is to impede or to penalise the exercise of the right to strike. Applying these principles to the facts of the present case, the committee can only conclude that the dismissal of 2,000 members of the complainant union in April 1988 was not compatible with the principles of freedom of association.[59]

The Committee also determined that the subsequent offer of re-employment on less favourable terms had no bearing upon whether the original dismissals were compatible with the principles, and expressly endorsed a 1989 observation of the Committee of Experts to the effect that s. 62 of the Employment Protection (Consolidation) Act did not provide adequate protection against dismissal on grounds of participation in strikes or industrial action.[60] It expressed a similar view in relation to s. 62A, which had been inserted in the 1978 Act subsequent to the P & O dispute.[61]

Protection against victimization on grounds of trade union membership or activity was also at issue in *Case No. 1618*, which was examined by the Committee at its meetings in May 1992 and May 1993.[62] In this instance the TUC alleged that British law and practice failed to meet the requirements of Article 1 of Convention No. 98 in that there is no effective legal protection against anti-union discrimination at the time of recruitment. It supported these allegations by reference to a number of workers in the construction industry who had been unable to find employment because they had been 'blacklisted' by the Economic League.

The Government asserted that it was 'important that employers should be able to obtain information in confidence from whatever source they consider appropriate about prospective employees', but went on to stress that 'there is a heavy responsibility on those who provide and those who use such information to ensure its accuracy'.[63] The Government also took the view that s. 1 of the Employment Act 1990[64] fully satisfied the requirements of Article 1 in that it makes it unlawful to refuse 'to employ persons on the grounds that they are, or are not, a trade union member, or because they refuse to become, or cease to be, such a member'. According to the Government 'there is no reason to believe' that these provisions would not also serve to protect an individual who was denied employment on grounds of past union activity.[65]

In its conclusions, the Committee expressed concern at the 'serious allegations presented by the complainant', and referred to its well-established jurisprudence on union blacklisting, etc.[66] It noted that s. 1 of the 1990 Act does provide some remedy in respect of acts of anti-union discrimination,[67] but did not seem entirely convinced that this was sufficient for purposes of Article 1:

> doubts may exist as to the efficiency of these procedures in those cases – which are probably numerous – where workers face practical difficulties in proving the real nature of their dismissal or of a denial of hiring. In order to make a fully informed decision, the Committee would appreciate obtaining more detailed information on the specific cases mentioned by the complainant organisation. The Committee therefore requests the Government and the complainant organisation to provide further information in this respect and, in particular, to indicate whether the workers in question did institute legal proceedings . . . and if so, to inform the Committee of the decisions issued and the reasons therefor.[68]

The further submissions of the Government and the TUC in relation to this matter were considered by the Committee in May 1993.[69] On the basis of that examination it came to the clear conclusion that:

> Whilst recognising that UK legislation . . . may provide some remedy against acts of anti-union discrimination, the Committee considers that workers do face many practical difficulties in proving the real nature of their dismissal or denial of employment, especially when seen in the context of blacklisting which is a practice whose very strength lies in its secrecy. Overall the Committee considers that the situation in this respect in the United Kingdom is not compatible with the requirements of Convention No. 98.[70]

The Committee of Experts and the Conference Committee on the Application of Conventions

The pattern of observations by the Committee of Experts in relation to the freedom of association Conventions ratified by Britain is very similar to that which has just been described in the context of complaints to the CFA. In other words, in the period prior to 1979 there were very few observations relating to either Convention, and even fewer which found the United Kingdom to be in breach of its international obligations.[71] Since the early 1980s, however, there have been observations relating to substantial breaches of one or both Conventions almost on an annual basis.[72]

CONVENTION NO. 87

The Committee directed its first substantive observation to the United Kingdom in relation to this Convention in 1985.[73] It concerned two sets of issues: the GCHQ case, and certain aspects of the Trade Union Act 1984 alleged by the TUC to be incompatible with the guarantees of trade union autonomy set out in Article 3 of the Convention.[74]

With regard to GCHQ, the Committee basically endorsed the decision of the CFA, which was noted earlier. As to the 1984 Act, it found that none of the issues raised by the TUC disclosed any breach of Article 3: (a) the union election provisions were found to be within the range of measures which were acceptable as being 'intended to promote democratic principles within trade union organisations or to ensure that the electoral procedure is conducted in a normal manner and with due respect for the rights of members'; (b) the strike ballot provisions did indeed restrict the rights of unions to initiate industrial action 'but it does not appear to the Committee that the procedures prescribed are so cumbersome as to render lawful strikes impossible and thus to conflict with the guarantees provided for in Convention No. 87'; and (c) while the provisions of Part III[75] undoubtedly constrain the use of union funds for political purposes they 'are not in breach of the Convention'.[76]

The Committee's comments on the GCHQ issue were repeated in essentially the same form in 1987, 1988 and 1989.[77] This latter observation is particularly significant in that it also contains a detailed examination of the compatibility of the Employment Acts 1980, 1982 and 1988 and the Trade Union Act 1984 with the Convention.[78] As indicated earlier, this examination was undertaken partly at the prompting of the CFA, which had adjourned its consideration of *Case No. 1439* pending scrutiny of the legislation by the Committee of Experts.

The Committee first determined that there was no incompatibility between Article 3 of the Convention and a number of the aspects of the legislation that were under challenge in *Case No. 1439*. These included the provisions relating to: (a) election of union officers; (b) removal of union trustees; (c) members' rights of access to accounting records; (d) political expenditure; (e) exclusion or expulsion from a union where a union membership agreement was in operation; (f) access to the courts for members with a grievance against their union; (g) ballots in respect of industrial action; and (h) 'the role, as presently defined, of the Commissioner for the Rights of Trade Union Members'. In relation to this latter functionary the Committee did, however, express concern at the possibility that the relevant provisions 'could be applied in a manner which would be inconsistent with the letter or the spirit of the Convention', and accordingly asked the Government in future reports to provide information on the practical operation of this aspect of the legislation.

Having found that there was no breach in these areas, the Committee then ruled that there was significant non-compliance in relation to: (a) the concept of 'unjustifiable discipline' in s. 3 of the 1988 Act, especially as applied to the disciplining of union members who refuse to participate in lawful industrial action; (b) the ban on indemnification of trade union members and officials in s. 8 of the 1988 Act;[79] (c) the erosion of legislative protection against civil liability for industrial action, for example in relation to boycotts and sympathy action, 'mixed motive' disputes, situations such as that in *Dimbleby* v *NUJ*[80] where a 'real' employer was sheltering behind a legal fiction, and industrial action in support of workers outside the United Kingdom; and (d) the lack of adequate protection for workers dismissed in connection with industrial action. The Committee also noted that as a consequence of repeated amendments the legislation had become so complex as almost to constitute an 'incursion on the rights guaranteed by the Convention' even though many of the changes were not in themselves contrary to the Convention.[81]

The Committee's comments on the narrowing of the statutory protections are particularly significant in that they constitute the first formal pronouncement by any of the supervisory bodies on the relationship between common law liabilities and the right to strike:

> The Committee notes that the common law renders virtually all forms of strikes or other industrial action unlawful as a matter of civil law. This means that workers and unions who engage in such action are liable to be sued for damages by employers (or other parties) who suffer loss as a consequence, and (more importantly in practical terms) may be restrained from committing unlawful acts by means of injunctions (issued on both an interlocutory and a permanent basis). It appears to the committee that unrestricted access to such remedies would deny workers the right to take strikes [*sic*] or other industrial action to protect and to promote their economic and social interests. It is most important, therefore, that workers should have some measure of protection against civil liability.[82]

These views have subsequently been endorsed by both the Committee and the CFA in relation to Australia,[83] and by the FFCC in relation to South Africa.[84]

The 1989 observation on GCHQ generated a protracted and heated debate in the Conference Committee on the Application of Conventions and Recommendations (the Conference Committee). The workers' group pressed strongly for the inclusion of a 'special paragraph' in the Committee's report to Conference as a mark of its strong disapproval of the Government's intransigence on this matter. Unusually, the matter was taken to a vote, and the attempt to insert a special paragraph was only narrowly defeated.[85]

In 1991 the Committee reiterated its 1989 observations in relation to both GCHQ and the legislative issues.[86] The continued lack of progress in relation to GCHQ again generated extensive debate in the Conference Committee, although on this occasion there was no formal attempt to adopt a 'special paragraph'.[87]

A further observation in 1992 was essentially similar to its predecessors of 1989 and 1991, albeit with a number of significant shifts of emphasis.[88] In particular, the Committee 'deplored' the fact that it had been unable to note any significant progress on GCHQ 'despite the very broad consensus that has emerged in the supervisory bodies'. In ILO terms this is exceedingly strong language, and clearly reflects the growing impatience of the Committee (and of the Conference Committee) at the Government's continuing refusal to make any concessions to international opinion on the GCHQ issue. This impatience was also evident in the Conference Committee in 1992, which expressed its 'deep concern at the continued refusal of the Government to implement the Convention as regards the situation of workers at GCHQ', 'deplored' the continued absence of 'genuine dialogue', and 'strongly hoped' that, following certain undertakings given to the Committee by the Government, there would be 'substantive, frank and constructive dialogue carried out in good faith, so that a solution in full conformity with the Convention could be found to this problem which had been raised by the Committee of Experts and discussed by the Conference Committee for many years'.[89]

In 1993 the Committee 'noted with interest' that 'high-level meetings took place between the Government and the unions in October 1992 and January 1993, and that other contacts are expected to follow'.[90] This presumably accounts for the absence of any discussion of the GCHQ issue in the Conference Committee in 1993. Press reports in late 1993 indicated that some 'other contacts' had indeed taken place, but that there appeared to have been little progress in relation to the central issue of the right of workers at GCHQ to become and remain members of the unions of their choice.[91]

A second shift of emphasis in the Committee's 1992 observation related to s. 3 of the 1988 Act. The Committee noted the Government's view that this provision did not encroach to an unacceptable degree upon union autonomy since 'unions are still able, if they wish, both to have rules which allow them to discipline members for refusing to take part in industrial action and to implement those rules - as is demonstrated by a number of instances, since the adoption of the 1988 Act, in which members have been disciplined in this way'. It appeared to see some substance in this argument, and requested further information on the matter. It did not resile from its previous position, but nor did it point to the inherent absurdity of the proposition that it is consistent with the guarantee of organizational autonomy in Article 3 to permit unions to adopt whatever rules they wish but then to grant a legal remedy to anyone to whom they are applied! It did, however, take this point in 1993.[92]

CONVENTION NO. 98

Apart from a number of comments on the development of collective bargaining in the banking industry,[93] it was not until the late 1980s that the Committee made its first substantive observation concerning the application of Convention No. 98 in the United Kingdom.

In 1986 and 1987 the WCOTP and the TUC raised concerns about the application of Article 4 of the Convention to collective bargaining for schoolteachers in England and Wales. The Committee examined these comments at its 1988 meeting, and concluded that the Teachers' Pay and Conditions Act 1987 was inconsistent with Article 4 on grounds that anticipated the decision of the CFA in *Case No. 1391*.[94]

In a 1989 observation the Committee noted that there had been no significant progress in relation to collective bargaining for teachers.[95] It also examined a further issue that had been raised in the context of *Case No. 1439* – namely, the lack of legislative protection against denial of access to employment on grounds of trade union membership or activity. It noted that ss. 23 and 58 of the Employment Protection (Consolidation) Act provided some measure of protection against dismissal and action short of dismissal on grounds of union membership or activity, but also ruled that the absence of specific protection against denial of access to employment on these grounds was not consistent with Article 1.

Two years later the Committee 'noted with interest' that s. 1 of the Employment Act 1990 went some way towards meeting these requirements, but asked the Government to indicate whether 'section 1 provides protection against denial of employment on grounds of past trade union membership or on grounds of trade union activity'.[96]

The Committee also addressed two collective bargaining issues in its 1991 observation. First, it endorsed the views of the CFA in *Case No. 1518* in relation to collective bargaining for schoolteachers. Second, it examined representations from the TUC (on behalf of the National Union of Journalists) relating to the absence of 'legislative provision whereby employers can be obliged to engage in collective bargaining with the trade unions to which their employees belong'. Recalling that it had 'always attached great importance to the principle that employers should, for the purposes of collective bargaining, recognise the organisations which are representative of the workers they employ', the Committee nevertheless reiterated that conformity with Article 4 does not require the adoption of provisions whereby employers could be obliged to negotiate with such organizations.

THE EFFICACY OF ILO STANDARDS AND PROCEDURES IN PROTECTING FREEDOM OF ASSOCIATION IN THE UNITED KINGDOM

The Traditional Approach

It is not surprising that the United Kingdom should have generated little activity on the part of the ILO's supervisory bodies prior to 1979. As indicated, both the standards and the procedures were strongly influenced by British law and practice, and by the contributions of government, employer and worker representatives at the conference and on the governing body. The development of the associated jurisprudence was also significantly influenced by a number of ILO officials who were of British origin, and who could be expected to be familiar with the British approach to industrial relations and the values that underpinned it. This suggests that as long as the basic approach to industrial regulation in Britain remained as it had been in the post-war period, it was inherently unlikely that there would be any serious divergence between British law and practice and ILO standards on freedom of association.

Other factors could also be expected to have exerted a significant influence on British compliance with freedom of association standards at this time. One was what appears to have been an unspoken assumption that significant breaches of the standards simply would not arise in a country like Britain. This is reflected, for example, in the extremely deferential tone of the observations of the CFA in the *NUBE case*, and in the lengths to which the Committee went to avoid actually making an adverse finding in that case. It may also help to explain the fact that the supervisory bodies never appear to have given serious consideration to the relationship between tort liability and the right to strike until the end of the 1980s, despite the serious gaps in the protections afforded by the Trade Disputes Act 1906, which were exposed during the period of judicial activism that followed the decision in *Rookes* v *Barnard*.[97]

Such assumptions were doubtless reinforced by the widespread perception that the strength of the British trade union movement was such that it did not need to fall back upon ILO standards and procedures in order to protect its organizational interests. Furthermore, these perceptions were not without substance. The union movement could rely upon an essentially favourable underlying consensus on industrial issues, even during periods of Conservative government.

While Labour held office, it could look to legislative support from a basically sympathetic government. Irrespective of which party was in power, it could rely on a relatively strong organizational base, a tradition of solidarity (particularly in areas such as mining, engineering, shipbuilding, steelmaking and the docks) and a legislative environment that was reasonably tolerant of industrial action. These considerations do much to explain why, in the thirty years to 1981, the TUC was party to only one complaint to the CFA, and had made virtually no representations to the Committee of Experts on freedom of association matters.

The situation changed dramatically after 1979. There was unprecedented public hostility towards unions in the aftermath of the 'winter of discontent' of 1978–9, and the newly elected Government was firmly committed to an agenda of radical economic, social and industrial change. The membership base in many of the areas of traditional union strength had been steadily eroded over number of years. This process accelerated markedly in the face of the economic policies of the new Government. The legislative environment within which the unions had to operate became steadily more hostile.[98] The Labour Party was seriously weakened as a political force, and could do little to stem the legislative tide. Indeed, for much of the 1980s it could hold out little realistic prospect of gaining office, let alone bringing law and practice into line with ILO standards on freedom of association.

In these circumstances it is hardly surprising that the unions should look to the ILO for some measure of protection of rights they had hitherto largely taken for granted.[99]

Britain in the ILO since 1979

It should be clear from the foregoing that the unions have not looked entirely in vain. For example, the supervisory bodies have repeatedly taken the view that the denial of the right of workers at GCHQ to join the unions of their choice is unacceptable in terms of Article 2 of Convention No. 87. They have also determined that denial of the right of school teachers in England and Wales to engage in free collective bargaining is incompatible with Article 4 of Convention No. 98, and have pointed to a substantial degree of non-compliance with freedom of association principles relating to the right to strike (including the inadequacy of protection against tort liability and against dismissal by reason of participation in industrial action), trade union autonomy and protection against victimization on grounds of trade union membership or activity.

On the other hand, the ILO standards offer little support in relation to one of the most vexed issues facing trade unions in Britain (and elsewhere), namely the refusal of employers to accord recognition for purposes of collective bargaining. The CFA and the Committee of Experts have repeatedly emphasized the desirability of both recognition and bargaining in good faith.[100] But they have consistently refused to take the next logical step and stipulate that refusal to recognize or to bargain in good faith is a breach of ILO standards on freedom of association.

Ironically, the jurisprudence on this issue was developed largely in the context of complaints relating to British dependent territories and to situations in Britain itself where small unions found themselves excluded from the bargaining process as a consequence of the operation of union security arrangements. It will be recalled that in the 1950s and 1960s the CFA seemed inclined to think that this latter factor was crucial, and that refusal to recognize *any* union for bargaining purposes might be qualitatively different from refusal to recognize a *particular* union where a closed shop was in operation. This explains why the Committee deliberately left this matter open in the *NUBE case*. However, it appears subsequently to have backed away from this position, and instead to have endorsed a general principle based on its observations in *Case No. 96*.[101]

This interpretation can clearly be sustained on the basis of the wording of Article 4, but it is equally clearly not *impelled* by it. For example, it could quite plausibly be argued that in order adequately to 'encourage and promote . . . voluntary negotiation . . . with a view to the regulation of terms and conditions of employment by means of collective agreements' it is necessary that there be some means whereby employers who refuse to negotiate with unions representing a significant proportion of their workforce can be forced to come to the negotiating table. This certainly seems to be more in tune with the notion of *promoting* collective bargaining than the rather formalistic approach that has been adopted by both the CFA and the Committee of Experts. Furthermore, it is not entirely logical to determine that it is contrary to Article 4 directly to deny certain groups of workers (such as schoolteachers in England and Wales) the right to engage in collective bargaining, but that it is consistent with the Convention for employers to achieve the same effect simply by refusing to negotiate with the unions to which they belong.

The argument for some element of 'compulsion' in relation to collective bargaining can also be sustained by reference to Article 3 of Convention No. 87. As indicated, both the CFA and the Committee of Experts have, on several occasions, ruled that the right of trade unions to 'organise their administration and activities and to formulate their programmes' should include the right to engage in collective bargaining. It seems to follow that it would be inconsistent with this guarantee for employers to be able to refuse to recognize a trade union for purposes of collective bargaining even though the great majority of their employees wish to be represented by that union for these purposes. This interpretation derives further substance from the fact that Article 3 (together with Articles 8 and 10) of Convention No. 87 has been held to protect the right to engage in strikes and other forms of industrial action. Given that the exercise of this right is commonly described as a weapon of last resort in the collective bargaining process, it is clearly arguable that compliance with Article 3 requires that there be in place mechanisms whereby employers can be obliged to engage in collective bargaining both in order to vindicate unions' right to organize their activities and to formulate their programmes, and in order to minimize the need to have recourse to the strikes or other forms of industrial action 'as a last resort'.

Further support for this analysis can be derived from Article III of the Declaration of Philadelphia:

> The Conference recognises the solemn obligation of the International Labour Organisation to further among the nations of the world programmes which will achieve . . .
>
> (e) the effective recognition of the right of collective bargaining, the co-operation of management and labour in the continuous improvement of productive efficiency, and the collaboration of workers and employers in the preparation and application of social and economic measures.

Attainment of these objectives could well be said to require that in appropriate circumstances employers should be obliged to engage in collective bargaining, and that they should be obliged to do so in good faith.

It is clear, therefore, that the freedom of association Conventions and the Declaration of Philadelphia could provide a sound basis for developing a jurisprudence that stipulates that respect for the principles of freedom of association requires that there be some mechanism whereby employers can be obliged to recognize trade unions for purposes of collective bargaining. As a consequence of a somewhat simplistic reading of Article 4 of Convention No. 98, and a failure to develop the possibilities afforded by Article 3 of Convention No. 87 and the Declaration of Philadelphia, the supervisory bodies have failed to avail themselves of this opportunity. They have, thereby, seriously undermined the efficacy of the entire structure of ILO freedom of association standards.

The Government Response

Notwithstanding the inadequacies of the jurisprudence on union recognition, the fact remains that both the CFA and the Committee of Experts have determined that the British Government has consistently breached its obligations both under ratified Conventions and as a member of the Organisation. The Government has also been subjected to increasingly rigorous criticism in the Conference Committee because of its obdurate refusal even to talk to the civil service unions about the GCHQ issue. Yet in terms of practical change, all these observations and adverse findings have had little visible impact upon the behaviour or attitudes of the Government.[102]

Not only has the Government declined to bring law and practice into conformity with its international obligations, it has consistently refused to accept that it is even in breach of those obligations. Indeed, in at least one instance, it has deliberately legislated in a manner that has served to exacerbate a breach which had already been brought to its attention by the supervisory bodies.[103]

The only legislative initiatives of recent years which could conceivably be presented as a positive response to ILO standards were: (i) the introduction of protection against denial of employment on grounds of trade union membership in s. 1 of the 1990 Employment Act. This was, however, a minimalist measure that probably owed more to a desire to appear to be even-handed in relation to the supposed 'right not to join' than to any concern to give effect to ILO obligations; and (ii) the introduction of the Trade Union and Labour Relations (Consolidation) Act 1992, which can be seen as at least a partial response to the Committee of Experts' criticisms of the complexity of the legislation,[104] although it should be noted that this was purely a consolidation measure and that as such it did not address any of the Committee's substantive criticisms of the post-1979 legislation.

It also seems reasonable to suppose that the Government's more recent preparedness at least to discuss the GCHQ issue with the relevant unions was largely in response to continued adverse criticism by the Committee of Experts and the Conference Committee, and to apprehension at the prospect of being singled out for mention in a 'special paragraph'. As indicated, however, it is far from clear that this renewed dialogue will yield any positive results as far as respect for Article 2 of Convention No. 87 is concerned.

This experience serves to emphasize the unpleasant but inescapable reality that international standards relating to freedom of association or any other aspect of human rights can be efficacious only to the extent that national governments are prepared to allow them to be so. The decisions of the CFA and of the Committee of Experts described in this chapter clearly indicate that ILO standards on freedom of association have exerted only a very marginal influence upon the policies and behaviour of the British Government in recent years. Such apparent indifference to its international obligations on the part of any government must inevitably be subversive of the integrity of the entire international regime for the protection of the principles of freedom of association, and of human rights in general. It is all the more disturbing when it emanates from the government of a country which played a pivotal role in the development of the very standards and procedures it now flouts with such apparent unconcern.

NOTES

1. Constitution, Article 41 (formerly Article 427 of the Treaty of Versailles). See now the preamble to the Constitution as revised in 1946.

2. The Declaration was adopted at the International Labour Conference held in Philadelphia in 1944. It was appended to the Constitution in 1946. See further M. Stewart, *Britain and the ILO: The Story of Fifty Years* (1969), pp. 57–62.

3. The Conference has also adopted a number of Recommendations dealing with various aspects of freedom of association. These include: Collective Agreements, 1951 (No. 91); Workers' Representatives, 1971 (No. 143); Rural Workers' Organisations, 1975 (No. 149); Labour Relations (Public Service), 1978 (No. 159); and Collective Bargaining, 1981 (No. 163).

4. See, for example, Article 8(3) of the International Covenant on Economic, Social, and Cultural Rights, 1966, and Article 22(3) of the International Covenant on Civil and Political Rights, 1966.

5. As of 31 December 1992 Convention No. 87 had attracted 102 ratifications, while No. 98 had attracted 116. New Zealand and the United States are the only OECD countries to have ratified neither Convention. Of the others, all except Turkey have ratified No. 87, and all except Canada, the Netherlands and Switzerland have ratified No. 98.

6. Governments that have ratified a freedom of association Convention remain subject to these special procedures but are also subject to the normal supervisory procedures relating to ratified Conventions.

7. Except in relation to cases brought under Article 26 of the Constitution, the FFCC can deal with complaints only where the government concerned has expressly accepted jurisdiction (see C. W. Jenks, *The International Protection of Trade Union Freedom* (1957), pp. 181–3). On the other hand, it can, with the agreement of the government, examine complaints against countries that are members of the United Nations, but *not* of the ILO. This now appears to be the principal role for the FFCC, as evidenced by the fact that the last three cases with which it has dealt all related to non-members: Lesotho (1973), the United States (Puerto Rico) (1978) and South Africa (1992). The jurisdiction of the CFA extends only to member states, but does not depend upon consent.

8. See also Jenks, *op. cit.*, pp. 561–2. For discussion of ILO standards and procedures relating to freedom of association in general see N. Valticos, International labour law. In R. Blanpain (ed.), *International Encyclopaedia for Labour Law and Industrial Relations* (Deventer, 1984), pp. 79–92, 239–53; and W. B. Creighton, Freedom of association. In R. Blanpain (ed.), *Comparative Labour Law and Industrial Relations* (4th edn, Deventer, 1990), Chapter 17.

9. See also Stewart, *op. cit.*, pp. 4–11.

10. Furthermore, the ILO's other principal supervisory body, the Committee of Experts on the Application of Conventions and Recommendations, was established at the joint suggestion of the British and Irish Governments in 1927.

11. No. 11 was ratified in 1923, No. 84 in 1950, No. 135 in 1973, No. 141 in 1977 and No. 151 in 1980. The Thatcher Government refused to ratify No. 154 on the ground that 'whilst wishing to facilitate bargaining, it would not take on an obligation to *promote* it by direct Government "intervention" ' (Lord Wedderburn of Charlton, *The Worker and the Law* (3rd edn, 1986), pp. 278–9).

12. Notably the Trade Union Act 1871 and the Conspiracy and Protection of Property Act 1875. For doubts as to whether there was in fact compliance with Convention No. 98 at the time of ratification or later see P. O'Higgins, International standards and British labour law. In R. Lewis (ed.), *Labour Law in Britain* (Oxford, 1986), Chapter 20.

13. Royal Commission on Trade Unions and Employers' Associations (Chairman: Lord Donovan). Report. Cmnd 3623 (1968). See also G. A. Johnston, The influence of international labour standards on legislation and practice in the United Kingdom (1968) 97 *International Labour Review* 465, 467–8.

14. C. W. Jenks, The application of international labour conventions by means of collective agreements. *Festgabe für A. N. Makarov* (1958), p. 199; and O. Kahn-Freund, *Labour and the Law* (3rd edn by P. L. Davies and M. R. Freedland, 1983), p. 55.

15. This was made all the easier by the habitual use of the term 'immunities', which served to obscure the essentially *protective* character of the 1906 Act and its successors.

16. See also O'Higgins, *op. cit.*, pp. 572–3 and 577–8, and K. D. Ewing, *Britain and the ILO* (Institute of Employment Rights, 1989), p. 7.

17. The recision of the Fair Wages Resolution necessitated the denunciation of the Labour Clauses (Public Contracts) Convention, 1949 (No. 94), while the repeal of the Truck Acts required the denunciation of the Protection of Wages Convention, 1949 (No. 95).

18. Indeed, no government anywhere has ever denounced a freedom of association Convention.

19. E. B. Haas, *Human Rights and International Action: The Case of Freedom of Association* (Stanford, CA, 1970), pp. 42–4 and 64–5, records that the United Kingdom was respondent to 48 complaints between 1950 and 1968. There were adverse findings in 11 cases. The decision of the Committee was implemented in all but three instances (p. 89).

20. 13th Report, paras 115–39.

21. ILC, 32nd Session, *Record of Proceedings*, at 468.

22. See also *Case No. 114 (United States)*, 15th Report, paras 36–64.

23. 13th Report, para. 137.

24. 26th Report, paras 12–19.

25. 30th Report, paras 101–8. Interestingly, one of the workers whose rights had allegedly been infringed in this case was the plaintiff in *Huntley* v *Thornton* [1957] 1 WLR 321.

26. The case was examined by the Committee on six occasions between October 1962 and November 1968: see 67th Report, paras 136–243; 70th Report, paras 280–4; 76th Report, paras 222–71; 87th Report, paras 122–6; 101st Report, paras 213–17; and 105th Report, paras 14–20.

27. 67th Report, para. 232.

28. *Ibid.*

29. 67th Report, paras 240–1.

30. 76th Report, para. 253.

31. 76th Report, paras 255–7.

32. 76th Report, para. 271.

33. 105th Report, para. 19.

34. *Case No. 680* related to the internment without trial of a Northern Irish schoolteacher in

August 1971. There was no evidence that the detention was related to the internee's trade union activities, and as such received short shrift from the Committee (see 127th Report, paras 93–9).

35. 211th Report, para. 133.

36. *Ibid.*

37. See also *Case No. 1469 (Netherlands)*, 265th Report, paras 161–209 at 204. See also the observation directed to the Netherlands Government by the Committee of Experts in 1989: ILC, 76th Session, Report III (Part 4A), at 196–201.

38. 211th Report, para. 135.

39. 211th Report, para. 141.

40. 284th Report, paras 341–60.

41. 284th Report, para. 360(c).

42. See 234th Report, paras 343–71; 236th Report, para. 33; 238th Report, para. 36; 244th Report, para. 21; 251st Report, para. 20; 253rd Report, para. 22; 259th Report, para. 14; and 275th Report, para. 11.

43. See, for example, S. Corby, Limitations on freedom of association in the civil service and the ILO's response (1986) 15 ILJ 161, pp. 163–5; P. O'Higgins, International standards and British labour law, *op. cit.*, pp. 578–81; K. D. Ewing, *Britain and the ILO* (1989), pp. 11–14; S. Fredman and G. Morris, *The State as Employer: Labour Law in the Public Services* (1989); and K. D. Ewing and C. A. Gearty, *Freedom under Thatcher: Civil Liberties in Modern Britain* (Oxford, 1990), pp. 132–4.

44. 234th Report, paras 361–4.

45. 234th Report, para. 271(b).

46. In *R* v *Secretary of State for Foreign and Commonwealth Affairs; Ex parte Council of Civil Service Unions* [1984] IRLR 353 the Court of the Appeal (at 358–9) unequivocally accepted the Government's view of the relationship between the three Conventions. Glidewell J had expressed no decided view on this issue at first instance ([1984] IRLR at 323–4), while the House of Lords simply declined to examine the matter in detail because 'the Conventions are not part of the law in this country' (*Council of Civil Service Unions* v *Minister for the Civil Service* [1985] ICR 14 at 30 (per Lord Fraser of Tullybelton)).

47. 256th Report, paras 39–89.

48. 256th Report, paras 84–5.

49. 256th Report, para. 89(a) and (b).

50. 275th Report, paras 53–79.

51. See now Trade Union and Labour Relations (Consolidation) Act 1992, s. 64.

52. 262nd Report, para. 9.

53. 265th Report, para. 10.

54. 268th Report, para. 9.

55. On the withdrawal of complaints in general, see ILO, *Freedom of Association: Digest of Decisions and Principles of the Freedom of Association Committee of the Governing Body of the ILO* (Geneva, 1985).

56. 277th Report, paras 47–98.

57. 277th Report, para. 88.

58. 277th Report, para. 90, citing ILO, *op. cit.*, para. 444.

59. *Ibid.*

60. 277th Report, paras 91–4.

61. 277th Report, para. 96.

62. 283rd Report, paras 422–52, and 287th Report, paras 224–67.

63. 283rd Report, para. 436.

64. See now Trade Union and Labour Relations (Consolidation) Act 1992, s. 137.

65. 283rd Report, paras 437–8.

66. See especially ILO, *op. cit.*, paras 544, 551 and 564. See also ILO, *Freedom of Association and Collective Bargaining: General Survey by the Committee of Experts on the Application of Conventions and Recommendations* (Geneva, 1983), paras 256, 259 and 279.

67. 283rd Report, paras 444–50.

68. 283rd Report, para. 451.

69. 287th Report, paras 224–67.

70. 287th Report, para. 264.

71. Normally, the Committee will have recourse to a formal observation only after engaging in dialogue with a particular government over a period of years through so-called 'direct requests'. For practical purposes these are identical to observations, except that they are sometimes more tentative in character (especially in the early stages of dialogue) and their content is confidential between the Committee and the government, unless the latter chooses to make the matter public. In the case of serious contraventions the Committee may 'short-circuit' the process and move straight to an observation.

72. There have also been several observations relating to Convention No. 151. These have identified a number of breaches of the Convention, notably in relation to the legal position of staff at the Houses of Parliament, and to various aspects of public-sector collective bargaining (see further Corby, *op. cit.*, pp. 165–72; Fredman and Morris, *op. cit.*, pp. 103–5). There do not appear ever to have been any observations in relation to the effect given to any of the other freedom of association Conventions ratified by the United Kingdom.

73. In a brief observation in 1971 (ILC, 56th Session, Report III (Part 4A), at 132) the Committee noted 'with satisfaction' the passing of the Merchant Shipping Act 1970, 'which affords merchant seamen the same protection as other workers in respect of acts done in contemplation or furtherance of a trade dispute'. The Committee also noted the impending introduction of what became the Industrial Relations Act 1971. Interestingly, despite the controversy it generated in Britain, that Act never seems to have formed the basis of even a direct request to the Government – nor did it give rise to any complaints to the CFA.

74. ILC, 71st Session, Report III (Part 4A), at 193–8.

75. See now Trade Union and Labour Relations (Consolidation) Act 1992, ss. 73–81.

76. According to P. Elias and K. D. Ewing (*Trade Union Democracy, Members' Rights and the Law* (1987), p. 267), these provisions did not seem to have 'sailed remotely close to the frontiers of Convention No. 87'.

77. See respectively ILC, 73rd Session, Report III (Part 4A) at 240–1; ILC, 75th Session, Report III (Part 4A), at 179–80; and ILC, 76th Session, Report III (Part 4A), at 234.

78. ILC, 76th Session, Report III (Part 4A), at 235–41.

79. See now Trade Union and Labour Relations (Consolidation) Act 1992, s. 15.

80. [1984] ICR 386.

81. For more detailed analysis of this observation see Ewing, *op. cit.*, pp. 19–22.

82. ILC, 76th Session, Report III (Part 4A), at 238.

83. In direct requests in 1989, 1991 and 1993 the Committee raised various concerns about the nature and extent of common law liability in Australia (there being no legislative protection against common law liability in that jurisdiction, apart from the minimal protection provided by s. 143a of the South Australian Industrial Relations Act 1972, and the even more marginal provisions of the Victorian Employee Relations Act 1992). For the views of the CFA see *Case No. 1511 (Australia)*, 277th Report, paras 151–246, at 235–6. See also W. B. Creighton, Enforcement in the federal industrial relations system: an Australian paradox (1991) 4 *Australian Journal of Labour Law* 197. The Industrial Relations Reform Act 1993 (Cth) goes at least some way towards meeting some of these criticisms.

84. Report of the Fact-Finding and Conciliation Commission on Freedom of Association concerning the Republic of South Africa, presented to the Governing Body at its 253rd Session (Geneva, May–June 1992), para. 666.

85. ILC, 76th Session, *Record of Proceedings*, at 26/54–26/59.

86. ILC, 78th session, Report III (Part 4A), at 217–23.

87. It was widely perceived that this was because the workers' group were aware that they did not have sufficient support successfully to do so. For the discussion see ILC, 78th Session, *Record of Proceedings*, at 24/58–24/64.

88. ILC, 79th Session, Report III (Part 4A), at 242–9.

89. ILC, 79th Session, *Record of Proceedings*, at 27/67–27/70. This form of words is very similar to that used in many 'special paragraphs'. However, the Government was again spared the ignominy of having the paragraph placed in the prominent place in the Committee's report which is reserved for particularly serious cases of repeated non-compliance.

90. ILC, 80th session, Report III (Part 4A), at 234–5.

91. See for example *Financial Times*, 11 November 1993, p. 7.

92. ILC, 80th Session, Report III (Part 4A), at 235–6. It should be noted, though, that the

Committee does seem to have drawn back somewhat from its earlier criticisms of the indemnification provisions in s. 15 of the 1992 Consolidation Act.

93. These observations reflected progress (or the lack thereof) in connection with the NUBE complaint to the CFA. See especially ILC, 53rd Session (1969), Report III (Part 4A), at 106, where the Committee noted 'with satisfaction' the establishment of national negotiating machinery in the industry.

94. See ILC, 73rd Session, Report III (Part 4A), at 300 and ILC, 75th Session, Report III (Part 4A), at 212–17.

95. ILC, 76th Session, Report III (Part 4A), at 302–3.

96. ILC, 78th Session, Report III (Part 4A), at 289–91. See also *Case No. 1618*, discussed above.

97. [1964] AC 1129.

98. For a highly perceptive analysis of the philosophical underpinnings of the Government's industrial relations policy, see Lord Wedderburn, Freedom of association and philosophies of labour law (1989) 18 ILJ 1.

99. No doubt these same factors also help explain why British unions have increasingly looked to developments within the EC as a means of protecting and promoting their interests.

100. See for example ILO, *Freedom of Association and Collective Bargaining* (1983), *op. cit.*, para. 296 and ILO, *Freedom of Association: Digest of Decisions* (1985), *op. cit.*, paras 617–19 and 589–90.

101. ILO, *Freedom of Association: Digest of Decisions* (1985), *op. cit.*, paras 614–15.

102. It is possible, of course, that there would have been even more radical change had it not been for the existence of the Conventions, and for the activities of the supervisory bodies. It must be said, however, that there is a singular lack of evidence to support this hypothesis.

103. Namely the introduction of s. 62A of the Employment Protection (Consolidation) Act just a year after the Committee of Experts' determination that s. 62 of the 1978 was already in breach of Convention No. 87.

104. See ILC, 80th Session, Report III (Part 4), at 238.

2

Freedom of Association and the Interests of the State

Gillian S. Morris

Freedom of association is regarded as a fundamental right under international human rights conventions. An important element of this right is the freedom of workers to associate in order to further and defend their interests. The Universal Declaration of Human Rights, adopted by the United Nations General Assembly in 1948, proclaims that 'Everyone has the right to form and to join trade unions for the protection of his interests.' The International Covenant on Economic, Social and Cultural Rights (ICESCR) and the International Covenant on Civil and Political Rights (ICCPR) of 1966 reiterate this principle. Freedom of association has been a fundamental principle of the International Labour Organisation (ILO) since its inception in 1919; the ingredients of the freedom are spelt out in a number of instruments, the most important being the Freedom of Association and Protection of the Right to Organise Convention, 1948 (No. 87) and the Right to Organise and Collective Bargaining Convention, 1949 (No. 98). The right is also expressed in treaties agreed at a regional level, including the European Convention on Human Rights (ECHR) and the European Social Charter (ESC).[1] Freedom of association for workers thus appears in both treaties that deal with civil and political rights and those that guarantee rights of an economic, social and cultural nature.

None of these treaties, however, extends the right to freedom of association to all workers; in the case of specific groups, or to meet specified objectives, they permit the freedom to be restricted or removed. The purpose of this chapter is to analyse when, according to the various treaties, the right to freedom of association may legitimately be restricted in the interests of the state. It will also incorporate discussion of those respects in which English law exceeds the permissible exceptions to the right and thus fails to comply with international standards. Restrictions on freedom of association that may be common to all workers within a national legal system (for example, the requirement imposed by some countries that a 'trade union' contain a minimum membership) will not be discussed; rather, the aim is to examine the extent to which differential treatment may be afforded to particular groups of workers. One striking and problematic feature is that the treaties are not consistent in the exceptions they permit. This disparity may have important practical implications; a finding that its law does not comply with one treaty may more easily be ignored by a contracting state where it does not constitute a violation of another. This is especially disturbing given that there are also radical differences in the procedures for supervising compliance with these treaties.

The chapter begins by outlining the general principles of freedom of association: its scope in international labour law; the supervisory machinery for monitoring compliance under each relevant treaty; and the framework of freedom of association in English law. It then explores in greater detail the scope of permissible exceptions under the respective treaties to the right to form and join trade unions and assesses the compatibility of English law with these provisions. There follows a comparative analysis of the treatment under three treaties of the ban imposed by the British Government in 1984 on membership of national civil service unions at Government Communications Headquarters (GCHQ), which safeguards the UK's military and official communications and provides signals intelligence for the Government. This study highlights the dangers of allowing differing criteria for excluding the application of the right to freedom of association under different treaties and supports the argument that these discrepancies can only jeopardize the impact of provisions that seek to protect the right most stringently. The conclusion makes a plea for the harmonization of international standards on freedom of association and, in particular, for measures to prevent the work of the specialist agency on labour issues, the ILO, being undermined by conflicting standards that emanate from other, less expert, sources.

FREEDOM OF ASSOCIATION: GENERAL PRINCIPLES

There is considerable debate about the extent of the concept of freedom of association as it applies to workers.[2] Is the core of the right confined merely to the right to form and join trade unions or does it also include a right to organize? Does it imply a right for trade unions to engage in collective bargaining? Does it imply a right to strike? This chapter is concerned primarily with the exceptions permitted under international instruments to the right to form and join trade unions, with a brief discussion of the right to strike. It is upon these areas that arguments about the legitimacy of restricting specific groups of workers have centred. The chapter does not therefore explore in detail all the implications of freedom of association in the employment context.[3] However, the significance of the exceptions can only be fully understood by first outlining the basic rights that each treaty guarantees. These rights are presented here without reference to the specified exceptions to them, which are discussed below. A brief summary is also given of the procedures for securing compliance with their respective guarantees and of the relationship between international standards and English law relating to freedom of association.

The Concept of Freedom of Association in International Law

The most detailed elaboration of freedom of association and the right to organize is contained in ILO Conventions Nos 87 and 98. Convention 87 provides that all workers, 'without distinction whatsoever, shall have the right to establish and, subject only to the rules of the organisation concerned, to join organisations of their own choosing without previous authorisation'. Such organizations also have the right to establish and join federations and confederations and to affiliate with international organizations of workers (Articles 1 and 5).[4] In addition, there are guarantees related to the free functioning of organizations (Article 3). Member states undertake to take 'all necessary and appropriate measures' to ensure that workers may exercise freely the right to organize, and the law of the land shall not impair the guarantees in the Convention (Article 8(2)). Convention 98 provides that workers should enjoy adequate protection against acts of anti-union discrimination in respect of their employment and their organizations should enjoy adequate protection against interference by other organizations and by employers in their establishment, functioning and administration (Articles 1 and 2). Again there is an obligation to establish 'machinery appropriate to national conditions', where necessary, to ensure respect for the right to organize (Article 3). The Convention also states that measures appropriate to national conditions should be taken, where necessary, to encourage and promote collective bargaining machinery (Article 4). There is no express reference in either Convention to the right to strike. However, ILO supervisory bodies have consistently affirmed that this is one of the essential and legitimate means by which workers and their organizations may promote and defend their economic and social interests and, as such, it is an integral part of the free exercise of the rights guaranteed by the Conventions (although in the case of public officials recognition of the freedom to associate does not necessarily imply the right to strike).[5]

Unlike the ILO instruments, the ICESCR explicitly guarantees the right to strike, although this is subject to the proviso that 'it is exercised in conformity with the laws of the particular country' (article 8(1)(d)).[6] The states party to the treaty also undertake to ensure: the right of everyone to form and join the trade union of their choice, subject to the union's rules; the right of unions to join federations, confederations and international union organizations; and the right of unions to function freely (article 8(1)(a–c)). The ICCPR and ECHR, which are concerned with civil and political rather than social, economic and cultural rights, deal with trade union freedom as a manifestation of a broader freedom to associate. Article 11 of the ECHR provides that 'Everyone has the right to . . . freedom of association with others, including the right to form and to join trade unions for the protection of his interests.' The European Court has adopted a narrow interpretation of this provision. Thus, it has held that the article does not give a right to collective bargaining; nor does it give a right for trade unions to be consulted. The Court denied that this rendered otiose the words 'for the protection of his interests' in Article 11. These words showed that

> the Convention safeguards freedom to protect the occupational interests of trade union members by trade union action, the conduct and development of which the Contracting States must both permit and make possible. . . . It follows that the members of a trade union have a right, in order to protect their interests, that the trade union should be heard. [However, the article] leaves each State a free choice of the means to be used towards this end. While consultation is one of these means, there are others. What the Convention requires is that under national law trade unions should be enabled, in conditions not at variance with Article 11, to strive for the protection of their members' interests.[7]

An analogous approach was taken in relation to the right to strike; such a right is not expressly enshrined in Article 11 and while it is 'one of the most important' of the means by which the occupational interests of trade union members may be protected, 'there are others'.[8] Where a state has chosen a particular means of enabling the protection of occupational interests, such as collective bargaining or rights of consultation, these facilities must be afforded without violating Article 14, which provides that the enjoyment of the rights and freedoms guaranteed under the Convention shall be secured 'without discrimination on any ground such as' (*inter alia*) political or other opinion.[9] However, where a legitimate aim is being pursued, and the disadvantage suffered by the applicant is not excessive in proportion to this aim, there will be no violation of the Convention. Thus in one case, even though the applicant union alleged that its exclusion from consultation rights led to a decline in membership, it was not established that this disadvantage was excessive in relation to the government's legitimate aim of reducing the number of organizations to be consulted.[10]

Insofar as the freedom to associate is protected under the ECHR, it is unclear how far the liability of the state for infringement of this right extends. It is clear that the state is liable for its actions as an employer, whether its relations with its employees are governed by public or by private law. Thus, if a state-employer dismissed or otherwise prejudiced union members in employment this would almost certainly violate the Convention,[11] although previous decisions would suggest that there would be no redress for individuals refused access to the civil service on grounds of union membership on the (curious) ground that there is no right to such access under the Convention.[12] Beyond this the position is unclear. First, the boundaries of state employment may be a matter for dispute.[13] More fundamentally, however, 'What has yet to be fully resolved is the extent to which a state is liable for violations of the guaranteed rights by *private* persons (on the basis that it should have acted to provide a remedy in its law)'.[14] The decision in *Young, James and Webster* v *UK*[15] may suggest that liability would lie. Here, the dismissal of three railwaymen for refusing to join a trade union pursuant to a closed shop agreement reached subsequent to their taking up employment was held to violate Article 11. The court found that the responsibility of the UK was engaged on the basis that 'it was the domestic law in force at the relevant time that made lawful the treatment of which the applicants complained'.[16] However, it may have been material that the dismissals in this case were specifically permitted under legislation (which had been enacted since the UK ratified the Convention) rather than there merely being no prohibition on such conduct.[17] (The law has since been changed and dismissal or other discriminatory treatment on grounds of non-membership of a union is now unlawful.[18])

The ESC, which provides the economic and social counterpart to the ECHR, protects trade union rights more extensively. Article 5 states that

> With a view to ensuring or promoting the freedom of workers . . . to form local, national or international organisations for the protection of their economic and social interests and to join those

> organisations, the Contracting Parties undertake that national law shall not be such as to impair, nor shall it be so applied as to impair, this freedom.

The Committee of Independent Experts (CIE) has stated that this provision contains both a negative and a positive obligation: the absence of any domestic law or practice that impairs freedom of association and 'adequate legislative or other measures' on the part of the state 'to guarantee the exercise of the right to organise, and in particular to protect workers' organisations from any interference on the part of employers'.[19] As in the case of the ILO Conventions on this matter, therefore, there is a clear obligation on the state to guard against infringement of the right by private employers as well as in relation to state employment. The CIE has held that the impairment of a union's capacity to engage in connective bargaining constitutes an infringement of Article 5.[20] It has not considered the right to take collective action, including the right to strike, to be within Article 5, but this may be because the *travaux préparatoires* indicate that this right would be protected only by Article 6.[21] (This point is significant because states do not have to be bound by every article: see ESC, Article 20.) Under Article 6, contracting states undertake: to promote joint consultation between workers and employers; to promote, where necessary and appropriate, collective bargaining machinery; to promote the establishment and use of appropriate machinery for conciliation and voluntary arbitration for the settlement of labour disputes; and to recognize 'the right of workers and employers to collective action in cases of conflict of interest, including the right to strike, subject to obligations that might arise out of collective agreements previously entered into'. The specific obligations contained in the ESC clearly exceed considerably those contained in Article 11 of the ECHR as interpreted by the European Court. Ironically, the existence of the ESC, because it allows contracting states some discretion as to the articles they accept, has been used by the European Court of Human Rights to bolster its narrow interpretation of Article 11. Thus, the Court took the view that, given that a state may not have accepted Article 6, to allow that a right to joint consultation derived directly from Article 11 would 'amount to admitting that the 1961 Charter took a retrograde step in this direction'.[22]

Supervisory Procedures

It is immediately apparent from the survey above that there are considerable discrepancies between the rights guaranteed under the respective treaties. There are also considerable variations in the supervisory procedures under each. Compliance with the ESC is monitored in the first instance by way of periodic reports from the contracting parties, which are then examined and commented upon by a committee of seven independent experts (the CIE), assisted by an ILO representative in a consultative capacity. In the last resort, the Committee of Ministers can make any necessary recommendations to an individual state. This procedure is open to a number of criticisms, including the fact that evidence of compliance with Charter obligations is produced solely by governments, unless some other body chooses gratuitously to furnish evidence, and that ultimately the parties are judges in their own cause.[23] Compliance with the ICESCR is also supervised by means of a periodic reporting procedure. By contrast, the ECHR is enforced by means of state and (more commonly) individual applications (provided the right of individual petition has been accepted), which go initially to the European Commission on Human Rights (independent experts from the contracting states) and, if admitted by the Commission for consideration, may go ultimately to the European Court of Human Rights.[24] There is a good record of compliance with the judgments of the European Court of Human Rights. The ICCPR is enforced by a mandatory reporting procedure, combined with an optional inter-state procedure and an optional individual communications procedure, to the Human Rights Committee (which the UK has not accepted).[25] The ILO has a more diversified supervisory machinery. First, states make periodic reports on the application of Conventions and of Recommendations, which are examined initially by a Committee of (independent) Experts; the Committee's reports are then submitted to a tripartite Committee on the Application of Conventions set up at each session of the International Labour Conference. Second, there are procedures by which a member state may file a complaint against another member state for non-compliance with a treaty which both have ratified; the Governing Body may also initiate this procedure. In addition, representations may be made by employers' or workers' organizations on the ground that a state is not securing the application of a ratified Convention. These are considered by a three-member committee of the Governing Body and then by the Governing Body itself. In relation to freedom of association there is also a special complaints procedure; because this freedom is a principle of the Constitution, the procedure may be invoked (by governments or by employers' or workers' organizations) against any member state of the ILO, not only those which have ratified the relevant Conventions. Complaints are examined in the first instance by the Committee on Freedom of Association, a tripartite body of nine members appointed by the Governing Body, which makes recommendations in a report that it presents to the Governing Body for approval. This Committee has formulated detailed principles in the course of examining a substantial volume of cases.[26] According to the ILO Constitution, any question or dispute relating to the interpretation of the Constitution or a Convention should be submitted to the International Court of Justice, but to date this has happened only once, in 1932. Ultimately, ensuring that Contracting Parties meet ILO standards, as with the other treaties, depends upon persuasion and voluntary compliance.

Freedom of Association in English Law

The United Kingdom is a signatory to all the treaties that have been outlined above. However, there is no positive right to freedom of association in English law, although, excepted groups apart, individuals have been free to join trade unions since 1824, when laws forbidding combinations for trade union purposes were repealed. There is statutory protection against anti-union discrimination by employers but this is limited in scope.[27] Employees (and certain other groups, such as those in Crown employment[28] - but not workers in general) have the right not to be dismissed for their membership of an independent trade union or participation in the activities of such a union at an appropriate time and the right not to have action short of dismissal taken against them to penalize or deter such conduct.[29] Persons who are refused employment because of union membership (but not union activities) also have protection.[30] In relation to the right to organize, there is no compulsory recognition procedure (although access to rights such as time off for union activities and statutory rights of consultation depends upon a union being 'recognized') and the state does not encourage collective bargaining by any other means. There is no positive right to strike. There are a number of respects, therefore, in which the general law does not comply with international standards even at a basic level. Obligations assumed under international treaties do not, by virtue of ratification, become incorporated into English law, although where domestic law is ambiguous or unclear such provisions may be taken into account by the courts. Thus, the influence of international standards upon domestic law depends, in practice, largely upon whether the government supports legislation to reflect them. It is probably fair to say that none of the treaties discussed has made any significant impact upon English law in the sense of the government introducing legislation to comply with treaty obligations when this did not serve its broader political objectives.[31]

RESTRICTIONS ON THE FREEDOM TO FORM AND JOIN TRADE UNIONS

An Overview

Laws that restrict the freedom of workers to form and join the organizations of their choice are clearly incompatible with freedom of association principles. However, all the treaties that guarantee this right also allow specified exceptions to it. This does not mean that excepted groups are necessarily forbidden to organize in all the ratifying states, merely that their position is then left for regulation by national law. The ICESCR, ICCPR, EHCR and ESC also allow the freedom to be restricted to meet specified objectives.

Restrictions on the freedom of specific groups to form and join trade unions are present in the majority of legal systems. Such restrictions may be absolute or partial in their form. At their most extreme, collective organization may be prohibited altogether. Many countries deny members of the armed forces the freedom to associate; some also extend such bans to the police.[32] At one time collective organization among civilian public servants was deemed incompatible with their status as representatives of the sovereign power and later with the doctrine of state sovereignty, which dictated that the state's right of action should not be challenged or trammelled by particular interest groups.[33] By the late 1970s most countries had removed comprehensive bans on association by public service workers, but many continue to prohibit trade union organization by specific groups[34] or those holding positions above a specified level in the administrative hierarchy. Even where collective organization is permitted, it may still be subject to restriction. In some countries public service workers are permitted to join only unions whose membership is confined to the public service or to a specific occupational category or hierarchical grade.

In English law, there is no general restriction on freedom of association among public service workers.[35] However, the police and workers in security and intelligence agencies are singled out for special treatment; in the case of the police this restriction derives from statute and for the latter group it is a term of their employment.[36] Members of the armed forces are permitted to join trade unions as individuals, provided that this does not involve them in activities that conflict with their military duties. They have no form of recognized collective representation, however, nor are they covered by the statutory protections against anti-union discrimination. Another group that is excluded from these protections against discrimination is prison officers, although this appears to have originated in a drafting oversight rather than deliberate policy.[37] In practice prison officers, like other civil servants, have been free to join trade unions. Following a judgment in November 1993 relating to industrial action which put into question the legal status of the Prison Officers' Association as a 'trade union', the Government has announced its intention to introduce legislation to clarify prison officers' trade union rights. Finally, government ministers have the right to issue a certificate in respect of persons in Crown employment stating that employment of a specified description or of a specified individual should be exempted from, *inter alia*, protection against anti-union discrimination 'for the purpose of safeguarding national security'.[38] The use of this power in relation to workers at GCHQ is discussed below. Additionally, if an employee in either the public or the private sector complains to an industrial tribunal of dismissal or action short of dismissal for trade union reasons the tribunal must dismiss the complaint if it is shown that the action was taken for the purpose of safeguarding national security; a certificate signed by or on behalf of a government minister is conclusive evidence of this.[39] Although these powers relating to national security have not been used on a comprehensive scale since 1984, their existence makes protection of the freedom to associate completely vulnerable to the exercise of ministerial discretion, which is most unlikely to be successfully challenged in the courts.[40]

Exceptions in the Treaties

SPECIFICALLY EXEMPTED GROUPS

In relation to the groups that are specifically exempted from the application of freedom of association principles contained in the treaties, one might have expected a measure of consensus. However, even between treaties that were reached under the aegis of a common organization there are startling discrepancies. Only the armed forces are universally excluded from the right to join a union. All the treaties allow some restriction on the police but the ESC is less permissive than the others; rather than allowing their freedom to associate to be inhibited completely, the Charter states that it must be left intact in its essentials (this interpretation is apparent from the wording and confirmed by the *travaux préparatoires*).[41] In its third cycle the Committee of Independent Experts took the view that

> legislation or regulations which:
>
> (i) forbid policemen to set up their own trade union or to join a trade union of their own choice
> (ii) obliged policemen to join a trade union imposed by statute, are contrary to the Charter because they effectively completely suppress the freedom to organise.[42]

Under English law members of police forces and cadets are banned from joining a trade union 'or any association having for its objects, or one of its objects, to control or influence the pay, pensions, or conditions of service of any police force'.[43] However, to provide an alternative channel for collective representation, a statutory body, the Police Federation, was established.[44] Membership of the Federation is compulsory for all police officers below the rank of superintendent. The compatibility of these arrangements with the Charter was a controversial issue for many years.[45] The CIE concluded in 1985 that, taking into account the nature of police negotiating machinery and what it perceived as greater flexibility as regards affiliation to international organizations, 'members of the police force in the United Kingdom could avail themselves of association bodies which were not totally deprived of certain functions of a trade union nature'.[46] However, the Committee continued to take the view that compulsory membership of the Federation was incompatible with the Charter. Finally, in 1987, the CIE decided not to revert to this issue again, having been informed that there was no obligation on the police to pay a subscription to the Federation and that failure to do this did not carry any penalty.[47] It is, perhaps, regrettable that the CIE took this view. As Harris[48] states, requiring workers to join a particular organization, whose constitution and membership is determined by the state, 'is not to limit the freedom to organize but to deny it entirely'. Confining collective organization within the police force can be justified by its disciplined status and role as an impartial law enforcement body. However, it does not follow from this that the choice of organization should be further constrained or, indeed, that membership should be compulsory. On this basis all the treaties, and not only the current interpretation of the ESC, require review.

For most treaties, the armed forces and the police are the only categories of worker specifically excepted from the right to freedom of association. However, the ECHR and the ICESCR also allow 'lawful restrictions' on the exercise of this right by 'members . . . of the administration of the State'.[49] In the case of the ECHR this is particularly anomalous given that the ESC, which grants no such exception, was also adopted under the aegis of the Council of Europe and was intended specifically to supplement the Convention in trade union matters. It can be argued that since the right to form or join a union is common to the Convention and the Charter, 'Article 60 of the Convention would require that . . . Article 11 be interpreted in like manner [to Article 5 of the Charter], in respect of any country party to both instruments'.[50] However, this has not occurred. The scope of 'members . . . of the administration of the State' was considered by the European Commission of Human Rights on the application relating to the ban on unions at GCHQ, described below. The Commission was unimpressed by the argument that the absence of this exception in other treaties was a ground to interpret this phrase narrowly; on the contrary, the differences demonstrated that there was no settled view under international law and other instruments could therefore be of no assistance.[51] The Commission conceded that the meaning and scope of the phrase was 'uncertain' and it did not attempt a detailed definition. Nevertheless, it considered that the purpose of GCHQ 'resemble[d] to a large extent' that of the armed forces and the police (the other excepted groups) insofar as staff directly or indirectly, by ensuring the security of the government's military and official communications, fulfilled 'vital functions in protecting national security'. It was therefore satisfied that GCHQ workers fell within the exception. It was argued for the applicants that the requirement for restrictions[52] to be 'lawful' under Article 11 meant that they must not be arbitrary; it was not sufficient that they were imposed in accordance with domestic law. The Commission found that, even if this was the case, any such requirement had been satisfied. The reasons for this finding, which reflect amply the view that states should be given 'a wide discretion when ensuring the protection of their national security', are explored below. The decision by the Commission, against which there was no appeal, rendered the application inadmissible. In the light of the uncertainties raised by this case it is unfortunate, to say the least, that the Commission took this course. It would seem to substantiate the view that given that 'the final word as to the interpretation of the Convention rest[s] with the European Court of Human Rights, not the Commission, there is a strong case for arguing that the Commission should be reluctant to reject an application on a ground that involves its interpretation of the meaning of the convention'.[53] (Note, however, that at the time of writing a protocol establishing a single court of human rights, removing the role of the Commission, is expected to be agreed in mid-1994.) On the basis of the Commission's decision in the GCHQ case, there would appear to be sufficient scope for restricting other groups whose duties embrace security matters of either an internal or external nature, such as civil servants who work in defence establishments or in some parts of the Home Office.

The inclusion of 'members . . . of the administration of the State' in Article 8(2) of the ICESCR is also curious given the further provision that 'Nothing in this article shall authorise States Parties to the [ILO] Convention of 1948 concerning Freedom of Association and Protection of the Right to Organise [No. 87] to take legislative measures which would prejudice, or apply the law as in such a manner as would prejudice, the guarantees provided for in that Convention.' (A similar clause appears in the ICCPR, which does not exempt this group.) ILO Convention No. 87 exempts only the police and armed forces from the freedom to associate; the presence of the additional exception may be explicable on the ground that Article 8 also incorporates the right to strike.[54] It is to be hoped that Article 8(2) would be interpreted in the light of Convention No. 87. It would be vastly preferable, however, for the text of the article to be revised.

Unlike Convention No. 87, ILO Convention 98 on the Right to Organise and Collective Bargaining, as well as excluding the armed forces and the police, 'does not deal with the position of public servants engaged in the administration of the State', although it should not 'be construed as prejudicing their right or status in any way' (Article 6). The Committee of Experts on the Application of Conventions and Recommendations has stated that this additional exception should be limited to persons who 'act as agents of the public authority' and has drawn a distinction between 'civil servants employed in various capacities in government ministries or comparable bodies and other persons employed by the government, by public undertakings or by independent public corporations'.[55] Convention 151 concerning Protection of the Right to Organise and Procedures for Determining Conditions of Employment in the Public Service was adopted in 1978 to govern persons employed by public authorities to the extent that they were not covered by more favourable provisions in other conventions (Article 1). This Convention includes provisions that parallel those in No. 98 relating to protection against anti-union discrimination for membership of a 'public employees' organisation'[56] and the independence of such organizations from public authorities (Articles 4 and 5). It also requires appropriate facilities to be afforded to the representatives of recognized organizations (Article 6).[57] Like Nos 87 and 98, Convention No. 151 also excludes the armed forces and the police. In addition it provides that 'the extent to which the guarantees provided for in this Convention shall apply to high-level employees whose functions are normally considered as policy-making or managerial, or to employees whose duties are of a highly confidential nature, shall be determined by national laws or regulations' (Article 1(2)). This exception is not sufficiently broad to justify the exclusion (at the time of writing) of prison officers under English law from protection against anti-union discrimination in employment.

The relationship between Conventions 87, 98 and 151 was considered by the Freedom of Association Committee of the ILO when the TUC complained that the ban on unions at GCHQ infringed Convention No. 87. The Committee upheld this complaint and rejected the argument that Nos 98 and 151 diluted the basic freedom of public service workers to associate.[58] The Government refused to accept this interpretation but has not, to date, taken up the suggestion that the matter should be referred to the International Court of Justice. In relation to countries that prevent higher-grade public servants associating with their juniors the Committee of Experts has stated that 'these categories should be entitled to establish their own organisations and . . . where association with other public servants is not allowed, the legislation should limit this category to persons exercising important managerial or policy-making responsibilities'.[59] However, such organizations should not be limited to employees of any particular ministry, department or service, and they should be free to join the federations and confederations of their choice (unless affiliation to the latter is linked to the obligation to use strike action).[60] Moreover, provisions stipulating that different organizations must be established for each category of public servant are incompatible with the right of workers to establish and join organizations of their own choosing.[61] This strict approach, which is also applied in relation to private sector managers,[62] seems amply justified; restrictions based on hierarchy clearly require careful scrutiny to ensure that they are not, in reality, a device to weaken collective organization among senior public service workers or, conversely, those below them.

RESTRICTIONS IMPOSED TO MEET SPECIFIED OBJECTIVES

The ECHR, ESC, ICESCR and ICCPR, as well as exempting certain groups by name, allow the freedom to associate to be restricted to meet specified objectives. This means that groups other than those for whom restrictions are specifically permitted may also have their freedom to associate limited (although in the case of the ICESCR and ICCPR this would be subject to the obligation not to prejudice the guarantees in ILO Convention No. 87). Article 11(2) of the ECHR provides that 'No restrictions shall be placed on the exercise of these rights other than such as are prescribed by law and are necessary in a democratic society in the interests of national security or public safety, for the prevention of disorder or crime, for the protection of health or morals or for the protection of the rights and freedoms of others'. For a state to claim that an interference with freedom of association falls within Article 11(2) it must show that it was 'prescribed by law', had an aim or aims that is or are legitimate under Article 11(2), and was 'necessary in a democratic society' for the aforementioned aim or aims. For the interference to be 'prescribed by law', the law must be adequately accessible to give individual citizens 'an indication that is adequate in the circumstances of the legal rules applicable to a given case' and sufficiently precise to enable them to regulate their conduct so that they can foresee, if necessary with appropriate advice, 'to a degree that is reasonable in the circumstances, the consequences which a given action may entail'.[63] To be 'necessary' in a democratic society, the interference must not be merely useful or desirable; rather it must arise from a 'pressing social need'. Moreover, the restriction must be 'proportionate to the legitimate aim pursued' and the reasons adduced by the national authorities to justify it must be 'relevant and sufficient'.[64]

In assessing whether these conditions are met, states have a 'certain margin of appreciation' but this 'goes hand in hand with a European supervision, embracing both the law and the decisions applying it, even those given by independent courts'.[65] The width of the 'margin of appreciation' is not identical in every case; it depends, rather, on the nature of the legitimate aim pursued and that of the interference at issue. Where national security is invoked, traditionally the Court has given states a wide 'margin of appreciation'.[66] However, in applications alleging an interference with Article 10 of the Convention (which guarantees freedom of expression), arising out of the *Spycatcher* litigation, the European Court for the first time displaced the judgment of a domestic authority that national security required the restriction in question.[67] It is possible that these decisions mark a more rigorous approach by the Court, although the circumstances of the case were highly unusual in that the interests of national security the British Government sought to protect shifted during the course of the litigation at issue.[68] The application of these exceptions to Article 11 has never been tested in the context of a ban on union membership; although arguments were put forward by both parties in the GCHQ case (the Government invoking the interests of national security as its aim), the finding that the workers there were 'members . . . of the administration of the State' made a decision on this aspect unnecessary.[69] The weight that may be attached to the arguments propounded there by the parties in the light of current case law is discussed below.

The ICESCR and ICCPR contain broadly similar exempting provisions to Article 11 of the ECHR, within Articles 8 and 22 respectively.[70] By contrast, the ESC contains a proviso of more general application: Article 31 allows all the substantive rights in the Charter to be subject to such 'restrictions and limitations' as are 'prescribed by law and are necessary in a democratic society for the protection of the rights and freedoms of others or for the protection of public interest, national security, public health or morals'. The interpretation of this article has not been discussed in detail by the CIE, although it is notable that in 1975 they opined that the denial of rights could not be considered necessary in a democratic society when 'no such denial is to be found in many democratic States that are Contracting Parties to the Charter'.[71] (The dangers for the maintenance of standards of a norm-reflecting approach of this nature should not be overlooked, however.) The Committee also appear to take the view that 'restrictions' in relation to the right to organize do not permit complete abolition of the right.[72] Article 31 was relied upon by the CIE in its finding that the ban on unions at GCHQ did not infringe the Charter,[73] although the reasons for this finding were not spelt out. The discussion below of the treatment of the ban demonstrates the dangers that provisions of this nature may present for freedom of association.

Finally, it should be noted that the ECHR, ESC and ICCPR all allow the right to freedom of association, among other rights, to be derogated from in times of war or other public emergency provided that certain procedures are observed.[74] Insofar as these provisions apply to all workers they will not be analysed further here. However, it should be observed that there is no provision for derogation from, or suspension of, the rights contained in ILO Conventions that relate to freedom of association, and the supervisory bodies have emphasized the dangers that emergencies may present for the continued exercise of legitimate trade union freedoms.[75] This may lend further weight to the argument, developed in the concluding section, that subsuming the right to form and join trade unions within a broader freedom of association may present risks to the preservation and promotion of that freedom.

GCHQ: A COMPARATIVE CASE STUDY

The ban imposed by the British Government in 1984 on membership of national civil service trade unions at Government Communications Headquarters is an instructive case study of the damage that may be caused by the discrepancies between international instruments as to the exceptions to freedom of association they permit. While, in theory, the most rigorous interpretation of exceptions to the right should be adopted[76] this does not, in practice, happen. It also supports the argument that broadly cast exemptions to the freedom to associate, some of which have been drafted to apply in a wide range of contexts, are inappropriate in relation to the freedom to form and join trade unions.

The facts of this notorious case can be summarized briefly.[77] From its inception in 1947, workers at GCHQ had been encouraged to join appropriate national trade unions in accordance with the traditional policy (no longer universally applied) of encouraging all civil servants so to do. In January 1984, with no prior warning, staff were informed that as from 1 March they would no longer be permitted to belong to national unions but would be allowed to join only a Departmental Staff Association approved by the organization's director, which would be unable to affiliate with other union bodies. (This Association was subsequently established as the Government Communications Staff Federation.) Two formal steps were taken to effect this change. First, the Prime Minister, as Minister for the Civil Service, by an oral instruction directed that the conditions of workers at GCHQ should be revised so as to exclude membership of national unions.[78] Second, the Foreign Secretary signed certificates exempting GCHQ workers on the ground of national security from legislation according, *inter alia*, protection against anti-union discrimination.[79] Four reasons were given for the ban: to avoid GCHQ operations being publicly discussed in industrial tribunals; to avoid any risk of its activities being disrupted; to confine negotiations, for security reasons, to departmental staff representatives answerable only to staff at GCHQ; and to avoid the staff being subject to conflicts of loyalty during national civil service disputes.[80] However, the factor most emphasized was the need to ensure continuous operations, which had allegedly been threatened seven times by industrial action between February 1979 and April 1981, mostly to further national disputes. Ministers acknowledged that the nation's security had not thereby been jeopardized but they were determined to remove any future risk. The civil service unions suggested that this requirement could be met by introducing a condition of service for GCHQ staff that they would take no action which might interfere with the uninterrupted operation of essential security and intelligence services, such services to be designated by the Government after consultation with local union representatives. However, the Government rejected this offer as inadequate and remained intransigent despite a unanimous recommendation from the House of Commons Select Committee on Employment that it should reconsider its position.[81] Recourse to the courts also failed. The lack of a positive right to belong to a trade union meant that the ban could be challenged only on the procedural ground that the minister's failure to consult the national unions before instructing that union membership should be excluded was a breach of natural justice, rendering the instruction void. The House of Lords accepted the unions' argument that they had a public law right to be consulted before their members' terms and conditions were varied but held that this duty could be outweighed by considerations of national security. Provided that there was evidence before the court that national security considerations were relevant, whether these considerations outweighed the duty to consult in any particular case rested with the Government. Here the court accepted the minister's evidence that consultation had been avoided to prevent the risk of provoking industrial action at GCHQ, which would have threatened national security.[82]

As well as challenging the ban in the domestic courts, the unions also challenged it in international forums. First the TUC complained to the Freedom of Association Committee of the ILO that it violated Convention No. 87.[83] The Committee upheld this complaint on three counts: the ban violated the right of all workers (other than the armed forces and the police) to form and join organizations of their own choosing; the Government, by issuing certificates withdrawing statutory employment rights and imposing new terms of employment, had contravened the obligation to take necessary and appropriate measures to ensure that workers could freely exercise that right; and the ability of staff to join an officially approved staff association did not meet the obligation to ensure that workers could form and join organizations without previous authorization. It also pointed out, however, that ILO standards did not prevent public servants being subjected to special rules as regards the settlement of disputes[84] and it urged the Government to attempt to reach an agreement with the unions, 'which would ensure not only the Government's wish as regards continuity of operations at GCHQ but also its full application of the freedom of association Conventions which it has ratified.' In June 1984 the governing body adopted this recommendation. However, despite regular and repeated exhortations by the ILO in subsequent years the

Government refused to reconsider its position and continued to argue that Convention No. 151, not No. 87, governed the position.[85]

An application under Article 11 of the ECHR seemed to carry greater hope for the unions given that the Government has a better history of compliance with judgments of the European Court. However, this avenue was blocked at the first stage by the Commission's finding that GCHQ workers were members of the administration of the state and that the restrictions were 'lawful' in the sense both of being in conformity with national law and of not being 'arbitrary'. In assessing the latter criterion, the Commission emphasized that states should have 'a wide discretion when ensuring the protection of their national security'. It

> considered the Government's position when issuing the certificates. In particular, the Government had to ensure that the functioning of GCHQ would no longer be vulnerable to disruption by industrial action. After industrial action had occurred in 1981, and once the Government had acknowledged the functions of GCHQ in May 1983 [following offences under the Official Secrets Act 1911 by a former employee], the time and means were lacking for the Government to conduct substantial negotiations with the trade unions. The guarantees offered by the latter were in the Government's assessment not adequate . . . it could not be excluded that industrial action could occur again at GCHQ at any moment. In this respect the Commission notes in particular that the House of Lords . . . unanimously accepted that the basis of the Government's actions related to the interests of national security . . . in this light and against the whole background of industrial action and the vital functions of GCHQ the action taken, though drastic, was in no way arbitrary.

This extract indicates clearly the perspective from which the action was being assessed; there was no enquiry equivalent to that of the ILO as to whether a lesser form of restriction, such as a limitation on industrial action, might have met the Government's case. It is interesting to speculate whether the outcome would have been any different had the ban been tested against the criterion of being 'necessary in a democratic society'. The unions argued that there was no pressing social need to deny trade union rights, particularly without negotiation or consultation. This was shown by the long history of trade unionism at GCHQ, the unaccountable delay in reacting had the industrial action in 1981 been truly felt to constitute a threat, the guarantees offered by the unions, and the Employment's Committee's recommendations that the Government should try to find another method of achieving its objective. Moreover, the action was disproportionate to the aim to be achieved, which could have been realized by the unions' proposals. The Government, for its part, argued that only when the role of GCHQ had been officially acknowledged could it fully reappraise the measures needed to prevent a recurrence of the threat to national security posed by the disruption; before that time, it had concluded that the need to take such measures was outweighed by the disadvantages of disclosing its true functions. The measures taken were not disproportionate: the House of Lords had found that the Government had legitimately concluded that the interests of national security required that there should be no prior notice of the ban;[86] before 1984 there had been no offer from the unions of a no-strike agreement; the measures merely brought staff at GCHQ into line with other security and intelligence workers; and the Staff Federation had been formed and recognized. It is hard to predict the fate of such arguments were they to come before the European Court today. Ultimately the task of the Court, in exercising its supervisory jurisdiction, 'is not to take the place of the competent national authorities but rather to review . . . the decisions they delivered pursuant to their powers of appreciation'.[87] It is thus concerned with the legitimacy under the Convention of the action taken by the state, not with consideration of the variety of alternative strategies which could be pursued to achieve the end in view. Although the Court has shown that it will not automatically defer to national security arguments one cannot be confident that it would gainsay the Government's view that only an outright ban could meet its aim, particularly if it viewed the Staff Federation as evidence of the Government's recognition of the basic right, albeit in a diluted form. The ILO, which is able to take a more subtle and differentiated approach to these matters, does not permit exceptions of this nature and their presence in other treaties can only risk subverting the freedom of workers to associate.

The ban was finally examined on the international plane by the CIE for conformity with the ESC. The response of the Committee also supports the argument above. Its conclusion, published in 1989, was as follows:

> the Committee noted that its [i.e. GCHQ's] Staff Federation, officially set up in 1985, has been registered as a trade union and given the right to negotiate on behalf of its members (at present 52% of the staff). It also noted that the membership of the Federation is optional and that its members belong to all the

> categories of staff employed. In the light of this information, the Committee concluded that the restrictions imposed on this category of civil servants did not exceed the limits prescribed in Article 31 of the Charter.[88]

This conclusion is perfunctory, to say the least, and its rationale obscure. Which of the exceptions under Article 31 is satisfied here? Which is the crucial factor that leads to the conclusion that the restrictions did not exceed the limits of that article? Did the Committee appreciate that being 'registered'[89] as a trade union means nothing; it is the organization's status as 'independent' that is the crucial issue. In December 1989 the Certification Officer refused to grant the Staff Federation's application for a 'certificate of independence' on the ground that it was established and continued to function subject to the approval of the Director of GCHQ, a fundamental constraint on its freedom to act independently.[90] An appeal against this decision to the Employment Appeal Tribunal was unsuccessful, the Federation being unable to convince the court that it was not vulnerable to interference by management.[91]

A comparative assessment of the treatment of the ban on national union membership at GCHQ amply demonstrates the dangers that the ECHR and ESC can present for trade union rights. The declaration by the European Commission that the unions' case was inadmissible under the Convention fatally weakened their chances of securing a modification of the Government's position. Had the ban been universally condemned by the relevant international supervisory bodies it would have been much more difficult for it to maintain its obdurate stance; in the event, it was able to use the findings by other bodies to minimalize and marginalize the impact of the findings by the ILO, for which, in any case, it has to date shown scant regard. At the time of writing, the Government and civil service unions have recently been engaged in discussions in an attempt to resolve the dispute, but the distance between the sides is great and it is hard to be optimistic about the prospects of a mutually satisfactory accommodation.

CONCLUSION

The right of workers to freedom of association is both a fundamental human right and an essential socio-economic right. As such, it should be restricted only when absolutely necessary and to the minimum possible extent. The exceptions to the right to form and join trade unions permitted in the treaties that have been examined in this chapter fail to meet this test. Three major reforms are required: the exceptions should be harmonized; they should be more narrowly confined; and they should be exhaustive and not susceptible to extension. The current lack of uniformity is in itself a threat to the basic right and, more broadly, to respect for international standards. As the GCHQ experience demonstrates, the discrepancies between treaties enable a government more easily to evade its obligations; indeed, the argument that other international bodies concerned with fundamental human rights have ruled in its favour has been cited by the British Government as a reason in support of its continued opposition to the ILO's findings on the matter.[92] The principle that treaties should not undermine the standards enshrined in other instruments is not translated into practice; indeed, the very lack of uniformity may encourage supervisory organs to examine a case without reference to the position under other treaties.[93] The need for a harmonized approach is, therefore, urgent. In terms of groups that are excluded from the right, complete exception should be confined to the armed forces; there seems no reason to forbid internal collective organization among the police (nor does compulsory membership of any particular organization seem justified). The exemption of 'members . . . of the administration of the State' appears to be a relic of the sovereignty argument; at most restrictions should be confined to persons exercising 'important managerial or policy-making' functions, who themselves should be permitted to form their own associations. These exceptions should be specific and exhaustive. Provisions that allow the right to be excluded to meet specified objectives are unnecessary in this context, as their absence from ILO conventions makes clear. Once more examination of the GCHQ affair shows the dangers that the existence of these provisions in international instruments, which are designed to deal with a wide range of situations beyond the labour area, can bring, particularly where national security is invoked. The considerations that may justify restricting freedom of association in other contexts are not the same as those applicable to union membership, which should be an unqualified right that cannot be eroded according to the priorities and perceptions of the government. Provisions of this nature are particularly dangerous in the hands of supervisory bodies that are not specialists in labour matters. The CIE, which supervises the ESC, has seven members, and so necessarily will not include among its number all contracting parties, and it is dependent upon governments to supply its information. It is thus at risk of failing to appreciate in all cases the fundamental issues; its findings in relation to GCHQ, for example, appear to be based upon confusion over crucial points. The organs that supervise compliance with the ECHR have the benefit of evidence presented in adversarial proceedings, and so are not reliant solely upon governments, but even so their predisposition towards an individualistic perspective, and caution in the face of argument about collective rights, makes their discretion in such an area undesirable and unhelpful to trade union rights.

The body that has the greatest claims to adjudicate upon labour standards is undoubtedly the ILO. This claim is based both upon its specialist nature and experience in this field and upon its tripartite structure, which ensures that the social partners as well as governments participate in the formulation of labour standards. It also has the advantage of an lengthy and worldwide perspective in considering a particular issue, unlike the European Court of Human Rights, for example, which deals only with the case in front of it. In the field of freedom of association the ILO has shown itself well able to appreciate the complexities of collective organization as demonstrated, in particular, by the principles it has developed in relation to industrial action. It is unlikely, therefore, that the development of common standards based upon ILO principles would present the risk of standards becoming diluted. Moreover, its supervisory bodies are not confined to making judgments upholding the position of one side or another; rather, they can seek to separate the issues and make recommendations of a more subtle nature.

The reports of the ILO's Freedom of Association Committee have been described as the 'cornerstone of the international law on trade union freedom and collective bargaining'.[94] The role of the ILO goes well beyond supervising compliance with specific labour standards; it also has important educational and proactive functions, particularly in developing countries. The existence of conflicting labour standards can only undermine its work. There is some benefit in including the freedom to form and join trade unions in other international instruments in order to emphasize the fundamental nature of the right, but exceptions to it should be individually specified, with no room for extension. A reference to ILO Conventions of the kind that currently exists in the ICESCR and ICCPR (but incorporating also Conventions Nos 98 and 151) may be helpful here. The main point, however, is that ILO standards should in no respects be compromised. If the cornerstone of the edifice is eroded, the whole building can tumble down. Restricting freedom of association in the interests of the state can be the thin end of a very insidious wedge. What may seem an issue that affects relatively few workers is of great significance for labour law and human rights in general.

NOTES

1. For other regional instruments see W. B. Creighton, Freedom of association. In R. Blanpain (ed.), *Comparative Labour Law and Industrial Relations in Industrialised Market Economies*, Vol. II, (4th edn, Deventer, 1990), para. 10.

2. Note that the freedom of employers to associate is also affirmed in ILO Conventions and the ESC and is implicit in general guarantees. The implications of this right will not be discussed here.

3. See Lord Wedderburn, Freedom of association or right to organise? (1987) 18 *Industrial Relations Journal* 244; T. J. Christian and K. D. Ewing, Labouring under the Canadian constitution (1988) 17 ILJ 73; and S. Leader, *Freedom of Association: A Study in Labor Law and Political Theory* (1992).

4. 'Organization' for this purpose means any organization of workers for furthering and defending the interests of workers: Article 10.

5. *Digest of decisions and principles of the Freedom of Association Committee of the Governing Body of the ILO* (Geneva, 1985), paras 360 *et seq.* (J. Hodges-Aeberhard and A. Odero de Dios, Principles of the committee on freedom of association concerning strikes (1987) 126 *International Labour Review* 543; R. Ben Israel, *International Labour Standards: The Case of Freedom to Strike* (Deventer, 1988)). It is important to note that although the right to strike may properly be considered a crucial element in freedom of association, ILO Conventions and the ESC permit more extensive restrictions upon the right to strike than those applicable to the right to form and join trade unions; while restriction of the latter implies restriction of the former, therefore, the converse is not the case. The ILO considers that the right to strike may be restricted in the case of public servants acting in their capacity as agents of the public authority or in essential services (defined as those whose interruption 'would endanger the life, personal safety or health of the whole or part of the population') provided that restrictions are accompanied by reciprocal guarantees to safeguard the interests of workers (*Digest of decisions*, *op. cit.*, paras 394, 397). See further G. S. Morris, *Strikes in Essential Services* (1986), Chapters 1 and 7, G. S. Morris and S. Fredman, Is there a public/private labor law divide? (1993) 14 *Comparative Labor Law Journal* 115, and, on the ESC, D. J. Harris, *The European Social Charter* (Charlottesville, VA, 1984), pp. 77–9.

6. See Ben-Israel, *op. cit.*, Chapter 2, for a discussion of the scope of this provision.

7. *National Union of Belgian Police* v *Belgium* (1975) 1 EHRR 578 at para. 39.

8. *Schmidt and Dahlstrom* v *Sweden* (1976) 1 EHRR 632 at para. 36. See also *X* v *Germany* (1985) 7 EHRR 461, Eur Comm. Ben-Israel (*op. cit.*, pp. 28–9), however, considers that the Court provided 'powerful support' for the argument that freedom to strike is essential to freedom of association.

9. These are the grounds most likely to be relevant to trade union rights in the European context. Others grounds include race, religion, national and social origin.

10. *Belgian Police*, above, note 7, paras 43–9. See also *Swedish Engine Drivers' Union* v *Sweden* (1976) 1 EHRR 617.

11. See M. Forde, The European Convention on Human Rights and Labor Law (1983) 31 *American Journal of Comparative Law* 301, at p. 311.

12. See *Glasenapp* v *Germany* (1986) 9 EHRR 25; *Kosiek* v *Germany* (1986) 9 EHRR 328 (the Court could not consider an allegation that the exclusion of the applicants from the German civil service violated the exercise of the right to freedom of expression guaranteed by Article 10). See generally I. Leigh and L. Lustgarten, Employment, justice and detente: the reform of vetting (1991) 54 MLR 613, esp. p. 625 *et seq.* Cf. the ICCPR, which provides that 'every citizen shall have the right and the opportunity . . . to have access, on general terms of equality, to public service in his country'.

13. In *Young, James and Webster* v *UK* (1982) 4 EHRR 28, outlined below, the argument that the state should be regarded as the employer or that British Rail was under its control was not discussed. In *Isabel Hilton* v *UK*, Application 12015/86 it was unnecessary for the European Commission to decide whether the state was responsible for the acts of the British Broadcasting Corporation. For general discussion of this problem in other contexts, see Morris and Fredman, *op. cit.*, and references therein.

14. S. H. Bailey, D. J. Harris and B. L. Jones, *Civil Liberties: Cases and Materials* (3rd edn, 1991), p. 757.

15. Above. See further F. von Prondzynski, *Freedom of Association and Indutrial Relations: A Comparative Study* (1987), and M. Forde, The European Convention on Human Rights and Labor Law (1983) 31 *American Journal of Comparative Law* 301. In *Sigurjonsson* v *Iceland* (1993) 16 EHRR 462 the Court held that Article 11 encompassed a negative right of association without determining whether this should be considered on an equal footing with the positive right. Here the obligation to join an association was imposed by law.

16. Para. 49.

17. Article 1 provides that the contracting states 'shall secure to everyone within their jurisdiction' the rights and freedoms defined in the Convention; hence 'if a violation of one of those rights and freedoms is the result of non-observance of that obligation in the enactment of domestic legislation, the responsibility of the State for that violation is engaged' (para. 49).

18. Trade Union and Labour Relations (Consolidation) Act (henceforth TULRCA) 1992, Part III, as amended by the Trade Union Reform and Employment Rights Act 1993 (TURERA 1993).

19. Conclusions I (1969–70), 31.

20. Conclusions III (1973), 31; Conclusions IV (1975), 40.

21. D. J. Harris, *op. cit.*

22. *Belgian Police*, above, note 7, para. 38.

23. D. J. Harris, *op. cit.* Also, P. O'Higgins, The European Social Charter. In R. Blackburn and J. Taylor (eds), *Human Rights for the 1990s* (1991).

24. See J. E. S. Fawcett, *The Application of the European Convention on Human Rights* (2nd edn, 1987). Note that at the time of writing a protocol establishing a single court of human rights, removing the role of the Commission, is expected to be agreed in mid-1994.

25. See D. McGoldrick, *The Human Rights Committee* (Oxford, 1991).

26. ILO, *op. cit.*

27. On these and other aspects of collective labour law see G. S. Morris and T. J. Archer, *Trade Unions, Employers and the Law* (2nd edn, 1993).

28. TULRCA 1992, s. 273. The armed forces are excluded: s. 274.

29. *Ibid.*, Part III, as amended by TURERA 1993.

30. *Ibid.*

31. On the ILO see K. D. Ewing, *Britain and the ILO* (1989), and D. Brown and A. McColgan, UK employment law and the International Labour Organisation: the spirit of cooperation (1992) 21 ILJ 265. On the low profile given to the ESC in Britain, see N. Burrows, UK. In A. Ph. C. M. Jaspers and L. Betten (eds), *25 Years: European Social Charter* (Deventer, 1988). The only adverse finding against the UK in this area under the ECHR has been *Young, James and Webster* v *UK*, above, note 13. By the time the case came before the European Court of Human Rights, the newly elected Conservative Government had already embarked upon a programme of legislation restricting the operation of the closed shop, which culminated eventually in its enforcement becoming unlawful: see above, note 18. In *Sibson* v *UK*, *The Times* 17 May 1993, the Court rejected a complaint that the applicant's treatment breached Article 11. For the argument that incorporation of the ECHR into domestic law could endanger collective rights see Lord Wedderburn, Freedom of association or right to organise? (1987) 18 *Industrial Relations Journal* 244; and T. J. Christian and K. D. Ewing, Labouring under the Canadian Constitution (1988) 17 ILJ 73. The relationship between the ECHR and European Community law lies beyond the scope of this chapter.

32. M. Ozaki, Labour relations in the public sector. In R. Blanpain (ed.), *Comparative Labour Law and Industrial Relations in Industrialised Market Economies*, Vol. II (4th edn, Deventer, 1990).

33. See further G. S. Morris and S. Fredman, Is there a public/private labor law divide?, *op. cit.*

34. Fire service and prison staff are frequently restricted, although under international standards this would not usually be justified: see further below and, in particular, ILO, *Freedom of Association and Collective Bargaining: General Survey by the Committee of Experts on the Application of Conventions and Recommendations* (Geneva, 1983), paras 78–89.

35. See, generally, S. Fredman and G. S. Morris, *The State as Employer: Labour Law in the Public Services* (1989).

36. This does not constitute a breach of the anti-union discrimination provisions because of the power of ministers to issue a certificate excluding such protection: see note 38, and see below for the use of this power in relation to workers at GCHQ.

37. The statute excludes persons who have 'the powers and privileges of a constable', who include prison officers: TULRCA 1992, s. 280; *Home Office* v *Robinson and the POA* [1981] IRLR 524, EAT.

38. TULRCA 1992, s. 275.

39. EPCA 1978, Schedule 9, para. 2 as amended by TULRCA, 1992.

40. There is no presumption that an administrative discretion should be exercised in a way which does not infringe the ECHR: *Brind and others* v *Secretary of State for the Home Department* [1991] 1 All ER 720, HL.

41. See D. J. Harris, *op. cit.*, pp. 60–1.

42. Conclusions III (1973), 3.

43. Police Act 1964, s. 47(1).

44. See further S. Fredman and G. S. Morris, *The State as Employer*, *op. cit.*, pp. 96–8.

45. See D. J. Harris, *op. cit.*, pp. 61–2.

46. Conclusions IX (1985), 49. It should be noted that any external association by the Police Federation or any branch thereof is subject to the approval of the Secretary of State: Police Act 1964, s. 44(2A) (inserted by the Police Act 1972).

47. Conclusions X-1 (1987), 68.

48. D. J. Harris, *op. cit.*, p. 62.

49. See also the exclusion of certain 'high-level employees' under ILO Convention No. 151 concerning Protection of the Right to Organise and Procedures for Determining Conditions of Employment in the Public Service, discussed below.

50. J. E. S. Fawcett, *op. cit.*, p. 285. The same argument could be made in relation to restrictions on the police. Article 60 states that 'Nothing in this Convention shall be construed as limiting or derogating from any of the human rights and fundamental freedoms which may be ensured under the laws of any High Contracting Party or under any other agreement to which it is a Party.'

51. *Council of Civil Unions* v *United Kingdom* Application No. 11603/85. See also S. Fredman and G. S. Morris, Union membership at GCHQ (1988) 17 ILJ 105, from which some of this discussion is taken.

52. Note that 'restriction' in this context covers complete prohibition of the exercise of the right; cf. the view of the CIE under the ESC in relation to Articles 31 and 5, below.

53. S. H. Bailey, D. J. Harris and B. L. Jones, *op. cit.*, p. 758.

54. See R. Ben-Israel, *op. cit.*

55. ILO, *Digest of decisions*, *op. cit.*, para. 598.

56. Defined as 'any organisation, however composed, the purpose of which is to further and defend the interests of public employees' (Article 3).

57. See more generally Recommendation No. 143 concerning Protection and Facilities to be Afforded to Workers' Representatives in the Undertaking. In relation to the determination of terms and conditions of employment, Convention No. 98 encourages collective bargaining whereas No. 151 gives more latitude in this respect.

58. Case No. 1261.

59. ILO, *Freedom of Association and Collective Bargaining*, *op. cit.*, para. 88.

60. *Ibid.*, paras 126, 248.

61. *Ibid.*, para. 126.

62. *Ibid.*, para. 131.

63. *Sunday Times* v *UK* (1979) 2 EHRR 245 at para. 49.

64. For a summary of the relevant principles, see *The Sunday Times* v *UK (No. 2)* (1991) 14 EHRR 229 at para. 50.

65. *Ibid.*

66. *Leander* v *Sweden* (1987) 9 EHRR 433 at para. 59.

67. *The Observer and the Guardian* v *United Kingdom* (1991) 14 EHRR 153; *The Sunday Times* v *UK (No. 2)*, above. See I. Leigh, Spycatcher in Europe [1992] PL 200 for a useful discussion of these decisions.

68. See the cases above, paras 69 and 55 respectively.

69. In *Young, James and Webster* v *UK*, above, the detriment suffered by the applicants for their lack of union membership was found not to comply with Article 11(2); see also *Sigurjonsson* v *Iceland*, above.

70. Legitimate objectives under the ICESCR are national security, public order and the protection of the rights and freedoms of others; the ICCPR also includes public safety and the protection of public health and morals.

71. Conclusions IV (1975), 49.

72. Cf. the CIE's approach to the right to strike guaranteed by Article 6(4), in relation to which Article 31 may be invoked to justify abolishing the right completely. However, it should be noted that no specific groups are exempted under Article 6(4).

73. Conclusions XI-1 (1989), 80.

74. Articles 15, 30 and 4 respectively. Curiously, the ICESCR contains no equivalent provision.

75. ILO, *Freedom of Association and Collective Bargaining, op. cit.*, paras 71-5; ILO, *Digest of decisions, op. cit.*, paras 192-6.

76. N. Valticos and K. Samson, International labour law. In R. Blanpain (ed.), *op. cit.*, Vol. I.

77. See S. Fredman and G. S. Morris, *The State as Employer, op. cit.*, Chapter 4.

78. Under the Civil Service Order in Council, Article 4.

79. EPCA 1978, s. 138(3); EPA 1975, s. 121(4). See now TULRCA 1992, s. 275, above.

80. Sir Geoffrey Howe, Foreign Secretary, HC Debs, 27 February 1984, col. 28.

81. House of Commons, First Report from the Employment Committee, Session 1983-4.

82. *Council of Civil Service Unions* v *Minister for the Civil Service* [1984] 3 WLR 1174, HL. See S. Fredman, Crown employment, prerogative powers, consultation and national security (1985) 14 ILJ 42 for a critique of this decision.

83. Case No. 1261.

84. See note 5.

85. See, most recently, Report of the Committee of Experts on the Application of Conventions and Recommendations, Report III, Part 4A, 1992, 242-3.

86. This is a little disingenuous; the House of Lords merely decided that whether national security considerations outweighed the duty to consult rested with the Government.

87. *Sunday Times (No. 2)*, above, note 64.

88. Conclusions XI-1 (1989), 80.

89. Presumably this is a reference to 'listing': see TULRCA 1992, ss. 2, 3.

90. For the criteria for a certificate of independence and the function of the Certification Officer, see G. S. Morris and T. J. Archer, *Trade Unions, Employers and the Law* (2nd edn, 1993), paras 4.5-6; 2.28-30.

91. *Government Communications Staff Federation* v *Certification Officer and another* [1993] ICR 163, EAT.

92. See Report of the Committee of Experts on the Application of Conventions and Recommendations, Report 111 (Part 4A), 1992, 242-3.

93. See back for the approach of the European Commission on Human Rights in the GCHQ case (although, by contrast, in *Cheall* v *UK*, Application No. 10550/83 8 EHRR 74, the Commission, in rejecting a complaint that expulsion from a trade union to honour an obligation under the Trades Union Congress's 'Bridlington Principles' violated Article 11, took into account articles 3 and 5 of ILO Convention No. 87). In an application under the ICCPR concerning the right to strike of public employees in Alberta, the Human Rights Committee in 1986 affirmed that each treaty 'has a life of its own' and the decision of the ILO Freedom of Association Committee on the matter was irrelevant (quoted by Wedderburn, *op. cit.*, at p. 248).

94. M. Forde, *op. cit.*, p. 302.

3

Trade Unions and Democracy in Transitional Societies: Reflections on Russia and South Africa

Bob Hepple

INTRODUCTION

Trade unions need democracy and democracy needs trade unions. This truism is apparent in two very different societies, in which independent workers' organizations were repressed but that are now in the process of transition to democracy. In Russia, the weakness of the new 'alternative' trade unions is one of the factors that make it unlikely that either industrial or political democracy will take root in the medium-term. In South Africa, by contrast, the grassroots strength of the union movement provides a spear for the development of a participative democracy and a potential shield against political repression by a new elite.

Both countries are in the process of transition from authoritarian or oligarchic rule. Students of such processes usually distinguish three stages of transition.[1] The first is that of liberalization, which involves the definition of rights such as freedom of association, freedom of speech, freedom of movement and the rule of law. The second stage is that of democratization, a period of popular mobilization in which the spaces opened by liberalization are used to establish participation and representation in political processes on the basis of equal citizenship. The third stage is socialization, the process of redistributing wealth and resources so as to achieve substantive and not merely formal equality. The first of these stages began in Russia with Gorbachev's *perestroika* after 1985, and in South Africa with De Klerk's lifting of political restrictions in February 1990. As the second stage develops in both countries, there is intensive debate about the relationship between trade unions, the political parties and the state.

Should the unions be closely involved through tripartite bodies including the government and the employers, in the formulation of economic and social policies, and then persuade their members not to pursue their own sectional interests? Or should the unions be a completely independent 'oppositional' force defending workers' interests? Or an oppositional force with the employers against government? If the unions are not to be a 'conveyor belt' between the ruling political party and the 'masses' (as in the former USSR), should they become affiliates of political parties, or simply pursue tactical or strategic 'alliances' (e.g. COSATU with the ANC and SACP in South Africa) or remain non-aligned? Should unions concentrate on collective bargaining with employers, or also engage in wider community and national objectives? And how should the law be structured so as to accommodate these sometimes conflicting union objectives?

The aim of this chapter is to develop a comparative analysis, using some 'models' of union forms and purposes, with illustrations from Russia and South Africa, as part of a wider project on the role of state and law in the restructuring of labour relations. It is hoped that this comparative approach will indicate some of the choices and possible outcomes in each of these transitional societies.

A FRAMEWORK FOR COMPARATIVE ANALYSIS

Trade unions were defined by the Webbs, in the revised edition of their classic work *The History of Trade Unions*,[2] as 'a continuing association of wage-earners for the purpose of maintaining or improving their *working lives*'. The emphasized words were intended to embrace aims of unions, such as socialism and syndicalism, that go beyond the 'perpetual continuance of the capitalist or wage system'.[3] Cella and Treu remark that in many developing nations, particularly when unions are weak in the labour market, and also, for different reasons, in centrally planned economies, 'the lack of union market power or the non-existence of a (fully operating) market account for the unions' quasi-total reliance on political, legislative or administrative action'.[4]

Many attempts have been made to develop 'models' of union forms and purposes in order to explain the differences between those countries in which unions have come to rely on collective bargaining as the main or even exclusive way to represent their members' interests and those in which political action predominates.[5] As Cella and Treu point out,[6] most situations in democratic industrialized countries fall somewhere in between these two extremes: 'the balance or combination of the two methods - which are not alternatives in principle but may be in fact - can be seen as a continuum'.

A wider range of 'models' along this continuum is needed if we are to understand the relationship between trade unions, the state and law in transitional societies. For present purposes, adapting the classifications suggested by Ross Martin,[7] unions may be seen as having combinations of the following objectives:

1 Industrial pluralism or joint regulation of industry, through the methods of collective bargaining and other forms of workers' participation such as works councils.
2 Social emancipation, which may include aims such as national democracy, socialism and syndicalism.
3 Moral persuasion, for example by spreading the ideas of social Christianity or Islam.
4 National or patriotic unity within the framework of an authoritarian or corporatist state.
5 Strengthening work and state discipline as the 'conveyor belt' to the 'masses' of the ruling of political party.

Models 1 and 2 are conflictual, but while the first sees agreement and compromise, to accommodate conflicting interests, as an end in itself, the second allows only for tactical compromises along the path to the strategic aim of social transformation. The other three models are consensual or unitary to varying degrees. But these models are no more than 'ideal types', and within each we find great differences of emphasis on conflict and cooperation.

The relationship between the unions, the state and political parties varies across a spectrum from complete independence through autonomy to total dependence. It is in the first, industrial pluralist model that we usually find the highest degrees of independence or, at least, autonomy. Ross Martin identified twelve union movements as 'autonomous', all of them in industrial market economies with liberal democratic political systems.[8] Where unions regard social transformation or moral persuasion (models 2 and 3) as a key purpose, they may have emerged as the offspring of political parties, or have developed close links with them. The way in which the law intervenes to regulate union activities is much influenced by the degree of ideological or political competition between unions.[9]

These models provide a basis for analysing current developments in Russia and South Africa.

RUSSIA

In the Soviet period, the orthodox Marxist-Leninist view (as expressed by one leading Soviet labour lawyer in 1972) was that 'trade unions are active assistants of the Communist Party, loyal executors of its policies, experienced organisers of the masses'.[10] Their 'tasks' as conveyor belts between the Party and the masses included (according to the same author) helping to raise productivity and to 'strengthen state and work discipline'.[11] In return for this role as an appendage of the Party and state-appointed management, they were given a central role in the application of labour legislation and over occupational health and safety. They had the right to apply sanctions to managers who did not observe the prescribed standards, in the 1980s annually demanding the dismissal of nine to ten thousand managers for violations.[12] The consent of the trade union committee was required for changes in works rules, working hours, methods of remuneration, job classifications and dismissals. The trade unions were in charge of the settlement of individual labour disputes, and had equal representation with management on enterprise labour dispute commissions. Their role as quasi-state institutions was ensured when, in 1933, Stalin conferred upon them the function of administering the state social security funds. This function, together with their powers to distribute vouchers to the extensive network of trade union convalescent and rest homes and tourist facilities, and to allocate all housing built by the state or individual enterprises, ensured that over 95 per cent of the 130 million workers, as well as students and pensioners, remained union members.

This system developed on the basis of an ideology that denied any divergence of interests between the managers of state property and the unions in a 'workers' state', and ruthlessly suppressed dissent.[13] The driving force behind this ideology was the Communist Party, which subjected the trade unions, like all other state and public bodies, to strict day-to-day control. Decisions taken by the unions had to be approved by the Party and were not infrequently dictated by it. Not surprisingly, the unions that had taken an active part in the Bolshevik revolution of 1917 and recruited millions of workers to its cause degenerated into tools of the state and the Party ready to accept decisions made by the leadership even though these were unpopular and neglected workers' interests. The severe restrictions on the autonomy of managers and unions in the administrative-command system meant that there was little scope for collective bargaining. The so-called 'socialist collective agreement' was negotiated within a rigid framework set by the central planners who provided the funds. Trade unions took part in the planning process as the representatives of *all* workers as a collective entity, not on behalf of particular sectional interests. Wage scales and basic salaries were largely determined by the state and were generally low partly because the state was also able to provide cheap housing, transport and basic services.

In the early stages of *perestroika*, when Gorbachev envisaged the 'development of socialist democracy' as the precondition for accelerated socio-economic development, trade unions began to reconsider their functions. At the Eighteenth Congress of Soviet Trade Unions in 1987, they claimed a role in *perestroika*, but did so simply by re-emphasizing such old slogans as socialist emulation, better product quality and savings in material resources. It was only after a wave of strikes swept the country in 1989, expressing workers' dissatisfaction with the slow process of reform and the neglect of their social needs, that the All-Union Central Council of Trade Unions responded, in September 1989, by declaring their 'independence' from political organizations and state, economic and administrative bodies. Since April 1992, the former All-Union Centre, with severely reduced resources, has officially been no more than an 'international centre' with affiliates from some of the former Soviet Republics.

In Russia, the Federation of Independent Trade Unions (FNPR) is the successor to the former official unions. It still claims a membership of 66 million, or about 90 per cent of the Russian workforce. As of September 1992, despite its proclaimed 'independence', the FNPR had not yet relinquished its quasi-state functions in respect of social security, convalescent and rest homes, housing and application of labour legislation. However, its influence and membership are rapidly declining and once it is deprived of its quasi-state functions (due to happen soon) it will be on an equal footing with the so-called 'alternative' trade unions.[14]

SOTSPROF (the Association of Socialist Trade Unions) is the main 'alternative' trade union. It was established in April 1989, as a means of channelling spontaneous strike action into permanent trade union activity, and it regards collective bargaining as its main function. Its leaders find it difficult to estimate its membership, but one indication is that 15,000 copies per month are sold of its newspaper, *Workers' Voice*. SOTSPROF has a highly decentralized organizational structure, with largely autonomous workplace organizations that send only small fixed financial contributions to the centre (compared with the 1 per cent of wages contributed by FNPR). The centre provides limited services, such as advice on collective bargaining and legal matters to its workplace affiliates. On visits to the FNPR headquarters in Moscow, and those of SOTSPROF, one is struck by the huge contrast in their resources, with the FNPR still occupying the large complex of buildings of its 'official' predecessors and SOTSPROF operating from small, cramped, back-street premises. SOTSPROF does not claim any right to the assets accumulated by the FNPR and its predecessors from membership dues, but it would like all the assets 'donated' by the state (such as rest homes) to be removed from FNPR control and privatized. When the social insurance funds are removed from FNPR control, SOTSPROF expects a sharp overall decline in union membership, but a relative increase in its own membership.

Despite the word 'socialist' in its name (a sop to the former Soviet regime), SOTSPROF is committed to the aims of the Yeltsin Government of building a capitalist market economy at breakneck speed. It is a strong supporter of privatization, and opposes the giving of enterprises to labour collectives. Their leaders, who have received much support from American unions, are uncertain about workers' participation in management and reject the idea of electing workers to the board of enterprises. (In this regard it is to be noted that while the Law on Enterprises of the former USSR provided for 50 per cent of the executive board to be appointed by the labour collective, the Russian Law on Enterprises of December 1990 is silent on this point.) SOTSPROF's influence in government is now far greater than that of the FNPR, and relations are particularly close with the small Russian Social-Democratic Party. The President of SOTSPROF, Mr Hramov, summed up his perspective in a conversation with me: 'FNPR opposes government. SOTSPROF opposes the employer.'

The FNPR have been strong critics of the Government's priorities and methods, in particular the inadequate social protection for workers in the face of steeply rising prices, and the unwaged 'holidays' forced on workers because of the absence of credits to enterprises. The FNPR has also formed alliances with the employers' organizations. In particular, they took an active part in promoting the Russian Assembly for Social Partnership, which held its first meeting in July 1992 with equal representation from the FNPR and the 'employers' of the still mainly state-owned enterprises, in particular those in the Russian Union of Industrialists and Entrepreneurs (headed by Mr Volsky, who is also leader of the opposition Civic Union). The aim of the Assembly (which now has a consultative council of equal numbers of FNPR and employers' representatives) is said to be to develop general principles relating to the role of trade unions and employers, and to comment on government-sponsored reforms. But the Government and SOTSPROF are deeply suspicious of the Assembly, which they see as an obstacle to reform, undermining the work of the Tripartite Commission (see below).

At enterprise level there is some evidence of practical collaboration between SOTSPROF organizations and FNPR members and officials. Workers who join SOTSPROF organizations do not at present leave FNPR because only the latter guarantees access to social insurance and welfare facilities. For example, at the Second Moscow Watch Factory I found (in July 1992) that 120 out of 300 workers had joined SOTSPROF but most of them also belonged to FNPR. SOTSPROF and the FNPR workplace organizations had made joint demands to management. SOTSPROF shop stewards claimed that FNPR officials were not tough negotiators, and that their success in winning 30 per cent wage increases had been due to what they termed a series of 'Italian' strikes (which turned out to be more akin to a British 'work to rule'). This is a recently privatized enterprise in which the workforce acquired 67 per cent of the shares, and the Moscow municipality has the remainder. Asked to explain the apparent contradiction in pushing up wages against their interests as shareholders in their 'own' enterprise, the SOTSPROF shop stewards laughed and said: 'We would prefer to own shares in other enterprises [non-union?] and to bargain purely as workers in our own!'

The government of Russia sees the present period in labour relations as one of transition from administrative regulation to collective bargaining, paralleling the move from a one-party state to political pluralism. At the end of January 1992, the government established a Tripartite Commission, consisting of fourteen government representatives, from various ministries that run state enterprises and from the Ministry of Labour, fourteen employers' organization representatives and fourteen trade union representatives. Nine of the latter are from the FNPR, three from SOTSPROF, one from the independent miners' union and one from the airline pilots' union. The Commission has no permanent staff or officers of its own, and the level of government representation appears to be relatively low. It has three main functions: (a) consultation on the main legislative proposals and on government socio-economic policies; (b) negotiation of a general agreement and sectoral agreements (40 of which had been concluded by July 1992) and territorial agreements (e.g. for municipalities; regional tripartite commissions are being established); and (c) the settlement of disputes at regional level.

The Ministry of Labour has adopted a three-stage legislative strategy to alter the institutions of labour relations. The first has been to secure amendments to the Labour Code in order to reflect changes in the economy and in the role of unions. Among the most important amendments adopted by the Supreme Soviet in July 1992 were: (a) the prohibition of forced labour; (b) a drastic reduction in the grounds upon which the trade union body in the enterprise (formerly the 'committee') must consent to termination of employment at the initiative of the employer (these are now limited to workforce reduction, incompetence of the worker and absence due to sickness for four months or more); (c) fixed-term contracts (which were being widely used to avoid labour standards) can only be concluded if the nature of the work is temporary; (d) a worker may terminate the contract at his or her initiative by giving two weeks' notice, instead of the previously prescribed two months; and (e) the hearing of individual labour disputes by trade union bodies has been abolished. The labour disputes commissions at enterprise level are now directly elected by the labour collective, and need not include any trade union representatives.

Second, the Ministry is attempting to develop laws on specific topics such as collective agreements, health and safety, payment of wages and individual labour contracts. The Law on Collective Agreements of 11 March 1992 is applicable to all enterprises, irrespective of forms of ownership, sector or number of employees. The law defines the legal grounds for the preparation, conclusion and implementation of collective agreements and covenants. A 'collective agreement' means a legal act governing labour–management relations at enterprise level for one to three years, and a 'covenant' means a legal act defining working conditions of employees in a particular occupation, industry or territory for not more than three years. Collective agreements are concluded bilaterally between one or more trade unions or workers' representative bodies and the employer, while covenants may be either bilateral or trilateral, including the government. A general covenant sets out general principles of socio-economic policy, while a sectoral covenant may cover a range of specific issues such as wages and working conditions, environment, safeguards for workers in the course of privatization and the development of tripartism and collective bargaining. Collective agreements may deal with matters such as the forms, systems and amounts of wages, workforce reduction, work and rest time, working conditions and workers' no-strike obligations. The only difference between sectoral covenants and enterprise agreements, therefore, is that the former can be, but need not be, trilateral. The law provides that where there are several trade union or other workers' representative bodies, each of them has the right to bargain in the name of their members or those whom they represent. This reflects the pressure exerted by SOTSPROF, supported by the government, to encourage trade union pluralism and to break the grip of the FNPR.

Third, the Ministry of Labour hopes to develop fundamentals of labour legislation and new labour codes for all 21 republics and regions that constitute the Russian Federation. This is a long-term and complex task, bearing in mind that a number of all-Union Acts are still in force insofar as they are consistent with Russian legislation. These include the Law on Trade Unions of 10 December 1990 and the Law on Collective Labour Disputes Settlement of 9 October 1989. The Commission on Social Policy of the Supreme Soviet is also examining a number of other areas that impact on labour relations, such as indexation, unemployment (the Law on Employment of 1991 provides for a very low level of benefits), child benefits, health insurance, the consequences of radiation and the removal of corruption.

Russian trade unions are thus in the painful process of transition from being the conveyor belt of a Party enjoying a monopoly of power, bound by a unitarist ideology to a situation of trade union pluralism and collective bargaining in a capitalist market economy. However, there are a number of reasons to doubt whether this transition can be successfully completed. A more likely outcome is the re-emergence of a relatively autocratic state with a high level of unilateral employer regulation of labour relations and only patchy collective bargaining.

One reason for this conclusion is the absence of genuine independent employers' organizations. More than 90 per cent of industrial enterprises are still state-owned. There are three major 'employer' organizations: the Russian Union of Industrialists and Entrepreneurs, representing the interests of directors of state-owned enterprises, which account in all for 65 per cent of commodity production; the Congress of Russian Business Circles, representing financial and stock-exchange businesses; and the Confederation of Entrepreneurs of Russia, representing small business interests. Only the first of these organizations specifically declares the objective of promoting the interests of its members as employers. Although the Russian Union includes 'social partnership' among its objectives and is willing to negotiate with the FNPR within the Russian Assembly (see above), its main role, and that of its President Mr Volsky, has been to oppose government measures. The Vice-President, Mr Kolmogorov, told me (in July 1992) that he regards many of the 'alternative' unions as 'imposters' and wants to deal only with 'representative' unions, which, at the present time, are likely to be the FNPR organizations. The Russian Union sees the development of disputes procedures largely as a matter for legislation rather than employer initiative. It has no experience of real collective bargaining, and it looks to the state to enact a new law on employers' organizations as a basis for its legitimacy, rather than by the voluntary development of its organizational base.

The government's privatization programme, described in its 'programme of economic recovery' as being 'at the heart of economic reform', will undoubtedly strengthen the 'entrepreneurs as a social stratum with specific interests in determining the basic directions of economic policy'. This new stratum is unlikely, however, to be much attracted by the values of industrial pluralism. The privatization programme envisages giving some shares to management and staff, then seeking a strategic investor willing to acquire a controlling interest and finally selling the residual shares. The mythical Russian 'entrepreneurs' will be either a small new acquisitive class who have got rich quickly in the collapse of the old regime, or foreign investors. One of the government's advisers has recently acknowledged that the government might be unable to resist the pressure of such economic interest groups. In order to maintain political and social stability while establishing a market economy, democratic forms might be suspended although appeals to populism. such as the referendum, could become more frequent.[15] Among the first casualties of an autocracy would be collective bargaining.

A second reason for doubting whether the collective bargaining model can be realized is the absence of genuine independent trade unions. As we have seen, the FNPR appears to be in terminal decline, although at enterprise level its organizations show signs of transformation into genuinely representative bodies working in alliance with the 'alternative' unions. However, the alternative unions are weak, have confused aims and are more influential on government policy than at the workplace.

The greatest change that would need to be made by both the employers' organizations and the trade unions in order to progress towards collective bargaining would be to lose their psychological dependence upon the state. The FNPR unions have to understand that they are no longer conveyor belts for other people's decisions; management has to be willing to accept responsibility for its own decisions, and negotiate with workers. An indication that this is not yet happening is the way in which sectoral covenants are developing. In practice most of these have been made with government participation and are highly detailed. They treat enterprise agreements as merely supplementary, to fill in details. Like the employers' reluctance to engage in voluntary negotiations over procedures, their unwillingness to negotiate independently of the state shows that the old system of administrative regulation is not dead, but is simply taking on new forms. This is, of course, inconsistent with the economic reforms (as embodied in the Russian Law on Enterprises of December 1990), which give the power to set wages to enterprises, to be exercised independently. The tendency to over-regulation, with state participation, at sectoral level is symptomatic of the problems that lie ahead. Genuine democratic trade unions will grow only if they have the confidence of their rank and file and vigorously defend their interests at enterprise level through negotiations with the employers. This is a lesson offered by the South African experience since 1979.

SOUTH AFRICA

Unlike in Russia, in South Africa the pluralist or joint regulation model has always been a major union objective but it was distorted by racialism, which denied legal support for collective bargaining to trade unions of black workers and imprisoned and victimized their leaders. The first unions were branches of British craft unions for immigrants who came to South Africa from 1880 onwards.[16] The often violent conflict between these unions and the Chamber of Mines, culminating in the 'Rand revolt' of 1922, was notable for the demands by these exclusively white unions for an industrial colour bar. As in Britain, the unions defended their political interests by helping to found a Labour Party (1909), but the 'socialist commonwealth' was firmly to exclude black, Asian and Chinese labour.

The labour legislation introduced in 1924 aimed to promote collective bargaining through joint industrial councils, on the model of the Whitley Councils in Britain but on a statutory rather than voluntary basis. However, this collective bargaining system excluded 'pass-bearing natives' (by an anomaly, until the 1950s, black women fell outside this class), debarred blacks from many skilled jobs and pursued a so-called 'civilized labour policy' to promote the interests of the recently urbanized 'poor whites', at the expense of the black majority. After 1929, Labour was excluded from government (apart from the war years) and by the 1950s had adopted non-racial policies that led to its rejection by the white electorate. On the other hand, the 'purified' Nationalists, through their 'Broederbond', infiltrated and secured control of many of the unions in which Afrikaners were in the majority. These unions were the 'conveyor belts' for the racially exclusive ideology that helped the Nationalist Government to power in 1948.

The excluded black majority had, from 1917, began to combine in the Industrial Workers of Africa (IWA) on the model of the American 'Wobblies'.[17] This organization was overtaken from 1918 by the Industrial and Commercial Workers' Union of South Africa (ICU), which at its height in 1927 claimed 100,000 members. It was more of a political than a trade union organization. According to one historian,[18] its collapse by 1930 'highlighted the weakness of general unionism; it failed to build working-class leadership and proper structures for democratic control; and related to this it allowed the development of individual leadership and personality cults.' During the 1930s and 1940s many attempts were made, particularly by the Communist Party, to organize black trade unions, despite their exclusion from labour law. These attempts met with fierce employer resistance and police repression.

From the 1950s, the Nationalist Government removed many communist and non-communist union leaders from their positions, enforced the break-up of 'mixed' unions into racially separate branches, intensified job segregation and legislated for a system of 'workers' committees' intended to 'bleed black trade unions white', although it never succeeded in this aim. The Minister of Labour prophetically declared: 'If there is a strong, well-organized [black] trade union movement in South Africa, and they utilize those trade unions as a political weapon, at a given time they can create chaos in South Africa.'[19] The Trades and Labour Council (TLC), which until then had united most of the registered white and mixed race unions, disintegrated. Some of its affiliates formed the Trade Union Council of South Africa (TUCSA) which over the years vacillated between exclusion of black trade unions and attempts to control them. Other TLC unions joined with right-wing nationalists and eventually formed the racially exclusive South African Confederation of Labour (SACLA). A small group of TLC affiliates joined with black unions in 1955 to form the South African Congress of Trade Unions (SACTU), which joined the ANC-led Congress Alliance and participated actively in mass political campaigns. SACTU grew from about 20,000 members in 19 unions in 1955 to 46,000 in 35 affiliated unions by 1959, despite bannings and official harassment.[20]

SACTU members were often also African National Congress (ANC) activists. During the 1960 State of Emergency, following the Sharpeville massacre, a large number of union activists were detained. After the banning of the ANC, in 1960, SACTU remained technically a legal organization, but many of its activists joined the ANC's military wing or were imprisoned or forced into exile. SACTU continued to operate in exile, but internally the unions entered a 'dark decade' until a series of strikes in 1973.[21] SACTU's legacy was 'planting the roots of non-racial trade unionism in the soil of apartheid South Africa' and the commitment to 'revolutionary struggle for political emancipation'.[22] While SACTU has been criticized for becoming 'captive of the nationalists',[23] it is mistaken to believe that involvement in politics diverted SACTU from building workplace organization. On the contrary, SACTU grew most rapidly in Natal and the Eastern Cape, where involvement with the ANC was closest at grassroots.[24]

The black workers' unions that re-emerged in the 1970s continued to face severe repression. Their organizers came from diverse groups, including former ANC and SACTU activists released after serving long prison sentences, white university students and a new generation of young workers. Their strategy was to build workplace union organization and to avoid overt political action, which, at the time, would have been suicidal. The Federation of South African Trade Unions (FOSATU), formed in 1979 with 20,000 workers in twelve unions, had strongly democratic structures based on the principles of worker control and accountability, emphasizing shopfloor organization and independence from political organizations.[25] Its foundation coincided with the publication of the Wiehahn Commission's Report, which resulted in the Labour Relations Amendment Act 1979 liberalizing labour relations, including freedom of association and rights of collective bargaining for all unions irrespective of race, while extending prohibitions on political activity. 'In reading the Report,' comments Sonia Bendix,[26] 'it becomes apparent that the Commission's point of departure was that the co-option of black trade unions into the existing system would make them more controllable and would prevent the flourishing of the system of plant-level agreements.'

Initially, however, most black unions refused to register (the precondition for participation in the industrial councils and certain other statutory benefits and protections) regarding this as a form of collaboration with the apartheid state's structures, and continued the previous strategy of securing recognition by employers plant-by-plant on the basis of strong shopfloor organization. Plant-level bargaining soon became widespread. Gradually, the advantages of registration became apparent, and unions were able to use their registered status to cover a substantial number of employees in particular industries. The membership of registered unions was 808,000 in 1980, and grew to 2.5 million in 1990 and 2.75 million in 1991.[27]

Another feature of the 1980s was the rise of black 'community unions', which differed from the more established unions by aligning themselves closely with residential (township) civic organizations and affiliating to the United Democratic Front (UDF). A study of shop stewards in 1985[28] found a significant difference between British shop stewards and their black South African counterparts. The latter were heavily involved in community politics, cutting across factory divisions. This, in turn, forced FOSATU to become involved in national political issues. Unions such as the South African Allied Workers' Union (SAAWU) and the Motor Assemblers and Component Workers

Union of South Africa (MACWUSA) argued against the 'economism' and 'workerism' that had confined activities to the workplace. The first significant political intervention by FOSATU was a two-day stayaway organized with civic and student organizations. Another federation, the Council of Unions of South Africa (CUSA), like FOSATU, grew rapidly. While CUSA was inspired by the philosophy of black consciousness, FOSATU emphasized non-racialism. After protracted negotiations, the Congress of South African Trade Unions (COSATU) was formed at the end of 1985 with half a million members from all FOSATU's affiliates and a number of other unions; by 1990 it had about one million members. The next largest federation, the National Council of Trade Unions (NACTU), was formed in 1986 from CUSA and two other black consciousness organizations; by 1990 it had 258,000 members; the Inkatha-backed Union of Workers of South Africa (UWUSA) claimed 28,000 members and SACLA 86,000. This left nearly a million union members in non-federated registered unions. Overall, one in four workers were unionized.

The trade union federations that emerged in the mid-1980s reflect the racial and political divisions in South Africa. The crucial factor, until February 1990, was that the union movement was the only legitimate organization of the voteless majority of South Africans. It was, therefore, natural for the black unions to pursue not only the objective of industrial pluralism, but also that of social emancipation, while the exclusively white unions remained a buttress of social reaction. Thus Cyril Ramaphosa, then General Secretary of the National Union of Mineworkers (NUM) who was later to become Secretary-General of the ANC, said at COSATU's inaugural congress that 'workers' political strength depends upon building strong militant organizations at the workplace', and that 'it is also important to draw people into a programme for the restructuring of society in order to make sure that the wealth of our society is democratically controlled and shared by its people'.[29] NACTU's declared aim is a 'non-exploitative democratic society based on the leadership of the working-class'.[30] Attempts at unity between COSATU and NACTU have so far failed, partly because of COSATU's political alliances with the ANC and SACP.

COSATU and NACTU have organized a number of strikes for the purposes of political protest, even after the unbanning of political organizations. It was COSATU that, in November 1991, organized the stayaway in protest against the imposition of value added tax, and in August 1992 helped to rescue the negotiations for a new constitutional dispensation by organizing mass action. COSATU showed that it could organize not only trade union members but also a wide range of community, business and other interests, for broad social objectives.

Perhaps the most impressive example of the combination of collective bargaining machinery and political mass action was the successful campaign against the Labour Relations Amendment Act of 1988, which had been designed, in the words of a recent ILO Fact Finding and Conciliation Commission,[31] 'to halt and even roll back the progress made by the trade unions since the Labour Relations Act (LRA) had been extended to black workers in 1981'. Shopfloor protests, demonstrations and a threat of a national stayaway were combined with intensive lobbying of individual employers. In this climate, the South African Consultative Committee on Labour Relations (SACCOLA), to which 90 per cent of private sector employers belong, approached the unions. The ensuing COSATU-NACTU-SACCOLA Accord was directly responsible for the repeal of all the most controversial 1988 amendments in March 1991. It was the first time that employers and unions representing black workers had made a 'social pact' in which the Government had to acquiesce. In the course of negotiations, the unions put forward further proposed changes to legislation, including coverage of farm and domestic workers. The State President established a tripartite working party and in another historic document, known as the Laboria Minute of September 1990, the Government agreed to implement most of the working party's recommendations. The Laboria Minute notes that 'legislation on labour relations cannot work unless there has been extensive consultation with at least the major actors in the labour relations arena and broad consensus on the legislative framework for the regulation of labour relations.'

Part of COSATU's strategy was to utilize the pressure of the International Labour Organisation (ILO) by submitting a complaint of breach of the international principles of freedom of association. The South African Government (although not an ILO member) consented to the establishment of an ILO Fact Finding and Conciliation Commission, which reported in mid-1992 that the Government 'is aware of the need for reform in the trade union and labour relations field'.[32] A further sign of the developing 'social pact' between government and unions was the bipartite agreement in November 1992 to implement all the ILO Commission's recommendations, to extend basic conditions of employment to domestic and farm workers, to reform the industrial court and to make the labour appeal court (with judges appointed by tripartite consensus) the final arbiter in labour law, so excluding the influence of 'common law' judges. A restructured tripartite National Manpower Commission (NMC) and national training body will have a vital role in the development of labour legislation.[33]

COSATU's growing power, as a mass base of the democratic

movement, has precipitated a fierce debate about the political role of trade unions. The 'typical' COSATU shop steward (of whom there are some 25,000) is male, in his mid-thirties, with some high school education, and considers himself to be a South African rather than in ethnic (Xhosa, Zulu, Sotho, etc.) terms. A survey of COSATU shop stewards conducted in September 1991[34] found that 78 per cent of stewards think that workers can influence the political system, 71 per cent think that union leaders should also be leaders of political parties and 70 per cent believe that COSATU can better represent their interests in the constitutional negotiations than the ANC or SACP.[35] COSATU has, in fact, formed a broad alliance with the ANC and the SACP, and the survey indicates that 94 per cent of shop stewards intend to vote for the ANC, compared to 3 per cent for the SACP, in democratic elections.[36] However, this support for the election of an ANC government does not indicate unqualified support for its policies. Indeed, on issues such as nationalization and the provision of welfare services, the survey revealed that shop stewards believe COSATU to be more likely to voice worker concerns on these matters than a multi-class national organization such as the ANC.[37] At the same time, an overwhelming majority of stewards in the survey favoured 'co-determination' models (with workers' committees and profit sharing) rather than a radical socialist transformation of ownership.

There has been criticism of COSATU's 'junior status' within the alliance. It was not independently represented in the early stages of the Conference for a Democratic South Africa (CODESA). At its June 1991 Congress COSATU reaffirmed the independence of the unions and expressed reservations about the ANC's handling of negotiations. In November 1991 the Central Executive Committee of COSATU resolved to attend CODESA either in its own right or not at all. There was also debate over the issue of whether COSATU officials should hold office in political parties and it was resolved to bar full-time paid COSATU officials from doing so. NACTU is resolved not to become aligned to any political party, while remaining committed to the struggle for black liberation. It has been far less influential than COSATU on the political scene, and internally suffers from divisions between black nationalists and 'Africanist' socialists. The most divisive element of all on the trade union scene has been the conflict between UWUSA and COSATU, reflecting the bloody political violence between Inkatha and ANC supporters in Natal and the Transvaal.

South Africa's trade unions have thus moved through a number of phases. From 1924, the pluralist collective bargaining model was predominant but was primarily a device for excluding the unskilled and semi-skilled black majority from economic and political power.

The harbingers of 'social movement' unionism can be found in the early ICU, in the attempts at black unionization in the 1930s and 1940s and in the policies of SACTU in the 1950s and early 1960s. After a 'dark decade' of repression, new black unions emerged with a strong shopfloor base, won plant-level collective bargaining rights without the aid of the law (and often in the face of severe state and employer repression) and were then compelled into the political sphere by the active community involvement of the shop stewards. The unions, particularly those grouped in COSATU, are now the power base of the democratic movement. There is an obvious contrast between the political violence of the Inkatha-impis and the 'young comrades' of the townships, on the one hand, and the disciplined organization represented by the shop stewards. The future political development of South Africa may well turn on how these workers' organizations react to the two social groups that flank them: on one side the rising black middle class soon to share political power with the white elite, and on the other the growing underclass of unemployed or partially employed workers who are not unionized.

CONCLUSIONS

An analysis based on models of the kind outlined at the beginning of this chapter suffers from the danger of presenting a static and unidimensional portrait of the processes of labour relations. One of the advantages of examining transitional societies, in which the rules of the game are unstable and in a period of redefinition, is that we are forced to examine union objectives *in motion*. The justification for focusing on union objectives is, as Wedderburn has pointed out,[38] that it is the character of labour movements and the different ways in which they have each emerged from repression that helps to account for the distinctive features of each system of collective labour law.

Liberalization, in both Russia and South Africa, has resulted in the assertion and extension of human rights, including freedom of association, although in Russia the severe restrictions on the right to strike imposed in the Gorbachev era remain in force in theory, if not in practice.[39] From the perspective of trade unions, the most important consequence has been the expansion of civil society. In Soviet Russia self-organized and autonomous trade unions had been destroyed, and organizations of that name existed mainly as conveyor belts of the state and Party apparatus. Authoritarian rule meant that there was no space for politics. Individuals became depoliticized, using the unions only as means to obtain welfare and social benefits, for which they paid the price of obedience to management and 'state and party discipline'. The former official unions have no tradition of industrial democracy on which to call in the period of transition, and the new 'alternative' unions are, as yet, too weak to provide a basis for democratic mobilization.

On the other hand, even at the height of repression in apartheid South Africa, some independent trade unions continued to resist. The tradition of industrial pluralism and collective bargaining, although enjoyed by only a privileged minority of workers, remained a dominant influence in shaping the objectives of the new black unions. The labour law reforms introduced under the pressure of the strikes and shopfloor organization were designed to incorporate those unions within an expanded, yet still limited, version of industrial pluralism. But the opening of this space on the industrial front facilitated grass-roots activity of a quasi-political nature. The liberalization of labour relations was the prelude to popular upsurge. The insurrection of 1985–6, in which the black people of South Africa rediscovered their own power and sense of freedom, might not have been possible without the growth in organization and self-confidence inspired by the expanding union movement. Despite the repressive state of emergency from 1986–7 onwards, popularly inspired democratization could no longer be avoided by the regime.

In the transitional period, following popular upsurge in both countries, there has not simply been a return to regime-inspired liberalization. There has been a period in which transitional pacts have been negotiated, and institutional arrangements have been made to involve trade unions and employers in the reform process. In Russia, this has been the function of the Tripartite Commission, while the Russian Assembly of Social Partnership appears to be more like an attempt by state-appointed managers and their allies in the former official unions to capture the reform process. In South Africa, a remarkable degree of tripartite accord now forms the social basis for continued labour law reform, in many ways running ahead of the democratization of the political system.

In one critical respect, the liberalization processes in the two countries is completely different. In Russia, liberalization involves the rapid introduction of a capitalist market economy, while in South Africa some form of socialization of the economy remains an aspiration of a significant section of the union and political movements. Paradoxically, Russia and other Eastern European countries are now witnessing a transition from state socialism to capitalism. Both the former official unions and the 'alternative' unions are, in varying degrees, committed to that transition. A pluralist collective bargaining system is their objective. The key questions that have to be resolved are whether the nascent 'corporatist' structures will come to dominate labour regulation, and whether the weakness of shopfloor organization will result in a large measure of unilateral employer regulation.

In South Africa, the main liberation parties are committed to a prolonged period of securing equal political rights, with equality of treatment and participation, and the gradual erosion of social and economic inequalities in a 'mixed' economy, through affirmative action and similar means. The largest question mark hanging over the future of South African trade unions is whether they will remain content with collective bargaining and industrial pluralism within a political democracy, or will press ahead, through the new tripartite institutions, with political demands for a radical redistribution of wealth and resources.

NOTES

This chapter is based on an Advisory Mission to the Russian Federation that I undertook on behalf of the International Labour Organisation in July 1992, and on a series of visits to South Africa between July 1990 and September 1992. Many people gave me the benefit of their knowledge and experience during these visits, but my special gratitude is due to Slava Egorov, Halton Cheadle, Clive Thompson and Martin Brassey. Neither they, nor the ILO, bear any responsibility for the contents. The essay was written before I had an opportunity to read Clive Thompson's valuable paper, 'Strategy and opportunism: trade unions as agents for change in South Africa', presented at the IIRA ninth World Congress, September 1992. Our conclusions about the South African situation are similar.

1. A. du Toit, Transitional societies and democracy. In I. de Villiers (ed.), *Collective Bargaining, Deregulation and Democracy* (Durban, Centre for Socio-Legal Studies, 1991); see, generally, G. O'Donnell *et al.* (eds), *Transitions from Authoritarian Rule* (Baltimore, 1986).
2. S. Webb and B. Webb, *The History of Trade Unionism* (revised edn, 1920), p. 1 note. In the first (1894) edition of their work the Webbs had confined the aims to the improvement of 'conditions of employment'.
3. *Ibid.*, p. 1 note.
4. G. Cella and T. Treu, 'National trade union movements'. In R. Blanpain (ed.) *Comparative Labour Law and Industrial Relations*, Vol. 2, 4th edn (Deventer, 1990), p. 56.
5. See esp. R. M. Martin, *Trade Unionism: Purposes and Forms* (Oxford, 1989).
6. *Ibid.*, p. 57.
7. *Ibid.*, pp. 246–51.
8. These were the United Kingdom, Ireland, the USA, Canada, Australia, New Zealand, four Scandinavian states, Germany and Austria (Martin, *ibid.*). See also H. Clegg, *Trade Unionism under Collective Bargaining* (Oxford, 1976), who shows the impact of collective bargaining on union government and workplace organization.
9. Martin, *op. cit.*
10. K. Batygin, *Soviet Labour Law and Principles of Civil Law* (Moscow, 1972), p. 75.

11. *Ibid.*, pp. 76–80.
12. G. Kanaev, in G. Standing (ed.), *In Search of Flexibility: The New Soviet Labour Market* (Geneva, ILO, 1991), p. 260.
13. See, generally, A. Bullock, *Hitler and Stalin: Parallel Lives* (1991), p. 454 *et seq.* on the power of ideology, and p. 511 *et seq.* on the terror that destroyed those (including trade unionists) who had made the revolution.
14. A decree by President Yeltsin in 1992 removing control of the social insurance funds from the trade unions was declared invalid by the Supreme Soviet in July 1992 because of failure to follow proper procedures of consultation. It seems likely, at the time of writing, that the transfer will be made later in 1992 to an independent fund, with a board of directors representing contributors, with professional management, so as to avoid direct state control. This is already the case with the pension fund.
15. V. Mau, Hazards of caution, *New Statesman and Society*, 9 October 1992, p. 18; see also J. Lloyd, The best one can hope for, *London Review of Books*, 22 October 1992, p. 14.
16. See, generally, A. Hepple, *South Africa: A Political and Economic History* (1966), pp. 221–53.
17. See L. Forman, *A Trumpet from the Housetops* (1992), pp. 62–9.
18. J. Baskin, *Striking Back: A History of COSATU* (Johannesburg, Ravan Press), 1991, p. 8.
19. Cited by A. Hepple, *Trade Unions in Travail* (Johannesburg, Unity Publications, 1954), p. 36.
20. Ken Luckhardt and Brenda Wall, *Organise or Starve: The History of the South African Congress of Trade Unions* (1980).
21. Baskin, *op. cit.*, p. 18.
22. Luckhardt and Wall, *op. cit.*, p. 441.
23. Steven Friedman, *Building Tomorrow Today* (Johannesburg, Ravan Press, 1987), p. 31.
24. This is the author's personal impression from close involvement in SACTU during this period. It is also that of Rob Lambert, cited by Baskin, *op. cit.*, p. 32, n. 12.
25. Baskin, *op. cit.*, p. 26.
26. *Industrial Relations in South Africa* (2nd edn, Cape Town, Juta, 1992), p. 342.
27. National Manpower Commission, Annual Report, 1991, p. 41.
28. E. C. Webster, *Cast in a Racial Mould: Labour Process and Trade Unionism in Factories* (Johannesburg, Ravan Press, 1985).
29. Cited by Bendix, *op cit.*, p. 373.
30. *Op. cit.*, p. 389.
31. *Prelude to Change: Industrial Relations Reform in South Africa.* Report of the Fact Finding and Conciliation Commission on Freedom of Association concerning the Republic of South Africa (Geneva, ILO, 1992), para. 564.
32. *Op. cit.*, para. 747.
33. *Weekly Mail*, 13–19 November 1992, p. 25.
34. Sm. Pityana and M. Orkin (eds), *Beyond the Factory Floor: A Survey of COSATU Shop Stewards* (Johannesburg, Ravan Press, 1992).
35. *Ibid.*, pp. 56–8.
36. *Ibid.*, p. 58.
37. *Ibid.*, p. 69.
38. Lord Wedderburn, Industrial relations and the courts (1980) 9 ILJ 65; and see A. Jacobs, in B. Hepple (ed.), *The Making of Labour Law in Europe* (1986), p. 195 *et seq.*
39. See K. Block, The legal status of strikes in the USSR (1991) 12 *Comparative Labor Law Journal* 133.

4

The Role of the European Court of Justice in the Development of Community Labour Law

Philippa Watson

INTRODUCTION

The purpose of this chapter is to discuss the contribution of the European Court of Justice (hereinafter the 'Court') to the development of labour law within the European Economic Community (EEC). This is not an easy task given the volume of the Court's case law in this area. Many methods of analysis suggest themselves but alas no single one will do justice to the subject.

An attempt to evaluate the Court's case law purely on a subject-by-subject basis has been discarded in favour of a two-step approach. This involves, first, an examination of the case law in the light of the major precepts of the Community legal order (many of which have been developed by the Court in the context of cases dealing with social and labour law matters). This is followed by an account of the Court's case law on the perimeters of four rights given to Community citizens under the EEC Treaty and the legislation implementing its objectives: freedom of movement; equality of treatment in pay and other employment related matters; vocational training; and employment protection. The result of this combined vertical and horizontal view of the case law of the Court will serve to indicate the extent to which the Court has created a body of social rights for Community citizens out of a few arid, and in some cases somewhat vague and seemingly meaningless, Treaty provisions.

For the sake of clarity, and to put the subsequent discussion in its proper perspective, the chapter begins with a brief description of the relevant provisions of the Treaty dealing with social and labour rights and the role and function of the Court in the Community legal system.

COMMUNITY LABOUR AND SOCIAL LAW: EEC TREATY PROVISIONS

Labour law and social policy are dealt with in many parts of the EEC Treaty but our discussion will centre upon the case law of the Court of Justice concerning those provisions contained in Part Two, Title III, Chapters I and II, dealing with the free movement of persons, and Part Three, Title III, which bears the caption 'Social Policy'.[1]

Free Movement

Articles 48–51 of the EEC Treaty provide for the free movement of workers. Such freedom entails, according to Article 48(2), the abolition of any discrimination based on nationality between workers of the member states as regards employment, remuneration and other conditions of work and employment. Article 48(3) further amplifies the content of this right by specifying that it includes the acceptance of offers of employment actually made, the right to move freely within the Community for that purpose and the right to stay in a member state for the purpose of employment and to remain there after having been employed.

Article 49 empowers the Council to adopt measures to implement the objectives set out in Article 48,[2] while Article 51 obliges the Council to adopt 'such measures in the field of social security as are necessary to provide for the freedom of movement for workers'.[3] The right of free movement does not apply to employment in the public sector (Article 48(4)) and is subject to whatever limitations individual member states may impose to safeguard their public policy, public security and public health.

Articles 52–66 grant the right of free movement to the self-employed: Article 52 prohibits restrictions on the freedom of establishment of nationals of member states, while Article 59 outlaws restrictions on the cross-border supply of services. Articles 54, 57 and 63 empower the Council to issue directives to achieve these objectives. The special treatment by member states of nationals from other member states on the grounds of public policy, public security and public health is permitted by Articles 56 and 66. Article 55 exempts from the scope of the provisions on the right of establishment all activities 'connected, even occasionally, with the exercise of official authority'.

Social Policy

Articles 117–122 of the EEC Treaty deal more generally with social policy. In contrast to the provisions of the Treaty on free movement, which are relatively clear and precise, conferring directly applicable rights upon Community citizens and empowering Community institutions to legislate to achieve free movement, the social policy chapter of the Treaty is, by contrast, rather weak. Its provisions are vague and repetitious, conferring no real powers upon the Community institutions and little by way of direct rights upon Community citizens. Article 117 states that the member states agree upon the need to promote improved living and working conditions and an improved standard of living for workers. It does not confer any specific powers on the Community institutions to bring about these ends nor does it impose obligations upon the member states to harmonize their social systems, but assumes that such harmonization will automatically arise from the 'functioning of the common market'.

Article 118 gives the Commission power 'to promote close co-operation between the Member States in the social field'. The Court has held these provisions to be 'more in the nature of a programme' rather than to be legally binding. As such, although they do not empower the Community to legislate in the social field they are not entirely without legal effect since 'they constitute an important aid in particular for the interpretation of the Treaty and other provisions in the social field'.[4] More importantly still, they can be used as an ancillary legal basis for measures based on the general law-making powers contained in Articles 100, 100a and 235 of the Treaty.[5] Article 118a empowers the Council to adopt directives for the improvement of the working environment. Article 118b institutionalizes the dialogue on social policy that has taken place for some years between management and labour. Article 119 provides for equal pay for men and women. Article 120 requires the member states 'to maintain the existing equivalence between paid holiday schemes' and Article 121 empowers the Council to assign certain tasks to the Commission. Article 122 requires the Commission to report on social developments to the European Parliament in its annual report.

Despite the absence of any clear commitment to social policy in the EEC Treaty the Community has managed to evolve such a policy, albeit in a somewhat haphazard manner. This policy has been the result of the political will of the member states to match economic achievement with improvements in living and working conditions and, perhaps more importantly, a desire to prevent distortions in competition arising out of divergencies in production costs between member states due to differences in national social measures, levels of health and social standards and social security costs.[6]

The Court of Justice[7]

The origins of the Court of Justice of the European Communities can be traced back to the Court of Justice of the European Coal and Steel Community (ECSC) set up under the Treaty of Paris in 1951. It came into being on 1 December 1952 and delivered its first judgment on 21 December 1954. When the European Economic Community (EEC) and the European Atomic Energy Commission (Euratom) were set up under two Treaties of Rome in 1957, a Convention was signed by the member states, providing that a single court should act as a Court of Justice of the two Communities and that it should take over the functions of the ECSC Court.

The function of the Court is to ensure that in the interpretation and application of the Treaties and in the rules laid down for their implementation the law is observed.[8] Cases come before the Court in a variety of ways, either by direct action, where a party seises the Court directly, or indirectly, where a case comes to the Court by way of reference for a preliminary ruling from a national court or tribunal. Less common in the field of social and labour law, but not by any means unknown, are infringement proceedings, brought by the Commission against member states for breach of their obligations under Community law. Examples that spring to mind are the two cases brought by the Commission against Italy in 1981[9] and 1984[10] for failure to implement the Collective Redundancies Directive.[11]

The overwhelming majority of cases in the social and labour sphere have come before the Court indirectly. Article 177 grants the Court jurisdiction to give rulings on questions referred to it by 'any court or tribunal' of a member state concerning (a) the interpretation of the Treaty, (b) the validity and interpretation of acts of the Community institutions, and (c) the interpretation of statutes of bodies established by an act of the Council where those statutes so provide. A body set up by a member state with jurisdiction to decide questions of law or fact will, in general, constitute a court or tribunal for the purpose of Article 177.[12] Article 177 provides that courts against whose decision there is no judicial remedy 'shall refer questions of Community Law to the Court of Justice',[13] whereas other tribunals 'may' make such a reference. In practice, references are made by a wide range of entities operating at all levels in the judicial hierarchy of the member states. It is for the national court or tribunal to decide whether there is a point of Community law at issue in the proceedings before it that requires interpretation and, if so, whether it will ask the Court of Justice to make a ruling on the matter. The parties to proceedings cannot make a reference, nor can they prevent the national court from doing so. The Court of Justice cannot compel a national court to make a reference to it, nor can it require the withdrawal of a case referred to it.

Currently pending before the Court are the first applications made under Articles 178 and 215 of the EEC Treaty in the social law field,[14] in which a number of large undertakings claim damages against the Commission and the Council in respect of losses they will incur in funding the equalization, as between men and women, of benefits payable under their pension schemes in accordance with Article 119 of the EC Treaty as interpreted by the Court in the Barber[15] case.

THE COMMUNITY LEGAL ORDER AND SOCIAL AND LABOUR LAW

Many of the essential characteristics of the Community legal order, its superiority over national law, the direct effect many of its provisions produce, and the general principles of law that govern the corpus of its rules, have been determined by the Court in its case law - no small measure of which has been concerned with social issues. In turn, those characteristics have contributed to the realization of the social objectives of the EC Treaty. The following sections will examine their development and application in the area of law under discussion.

Direct Effect

The term 'direct applicability' is used in Community law to denote a provision that becomes law in each member state simply by being adopted by the competent Community institution. No implementing measures are required on the part of the member states; in fact such measures are prohibited except where the particular instrument in question requires them to be adopted.[16] Article 189 of the EEC Treaty provides that, of all the possible types of Community measure that may be used by the Council or the Commission in carrying out the tasks entrusted to them, only regulations are directly applicable.[17] Directives are expressed to be binding upon each member state 'as to the result to be achieved', while decisions are stated to be binding in their entirety upon their addressees. The Court has, however, held that other categories of legal measure may be directly applicable.[18]

Closely linked to the concept of direct applicability but differing from it is the concept of direct effect, which finds no mention in the EEC Treaty but is a creature of the case law of the Court.[19] It is of the utmost importance, constituting one of the fundamental principles of Community law. Provisions of Community law having direct effect create rights and obligations, which may be enforced by individuals before their national courts. To produce direct effects a provision of Community law must have the following characteristics:

- it must impose a clear and precise obligation on member states;
- it must be unconditional (in other words subject to no limitation), but if subject to certain limitations their nature and extent must be defined;
- the implementation of the Community rule must not be subject to the adoption of any subsequent rules or regulations on the part of either the Community institutions or any of the member states, so that, in particular, member states must not be left any real discretion with respect to the application of the rules in question.[20]

The area of social and labour law has provided fertile ground for the development, by the Court, of the concept of direct effect, which in turn has considerably enhanced the scope of rights available to Community citizens. It has proved particularly useful in those situations where either the Community institutions have failed to adopt legislation implementing EEC Treaty provisions or, even where such legislation has been adopted, the member states have failed to implement it. In the absence of such a concept (and the willingness of the Court to recognize its applicability to a multitude of measures) an individual would be totally reliant upon the Community institutions' readiness to propose, and the member states acting in Council to adopt and subsequently implement, legislative measures implementing basic Community objectives. The concept of direct effect enables the individual to assert his or her rights before national courts on the basis of many of the Treaty provisions themselves and some implementing measures.

In the field of free movement many of the Treaty provisions intended to regulate and protect the rights of individuals have direct effect. Articles 48,[21] 52,[22] 53,[23] 55(1),[24] 56(1),[25] 59 (1) and 60(3),[26] all of which concern the rights of workers and the self-employed to move within the Community for the purpose of exercising an economic activity, have been held to have this quality. By contrast, the provisions of the Treaty requiring the Community institutions to take action to ensure the realization of the right to free movement are not capable of producing direct effects.

While the Community institutions may be empowered to adopt measures to facilitate the attainment of a Community objective, if Treaty provisions setting out that objective possess those characteristics attaching to direct effect, those rights can be enforced by individuals even in the absence of implementing legislation. Thus in *Reyners* v *Belgium*[27] the Court ruled that 'Article 52 . . . imposes a duty to attain a precise result the fulfilment of which was made easier by, but not dependent on, the implementation of a programme of progressive measures', with the result that, for example, a British architect whose qualifications were recognized under French law was entitled to practise his profession in France despite the fact that no Community directive had been issued under Article 57 providing for the mutual recognition by the member states of architectural qualifications.[28]

The area of equal pay and equal treatment for men and women in pay and employment matters is illustrative of the efficacy of the principle of direct effect. With respect to the principle of equal pay for equal work, it will be recalled that Article 119 does not endow the Community with any legislative power; rather it places the onus of implementing that principle on each member state. The member states were required to complete this task 'during the first stage'; that is, by 1 January 1962. In fact, most of them did not do so, in spite of the repeated exhortations of the Commission during the 1960s and early 1970s.[29] Consequently, in November 1973 the Commission proposed to the Council the adoption of the measures that eventually became Directive 75/117 on the approximation of the application of the principle of equal pay for men and women.[30] The date by which member states were required to comply with its provisions was 12 February 1976. Meanwhile, in *Defrenne* v *Sabena*[31] the Court of Justice was asked, in the context of a dispute between a Belgian air hostess and her employer, Sabena, whether Article 119 had direct effect. The Court held that it had: 'Article 119 may be relied on before the national Courts. These Courts have a duty to ensure the protection of rights which that provision vests in individuals.'

The application of Article 119 was to have been fully secured by the original member states as from 1 January 1962 (1 January 1973 in the case of Denmark, Ireland and the United Kingdom). Consequently, the member states could not, as they had sought to do in their Resolution of 30 December 1961, modify that date. In spite of the firm stance of the Court on the date from which Article 119 had direct effect, mindful of the arguments of the United Kingdom and Ireland that the consequences of holding that Article 119 produced direct effects could seriously prejudice the viability of many undertakings in those countries, the Court limited the temporal effect of its judgment: 'the direct effect of Article 119 cannot be relied upon in order to support claims concerning pay periods prior to the date of this judgment except as regards those workers who have already brought legal proceedings or made an equivalent claim.'[32] Less successful was the attempt by the Court in *Barber* v *Guardian Royal Exchange Insurance*[33] to limit the effect of its ruling that occupational pensions were within the concept of 'pay' within Article 119, with the intention of avoiding financial disaster for many of the funds of contracted-out pension schemes. In the now notorious paragraph 45 of its judgment it ruled that the direct effect of Article 119 of the Treaty could not be relied upon with effect from a date prior to that of the judgment, 'except in the case of workers or those claiming under them who have before that date initiated legal proceedings or raised an equivalent claim under the applicable national law'. Of all the hundreds of thousands of dicta of the Court none has given rise to such fierce debate as paragraph 45 of the *Barber* judgment. Six or seven different interpretations of it have been advanced and a number of preliminary rulings, notably from courts and tribunals in the United Kingdom, Germany and The Netherlands, asking for the clarification of its meaning are currently pending before the Court.

Prompted by this confusion the member states decided to clarify by way of a Protocol to the Treaty on European Union, the scope of application of Article 119 to occupational pensions. Accordingly, Protocol No. 2 to that Treaty provides

> For the purposes of Article 119 of this Treaty, benefits under occupational social security schemes shall not be considered as remuneration if and in so far as they are attributable to periods of employment prior to 17 May 1990, except in the case of workers or those claiming under them who have before that date initiated legal proceedings or introduced an equivalent claim under the applicable national law.

The adoption of this Protocol does not so much overrule the judgment of the Court in *Barber*, which (even if unclear) still stands, but it does create a rather interesting situation *vis-à-vis* those cases currently pending before the Court seeking clarification of the meaning of paragraph 45: is the Court bound to take cognizance of Protocol No. 2 in giving judgment in these cases or has it a free hand to say precisely what it meant (but sadly did not articulate) in paragraph 45, leaving Protocol No. 2 to come into effect as and when the Treaty on European Union is ratified by all the member states as required by Article 236 of the EEC Treaty? It is difficult to avoid concluding that somewhat more analysis of the complexities of pensions law would have revealed to the Court the futility of making a ruling such as it did in paragraph 45 in *Barber*, which has only led to confusion, much criticism of the Court and an unprecedented step by the member states to dictate to the Court the interpretation to be given provision in the EEC Treaty, on the meaning of which the Court had already ruled.

Equality of treatment in social security has, like the right of equal pay, been established only after many years of struggle and then only following the bold intervention of the Court. Following the judgment in *Defrenne* v *Sabena*[34] to the effect that benefits payable under a social security system were not pay, attempts were made by the Commission to include social security among the matters dealt with by Directive 76/207 on equal treatment for men and women.[35] They failed because of opposition from the member states, and the Commission was subsequently obliged to propose a separate directive on equality of treatment between men and women in social security, which was eventually adopted on 23 December 1978.[36] The member states were obliged to bring their laws and practices into line with the provision of the Directive by 23 December 1984. In fact by that date little had been done. Inequalities still abound, leading to litigation before the national courts, which in turn results in references for preliminary rulings to the Court.

The essential question raised in earlier cases concerned the direct effect of the principle of equality of treatment set out in Article 4(1) of the Directive. Could that provision be relied upon by claimants to enforce their right to equal treatment after 23 December 1984 in the absence of national implementing measures? The Court held that it could. In the *FNV*[37] case it held that Article 4(1) precludes generally and equivocally all discrimination on the grounds of sex from the date of its required implementation into national law:

> Article 4(1) of the Directive does not confer on Member States the power to make conditional or to limit the application of the principle of equal treatment within its field of application and so is sufficiently precise and unconditional to allow individuals, in the absence of implementing measures adopted within the prescribed time, to rely upon it before national courts as from 23 December 1984 in order to preclude the application of any national provisions inconsistent with that Article.

The Court confirmed that ruling in the subsequent cases of *Borrie Clark*[38] and *McDermot and Cotter*,[39] stressing in the latter that in the absence of national measures implementing the principle of equal treatment women were entitled to have the same rules applied to them as men who were in the same situation since, where the Directive had not been implemented, these rules remain the only valid point of reference. In *Emmott*[40] the Court ruled that the direct effect of the principle of equal treatment on Article 4(1) meant that national procedural rules could not bar any claims made on the basis of the Directive where it had not been implemented.

Much of the employment legislation has been adopted by means of directives. The extent to which directives can produce direct effects in favour of individuals is thus of considerable importance. Although it has been established for some time that a provision in a directive that is unconditional and sufficiently precise for it to be pleaded against a member state has what has become known as 'vertical direct effect',[41] the question whether such a provision has 'horizontal direct effect' (that is, if it can confer rights or impose obligations upon private individuals which may be enforced by another private individual) remained the subject of considerable debate.[42] The position was clarified by the Court in 1986. In *Marshall* v *Southampton and South-West Hampshire Area Health Authority*[43] it was held that directives may not confer rights on individuals *vis-à-vis* other individuals:

> according to Article 189 of the EEC Treaty the binding nature of a directive, which constitutes the basis for the possibility of relying on the directive before a national court exists only in relation to each Member State to which it is addressed. It follows that a directive may not impose obligations on an individual and a provision of a directive may not be relied upon against such a person.

This in effect means that while public sector employees may invoke the provisions of Community directives that have direct effect against their employer, private-sector employees cannot. To a certain extent this discrimination has been alleviated by the broad interpretation that the Court has given to the concept of 'State'[44] but the truth remains that those employees who can be considered to be employed by the state are more advantageously treated within the Community legal order than private sector employees with respect to the enforceability of their rights under Community law.

General Principles of Law

There are a number of general principles of law underpinning the entire Community law system to which all rules contained therein are subject, both in substance and in form. Some of these find expression in the Community Treaties themselves; others have been enunciated and developed by the Court of Justice on the basis of principles of law common to all Member States. Two of these general principles, equality of treatment and proportionality, have special significance in the social and labour law field.

EQUALITY OF TREATMENT

Central to the provisions of the Community on the free movement of workers and employment is the principle of equality of treatment, a principle interpreted imaginatively and constructively by the Court. Equality of treatment means that identical or comparable situations must not be treated differently[45] and that different situations must not be treated identically.[46] Moreover, it requires not only that unlawful discrimination should be avoided but also that possible steps should be taken to remove unlawful differences in treatment when they arise.[47]

The concept embraces both overt (or direct) discrimination based on nationality and covert (or indirect) discrimination, which, by the application of other criteria of differentiation, such as residence, has a discriminatory impact.[48] In *Pinna* v *Caisse d'allocations familiales de la Savoie*,[49] although neither French legislation nor the relevant Community rules differentiated between the entitlement of French nationals and nationals of other member states to receive family allowances for family members resident outside France, the imposition of restrictions on the exportability of those benefits amounted to unlawful discrimination since 'the problem of members of the family resident outside France arises essentially for migrant workers'. Therefore, the Court held that employed persons subject to French legislation must be entitled to French family benefits for all members of their family resident in the territory of another member state in spite of a provision in Regulation 1408/71 decreeing otherwise.[50] In *Allue and Coonan* v *Università degli Studi di Venezia*[51] the Court found that the principle of equality of treatment was not respected when a defined group of workers, namely foreign-language lecturers who were predominantly nationals of other member states, were excluded from the social security system of the member state in which they were employed. Similarly, in *URSAFF* v *Société à Responsabilité limitée Hostellerie Le*

Manoir[52] the Court held that the prohibition on any discrimination based on nationality

> precludes national rules which require a body responsible for recovering social security contributions to take into account, for a trainee worker who does not come under the national educational scheme, a basis for calculating employers' social security contributions which is less favourable than that applied in respect of a trainee worker who comes under the national educational system.

On the question of which situations can be compared for the purpose of ascertaining whether there has been unlawful discrimination the Court has been flexible. It has had no difficulty in comparing part-time workers to full-time workers in examining rates of pay,[53] and in *Murphy* v *An Bord Telecom*[54] it held that a worker could compare his or her pay with that of another worker who was paid more for performing work that had been evaluated as being of lesser value. The complainants were women whose job it was to dismantle, clean and assemble telephones, who wished to compare themselves to male stores labourers. Likewise there is no requirement that the situations being compared should be contemporaneous. In *Macarthys Ltd* v *Smith*[55] the Court allowed Mrs Smith to compare her rate of pay with that of her male predecessor.

PROPORTIONALITY

The principle of proportionality requires that the means used to attain a given end should be no more than is appropriate and necessary to attain that end.[56] The Court has used this principle to ensure that the limitations permitted on the exercise of Community law rights are applied as narrowly as possible.

Consequently, while it may be lawful to discriminate in the matter of pay between different groups of workers 'on economic grounds which may be justified',[57] an employer must show that the measures he or she adopted were 'appropriate with a view to achieving the objective in question and necessary to that end'.[58] Likewise, in *Johnston* v *Chief Constable of the Royal Ulster Constabulary*[59] the Court, in replying to a question put to it by the Industrial Tribunal for Northern Ireland, held that 'A Member State may take into consideration requirements of public safety in order to restrict general police duties, in an internal situation characterized by frequent assassinations, to men equipped with firearms', but it was for the national court 'to ensure that the principle of proportionality is observed and to determine whether the refusal to renew Mrs Johnston's contract could not be avoided by allocating to women duties which, without jeopardising the aims pursued, can be performed without firearms'.

Proportionality has been used by the Court to eliminate unnecessary restrictions imposed by the member states on the right of establishment and the right to provide services within their territory by non-nationals. Although a member state is entitled to protect its general interests it must do so in the manner least restrictive of Community rights. In *Klopp*[60] the Court refused to accept that a member state could require a lawyer to have only one set of chambers, which had to be situated within a given radius of the court before which he was registered to practise, on the ground that such a rule was necessary in order that clients could maintain contact with their lawyers, since 'modern means of transport and telecommunications made this possible'. Similarly, although a member state could, in the interest of road safety, require a national of another member state established in its territory to acquire a driving licence, such an obligation could contravene Community law if 'the conditions imposed by national rules on the holder of the driving licence issued by another Member State are not in due proportion to the requirements of road safety'.[61] In the same way, the Court has held that although a member state may control the entry and residence of Community nationals it must not do so in a manner that is disproportionate to the objective to be achieved, and that may therefore constitute an obstacle to free movement: the failure of a national of a member state to comply with the formalities laid down in a member state for the entry, movement and residence of aliens cannot justify expulsion from its territory or even temporary imprisonment.[62] In *Watson* v *Bellmann*[63] the Court elaborated further on the type of sanctions a member state could impose for failure to comply with entry formalities, ruling that these must not be 'disproportionate to the gravity of the offence' or include 'deportation'. Moreover, the period allowed for the discharge of immigration formalities must be 'reasonable'.

Remedies for Breach of Community Law

The availability of remedies to the individual for denial of his or her Community law rights is a most hotly debated issue and not without good reason. Community competence is expanding to include within its sphere many matters that were previously the responsibility of national authorities and, therefore, subject to control by national judicial and administrative authorities.

Little scope is given in the EEC Treaty to the individual, as opposed to either a member state or a Community institution, to challenge the validity of Community measures applicable to them, or to obtain damages for loss incurred as a result of an illegal Community law measure. *Locus standi* is difficult to establish and the burden of proof of wrongdoing on the part of the Community institutions is difficult to discharge. Regarding the rights of the individual to enforce his or her Community law rights against his or her own member state or the remedies that ought to be offered if these are breached, nothing is stated in the EEC Treaty or in implementing legislation. The matter of national remedies has traditionally been left to each member state to organize according to its own legal system. Situations have arisen, however, where the limited availability or lack of adequate remedies has threatened to jeopardize the fundamental objectives of the EEC Treaty and here, happily, the Court has stepped in, laying down that there must be no discrimination in the remedies available to those wishing to exercise their Community law rights[64] and that such remedies as are available under national law must be 'effective': 'compensation must in any event be adequate in relation to the damage sustained and must therefore amount to more than purely nominal compensation'.[65] In *Francovich* v *Italy*[66] the Court went further and held that a member state was obliged to make good the damage suffered by an individual as a result of its failure to implement a directive.

SUBSTANTIVE SOCIAL RIGHTS

In this section a selection of the Court's cases dealing with four substantive social rights - the right to free movement, equality of treatment between men and women in the employment field, vocational training and employment rights - will be examined.

Free Movement of Persons

The scope and strength of any right depends upon the interpretation given to the basic concepts constitutive of that right and the extent to which its exercise can be legitimately limited or denied. In the case of the rights of Community citizens to move freely for employment purposes throughout the Community, much depends upon the meaning given to 'worker', and yet no definition is given to that term either in the EEC Treaty itself or in secondary legislation.

It *is* clear from the structure of the free-movement provisions of the EEC Treaty, which deal with workers and the self-employed separately, that a worker must be a salaried employee, and that for the purpose of ascertaining his or her social security rights a worker is an employed person insured as such under the social security system of a member state.[67] But apart from these general indications no clue is given of the precise attributes a person must have in order to be able to claim the right of free movement under Article 48 of the EEC Treaty. The Court has been entrusted with the task of elaborating the profile of a worker in the course of a number of requests for preliminary rulings from courts and tribunals up and down the Community. This it has done, giving 'worker' its ordinary meaning in the light of the objectives of the EEC Treaty[68] and, since that concept defines the limits of one of the fundamental freedoms guaranteed by the Treaty, it has held that it must not be interpreted restrictively.[69]

Emphasizing some thirty years ago that 'worker' is a Community law concept whose meaning is not to be determined solely by national law,[70] the Court has gone on to hold in the intervening years that the essential criterion in establishing whether a person is a worker is whether he or she is in 'effective and genuine employment'.[71] The nature[72] or duration of that employment[73] and the fact that it yields an income lower than that considered in the member state in which it is carried out to be required to meet essential needs are all irrelevant factors.[74] Similarly, the motives that may have prompted a citizen of a member state to seek employment in another member state are of no account provided that the employment in question is a genuine economic activity.[75] Thus a part-time music teacher giving twelve lessons a week, who was at the same time in receipt of unemployment benefit, was held to be engage in work that was not 'purely a marginal and ancillary activity',[76] and a trainee teacher who did some teaching as part of her course of study was held to be a worker within the meaning of Article 48, even though her employment was subject to public law and formed the last stage of her professional training.[77] A professional sportsman is a worker but an amateur is not.[78] A national of a member state employed by an undertaking established in a member state who temporarily works outside the territory of a member state remains a 'worker' for the purposes of Article 48 of the EEC Treaty even if he works temporarily outside the territory of the Community.[79] Movement from one member state to another is essential to qualify a person as a worker within the meaning of Article 48,[80] but the temporary movement of workers who are sent to another member state to carry out construction or other types of work as part of a contract to provide services concluded by their employer falls within the scope of Article 59 as opposed to Article 48 of the EEC Treaty.[81]

Although the legislation implementing Article 48 abounds with rules referring to the rights of entry and residence of workers and their families, all such rules are based upon the assumption that a worker who moves to another member states does so after finding employment there. No mention is made of the right of a worker to move to another member state in search of employment. At the time of the adoption of Regulation 1612/68[82] and Directive 68/360,[83] which implemented Article 48, the member states made a declaration to the effect that nationals of a member state were allowed to move to another member state in order to seek work for a period of three months. This implied that the member states did not regard a person seeking employment as a 'worker' within the meaning of Article 48. The Court, however, in February 1991 in *R* v *Immigration Appeal Tribunal, ex parte Antonissen*,[84] ruled otherwise, holding that a national of a member state did have the right to move freely within the Community and to stay in another member state in order to seek employment there. However, such a right is limited in time: the Court considered that a period of six months was 'not insufficient to enable the persons concerned to apprise themselves . . . of offers of employment corresponding to either occupational qualifications' but that if, after the expiry of that period, evidence was adduced showing that the Community citizen in question was seeking employment and that he or she had genuine chances of being engaged, he or she could not be required to leave the territory of the host member state.

If the Court has taken a liberal view of what constitutes a worker it has been proportionately restrictive in its view of the circumstances in which a worker may be deprived of his or her right to free movement. It has already been pointed out that the right to free movement can be limited by the member states on grounds of public policy, public health or public security (Article 48(3), Articles 56 and 66) and that it is not applicable to employment in the public sector (Article 48(4)) or to activities connected with the exercise of official functions (Articles 55 and 66). These are broadly phrased provisions, potentially giving member states a considerable degree of discretion. The Court has insisted that they be interpreted restrictively to ensure that they are used only for the purposes for which they were granted in the EEC Treaty, i.e. the protection of vital national interests. A person's past association with an organization or body whose activities are regarded as being contrary to public policy does not justify expulsion from a member state but a present association can.[85] Criminal convictions in themselves do not permit a member state to deny a Community citizen his or her rights under Article 48 but they may be evidence of personal conduct that is a threat to the public security of a member state.[86]

With respect to employment in the public service, which is exempt from the principle of free movement by Article 48(4) and its sister provision, Article 55, the Court has been equally vigilant. In a series of judgments handed down over the past twenty years[87] it has developed two main principles: (a) public service is a Community law concept that extends only to 'the posts . . . typical of the specific activities of the public service in so far as the exercise of powers conferred by public law and responsibility for safeguarding the general interests of the State are vested in it';[88] and (b) the nature of the relationship between the employee, whatever his or her status, and the employing organization is not relevant. Consequently it is of no importance whether a public service employee is employed under private or public law.[89] In *Reyners*[90] the Court held that the exception from the right of establishment contained in Article 55 of the EEC Treaty must be restricted to those activities which in themselves involve a direct and specific connection with the exercise of official authority.

Equality of Treatment between Men and Women in Pay, Working Conditions and Social Security

The scope of the right to equality of treatment between men and women in pay, social security and working conditions is largely dependent on the meaning to be given to those latter three concepts and the application of the principle of non-discrimination. The last has been discussed in general above: any further discussion of its specific application to the field of equal treatment is beyond the scope of this chapter.[91]

In interpreting the concept of 'pay' in Article 119 and Directive 75/117 on the principle of equal pay for men and women,[92] the Court has ruled that it includes all consideration, direct and indirect, that an employee receives from his or her employer in respect of work done. In *Worringham and Humphries*[93] it was held that 'Sums . . . which are included in the calculation of advantages linked to salary such as redundancy payments, unemployment benefits, family allowances and credit facilities form part of a worker's pay . . . even if they are immediately deducted by the employer and paid to a pension fund on behalf of the employee.'[94] However, conditions of employment[95] or social security benefits paid out under general schemes applicable to all categories of workers are not encompassed. Nor, strangely and in apparent contradiction to *Worringham and Humphries*, is the deduction of social security contributions from the net salary of an employee necessarily covered.[96] It seems somewhat contradictory to rule that contributions paid to a pension scheme out of gross salary are 'pay' whereas those paid out of net salary are not, since the result of either deduction is the same: less money in the pocket of the employee.

In determining what types of work can be compared with a view to ascertaining whether they are equal or not the Court has been generous.[97] Likewise, it has not hesitated to condemn member states that do not have job evaluation schemes, thereby preventing comparisons being made.[98]

Directive 79/7 established the principle of equal treatment for men and women in social security matters.[99] That principle applies to statutory social security schemes which provide protection against sickness, invalidity, old age, accidents at work and occupational diseases, and to social assistance insofar as it is intended to supplement or replace any of these schemes. In determining which benefits fall within the scope of Directive 79/7 the Court has adopted a functional approach, ruling that it covers all benefits designed to cover any of the risks enumerated in the Directive, regardless of to whom and how they are paid.[100] Benefits must be specifically aimed at the alleviation of one of the risks covered by the Directive: a benefit that is general in nature (one that provides a minimum income for those in need for whatever reason) is not covered by the Directive.[101]

Vocational Training

Apart from Article 128 of the EEC Treaty, which empowers the Council to 'lay down general principles for implementing a common vocational training policy' and has a more specific provision for vocational training measures for agricultural workers,[102] the original EC Treaty is silent on the question of education, although Articles 130f to 139q, inserted into the Treaty by the Single European Act, provide for the funding of research and technological projects. More specific are the provisions of the ECSC Treaty[103] and the Euratom Treaty. The promotion of research is one of the main tasks of Euratom.[104]

The Community Treaties, in providing only for that type of education linked to employment, thus reflected the traditional view that education was a matter for the member states to regulate according to national, cultural, religious and philosophical norms. Educational policy in general is therefore not considered to be a matter for Community competence.[105] Yet it is arguable that a pluralist education is necessary for the successful creation of a single integrated market in that it spawns the cross-fertilization of ideas among the peoples of the member states, which in turn generates the degree of mutual understanding required for harmonious social and economic coexistence. Whatever the inherent merits of encouraging the Community's youth to pursue their studies outside their home member state, the Community legislative bodies, until recently, and then only in the wake of a considerable body of case law of the Court of Justice establishing the right of students to a Community-wide education of a vocational nature, have done little to encourage the movement of students.

Whatever rights students have to move in pursuit of learning outside their own member state derives from the case law of the Court over the past nine years. The nature and extent of these rights will very much depend upon the status of the person wishing to exercise them – whether he or she is a migrant worker, a member of the family of a migrant worker, or a Community citizen simply wishing to take advantage of educational opportunities outside his or her home country. Migrant workers have the greatest body of rights: they have the right to vocational training on an equal footing with nationals of the host member state[106] and the right to continue to reside in a member state to pursue studies of a vocational training nature after they have ceased to be in employment. Moreover, by virtue of Article 7(2) of Regulation 1612/68, which grants the right to the same 'social and tax advantages' as nationals of the host member state, they have the right to receive from the latter grants and scholarships for both tuition fees and living expenses for the duration of the studies, provided that (a) the studies in question are linked to previous employment and (b) the employment endowing the status of worker was undertaken independently of the course of studies for which the grants are claimed.[107]

The children of migrant workers enjoy the right to 'general, apprenticeship and vocational training courses under the same conditions as nationals of [the host] State'.[108] This has been interpreted to include equality of treatment with respect to all types of education grants, whatever their purpose, available to nationals of the host state.[109] The body of rights attaching to the spouse and other members of the migrant worker's family is less extensive: they have the right of equality of access to vocational training courses only and to financial assistance to meet the cost of registration and tuition fees.[110]

Community citizens who are not exercising their right to free movement under Article 48 nevertheless have, on the basis of Articles 7 and 128 of the EEC Treaty, the right to enter and take up residence in a member state to pursue vocational training therein.[111] They have equality of access to such courses and the right to the same range of grants for registration and tuition expenses as nationals of the member state in which they are pursuing their studies,[112] but not to maintenance grants. Vocational training has been interpreted broadly by the Court in *Gravier* v *City of Liège*:[113] 'any form of education which prepares for a qualification for a particular profession, trade or employment or which provides the necessary skills for such a professional trade or employment is vocational training whatever the age and level of the pupil or student.' Some years later the Court refined its thinking on the concept of vocational training, holding that it encompassed most university studies. The only exception might be 'certain courses of study which, because of their particular nature, are intended for persons wishing to improve their general knowledge rather than to prepare themselves for an occupation'.[114] In assessing whether a particular course of studies is of a vocational training nature or not the Court has insisted that it must be considered as a whole; the various years of a study programme that forms a 'single coherent unit' cannot be split up into 'academic years' and 'vocational training years'.[115]

Employment Protection

Following the pledge made by the Community in its Social Action Programme[116] to improve 'living and working conditions', three directives were adopted: (a) Directive 75/129 on the approximation of the laws of the member states relating to collective redundancies ('the Collective Redundancies Directive');[117] (b) Directive 77/187 on the laws of the Member States relating to the safeguarding of employees' rights in the event of transfers of undertakings, businesses or parts of businesses ('the Acquired Rights Directive');[118] (c) Directive 80/987 on the approximation of the laws of the member states relating to the protection of employees in the event of insolvency of their employer ('the Insolvency Directive').[119] The Court has had occasion to consider all these Directives but most of its case law in this particular area concerns the Acquired Rights Directive.

The case law on collective redundancies has been, for the most part, concerned with the adequacy of measures adopted by the member states to implement the Directive, rather than with the interpretation of its particular provisions. With respect to the duty of member states to execute the provisions of the Directive, it is quite clear from the judgments of the Court that it requires the Directive to be fully and properly implemented, regardless of socio-economic difficulties or industrial practices prevailing in the member states[120] or the level of social security benefits in the case of unemployment.[121] However, the Court does not demand the impossible. An employer cannot be condemned for failing to foresee collective redundancies: he is at liberty to decide whether and when he should first formulate his plans to dismiss his workers.[122]

The Acquired Rights Directive has been the subject of a considerable number of requests for preliminary rulings, almost exclusively from courts in either The Netherlands or Denmark. They concern mainly the scope of the Directive, including in particular the question of what types of transactions will be deemed to be transfers for the purpose of the Directive. From this case law the following principles emerge:

1 The Directive does not apply to insolvency proceedings but may extend to other similar types of proceedings which are not designed to liquidate the undertaking but to safeguard its continued existence.[123]

2 When a transfer falls within the scope of the Directive, only those obligations existing on the date of the transfer with respect to employees whose employment relationship was transferred to the transferee are the responsibility of the transferee. The Directive will not cover obligations arising after the date of the transfer or concerning employees who were not transferred with the undertaking but who retain a relationship – but not an employment relationship – with the new undertaking.[124] Similarly, the employment relationship out of which the obligations claimed arose must have existed at the time of the transfer.[125]

3 The transferee must acquire a going concern for the transaction to be considered a transfer for the purpose of the Directive.[126] Whether a business is transferred as a going concern or not is a matter of fact to be decided by the national courts.[127]

4 The Directive can extend to a transfer taking place in two stages provided the undertaking transferred retains its identity.[128]

5 Employees may not contract out of the rights accorded to them by the Directive.[129]

The Acquired Rights Directive has been the subject of two judgments in which the Court has condemned Italy[130] and Greece[131] for failure to implement its provisions properly.

CONCLUSIONS

This chapter has attempted to described and assess the contribution of the European Court of Justice to the development of Community social and labour law. The exercise has been carried out by means of a vertical and horizontal examination of the Court's case law in four main areas of Community competence in labour law: the free movement of persons, equality of treatment between men and women in pay and other employment-related matters, vocational training and employment protection. The selection of the cases to be discussed has been difficult: readers will no doubt be disappointed that some of their favoured cases, which they believe to have made a contribution to the development of Community labour law, have been omitted. Despite the cursory treatment of some cases and the failure to mention others, it can be fairly concluded that the Court has made a considerable contribution to the development of Community labour law. Further, and most importantly, many of the cases in this area have been instrumental in evolving the Community legal order as we know it today, in particular the means whereby Community citizens can enforce their Community law rights.

By adopting a functional approach in interpreting the scope, both *ratione personae* and *ratione materiae*, of employment law rights available to the individual under Community law broadly, and in restricting the limitations imposed on those rights to what is strictly necessary to satisfy the legitimate concerns of the member states, the Court has managed to go a considerable way towards attaining the objectives of the EEC Treaty and implementing legislation. Essential concepts such as 'worker', 'pay', 'vocational training' and 'transfer of an undertaking' have been given a wide interpretation: conversely, 'public policy', 'public security' and 'public service' have been interpreted in a manner which ensures that they protect the legitimate interests of member states but in a manner which restricts as little as possible the movement of persons. The principle of equal treatment stated in general in Article 7 of the EEC Treaty and given specific expression in other areas of the Treaty has been developed to embrace both overt (or direct) and covert (or indirect) discrimination in law and in fact.

In addition to ensuring the effectiveness of the Community rights granted under the EEC Treaty itself and in implementing legislation, the case law of the Court has had an energizing effect on the Community's legislative organs; in indicating to them the extent of their competence in specific areas the Court has encouraged them to exercise their powers. An example of such a development is vocational training, which until the line of cases beginning with *Forcheri*[132] had hardly been the subject of any legislative measures but in which there is now a substantial corpus of measures providing for Community training programmes, some general (e.g. ERASMUS[133]) and others specific (e.g. COMMETT[134] and LINGUA[135]). These programmes provide generous Community funding and have given thousands of students the opportunity to study outside their own member state. Their legality has been challenged[136] but the Court has stood firm on the right of the Community to organize and finance such efforts. More importantly still, the Treaty on European Union, in providing for a new chapter on vocational training to be inserted into the EEC Treaty, reflects the Court's case law and the political will of the member states to build on it.

In any discussion of the work of any constitutional court the question invariably arises as to the pattern of behaviour of the court in question, in particular the factors that may have a bearing on its decisions. With specific reference to the Court of Justice one can ask whether the Court has been bolder at some times than others in its approach to employment law issues and, if so, why. The starting point in answering this question must be the characteristics of the members of the Court. Are there some judges who have had a more profound influence on the development of labour law than others? If so, who are they and what are the attributes they possess that make them more inclined to adopt a constructive approach rather than a literal interpretation of certain provisions? These are difficult questions to answer with respect to the Court, where the bench is composed of thirteen judges, one from each of the member states and a thirteenth appointment shared in turn among the larger member states, all of whom are men (the court has known a female Advocate-General but never a female judge) whose expertise in legal matters cannot be doubted but who may, prior to their appointment to the bench, have had widely differing experience of the law.

The Court is assisted in its functions by six Advocates-General, four of whom are appointed by the larger member states (France, Germany, Italy and the United Kingdom) and two from the other, smaller member states. The Court is therefore multinational and culturally rich. Article 167 of the EEC Treaty requires judges to be 'chosen from persons whose independence is beyond doubt and who possess the qualifications required for appointment to the highest judicial office in their respective countries or who are jurisconsults of recognised competence'. In effect judges come from a variety of backgrounds - the practising profession, academic life, the bench or government service - thereby affording the Court in its deliberations a wide breadth of legal opinion garnished from a multitude of sources. Quite what effect the multiplicity of cultures and experiences of the bench has on the judgments of the Court is hard to determine. The Court delivers only one judgment and that is generally rather terse. There are no dissenting judgments. It is, therefore, rather difficult to discern what views particular judges have on the issues before them or even why the Court came to its conclusions. More illuminating are the Opinions of the Advocates-General, which are fully reasoned, reflecting the common law style of judgments.

Turning now to the pattern of the Court's case law, can it be said that in developing social and employment policy the Court has been more dynamic at some points in time than others? In the early days of the life of the Community the Court occupied itself with constructing the framework of the Community legal order, moving in the early 1980s to reinforcing the rights of the individual to seek effective remedies for breach of their Community law rights. This case law mirrors the growth of the Community law system with its perceived penetration into national legal systems[137] and the acknowledgment that citizens must be given adequate means of redress within those systems when their Community law rights are violated. Following the political commitment of the Heads of State and Government at the Paris Summit in December 1992 to ensure that the Community acquired a 'human face' and the subsequent adoption of a sizeable body of Community law measures concerning employment conditions, leading in turn to an increase in cases concerning this issue before the Court, we see a certain increased boldness in the Court's judgments: member states are condemned for failure to fulfil their obligations, the right of the individuals to rely in Community law directly to enforce their rights is confirmed and the principle of effective remedies is established.

Following the publication of the Commission's White Paper on the Completion of the Internal Market in 1985 and the increased commitment of the member states to the creation of a Community social policy, the pattern of which was seen as an essential element in a single integrated market, we discern again a new phase in the case law of the Court, in which the Court is seen to be making a positive contribution to the development of a social Europe in line with the political wishes of the member states: the perimeters of the rights set out in the EEC Treaty and implementing legislation are further pushed back; issues that in the past the Court had been reluctant to confront are tackled positively and with firmness and conviction. Regrettably, as fierce debate swept the Community after the signing of the Treaty on European Union, followed by a surge in nationalism and a corresponding hostility towards the Community, resulting in the espousal of the principle of subsidiarity so aptly and amusingly described by Lord Wedderburn as 'that principle of feline inscrutability and political subtlety',[138] we note too a new timidity in the Court's judgments.[139] Given the paralysis of the Community legislature in the face of social policy measures, it is to be hoped that it does not herald a new conservatism on the part of the court, since otherwise the battle for a social Europe will surely be lost.

NOTES

1. Among the other provisions of the EEC Treaty concerning social policy are Article 39(1)(b), which reads 'The objective of the common agricultural policy shall be: . . . (b) . . . to ensure a fair standard of living for the agricultural community, in particular by increasing the individual earnings of persons engaged in agriculture', Article 123, which provides for the setting up and operation of the European Social Fund, and Article 128, empowering the Council to lay down a general policy for implementing a common vocational training policy.

2. The following are the principal measures adopted to implement Article 48: Regulation 1612/68 on the free movement of workers within the Community (OJ Eng.Sp.Ed. 1968 (II) 475) as amended by Regulation 2434/92 (OJ 1992 L245/1); Directive 68/360 on the abolition of restrictions on movement and residence within the Community for workers and their families (OJ Eng.Sp.Ed. 1968 (II) 485); Regulation 1251/71 on the right of workers to remain in the territory of a member state after having been employed in that state (1970 (II) 402).

3. Regulation 1408/71 on the application of social security schemes to employed persons, to self-employed persons and to members of their families moving within the Community as consolidated by Regulation 2001/83 (OJ 1983 L230/6); Regulation 574/72 laying down the procedure for implementing Regulation 1407/71 as consolidated by Regulation 2001/83.

4. Case 170/84, *Bilka-Kaufhaus GmbH* v *Weber von Hartz* [1986] ECR 1607; Joined Cases 281, 283, 285 and 287/85, *Germany and Others* v *Commission* [1987] ECR 3203; Case 126/86, *Zaera* v *Instituto Nacional de la Seguridad Social y Tesorería General de la Seguridad Social* [1987] ECR 3697.

5. Article 235 provides that if action by the Community should prove necessary to attain one of the objectives of the common market and the Treaty has not provided the necessary powers, the Commission can adopt directives 'for the approximation of national provisions which directly affect the establishment and functioning of the common market'. Article 100 empowers the Council to issue directives for the approximation of national measures that directly affect the establishment and functioning of the common market. Measures based upon either of these two provisions must be adopted by unanimous vote in the Council. Article 100a provides that in order to establish the internal market, the Council acting on a qualified majority on a proposal from the Commission must adopt measures for the approximation of national laws that have as their objective the establishment and functioning of the internal market. But the legislative competence granted in Article 100a is of limited application; it does not extend to fiscal provisions, to measures relating to the free movement of persons or to those pertaining to the rights and interests of employed persons.

6. For an account of the development of Community social policy see Teague, *European Community Social Policy* (1989), Chapters 2 and 3; P. Watson, The Community Social Charter (1991) 28 CML Rev 37, at pp. 39–45.

7. It is beyond the scope of this chapter to give a full account of the nature and workings of the Court of Justice. See Lasok, *The Court of Justice of the European Communities* (1986); Brown and Jacobs, *The Court of Justice of the European Communities*, 3rd edn (1990).

8. Article 31 of the ECSC Treaty; Article 164 of the EEC Treaty; Article 136 of the Euratom Treaty. In addition, jurisdiction is conferred on the court to give preliminary rulings in the interpretation of the Convention on the Jurisdiction and Enforcement of Judgments in Civil and Commercial Matters (Protocol on the Interpretation by the Court of Justice of the Convention on Jurisdiction and Enforcement of Judgments in Civil and Commercial Matters, OJ 1983 C97/24) and jurisdiction will be conferred on the Court to give preliminary rulings on the interpretation of the mutual recognition of companies and legal persons when this convention comes into force. In addition, various other specific functions are conferred upon the Court.

9. Case 91/81, *Commission* v *Italy* [1982] ECR 2133.

10 Case 131/84, *Commission* v *Italy* [1985] ECR 3531.

11. Directive 75/129 on the approximation of the laws of the member states relating to collective redundancies (OJ 1975 L48/29).

12. Case 138/80, *Borker* [1980] ECR 1975; Case 246/80, *Broekmeulen* v *Huisarts Registratie Commissie* [1981] ECR 2311; Case 102/81, *Nordsee* [1982] ECR 1095. From these cases it is clear that in order to be able to refer a question to the Court under Article 177 the court or tribunal in question must be linked to the state, its proceedings must be adversarial and its decisions must be binding. Bodies that give opinions or private arbitrators thus cannot refer questions.

13. There is no obligation on such a Court to make a reference where 'the Community provision in question has already been interpreted by the Court of Justice or . . . the correct application of Community law is so obvious as to leave no scope for any reasonable doubt' (Case 283/81, *CILFIT* [1982] ECR 3415).

14. Case C 298/91, *British Petroleum* v *Council and Commission* (OJ 1992 C24/1); Case 315/91, *Stichting Bedrijfspensioenfonds voor het Glazenwassers- en Schoonmaakbedrijf* v *Council and Commission* (OJ C 1992 24/7); Case 324/91, *Eastern Electricity* v *Council and Commission* (OJ 1992 C57/6).

15. Case C 262/88, [1990] ECR I-1889.

16. Case 34/73, *Variola SpA* v *Amministrazione italiana delle Finanze* [1973] ECR 981; Case 31/78, *Bussoni* v *Italian Ministry for Agricultural and Forestry* [1978] ECR 2429.

17. The term 'direct applicability' has been used on occasion with respect to provisions of the Treaty itself (see Case 2/74, *Reyners* v *Belgium* [1974] ECR 631) but it is somewhat inappropriate given that the Treaty has been incorporated in its entirety into the legal systems of all the member states in accordance with the constitutional practices of the member states. See Article 236, EEC Treaty.

18. Case 9/70, *Grad* v *Finanzamt Traunstein* [1970] ECR 825, at p. 837. In Case 41/74, *Van Duyn* v *Home Office* [1974] ECR 1337, the Court ruled, 'If however by virtue of the provision of Article 189 regulations are directly applicable and consequently, by their very nature have direct effects it does not follow that other categories of acts mentioned in that Article can never have similar effects. It would be incompatible with the binding effect attributed to a directive by Article 189 to exclude, in principle, the possibility that the obligation which it imposes may be invoked by those concerned.'

19. The theory of direct effect was first articulated by the Court in Case 26/62, *NV Algemene Transport en Expeditie Onderneming van Gend en Loos* v *Netherlands Inland Revenue Administration* [1963] ECR 1. There is a considerable body of literature on the concepts of direct applicability and direct effect. The leading article is J. W. Winter, Direct applicability and direct effect: two distinct and different concepts (1972) CML Rev 425.

20. Opinion of Advocate General Mayras in Case 41/74, *Van Duyn* v *Home Office* [1974] ECR 1337, at p. 1354.

21. Case 167/73, *Commission* v *France* [1974] ECR 351; Case 41/74, *Van Duyn*, *op. cit.* note 18.

22. Case 2/74, *Reyners* v *Belgian State* [1974] ECR 631.

23. Case 6/64, *Costa* v *ENEL* [1964] ECR 585.

24. *Reyners*, *op. cit.* note 22.

25. Case 46/75, *Royer* [1976] ECR 495.

26. Case 33/74, *Van Binsbergen* [1974] ECR 1299.

27. *Op. cit.* note 22.

28. Case 11/77, *Patrick* v *Ministère des Affaires Culturelles* [1977] ECR 1199. See also Case 271/82, *Auer* v *Ministère Public* [1983] ECR 2727.

29. A Recommendation of 20 July 1960 reminded the member states of their need to fulfil the duty imposed by Article 119 and indicated the means whereby this aim could be achieved.

Subsequently the member states considered that they were not in a position to comply with the prescribed time and in a Resolution adopted on 30 December 1961 decreed 31 December 1984 as the date by which discrimination between men and women in pay had to be abolished. Both the Recommendation and the Resolution emphasized the need for the member states to establish the principle of equal pay for equal work: in the opinion of both the Commission and the member states Article 119 was not self-executing. Subsequently the Social Action Programme 1974 (OJ 1974 C13/1) included among its many objectives the attainment of principle of equal pay for equal work. See Opinion of Advocate-General Trabucchi in Case 43/73, *Defrenne* v *Sabena* [1976] ECR 455, at p. 485; S. Prechal and N. Burrows, *Gender Discrimination Law of the European Community* (Aldershot, 1990), at pp. 81–2.

30. OJ 1975 L45/11. The legal basis chosen for this Directive was Article 100.

31. Case 43/75, *Defrenne* v *Sabena* [1976] ECR 455.

32. The Court made a similar ruling in Case 41/84, *Pinna* v *Caisse d'Allocations familiales de la Savoie* [1986] ECR 1. In finding that Article 73(2) of Regulation 1408/71 on the application of social security schemes to employed persons and their families moving within the Community (OJ Eng.Sp.Ed. 1971 (II) p. 416) precluding the award to persons subject to French legislation of French family benefits for members of their families residing in the territory of another member state was invalid, the Court held that such invalidity could not be relied upon by workers in order to claim French family allowances for their children resident in another member state, for periods prior to the date of the judgment (15 January 1984), except where such claims had already been made by that date.

33. Case 262/88, [1990] ECR 1-1889.

34. Case 80/70, *Defrenne* v *Belgian State* [1971] ECR 445.

35. Directive 76/207 on the implementation of the principle of equal treatment for men and women as regards access to employment, vocational training and promotion and working conditions (OJ 1976 L39/40). See original proposal in COM 75(36) Final.

36. Directive 79/7 on the principle of equal treatment for men and women in social security (OJ 1979 L24).

37. Case 71/85, 1986 ECR 3855.

38. Case 384/85, 1987 ECR 2863.

39. Case 286/85, 1987 ECR 1453.

40. Case C-208/90, [1991] ECR I-4269.

41. Case 41/74 *Van Duyn* v *Home Office* 1974 ECR 1337; Case 8/81, *Becker* v *Finanzamt Munster-Innenstadt* [1982] ECR 53.

42. A. J. Easson, Can directives impose obligations on individuals? (1979) 4 EL Rev 67. C. W. A. Timmermans, Directives: their effect within the national legal systems (1979) 16 CML Rev 533; D. Wyatt, The direct effect of Community social law (1983) 8 EL Rev 241.

43. Case 152/84, [1986] ECR 723.

44. In *Marshall* the Court rejected the argument of the United Kingdom government that a directive can only have direct effect against a member state *qua* public authority, holding that an individual may rely on a directive as against a member state regardless of the capacity in which the latter is acting, whether as an employer or a public authority. In the subsequent case of *Foster* v *British Gas*, Case 188/89, [1991] ECR I-3313 the Court held, in the context of a dispute between a group of women and their employer, British Gas plc, that Directive 76/207 on equal treatment could be relied upon by an individual in a claim for damages 'against a body whatever its legal form, which has been made responsible, pursuant to a measure adopted by the State for providing a public service under the control of the State and has for that purpose powers beyond those which result from the normal rules applicable to individuals'.

45. Joined Cases 117/76 and 16/77, *Ruckedeschel* v *Hamptzollamt Hamburg St Annex* [1977] ECR 1753, at p. 1769. Joined Cases 198/202/81, *Michele* v *Commission* [1982] ECR 4145, at p. 4157.

46. Case 13/63, *Italy* v *Commission* [1963] ECR 165, at p. 178.

47. Joined Cases 50–60/74, *Kampffmeyer Muhlenvereinigung KG* v *Commission and Council* [1976] ECR 711, at p. 744.

48. Case 152/73, *Sotgiu* v *Deutsche Bundespost* [1974] ECR 153, at p. 164. Case 61/77, *Commission* v *Ireland* [1978] ECR 417 at p. 450; Case 22/80, *Boussac* v *Gertenmeier* [1980] ECR 3427.

49. Case 41/84, [1986] ECR 1.

50. Article 73(2) of Regulation 1408/71 (note 3 above) provided at the time of this dispute that an employed person subject to French legislation was entitled to family allowances provided for by the law of the member state in whose territory the members of the family resided. Following the *Pinna* judgment this provision was amended by Regulation 3427/89 (OJ 1989 L33/11). The general rule now is that employed or self-employed persons are entitled to family benefits provided by the social security system to which they are affiliated regardless of where their children are resident within the Community.

51. Case 33/88, [1989] ECR 1591.

52. Case C-27/91, Judgment of 21 November 1991.

53. Case 96/80, *Jenkins* v *Kingsgate Clothing* [1981] ECR 911.

54. Case 157/86, [1988] ECR 673.

55. Case 129/79, [1980] ECR 1275.

56. *Halsbury's Laws of England*, Vol. 51, at para. 2.296. It has been described by the Court as early as 1955 as a 'generally accepted rule of law' (Case 8/55, *Fedechar* v *High Authority* [1954–6] ECR 245). For its application in the United Kingdom, see *R* v *Goldstein* [1983] 1 WLR per Lord Diplock: 'You must not use a steel hammer to crack a nut if a nutcracker will do.'

57. Case 96/80, *Jenkins* v *Kingsgate Clothing* [1981] ECR 911.

58. Case 170/84, *Bilka-Kaufhaus* v *Weber* [1986] ECR 1607.

59. Case 22/84, [1986] ECR 1651.

60. Case 107/83, [1984] ECR 2971.

61. Case 16/78, *Choquet* [1978] ECR 2293. For an example of the requirements that would fall into this category, the Court said: 'Insistence on a driving test which clearly duplicates a test taken in another Member State for the classes of vehicle which the person concerned wishes to drive or linguistic difficulties arising out of the procedure laid down for the conduct of any checks or the imposition of exorbitant charges for completing the requisite formalities could all be examples of this. Such obstacles to the recognition of a driving licence issued by another Member State are not in fact in due proportion to the requirement for the safety of highway traffic.'

62. Case 48/75, [1976] ECR 497.

63. Case 118/75, [1976] ECR 1185.

64. Case 130/79, *Express Dairy Foods Ltd* v *Intervention Board for Agricultural Produce* [1980] ECR 1887.

65. Case 14/83, *von Colson and Kamann* v *Land Nordrhein-Westfalen* [1984] ECR 1891. See further Case C-271/91, *Marshall* v *Southampton and South-West Hampshire Area Health Authority*, Judgment of 2 August 1993.

66. Case C-6/90, [1991] ECR I-5357.

67. Regulation 1408/71 (note 3), Article 1(1).

68. Case 53/71, *Levin* [1982] ECR 1033.

69. *Ibid.* and Joined Cases 389 and 390/81, *Ecternach and Moritz* [1989] ECR 723.

70. Case 75/63, *Hoekstra (née Unger)* v *Bestuur der Bedrijfsvereniging Detailhandel* 1964 ECR 177.

71. Case 53/81, *Levin* v *Staatssecretaris van Justitie* [1982] ECR 1035.

72. Case 66/85, *Lawrie Blum* v *Land Baden-Württemberg* [1986] ECR 2121.

73. Case 139/85, *Kempf* v *Straatsecretaris van Justitie* [1986] ECR 1741; Case C-3/90, *Bernini* v *Minister van Onderwijs en Wetenschappen* [1992] ECR I-1071; Case C-357/89, *Raulin* v *Minister van Onderwijs en Wetenschappen* [1992] ECR I-1027.

74. Case 53/81, *op. cit.*

75. *Levin*, *op. cit.*, at para. 23.

76. *Kempf*, *op. cit.*, note 73.

77. Case 66/85, *Lawrie Blum* v *Land Baden-Württemberg* [1986] ECR 2121.

78. Case 36/74, *Walrave and Koch* v *Association Union Cycliste Internationale Koninklijke* [1974] ECR 1405.

79. Case 237/83, *Prodest* v *Caisse Primaire d'Assurance Maladie de Paris* [1984] ECR 3153.

80. Case 175/78, *Regina* v *Vera Ann Saunders* 1979 ECR 1129; Joined Cases 35 and 36/81, *Morson and Jhanjan* [1982] ECR 3273; Case 298/84, *Iorio* v *Azienda Autonoma delle ferrovie dello Stato* [1986] ECR 247.

81. Case C-113/89, *Rush Portuguesa Lda* v *Office National d'Immigration* [1990] ECR I-1417. Proposal for a Council Directive concerning the posting of workers in the framework of the provision of services COM (91) 230 Final.

82. Note 2.
83. *Ibid.*
84. Case C-292/89, [1991] ECR I-745.
85. Case 41/74, *Van Duyn* v *Home Office* [1974] ECR 1337, at p. 1349.
86. Case 30/77, *R* v *Bouchereau* [1977] ECR 1999.
87. Case 152/73, [1974] ECR 153; Case 149/79 (No. 1), *Commission* v *Belgium* [1980] ECR 3881; Case 149/79 (No. 2), *Commission* v *Belgium* [1982] ECR 1845; Case 307/84, *Commission* v *France* [1986] ECR 1725; Case 66/85, *Lawrie-Blum* v *Land Baden-Württemberg* [1986] ECR 2121; Case 225/85, *Commission* v *Italy* [1987] ECR; Case 33/88, *Allue and Coonan* v *University of Venice* [1989] ECR.
88. *Sotgiu* (*op. cit.*, note 48) at para. 12 of the Judgment.
89. Case C-149/79 (No. 1) *Commission v Belgium*, *op. cit.*, note 87, at para. 12.
90. Case 2/74, [1974] ECR 631.
91. See Prechal and Burrows, *Gender Discrimination Law of the European Community*, *op. cit.*; Ellis, *European Community Sex Equality Law* (1991).
92. OJ 1975 L45.
93. Case 80/71, [1971] ECR 445.
94. Case 69/80, [1981] ECR 767; Case 23/83, *Liefting* v *Academisch Ziekhuis bij de Universiteit van Amsterdam* [1984] ECR 2225.
95. Case 149/77, *Defrenne* v *Sabena* [1978] ECR 1765.
96. Case 192/85, *Newstead* v *Department of Transport* [1987] ECR 4753.
97. See p. 87 above.
98. Case 61/81, *Commission* v *United Kingdom* [1982] ECR 2601.
99. OJ 1979 L6/24.
100. Case 150/85, *Drake* v *Chief Adjudication Officer* [1986] ECR 1995.
101. Case 243/90, *The Queen* v *Secretary of State for Social Security ex parte Smithson* Judgment of 4 February 1992; Joined Cases C-63/91 and C-64/91, *Jackson and Cresswell* v *Chief Adjudication Officer* Judgment of 16 July 1992.
102. Article 41(a) EEC Treaty.
103. Article 56.
104. Article 2(a) and Articles 4–11 Euratom Treaty.
105. A view endorsed by the Court in Case 93/83, *Gravier* v *City of Liège* [1985] ECR 595: 'educational organisation and policy are not as such included in the spheres which the Treaty has entrusted to the Community institutions'.
106. Regulation 1612/68, Article 7(3).
107. Case 39/86, *Lair* v *Universität Hannover* [1988] ECR 2121.
108. Regulation 1612/68, Article 12.
109. Case 9/74, *Casagrande* v *Landeshaupstadt München* [1974] ECR 773; Case 68/74, *Alaimo* v *Préfet du Rhône* [1975] ECR 109.
110. Lair, *op. cit.*
111. Case 152/82, *Forcheri* v *Belgian State* [1983] ECR 2323.
112. Directive 90/366 on the right of residence for students, OJ 1990 L180/30. Case C-3/90, *Bernini* v *Minister van Onderwijs en Wetenschappen* Judgment of 26 February 1992; Case C-257/89, *Raulin* v *Minister for Education and Science* Judgment of 26 February 1992.
113. Case 293/83, [1985] ECR 606.
114. Case 24/86, *Blaizot* v *University of Liège* [1988] ECR 355.
115. Blaizot, *ibid.*, and Case 263/86, *Belgian State* v *Humbel* [1988] ECR 5365.
116. OJ 1974 L13.
117. OJ 1975 L48/29.
118. OJ 1977 L61/26.
119. OJ 1980 L283/23.
120. Case 131/84, [1985] ECR 3531.
121. Case 215/83, *Commission* v *Belgium* [1985] ECR 1039.
122. Case 284/83, *Dansk Metalarbedejderforbund and Specialaedbejderforbundet i Denmark* v *Nielsen & Son Maskin-fabrik A/S in Liquidation* [1984] ECR 553.
123. Case 135/83, *Abels* [1985] ECR 469; Case 179/83, *FNV* [1985] ECR 511; Case 186/83, *Botzen* [1985] ECR 519.

124. Abels and Botzen, *ibid.*; Case 19/83, *Wendelboe* v *L. J. Music Aps* [1985] ECR 457.
125. Case 105/84, *Mikkelsen* [1985] ECR 2639.
126. Case 24/85, *Spilkers* [1986] ECR 1119.
127. Case 287/86, [1987] ECR 5465.
128. Case 324/86, [1988] ECR 739.
129. Joined Cases 144 and 145/87, *Berg* [1988] ECR 2559. See also Joined Cases C-132/91, C-138/91 and C-139/91, *Katsikas and Others* [1992] ECR I-6577.
130. Case 22/87, *Commission* v *Italy* [1989] ECR 143.
131. Case 53/88, [1990] ECR 1-3917.
132. See note 109.
133. OJ 1987 L166/20; Case 242/87, *Commission* v *Council* [1980] ECR 1425.
134. Decision 86/365 (OJ 1986 L222/17); Decision 89/27 (OJ 1989 L13).
135. Decision 89/489 (OJ 1989 L239/24).
136. *Commission* v *Council*, note 133; Joined Cases C51–89, C90/89 and C94/89, *United Kingdom* v *Council* [1991] ECR I-2757.
137. Although many provisions of Community law are directly applicable and have direct effect it was some time before they were fully exploited by Community citizens.
138. Wedderburn, *The Social Charter, European Company and Employment Rights* (Institute of Employment Rights 1990), p. 14.
139. See Joined Cases C-63/91 and C-64/91, *Jackson and Cresswell* v *Chief Adjudication Officer*, Judgment of 16 July 1992; Case C-9/91, *The Queen* v *Secretary of State for Social Security ex parte Equal Opportunities Commission*, Judgment of 7 July 1992.

5

Collective Bargaining and the Protection of Social Rights in Europe

Brian Bercusson

The history of British labour law is the attempt, from the late nineteenth century up until the legislation of the 1970s, to come to terms with the reality of collective regulation of labour conditions. The dialectic between law and collective bargaining is emerging as central to the process of formulating and implementing social and economic rights in the European Community. This chapter begins by describing the long process up to 1989 whereby collective agreements were introduced as an element in Community labour law.

Following the Community Charter of Fundamental Social Rights of Workers of December 1989, the Commission began producing proposals that reflected the renewed interest in collective bargaining as an instrument of Community labour law. These proposals went beyond the passive role for collective agreements envisaged before by Community law, which merely recognized agreements as valid instruments for the legal implementation of Community labour law directives. Instead, the new proposals integrated collective agreements in member states into Community law as the source of Community labour law standards. The second part of the chapter examines these proposals.

The Conclusion describes how the Maastricht Agreement on Social Policy is the most recent and dramatic step in the dialectic between Community law and collective bargaining, potentially articulating the formulation of Community labour law through social dialogue between the social partners at European level with collective bargaining within the member states.

COLLECTIVE BARGAINING AND COMMUNITY LAW UP TO 1989: IMPLEMENTATION OF DIRECTIVES THROUGH COLLECTIVE BARGAINING

Article 189 of the Treaty of Rome stipulates that 'A directive shall be binding, as to the result to be achieved, upon each Member State to which it is addressed, but shall leave to the national authorities the choice of form and methods.' Non-compliance with this obligation allows the Commission eventually to make a complaint to the European Court. Directives habitually referred to the obligation of member states to implement their provisions through 'legislative, regulatory or administrative provisions'.[1]

In *Commission of the European Communities* v *Italian Republic*,[2] the Italian Government argued 'in substance' that legislation, regulatory provisions and collective agreements combined to achieve adequate implementation of Directive 75/129 on collective dismissals. The Italian Government argued that to take the contrary view was formalist:

> In its opinion, the Commission set out from the formalistic standpoint that the directive can be complied with only by the adoption of implementing measures, irrespective of whether the provisions of directives are already complied with in the legal order of a Member State. It contends that the Commission inferred purely from the fact that the implementing measures were not put into effect that the Italian Government had not complied with the obligations arising out of the directive, without ascertaining whether the aims of the directive were already ensured in the Italian legal order.[3]

Responding to this argument, Advocate-General Verloren Van Themaat came to a specific conclusion regarding the role of collective agreements in implementing Directives: 'with regard to Article 100 of the EEC Treaty and Article 6 of the directive, they cannot be regarded as "methods" within the meaning of Article 189 of the Treaty or as "laws, regulations or administrative provisions" within the meaning of Article 6 of the directive.'[4] To the contrary, the Court seemed to respond in some degree to the substantive argument of the Italian Government. Upholding the Commission's complaint, the European Court pointed out that certain sectors were not covered by agreements, and that the agreements did not include all the provisions required by Community law.[5] The conclusions of Advocate-General Verloren Van Themaat had also pointed out the defects of the Italian agreements regarding their coverage and scope. But, significantly, there was no reference in the Court's judgment to his conclusion regarding the formal role of collective agreements. It appeared that the Court was unwilling to hold collective agreements formally inadequate when there was no need to, as they were, on the facts of the case, in any event substantively inadequate.

This preference for substantive over formal logic was again manifested in the well-known case of *Commission of the European Communities* v *United Kingdom of Great Britain and Northern Ireland.*[6] The European Court held that the failure of the UK Government to enact legislation providing for the nullification of collective agreements violating the provisions of Directive 76/207 on equal treatment of men and women constituted non-fulfilment of its obligations under Article 189. Although collective agreements in the UK lacked legal effect, the European Court stated:

> The directive thus covers all collective agreements without distinction as to the nature of the legal effects which they do or do not produce. The reason for that generality lies in the fact that, even if they are not legally binding as between the parties who sign them or with regard to the employment relationships which they govern, collective agreements nevertheless have important *de facto* consequences for the employment relationships to which they refer, particularly in so far as they determine the rights of the workers and, in the interests of industrial harmony, give undertakings satisfy or need not satisfy [*sic*]. The need to ensure that the directive is completely effective therefore requires that any clauses in such agreements which are incompatible with the obligations imposed by the directive upon the Member States may be rendered inoperative, eliminated or amended by appropriate means.[7]

In this the Court reflected the realist view of Advocate-General Rozes, who stated:

> a situation in which possibly discriminatory provisions continue to exist in documents such as collective agreements . . . is just as ambiguous – above all for workers who in most cases have no legal training . . . workers have easier access to collective agreements . . . than to Directive 76/207 or to the United Kingdom laws depriving those documents, in general, of legally binding force. Thus, workers may believe that because their contracts of employment reproduce possibly discriminatory provisions from the types of document referred to they are legal and may not be challenged at law and the workers may therefore be deprived of the advantages of a directive which was in fact adopted for their benefit. In order to avoid such risks of confusion, the best course is to make it possible for such discriminatory provisions to be removed from those documents, as required by the directive.[8]

A definitive step towards formal recognition of collective agreements was taken in *Commission of the European Communities* v *Kingdom of Denmark*.[9] In that case, the Danish Government's position was explicitly that collective agreements were its choice of form and method for implementation of the obligations of Council Directive 75/117 on equal pay. It was argued that the Danish legislation was but a secondary guarantee of the equality principle in the event that this principle was not guaranteed by collective agreements. An agreement of 1971 made such provision and covered most employment relations in Denmark.[10] Significantly, in this case Advocate-General Verloren Van Themaat did not refer to his earlier conclusion excluding collective agreements as measures implementing Council Directives. He merely noted that 'From the point of view of legal certainty it would undoubtedly have been preferable had Denmark simply incorporated in its legislation the interpretation of the principle of equal pay laid down in Article 1 of the directive, in accordance with the view of the Commission.'[11] The Court held

> that Member States may leave the implementation of the principle of equal pay in the first instance to representatives of management and labour. That possibility does not, however, discharge them from the obligation of ensuring, by appropriate legislative and administrative provisions, that all workers in the Community are afforded the full protection provided for in the directive. That State guarantee must cover all cases where effective protection is not ensured by other means, for whatever reason, and in particular cases where the workers in question are not union members, where the sector in question is not covered by a collective agreement or where such an agreement does not fully guarantee the principle of equal pay.[12]

However, in a second case involving Italy, *Commission of the European Communities* v *Italian Republic*,[13] Advocate-General Sir Gordon Slynn returned to the attack. He invoked the conclusion of Advocate-General Verloren Van Themaat in the earlier case involving Italy: 'a collective bargaining agreement is not a "method" for implementing a directive under Article 189 of the Treaty'.[14] He also cited the text of the Directive in question (Directive 77/187), which, following the language normally used in Directives, specified implementation through laws, regulations or administrative provisions – not mentioning collective agreements.[15] Despite this, the Court cited its own judgment in *Commission of the European Communities* v *Kingdom of Denmark* and reiterated that

> it must be remembered that, as the Court held in its judgment of 30 January 1985 in Case 143/83 (*Commission* v *Denmark* [1985] ECR 427), it is true that the Member States may leave the implementation of the social policy objectives pursued by a directive in this area in the first instance to management and labour. That possibility does not, however, discharge them from the obligation of ensuring that all workers in the Community are afforded the full protection provided for in the directive. The State guarantee must cover all cases where effective protection is not ensured by other means.[16]

The substantive logic received a further impulse in *Commission of the European Communities* v *French Republic*.[17] The Commission challenged the French Government's delegation to the social partners of the task of amending agreements violating the provisions of Directive 76/207 on equal treatment. This time Advocate-General Sir Gordon Slynn argued that 'it was not sufficient to leave it to labour and management without specific requirements as to the time or methods of enforcement'.[18] Moreover, he pointed out, 'There is no State guarantee of effective enforcement of the principle of equality should the negotiation process between the two sides of industry fail'.[19] To support this he added:

> The results of the legislation in practice demonstrate the absence of any effective State guarantee of compliance, notwithstanding the existence of a procedure for government approval of collective agreements. It appears that in 1983 in France 1,050 collective agreements were concluded in branches of working activity and 2,400 in individual undertakings. In 1984 the figures were 927 and 6,000 respectively. By contrast, only 16 collective agreements were renegotiated on a non-discriminatory basis.[20]

Citing these figures, the Court concluded:

> Such figures are extremely modest when compared with the number of collective agreements entered into each year in France . . . The requirement that collective agreements must be approved and the possibility that they may be extended by the public authorities have therefore not led to a rapid process of renegotiation.
>
> The French Government's argument that collective negotiation is the only appropriate method of abolishing the special rights in question must be considered in the light of that conclusion.

> In that regard, it is enough to observe that, even if that argument were to be accepted, it could not be used to justify national legislation which, several years after the expiry of the period prescribed for the implementation of the directive, makes the two sides of industry responsible for removing certain instances of inequality without laying down any time-limit for compliance with that obligation.
>
> It follows from those considerations that the French Government's argument that the task of removing special rights for women should be left to the two sides of industry working through collective negotiation cannot be accepted.[21]

This case also illustrates the limitations of the litigation procedure. The figures cited do not indicate what proportion of agreements contained discriminatory clauses. The figure of sixteen agreements amended has to be assessed not against the total number of agreements, but against those containing clauses requiring amendment. Research by the French Commission Nationale de la Negociation Collective has produced reports on the number of agreements containing such clauses.[22] These indicate that relatively few contain clauses pertaining to equality. This puts the evaluation by the Court and the Advocate-General in a different light.

Subsequently, there has been a series of other decisions of the European Court reinforcing the substantive approach to collective agreements in the area of equal pay and equal treatment. Collective agreements are condemned if they make unequal provision for men and women,[23] provide for discriminatory criteria for pay calculations and lack transparency as regards pay determination.[24] Each case involved the Court making a close examination of the practical workings of a collective agreement. In each case it was the substance of the agreement that was condemned. But it was already clear by 1989 that collective agreements were formally acceptable as instruments for the implementation of Community law obligations.

This was evident in the Preamble to the Community Charter of Fundamental Social Rights of Workers of 1989: 'Whereas such implementation may take the form of laws, collective agreements or existing practices at the various appropriate levels and whereas it requires in many spheres the active involvement of the two sides of industry.' The Charter further declared in Article 27: 'It is more particularly the responsibility of the Member States, in accordance with national practices, notably through legislative measures or collective agreements, to guarantee the fundamental social rights in this Charter.'[25] The Commission followed suit. In proposals under the Action Programme to give effect to the Charter, it has begun to insert an implementation provision, which accords a role to collective bargaining.[26] One such proposal has already been approved by the Council of Ministers:

> Member States shall adopt the laws, regulations and administrative provisions necessary to comply with this Directive no later than 30 June 1993, or shall ensure by that date that the employers' and workers' representatives introduce the required provisions by way of agreement, the Member States being obliged to take the necessary steps at all times to guarantee the results imposed by this Directive.[27]

Article 2(4) of the Agreement annexed to the Protocol on Social Policy of the Treaty on European Union, signed at Maastricht on 7 February 1992, stipulates:

> A Member State may entrust management and labour, at their joint request, with the implementation of directives . . .
>
> In that case, it shall ensure that, no later than the date on which a directive must be transposed in accordance with Article 189, management and labour have introduced the necessary measures by agreements, the Member State concerned being required to take any necessary measure enabling it at any time to be in a position to guarantee the results imposed by that directive.[28]

It provides the concluding point of a long process whereby first individual member states, then the European Court, then eleven member states in Article 27 of the Community Charter and Maastricht Agreement and finally the Commission and Council have formally recognized the role of collective bargaining in the implementation of Community labour law.

PROPOSALS OF THE COMMISSION AND COUNCIL AFTER 1989: THE INCORPORATION OF COLLECTIVE BARGAINING INTO COMMUNITY LABOUR LAW INSTRUMENTS

The proposals of the Commission and Council after 1989 demonstrate a new development in the use of collective bargaining as an instrument of Community labour law. I have argued elsewhere that the significance of this development is potentially profound: that the policy emerging is that the employment conditions of workers in general, where these derive from national labour law instruments, including certain collective agreements, are to be protected by Community law.[29] The argument will be illustrated by examination of two recent Community proposals: (a) Council Directive on an employer's obligation to inform employees of the conditions applicable to the contract or employment relationship;[30] and (b) Commission Proposal for a Council Directive concerning the posting of workers in the framework of the provision of services.[31]

Council Directive on an Employer's Obligation to Inform Employees of the Conditions Applicable to the Contract or Employment Relationship[32]

In its original proposal for what became the Council Directive on an employer's obligation to inform employees of the conditions applicable to the contract or employment relationship, the reasons for the proposal were set out in an Explanatory Memorandum as follows:

> Certain long-standing forms of work, such as part-time or home working, have now been supplemented by such new forms as 'part-time vertical work', i.e. work organized on a daily, weekly, monthly or annual basis, job-sharing, job-splitting, on-call work, work-training contracts and training schemes . . .
>
> Moreover . . . new production methods and the explosive development of the service industry have both played a part in making the labour market considerably more flexible, thus generating new possibilities for 'black work' and other illicit practices . . .
>
> These developments, to which must be added the greater flexibility in the time reference frame (adaptation of working time or development of intermittent and maintenance work), have also tended to cloud the position of many workers, leading to confusion, uncertainty and instability. They tend, a fortiori, for those workers without written proof of their working relationship, to make workers unaware of certain social and professional rights linked to this relationship.
>
> The provision of a written declaration relating to a form of proof of an employment relationship is designed, in consequence, to clarify the legal position of employees who are not covered by a written employment contract or letter of appointment, and, in

> particular, to give them a better idea of when, where and for whom they are supposed to be working, and, more generally, to give them written proof of the essential elements of this relationship. This will do a lot towards improving the transparency of the Community labour market, while at the same time giving workers more security, a better idea of their rights and more mobility within the Community.[33]

Collective agreements were seen as one instrument in achieving the objectives of the proposal. This emerges from the provisions of both the proposal and the final text of the Directive, which contained a number of changes. The final Directive exerts considerable pressure for use of collective agreements as reference points in four ways:

1 Reference to collective agreements applicable is probably compulsory.
2 There is a possibility of using agreements as sources of information on specific terms of employment.
3 Modification of terms of employment need not be individualized if collective agreements are used as the reference document.
4 Fifteen days' notice of legal action is required if workers are covered by collective agreements, but direct recourse to the court is available if collective agreements do not apply.

COLLECTIVE AGREEMENTS AS AN ESSENTIAL ASPECT OF EMPLOYMENT

Collective agreements themselves are specified as an essential aspect of the contract or employment relationship. Article 2 prescribes an obligation for the employer to provide information and Article 3 requires that this be in written form. The employee must be notified 'of the *essential aspects* of the contract or employment relationship' (Article 2(1)). The information is to include '*at least* the following' items listed in Article 2(2). Article 2(2) in the first draft of the proposed Directive provided that the information specified include 'a reference to the collective agreements applicable'. The final text reads instead:

> *Where appropriate*:
> i) the collective agreements governing the employee's conditions of work; or,
> ii) in the case of collective agreements concluded outside the business by special joint bodies or institutions, the name of the competent body of joint institution within which the agreements were concluded.

A first key question is whether the words 'where appropriate' mean that it is *discretionary* for the employer to notify the employee of collective agreements, or is to be read as meaning that where they exist it *is* appropriate. Second, it is not clear whether the information to be given consists of the agreements themselves or information about the agreements: e.g. parties to the agreement, date, geographical area covered (enterprise, region, industry, national) and where these agreements may be found. That the alternative requires only mention of the relevant negotiating body implies perhaps a restrictive interpretation. But it would seem doubtful that a statement merely that there exist collective agreements governing working conditions would suffice. It is not clear whether it covers non-legally binding collective agreements, but the decision of the European Court in *Commission of the European Communities* v *United Kingdom of Great Britain and Northern Ireland* probably means it does.[34]

COLLECTIVE AGREEMENTS AS A SOURCE OF INFORMATION

Article 2(3) provides that the information on (f) leave, (g) notice, (h) remuneration and (i) working time 'may, where appropriate, be given in the form of a reference to the laws, regulations and administrative or statutory provisions, or collective agreements governing those particular points'. Again, does 'where appropriate' imply a discretion to refer to the agreements, or that it *is* appropriate (i.e. obligatory) where agreements exist and regulate working conditions?

In the UK, discretionary substitution is allowed by the Employment Protection (Consolidation) Act 1978 (EPCA), section 2(3). Research found that many employers provided the detailed information even where collective agreements existed.[35] This may not be permitted under the Directive if reference is deemed obligatory as 'appropriate'.

One argument that it is obligatory derives from Article 4(1) (c and d), requiring the employer to provide information, '*where appropriate*', to expatriate workers on conditions of employment of particular importance to such workers (e.g. payment in kind linked to expatriation and conditions of repatriation). The implication is that where these terms of employment are agreed, the employer *must* provide the information. Similarly, Article 2(2)(b): in this provision 'where appropriate' offers a choice between notifying the domicile or the principle of multiple workplaces, but one is obligatory.

Article 3 specifies the means of providing the requisite information. The first draft of the directive required a written declaration, signed by the employer who keeps a copy. The final text prescribes instead optional methods. The methods are specified in Article 3(1): (a) '*a written contract of employment*'; and/or (b) '*a letter of engagement*'; and/or (c) '*one or more other written documents*, where one of these documents contains at least all the information referred to in Article 2(2)(a), (b), (c), (d), (h) and (i)'.

The first draft allowed for the option of a written contract instead of a written declaration. But as regards the letter of engagement or other document – these were permitted if they referred 'to a collective agreement or other regulations governing employment relationships, copies of which are easily accessible' (draft Directive, Article 3). The reference to a collective agreement has been dropped, presumably replaced by the general provision regarding reference to collective agreements (Article 2(3)).

In sum, as regards collective agreements:

- '*where appropriate*', information is required (2(2)(j));
- *some items* of the information may, '*where appropriate*', be provided through reference to collective agreements (Article 2(3)).

The question remains as to whether 'where appropriate' implies a *discretion* to refer to the agreements, or that it *is* appropriate (i.e. *obligatory*) where an agreement exists and regulates working conditions.

COLLECTIVE AGREEMENTS AS THE MEDIUM FOR CHANGES IN EMPLOYMENT CONDITIONS

Article 5 is concerned with the employer's obligation to notify the worker in writing about modification of aspects of the contract or employment relationship. But Article 5(2) provides that such a document is not compulsory 'in the event of a change in the laws, regulations and administrative or statutory provisions or *collective agreements* cited in the documents referred to in Article 3'.

So use of collective agreements obviates the need for updating documentation. The implication is that Article 3, *which does not mention collective agreements*, could (and in practice should) be used as the point of reference for information generally, as this will obviate any need for updating notification. This has an analogue in section 4(3) of the EPCA (as originally enacted), which exempts the employer from the obligation to notify changes if 'the employer indicates to the employee that future changes in the terms of which the particulars are given in the document will be entered up in the document' (in the case of the document being a collective agreement). As mentioned above, the first draft of Article 3 of the Directive even included an explicit reference to collective agreements, but this was deleted in the final draft.

Article 7 allows for more favourable provisions. This was also provided in the first draft, but the final text added that member states have the prerogative to 'encourage or permit the application of *agreements* which are more favourable to employees'. While this clearly excludes less favourable provisions, the problem remains of how to assess whether an agreement is more or less favourable. Second, the wording does not seem to be confined to *collective* agreements. Previously all references to agreements stated collective explicitly. Now it seems to allow for improvement by individual parties.

INCENTIVES TO EMPLOYERS TO ADOPT COLLECTIVELY AGREED STANDARDS

Article 8 is concerned with enforcement of the rights provided in the Directive. Article 8(2) is a new provision. Paragraph 1 provides that member states may stipulate that access to means of redress envisaged by Article 8(1) (judicial process or other recourse to competent authorities) is 'subject to the notification of the employer by the employee and the failure by the employer to reply within 15 days of notification'. However, para. 2 allows for exceptions to the requirement of prior notification:

> The formality of prior notification may in no case be required in:
> • the cases referred to in Article 4 [*expatriate workers*],
> • neither for workers with a *temporary* contract or employment relationship,
> • nor for employees *not covered by a collective agreement or by collective agreements relating to the employment relationship.*

This is a clear recognition of the role of collective agreements in providing protection, for collective agreements imply a trade union presence at the workplace, or at least some recognition of collective regulation limiting the unilateral power of the employer. The absence of such presence or recognition implies an unrestrained exercise of employer power. Prior notice might be dangerous for an employee so exposed to employer retaliation for daring to claim a (perhaps disputed) right. Hence, prior notice is not required where collective agreements do not apply, and the employee can seek 'instant' judicial protection. Without some evidence of collective regulation, prior notice might be dangerous, so it is not required.

This is an inducement to employers to come under agreements so as to require employees to give prior notice. There is, however, the further problem of knowing when workers *are* covered. A similar problem of knowing whether workers are covered arises in those provisions where agreements are to be referred to 'where appropriate': Article 2(2)(j) requiring information about agreements 'where appropriate'; and Article 2(3) allowing for requisite information to be provided, 'where appropriate . . . in the form of a reference to . . . collective agreements'. Here the problem is also to know if the worker is covered, and, hence, reference *is* appropriate. The problem can be formulated as follows.

1 Employer invokes Article 8(2)(2) requiring notice.
2 Employee invokes exception – not covered by collective agreement; also, he or she may or may not refer to failure to mention agreement as per Article 2(2)(j).
3 Employer invokes Article 2(3) – does this mean the employee is covered by the agreement, or only that the agreement is the source of information referred to?
4 Employee argues that wrong collective agreement is referred to; or that one or more, or no, relevant agreements are accepted by the employer. Is he still 'covered' within the meaning of the exception?

IMPLEMENTATION THROUGH COLLECTIVE AGREEMENTS

Finally, Article 9(1) provides that member states shall 'adopt the laws, regulations and administrative provisions . . . *or* ensure by that date that the employers' and workers' representatives introduce the required provisions by way of agreement, the Member States being obliged to take the necessary steps enabling them at all times to guarantee the results imposed by this Directive'. In sum, these new provisions of European Community labour law have numerous implications for member state collective bargaining systems and collective agreements.

Working Conditions Applicable to Workers from Another State Performing Work in the Host Country

On 1 August 1991, the Commission published a Proposal for a Council Directive concerning the posting of workers in the framework of the provision of services.[36] This was concerned to implement the commitment in the Commission's Action Programme relating to the Community Charter of Fundamental Social Rights of Workers, as regards the 'working conditions applicable to workers from another State performing work in the host country in the framework of the freedom to provide services, especially on behalf of a subcontracting undertaking'.[37] In plain English, this protects local working conditions where workers are imported by foreign sub-contractors, or, even plainer, protects workers from the lump.

The Commission posed the question 'as to which national labour legislation should be applied to undertakings which post a worker to carry out temporary work in a Member State'.[38] Formally, the solution depends on conflict of law rules, but given that these vary among member states, the outcome may give rise to distortions of competition between national and foreign undertakings. The Commission therefore proposed to coordinate the laws of the member states 'to eradicate practices which may be both detrimental to a fair competition between undertakings and prejudicial to the interests of the workers concerned'[39] The element of competition between firms as regards labour conditions was described as follows:

> A particular problem arises, however, where a Member State places obligations, notably with regard to pay, on firms based in and working on its territory, and these firms are faced with competition - for a specific task carried out within that same Member State - from a firm based elsewhere and not subject to the same obligations. Legitimate competition between firms is then overlaid by potentially distortive effects between national requirements.
>
> The question is therefore one of finding a balance between two principles which find themselves in contradiction. On the one hand, free competition between firms, including at the level of subcontracting across borders, so that the full benefits of the Single Market can be realised, including by firms based in Member States whose main comparative advantage is a lower wage cost. On the other, Member States may decide to set and apply minimum pay levels applicable on their territory in order to ensure a minimum standard of living appropriate to the country concerned.[40]

This competition between firms would not occur, of course, if national labour laws were harmonized. The fact is, however, that the disparities among member states regarding labour standards are such as to produce what has been termed 'social regime competition' - competition among member states as to the costs imposed on employers by national regimes of social and labour regulation.[41] The Commission's Explanatory Memorandum elaborates this difference as regards pay levels and working time standards. The conclusion was:

> National differences as to the material content of working conditions and the criteria inspiring the conflict of law rules may lead to situations where posted workers are applied lower wages and other working conditions than those in force in the place where the work is temporarily carried out. This situation would certainly affect fair competition between undertakings and equality of treatment between foreign and national undertakings; it would from the social point of view be completely unacceptable.[42]

The legal framework proposed by the Commission to combat this problem drew upon a number of sources of inspiration. One in particular is of interest, the case of *Rush Portuguesa Lda* v *Office national d'immigration*,[43] not least because it derives from the European Court, which may eventually be faced with interpretation of the Community instrument regulating this issue.

Rush Portuguesa Lda, a building and public works undertaking, was a company governed by Portuguese law, whose registered office was in Portugal. It entered into a sub-contract with a French company for works in France and, to carry out these workings, brought its Portuguese workforce from Portugal. However, it failed to obtain work permits for these workers, as prescribed by the French Labour Code, and was therefore informed by the Director of the Office national d'immigration that it was required to make certain payments. The company challenged this before the French Administrative Tribunal, arguing that the effect of applicable provisions of the EEC Treaty (Articles 59 to 66) was that a provider of services may move freely from one member state to another with his employees. The Tribunal considered that their decision depended on the interpretation of the applicable Community law and referred the issue to the European Court. One of the questions put to the Court was the following: 'May the right of a Portuguese company to provide services throughout the Community be made subject . . . to conditions, in particular relating to the engagement of labour *in situ*, the obtaining of work permits for its own Portuguese staff or the payment of fees to an official immigration body?'[44]

The issue was complicated by the fact that the transitional provisions regarding Portuguese accession were still in force so that free movement of workers was not available, whereas the freedom to provide services was available. The Portuguese company argued that 'a person providing services may go from one Member State to another with his work-force. The application to that work-force of the restrictive provisions of the *code du travail* is therefore contrary to Community law.'[45] The French Government argued

> that right does not impede the application of all national rules concerning the economic activity in question . . . an undertaking cannot be allowed, under the cloak of subcontract work, to evade national provisions concerning the supply of labour, in particular those relating to temporary work . . . a distinction must be drawn between the activity of the undertaking, which is entitled to freedom to provide services, and the status of the undertaking's employees.[46]

The Portuguese Government argued against the French Government's position:

> The availability of such an undertaking's work-force as a whole determines its production capacity and therefore its capacity to provide the service in question. Any condition restricting the use of a company's workers consequently limits its freedom to provide services . . . The terms of their employment are, moreover, governed entirely by Portuguese law.[47]

The Commission sought an intermediate position by seeking to distinguish among the workforce those workers who, by virtue of their special position, can be associated with the employer's freedom to provide services, and other workers who cannot.[48]

Advocate-General Van Gerven in his Opinion emphasized that the French national legislative provision, which effectively restricted the freedom to provide services, could be justified in terms of the general good: 'the restriction introduced by the national provision must be objectively necessary in order to protect an interest which is acceptable from a Community point of view'.[49] The Advocate-General then proposed to differentiate among the workforce, albeit using criteria differing from those suggested by the Commission.

The Court of Justice, on the one hand, accepted that the Portuguese company could not be precluded from bringing its workers into France by

> making the staff subject to restrictions such as conditions as to engagement *in situ* or an obligation to obtain a work permit. To impose such conditions on the person providing services established in another Member State discriminates against that person in relation to his competitors established in the host country who are able to use their own staff without restrictions, and moreover affects his ability to provide the service.[50]

On the other hand, the Court made the following profoundly important statement:

> Finally, it should be stated, in response to the concern expressed in this connection by the French Government, that Community law does not preclude Member States from extending their legislation, or collective agreements entered into by both sides of industry, to any person who is employed, even temporarily, within their territory, no matter in which country the employer is established; nor does Community law prohibit Member States from enforcing those rules by appropriate means.[51]

The substantive outcome of the judgment is that restrictions on entry would not be permitted, but regulation of terms and conditions of employment, by law or collective agreement, was permissible.

Unlike the Commission in its later proposal, the Court did not address the implications of this judgment, and particularly the statement as to the possibility of regulating employment conditions of foreign contractors, for freedom to provide services. Effectively, such regulation would undermine foreign contractors, since it eliminated their main competitive advantage, derived from less costly labour and social regulation of working conditions. The Commission obviously appreciated this. But it clearly opted to subordinate the competition imperative to a social policy – a profoundly important policy choice:

> the need to eradicate discrimination between national and non-national undertakings and workers with respect to the application of certain working conditions, justify a Community proposal which . . . intends to create a hard core of mandatory rules laid down by statutes or by erga omnes collective agreements, without disrupting the labour law systems of the Member States and particularly their legislative or voluntaristic approach and their collective bargaining systems.[52]

Hence Article 3(1) of the proposed Directive provided:

> Member States shall see to it that, whatever the law applicable to the employment relationship, the undertaking does not deprive the worker of the terms and conditions of employment which apply for work of the same character at the place where the work is temporarily carried out, provided that:
> (a) they are laid down by laws, regulations and administrative provisions, collective agreements or arbitration awards, covering

the whole of the occupation and industry concerned having an 'erga omnes' effect and/or being made legally binding in the occupation and industry concerned, and

(b) they concern the following matters:

(i) maximum daily and weekly hours of work, rest periods, work on Sundays and night work;

(ii) minimum paid holidays;

(iii) the minimum rates of pay, including overtime rates and allowances, but excluding benefits provided for by private occupational schemes;

(iv) the conditions of hiring out of workers, in particular the supply of workers by temporary employment businesses;

(v) health, safety and hygiene at work;

(vi) protective measures with regard to the working conditions of pregnant women or women who have recently given birth, children, young people and other groups enjoying special protection;

(vii) equality of treatment between men and women and prohibition of discrimination on the grounds of colour, race, religion, opinions, national origin or social background.

There remain many issues of interpretation and application of the requirement that certain collective agreements be observed - not least arising from the differences in the nature and legal effects of collective agreements in different member states. But the proposal by the Commission requiring employers to adhere to collectively agreed standards as those which Community law demands is of fundamental significance.

CONCLUSION: FORMULATION OF COMMUNITY SOCIAL POLICY THROUGH COLLECTIVE BARGAINING

Each of the two developments described above has served to emphasize the dialectic between collective bargaining and Community labour law. The recognition of collective agreements as one of the instruments legally available to implement Community labour law was an important step. It none the less still formally relegated collective bargaining to a secondary role, though, as in the case of judicial interpretation and implementation of legislative texts, the borderline between law-applying and law-making is not always clear. The role of the social partners in applying Community labour law thus also allows some scope for the indirect formulation of Community labour law.

In the case of Community instruments using collective agreements as the basis for Community labour law standards, this delegation of the capacity effectively to formulate policy becomes more explicit. Collective regulation of conditions of employment is perceived as an essential element of the employment relationship and collective agreements as the potential source of essential terms of employment. Incentives are provided to employers to acknowledge the role of collective regulation.[53] A second proposal, drawing on the jurisprudence of the Court of Justice, regards Community law as requiring the maintenance of certain collectively agreed national standards, even where this conflicts with the imperatives of competition. Again, this may be seen as a preliminary recognition of the role of the social partners in defining Community labour law standards.

Definitive recognition has arrived in the form of the Agreement on Social Policy between Member States of the Community, with the exception of the UK, annexed to the Protocol on Social Policy of the Treaty on European Union, signed at Maastricht on 7 February 1992. As described above, Article 2(4) provides the conclusive statement that management and labour may be entrusted with the implementation of directives. Further, Article 3(1) of the Agreement requires the Commission to promote the consultation of the social partners at Community level and to take any relevant measure to facilitate their dialogue. Article 3(2, 3) of the Agreement also requires the Commission to incorporate the social partners in the process of formulating Community social policy.

In a definitive step, Article 3(4) enables the social partners to begin a procedure for the independent formulation of Community social policy in the form of European collective agreements.[54] These agreements, in the words of Article 4(2), 'shall be implemented' in one of two ways specified, the first of which is stated to be 'in accordance with the procedures and practices specific to management and labour and the Member States'. This seems to envisage articulation of European agreements with systems of collective bargaining specific to each member state.

It may be that member states are obliged to develop formal machinery of articulation of national standards with those laid down in the agreements or to use existing machinery of articulation. Alternatively, given the nature of the authors of the standards (Community-level organizations of employers and workers), the procedures and practices peculiar to each member state may consist of mechanisms of articulation of Community agreements with collective bargaining in the member state concerned. Member states are not obliged to create such mechanisms, but national law may not interfere with mechanisms that already exist, or that may be created by the social partners within the member state to deal with the new development at Community level.

This is the logical conclusion of the process whereby collective bargaining and collective agreements have moved from being merely formal means of implementation of Community instruments to vehicles for the substantive definition of Community labour standards and, finally, to becoming independent sources of Community labour law and social policy.

NOTES

1. For example, Council Directive 77/187 of 14 February 1977 on the approximation of the laws of member states relating to the safeguarding of employees' rights in the event of transfers of undertakings, businesses or parts of businesses (OJ 1977, L61/26, Article 8): '1. Member States shall bring into force the laws, regulations and administrative provisions needed to comply with this Directive'.
2. Case 91/81, [1982] ECR 2133.
3. *Ibid.*, p. 2142.
4. *Ibid.*, p. 2145.
5. *Ibid.*, p. 2140, paras 8–9.
6. Case 165/82, [1983] ECR 3431.
7. *Ibid.*, p. 3447, para. 11.
8. *Ibid.*, p. 3454.
9. Case 143/83, [1985] ECR 427.
10. *Ibid.*, p. 434, para. 7.
11. *Ibid.*, p. 430.
12. *Ibid.*, pp. 434–5, para. 8.
13. Case 235/84, [1986] ECR 2291.
14. *Ibid.*, p. 2295.
15. *Ibid.*
16. *Ibid.*, p. 2302, para. 20.
17. Case 312/86, [1988] ECR 6315.
18. *Ibid.*, p. 6329.
19. *Ibid.*
20. *Ibid.*
21. *Ibid.*, pp. 6337–8, paras 20–3.
22. Commission Nationale de la Negociation Collective, *Bilan Annuel de la Negociation Collective 1984, L'égalité professionnelle entre les femmes et les hommes* (Ministère des Affaires Sociales et de l'Emploi, June 1985, mimeo), and similar reports published in following years.
23. Case 170/84, *Bilka-Kaufhaus GmbH* v *Karin Weber von Hartz* [1986] ECR 1607. Case 33/89, *Maria Kowalska* v *Freie und Hansestadt Hamburg* [1990] ECR 3199.
24. Case 109/88, *Handels og Kontorfunktionaerenes Forbund i Danmark* v *Dansk Arbejdsgiverforening* [1989] ECR 3199.
25. The text of the Charter is published in *Social Europe*, 1/90.

26. Proposal for a Council Directive on certain employment relationships with regard to distortions of competition, Article 6; COM(90) 228 final–SYN 280, Brussels, 13 August 1990. Proposal for a Council Directive concerning certain aspects of the organization of working time, Article 14; COM(90) 317 final–SYN 295, Brussels, 20 September 1990.

27. Council Directive 91/533 of 14 October 1991 on an employer's obligation to inform employees of the conditions applicable to the contract or employment relationship (OJ 1991 L288/32), Article 9(1).

28. This version was derived from the ETUC/UNICE/CEEP accord of 31 October 1991, and differs from that initially proposed by the Dutch Presidency: 'A Member State may entrust management and labour with the implementation of all or part of the measures which it has laid down in order to implement the directives adopted in accordance with paragraphs 2 and 3.' *Europe Documents* No. 1734, 3 October 1991, proposal for new Article 118(4).

29. B. Bercusson, Maastricht: a fundamental change in European labour law (1992) 23 *Industrial Relations Journal* 177, at pp. 180–1.

30. Council Directive 91/533 of 14 October 1991 (OJ L 288/32). This began life as Commission Proposal for a Council Directive on a form of proof of an employment relationship, COM(90) 563 final, Brussels, 8 January 1991.

31. COM(91) 230 final–SYN 346, Brussels, 1 August 1991.

32. For a general account of this Directive and its implications for British labour law and industrial relations, see J. Clark and M. Hall, The Cinderella directive? Employee rights to information about conditions applicable to their contract or employment relationship (1992) 21 ILJ 106.

33. Note 31, paras 4–7.

34. Case 165/82, [1983] ECR 3431.

35. P. E. Leighton and S. L. Dumville, From statement to contract: some effects of the Contracts of Employment Act 1972 (1977) 6 ILJ 133.

36. COM(91) 230 final–SYN 346, Brussels, 1 August 1991.

37. Action Programme, Part II, Section 4B.

38. Explanatory Memorandum, above, note 36, para. 2.

39. *Ibid.*, para. 3.

40. *Ibid.*, para. 9 bis.

41. W. Streeck, La dimensione sociale del mercato unico europeo: verso un'economia non regolata? [1990] *Stato e Mercato*, no. 28, pp. 31–68.

42. *Op. cit.*, para. 12.

43. Case 113/89, [1990] ECR 1417.

44. *Ibid.*, p. 1420.

45. *Ibid.*, p. 1421.

46. *Ibid.*

47. *Ibid.*, p. 1422.

48. *Ibid.*, pp. 1422–4.

49. *Ibid.*, p. 1429.

50. *Ibid.*, p. 1443, para. 12.

51. *Ibid.*, p. 1445, para. 18.

52. Explanatory Memorandum, *op. cit.*, para. 18.

53. Another example is in the Commission's proposal for a Council Directive concerning certain aspects of the organisation of working time, Article 12(3) of which allowed for the social partners to opt out of state regulation by substituting a collective agreement. COM(90) 317 final–SYN 295, Brussels, 20 September 1990.

54. I have called this a process of 'bargaining in the shadow of the law' (see note 29).

6

Using Community Law to Protect Workers' Rights: A Case Study[1]

B. W. Napier

INTRODUCTION

Writing in 1986, Paul O'Higgins drew attention to the many different ways in which UK labour law was falling short of standards set by international bodies for the protection of workers.[2] In the years since then, the substance of his criticisms has been confirmed on a number of occasions, as predictable conflicts have developed between a government determined to pursue labour law policies based on deregulation and market forces, and international standards giving priority to the need to make provision for the protection of workers' rights.

On the whole, the UK Government has resisted criticism coming from bodies and institutions where the standards they defend do not give rise to enforceable rights under domestic law. The negative response given to the condemnation by the ILO of various aspects of the UK's legislation on trade union rights and industrial relations is perhaps the best-known example of official intransigence in the face of international criticism.[3]

In one specific area, however, the results have been different. In connection with the standards set by the law of the European Communities, the Government has not had the option of rejecting standards set.[4] The reason, of course, is that Community law is not something that stands separate from domestic law; it is part of it, and enforceable as much before the courts and tribunals of the United Kingdom as before the European Court of Justice in Luxembourg.

Until recently, the law relating to sexual discrimination gave the best illustration of how Community law could operate to protect and extend workers' rights, with cases such as *Barber*[5] and *Marshall*[6] illustrating the power it has to compel changes in domestic employment law far removed from the objectives pursued by government under the banner of deregulation and job creation. But now it is increasingly clear that Community law impacts beyond sex discrimination to shape many other areas in which workers' rights are in issue. In the initial litigation over the coalmine closure programme announced in 1992, for example, we can see how the EC Directive on Collective Redundancies[7] had an important part to play in shaping the decision of the Divisional Court to restrain the closures proposed by British Coal.[8]

The protection of workers' rights in the event of the transfer of a business is another area where Community law is of increasing importance, and it is with this particular part of the law and, in particular, the role that the Acquired Rights Directive (EEC/77/117) has played in the interpretation of the Transfer of Undertakings (Protection of Employment) Regulations 1981 (TUPE) that the present chapter is concerned.

THE BACKGROUND: BUSINESS TRANSFERS AND THE MARKET TESTING PROGRAMME

Although TUPE has been in force for over a decade, it is only in recent times that it has been seen as posing particular problems for government. The main reason for this is its interaction with the privatization programme that is central to the British Government's policy. The subjection of public services to the discipline of the market has proved to be one of the most controversial features of Conservative economic policy in the 1980s and 1990s. The policy, under a variety of names, has been constantly evolving for more than a decade, and it extends to the widest range of activities. To give just a few examples, market testing has been applied to provision of refuse collection and to the management of prisons, to the running of computer systems and to the provision of typing facilities.[9] The programme extends to the services provided by both central and local government, and large numbers of staff are involved. It was announced in Parliament in March 1993 that market testing in central government would, in the period to September 1993, extend to activities valued at about £1.5 billion and employing 44,000 staff. It follows that the legal framework within which such commercialization of public-sector services takes place is already and will remain a subject of the highest significance.

MARKET TESTING AND CCT

What is sometimes loosely referred to as 'privatization' has radically altered management practices and the organization of the labour market in the public sector. The process is known under a variety of names: externalization of services, facilities management, contractorization, compulsory competitive tendering and contracting-out are all terms encountered. CCT (compulsory competitive tendering) usually denotes a market testing programme linked with the provision of local government services.

Market testing itself, when not used as shorthand to describe the process of putting out to tender of work, is usually specifically associated with the restructuring of central government services, and thus changes affecting the employment of civil servants. Unlike CCT it is a voluntary process, in the sense that it is carried out as a matter of policy and not because of the requirements of legislation.[10] But it is a procedure based on the same competitive principles that underpin CCT, namely that competition in the open market, relying upon a process of tendering, provides the best guarantee of value for money.

Tendering for public sector work is usually only commercially attractive for companies because they hope to be able to do the work with reduced labour costs. In practice, this means that the conditions of employment of affected staff typically worsen following such a market testing; indeed, in many cases, the process will entail redundancies of staff not needed by the new employer and for whom there is no place in the local or central authority's reduced operations. TUPE, which broadly operates to maintain terms and conditions after a change in the identity of the employer following a business transfer, has the potential to inhibit such cost-cutting. It may thus significantly reduce the commercial attraction of tendering for public sector contracts, and it is precisely for this reason that its operation has caused so much alarm in Government circles.

THE GROWING DEBATE

In the course of the past two years the employment law implications of the market testing programme have become of increasing importance to government, employers and workers, and this can be seen as a result of changes in two different areas.

The Legal Context

The period saw the emergence of a series of important cases, decided by both the UK courts and the European Court of Justice, dealing with the interpretation of the domestic and Community instruments. A first point to note is the existence of significant differences in the content of these. TUPE in its original version (i.e. before the amendments made by s. 33 of the Trade Union Reform and Employment Rights Act 1993) did not apply to transfers of undertakings 'not in the nature of a commercial venture'. There is no such limitation to be found in the EC Directive.[11]

For some time it was widely assumed that, because of this and certain other differences, many contracting out and privatization exercises were not covered by TUPE. This meant, broadly, that the employment rights of such employees were not protected when transfers took place and their employment was carried over or terminated. Although the 'commercial undertaking' limitation feature of UK law was criticized some time ago as incompatible with the parent Directive, it was not until the late 1980s that public awareness began to focus on the particular implications this exclusion might have for privatization and competitive tendering exercises. At around this time a number of EAT decisions seemed to confirm that TUPE excluded many – though not all – transfers consequent upon competitive tendering.

In *Expro Services Ltd* v *Smith*,[12] it was held that the contracting out of a catering function by a public body did not create the necessary conditions for the application of TUPE because it was not an operation in the nature of a commercial venture. The Court held that it mattered not that, subsequent to the privatization, it was operated commercially; the court ruled that it had to have that characteristic beforehand. A somewhat different argument, leading to the same conclusion, emerged in *Stirling* v *Dietsmann Management Systems Ltd*,[13] where the absence of transfer of either physical assets or goodwill was held conclusive against the application of TUPE. There the facts concerned the transfer of workers under an agreement to staff and operate a diving vessel. Again, the particular circumstances of the ensuing changeover were thought not to meet the 'commercial venture' requirement of TUPE, and an argument that a contrary conclusion could be reached by taking account of Community law was rejected.[14]

In the important decision in *Woodcock* v *Friends' School*,[15] it was said that defining what is an undertaking 'not in the nature of a commercial venture' was very much a matter of first impression for the industrial tribunal. The fact that the managers of an undertaking were interested in financial return rather than artistry would be a pointer in favour of identifying an operation as being in the nature of a commercial venture. In that case the operation of a charitable school was held not to give rise to a TUPE transfer when it was sold.

This line of domestic authority is now to be seen as controverted by the approach taken by the European Court of Justice. In the course of 1992 the European Court delivered three significant judgments concerned with the interpretation of the Acquired Rights Directive. These have radically altered the general perception of the scope of TUPE in the United Kingdom, and, taken together with the NATFHE case in the British courts (below), indicate ways in which direct access to Community law might be a useful aid available to workers who are faced with deteriorating terms and conditions of employment as a result of contracting out. The decisions have confirmed earlier jurisprudence to the effect that the protection of employees is an aim fundamental to the Acquired Rights Directive's proper interpretation.[16]

The European Court ruled in *Sophie Redmond*[17] that a transfer from one body subsidized by a public authority to another body could fall within the Acquired Rights Directive. Although the facts of the case did not concern privatization as such (or indeed any move from the public to the private sector), the decision established that the Directive was capable of applying to non-commercial undertakings. The terms of the judgment referred to earlier authority[18] to emphasize that the key issue was whether the transfer showed that a business had retained its identity. This in turn required consideration of a range of questions,[19] with a large measure of discretion in the application of these criteria to particular facts being reserved for the national court.

The judgment in *Sophie Redmond* alerted many British commentators to the fact that market testing exercises (and CCT in particular) could be covered by the Directive to an extent that had not previously been widely appreciated. Insofar as such transfers were excluded by the words of TUPE, there was clear evidence that UK law was defective by Community standards - since it is fundamental that UK law may not provide less favourable treatment than that required by Community law. This finding further raised the possibility that individuals who were worse off in new jobs after privatization transfers (or who had no jobs at all following dismissal) might be able to take legal action by relying on the Acquired Rights Directive and the rights it gave under Community law.

Subsequent to the *Sophie Redmond* case, the ECJ in *Rask and Christensen* v *ISS Kantineservice A/S*[20] held that the Directive could apply where an employer contracted out the operation of its canteen service. The company (Philips) ceded to a contractor the responsibility for operating its staff canteens, including responsibility for menu planning, purchasing, preparation service, all administrative functions and the recruitment and training of staff. As part of the contract the contractor undertook to take on the staff permanently employed by Philips in its canteens, maintaining the same wages and conditions. Philips in return paid a fixed monthly fee to cover staff remuneration and administrative costs, as well as the costs of disposables. Philips also provided access free of charge to premises, operating equipment, electricity, telephones and refuse collection, and held itself responsible for the maintenance of the premises used.

In these circumstances it was held by the ECJ that the Acquired Rights Directive *could* apply. The *Rask* decision, it should be noted, stopped short of saying that contracting out *was* covered by the Directive. It merely indicated that it might be, the actual decision being one left for the appreciation of the national court, according to the application of the appropriate criteria.[21]

The decision in *Rask* was taken by several commentators as showing that many instances of market testing and CCT would be caught by the Directive, with, of course, the corollary that any rule to the contrary in the British regulations or case law was untenable. In particular, the decision stands in contrast to, and effectively overrules, a ruling made under TUPE in *Hadden* v *University of Dundee Students' Association*,[22] where the EAT indicated that a transfer following on from the provision of services by an outside contractor, involving the supply of a manager, would not be within the TUPE framework.

The third ECJ decision is *Katsikas* v *Konstantinidis*.[23] The facts concerned the rights under the Directive of an employee who declined to go to a transferee, in circumstances where the transfer was clearly within the scope of the instrument. A key question was what the effect of the employee's refusal was. The Court reasoned that the Directive did not oblige the employee to accept the transfer, and it pointed out that the contrary view 'would place in question the fundamental rights of the employee, who must be free to choose his employer and may not be required to work for an employer whom he has not freely chosen'.[24] The Court went on to hold that what happened to the employee's contract was a matter for the member state to decide, and that national law might provide for the contract to be seen as repudiated at the instance of the employee or the transferor; alternatively, national law might provide that the contract was continued with the transferor.

In the British context, it has long been assumed that the effect of TUPE (Regulation 5 (1)) was to require, in a relevant transfer, the employee to go across to the transferee.[25] 'The contract is automatically continued by operation of the Regulations even if the transferee has no wish to continue the employment.'[26] It is clear, however, that but for Regulation 5(1) no right exists on the part of an employer to insist on a transfer to a new employer.[27] It was assumed, almost without question, that, subject only to tendering a resignation or the limited right to complain of constructive dismissal in the limited circumstances falling within Regulation 5(5), the employee must accept transfer as a *fait accompli* once TUPE applies. On one reading of the decision in *Katsikas* it was possible to challenge this interpretation of the Regulations. The main argument was that, following the *Litster* principle requiring a purposive construction of TUPE that is in line with the Acquired Rights Directive,[28] it might have been possible to make the effect of Regulation 5 in transferring across an employee subject to the right of the individual to object. There was also a point on *ultra vires*, as arguably, by making provision for automatic transfer even where the employee objected, TUPE went further than permissible under s. 2(2) of the European Communities Act 1972. These arguments were never accepted by Government, but they certainly contributed to the amendment of Regulation 5 introduced by s. 33(4) of the TURER. That amendment is to the effect that an objection by an employee, of which the transferor or transferee is informed, has the effect of preventing a transfer of the employee's contract of employment. This is of little benefit to the employee, however, for it is also provided that in such circumstances the contract will be terminated, but the individual shall not be treated as having been dismissed by the transferor. In other words, he will find himself without a job, in circumstances where he will be unable to claim in respect of either unfair dismissal or redundancy - a situation which effectively combines the worst of all worlds. Had the amendment not been made, it is arguable that the objecting employee might have been able to maintain that his employment with the transferor continued (until he voluntarily left or was dismissed). But that reading of the legal position is no longer tenable in the light of the changes made to Regulation 5.

In addition to these three decisions of the European Court of Justice, there have also been several important developments before UK domestic courts. In October 1992 the education union, NATFHE, succeeded in proceedings brought against the Crown in respect of the transfer of staff from local education authorities to further education corporations. The union maintained, and the government finally conceded, in the light of the *Sophie Redmond* decision, that such a transfer was caught by the Acquired Rights Directive and that, moreover, certain terms of the Directive had direct effect, giving enforceable rights to individuals. That decision, like *Sophie Redmond* itself, does not concern market testing or CCT in the sense in which these terms are used here. But the concession[29] made by the Crown has considerable importance for the employment rights of staff affected by the statutory transfer of public functions. It means that TUPE almost certainly also applies to staff transferred from the NHS service to an NHS trust, and probably in other statutory transfer situations too.[30] The legislation that accomplishes such transfers typically transfers existing contracts of employment to the new employer.[31] That gives some protection to existing staff, but a protection that falls far short of that available through the application of TUPE. It also fails to make any provision for the continuation of trade union rights after the transfer. It is understood that in practice the passing of staff to NHS trusts is regarded as a 'TUPE transfer' by at least some of the unions involved.

In March 1993 the Government suffered a setback to the implementation of its market testing program when the High Court made a declaration that the contracts of employment of staff involved in prison education were transferred subsequent to the carrying out of a competitive tendering exercise. In *Kenny v South Manchester College*[32] the transfers came about when the Home Office changed the contractors whom it paid to provide education services at a particular prison. The decision was certainly unwelcome and an embarrassment to the Government. The decision not to take it to appeal is perhaps to be understood on the ground that it was feared the substantial risk that the ruling would be confirmed by a higher authority was unacceptable. One of the many interesting features of the case is that it was argued and decided on the basis of the direct applicability of the Acquired Rights Directive, and not under TUPE itself.

Action by the Commission

In 1992, the European Commission produced a report examining the treatment of the Acquired Rights Directive in the different member states.[33] This contained criticism, based on an earlier study of the application of Community law in the EC,[34] of the UK's Regulations, which were said not to conform adequately with what the Directive required in five detailed respects. Subsequently proceedings against the UK were initiated by the Commission before the ECJ. The Commission's complaint against the UK rested on the following five points:

- The British system for appointing workers' representatives was said not to be compatible with the aim of the Directive. Basically, the employer in Britain was free in law to derecognize a union whenever he liked; this was said to be out of line with what the Directive required.

- The UK legislation did not state that consultation with workers' representatives had to be 'with a view to seeking agreement', as required by Article 6(2) of the Directive.
- The British courts had held that for TUPE to apply, the transferor must be the owner of the undertaking in question (this was seen as unduly restrictive).
- The exclusion of undertakings 'not in the nature of a commercial venture' was not acceptable, given the absence of any such exclusion in the Directive.
- The sanctions provided for in order to ensure that TUPE is observed were inadequate.

The Government, while not accepting that it was in breach of its duties, accepted most of the criticisms made (with the exception of the first) and gave an undertaking to amend the law. That reform was carried out by provisions contained in the Trade Union Reform and Employment Rights Act. The Act makes a number of detailed changes, including removing the 'commercial venture' requirement found in the regulations as originally drafted, and clarifying the rule that a relevant transfer may be effected by a series of two or more transactions and could take place whether or not any property is transferred. The Act also makes changes in the rules relating to the consultation with recognized unions and in the penalties provided for failure to comply with the same.[35] Other changes designed to meet the possible consequences of the *Katsikas* decision have already been discussed.[36] Although the changes do much to rectify the position of the UK for the future, no retrospective changes are made in the law. It is left to the general principles of Community law to provide compensation for individuals who can show that they have suffered loss because of any gap between the level of protection set by TUPE and that required by the Directive. The limits, both substantive and procedural, on such claims are complex and controversial. In any event it should be noted that the Commission has not dropped its infraction proceedings against the UK, which are continuing before the ECJ. One good reason for this could be said to be the absence of any provision dealing with retrospective claims, though as it happens this is not a point that the Commission itself has sought to make.

LEGAL RIGHTS FOR STAFF IN TRANSFERS

The significance of the impact of the Acquired Rights Directive on TUPE can only be properly appreciated against an awareness of the basic common law and statutory rules applicable to workers following a change of employer.

Common Law

A change of identity[37] of an employer has very important legal consequences for the legal rights of employees. The basic rules are well established: individuals cannot be sold like bricks and mortar, and any attempt to enforce a change in identity will result in a termination of the contract of employment. The common law here reflects the famous words found in the ILO's constitution: 'labour is not a commodity'. An employer who imposes a change by the transfer of his business (otherwise than by disposing of the shares in it) to another will thus commit a repudiatory breach of contract, in the absence of a special term allowing such behaviour, because he is in effect telling his staff that he will not continue to employ them: 'a man cannot be transferred from one employer to another without his consent. Hence comes the rule that the sale or transfer of an undertaking determines the contract of employment of employees.'[38]

Whether, as Balcombe LJ states, the transfer actually determines the contract or, as is suggested here, the transfer merely amounts (in cases where it leads to a ceasing of employment) to a unilateral repudiation of contract is a moot point.[39] The effect of a repudiatory breach on a contract of employment is simply that it gives to the innocent party the right to terminate; it does not terminate the contract itself.[40] But it is worth noting that Regulation 5(1) of TUPE proceeds, arguably erroneously, on the basis that it is the transfer that terminates the contract - except, of course, where TUPE itself applies to keep the contract alive.

Where Regulation 5 applies, the effect is to make the contract of employment continue with the new employer substituted for the old; it has for that reason been described as the 'ultimate "commodification" of labour, for apparently employees become as it were intangible assets of the business, to be sold along with lock, stock and barrel and the transferor's discretion'.[41] In the context of market testing, however, the effects will often be welcome to the workforce, since the continuation of contractual rights will usually mean the enjoyment of more favourable conditions of employment than would otherwise be on offer from the private-sector contractor who takes over.

A recent decision of the Court of Appeal gives useful general guidance on the employment law implications of takeovers at common law, as affected by the impact of TUPE. In *Newns* v *British Airways plc*[42] an unsuccessful attempt was made by an employee to restrain a business reorganization that would have meant his transfer to a new employer. The employee argued that, because of the application of TUPE, the result of the sale of the part of the business in which he worked would mean his transfer to another employer - and maintained that he had a right to object to what was a repudiatory breach by the employer of his contractual obligations. It was accepted by the Court that no right to transfer without agreement exists at common law, but also that the effect of TUPE (where applicable) was to cancel out any breach of contract associated with a change of employer that was unwanted by an employee. (This, of course, is a point that must now be reconsidered, taking into account the decision in *Katsikas* and the arguments deployed above.) The Court in *Newns* held that an employee had never had a right to object to a transfer taking place and had not acquired such right by virtue of TUPE. But, interestingly, it left open the possibility that, exceptionally, a proposed transfer might amount to a breach by the employer of his implied duty of good faith. This did not arise on the particular facts of the case, but it could if, for example, the transfer was going to result in a worsening of the employee's legal rights. Such a result might arise when the transferee employer states that he is not prepared to maintain pension arrangements in the new job, and yet the transferor is prepared to go ahead with the transfer.[43]

Redundancy

The fact of a change of employer may have an important impact on redundancy entitlements. Redundancy will often result from a transfer, where an employee finds that his contract is ended and there is no further work for him to do with his own employer. A transfer may also provoke redundancy in the workforce of the transferee, because incoming staff displace existing job-holders from their positions. But where TUPE applies and a 'relevant transfer' takes place, there is of course no dismissal and no break in the contract, which by operation of Regulation 5(1) is carried over to the transferee. If there is a right on the part of an individual to object to being transferred (as argued above[44]) then by the exercise of that right it may be possible for the employee to ensure that he receives a redundancy payment; for arguably the result of objecting will be that the unwilling employee stays with his original employer, unless and until his contract is determined by either a direct or constructive dismissal. In practice there is unlikely to be work available for him to do if a transfer has taken place, and dismissal is likely unless some alternative employment is possible.

Where TUPE applies and a dismissal by reason of redundancy is effected by the transferor or transferee, then the dismissal may in addition be automatically unfair, by reason of Regulation 8, discussed below. In this situation any redundancy payment that may be made will not by itself satisfy the employee's claims, as the compensatory elements available in a claim for unfair dismissal are additional to the sums awarded in respect of past service by reference to redundancy.[45] The prospect of having to pay redundancy compensation to staff has encouraged certain public sector authorities to favour the application of TUPE to CCT and other market testing situations. Conversely, the belief (arguably mistaken) that the existence of a TUPE transfer will prevent recovery of a redundancy claim has been seen as a disadvantage by some unions. Where a transferee reorganizes the way in which work which comes to him is to be done, this may be sufficient to prevent the transfer of an economic entity, as TUPE Regulation 3(1) requires. On the other hand, not every small organizational change will have this effect. A change that is not sufficiently important to prevent a finding that a 'relevant transfer' has taken place may yet provide the basis for a redundancy dismissal if staff who worked for the transferee are not equipped with the skills needed in the new jobs. Such dismissals may be for an 'economic technical or organisational reason entailing changes in the workforce', and thus may not be automatically unfair, although made for a reason connected with the transfer.[46]

Where a transferee employer offers alternative employment to an employee who is dismissed by his original employer, this offer may have the effect of removing the entitlement to redundancy payment that would otherwise accrue. The law used to be that an offer of suitable alternative employment by the transferee, if unreasonably refused by the employee, would remove the employee's redundancy entitlement. For this to happen, the offer had to be made before the dismissal took effect, and of employment to start within four weeks of the end of employment with the transferor. Repeal of the relevant section (Employment Protection (Consolidation) Act 1978, s. 94) is, however, effected by the Trade Union Reform and Employment Rights Act, Schedule 10. In the context of market testing and CCT, however, it is unlikely that the old law posed much of a trap for unwary employees, since any offer likely to be made by a successful bidder was likely to involve significantly less favourable terms than were enjoyed by the employee with the transferor.

One area that illustrates this last point arises in relation to pensions. Under TUPE Regulation 7, certain occupational pension rights do not pass over on a relevant transfer.[47] And it is extremely improbable that any non-public-sector contractor would wish to contemplate the scale of liability that would follow from offering pension entitlements equivalent to those available to those directly employed in central or local government. However, an offer of employment that did not match in pension terms the old employment would be very hard to describe as suitable, and it would be equally difficult to maintain that a refusal to accept such an offer was unreasonable.

Refusal to ensure that comparable pension terms will be maintained after the transfer could also be seen as a fundamental breach of contract on the part of the transferor, and might set the scene for a constructively unfair dismissal should the employee choose to leave. This important point is further considered below.

There may be difficult problems arising in the situation where a redundancy payment is made by an employer who believes, wrongly, that a transfer consequent upon a contracting out of work is one to which TUPE does not apply. It is common for such changes to lead to a staff surplus, and this would normally be dealt with by the making of redundancy payments. What, however, if it is subsequently established that TUPE did apply to the transfer, so that no true redundancy situation actually arose on the facts? The matter was raised in Parliament in the course of the passage of the Trade Union Reform and Employment Rights Act,[48] and the Government gave the answer that in such circumstances both the redundancy payment and the dismissal would stand, notwithstanding the fact that TUPE operated to continue the contract of employment. But it is arguable that, in such circumstances, the employee should have an additional remedy of compensation, since the dismissal would be unfair by reason of the operation of TUPE, Regulation 8, as discussed below.

Unfair Dismissal

The statutory protection against unfair dismissal is also very substantially affected by the application of TUPE. A dismissal that is by reason of the transfer is deemed by regulation to be automatically unfair,[49] except when it falls into the special category envisaged by Regulation 8(2). This circumstance transfers the dismissal into one that is potentially fair, in the sense that it is then deemed to be for a 'substantial reason', and as such deserving of inquiry by the tribunals and courts. Whether it is in the end classed as fair or unfair depends on the application of general principles of unfair dismissal law - broadly, the industrial tribunal hearing the case will have to be satisfied that the employer acted reasonably in relying upon it as a reason for dismissal.

The dismissal may be effected by the transferor before the transfer takes place, or by the transferee after it happens. It is important to appreciate that not only the employee who 'goes across' is protected by Regulation 8. If there is a 'relevant transfer', then protection extends to 'any employee of the transferor or transferee dismissed for a reason connected with the dismissal'. It may indeed be that no employees 'go across'. Nevertheless, if the transaction amounts to a 'relevant transfer' then the protection against dismissal will avail all employees in both establishments. Any dismissal for any reason connected with the transfer is potentially automatically unfair, by reason of Regulation 8. When it is the transferor who dismisses unfairly under Regulation 8(1), liability passes to the transferee by operation of the principle elaborated in *Litster* v *Forth Dry Dock & Engineering Co. Ltd.*[50] In that case it was held that a pre-transfer dismissal, unfair because it fell within Regulation 8, did not have the effect of terminating the contract of employment of the employee. Accordingly, the employee remained employed until the transfer took place, with the result that liability for the unfair dismissal fell on the transferee. Such a reading of the Regulations was necessary in order to give effect to the demands of Community law, for Article 3 of the Directive was intended, said the House of Lords, to prevent an insolvent old employer from dismissing a workforce at the behest of a solvent new owner so as to deprive the workforce of their rights.

There is a substantial case law surrounding the meaning of 'economic, technical or organisational' - the words used in Regulation 8(2) to qualify a finding of automatically unfair dismissal under Regulation 8(1). If an employer can show that the reason or principal reason for the dismissal was an 'economic, technical or organisational reason' entailing changes in the workforce, then, even though it was for a reason connected with the transfer the dismissal will not be automatically unfair.[51] The courts have shown themselves mindful of the need to extend legal protection to employees subject to transfers, and have thus given the provision a relatively narrow construction. It is not enough for an employer to show that he was dismissing at the request of the transferee, even if he was being faced with an ultimatum that, without the dismissal, the sale of the undertaking would not go ahead.[52] Neither will a dismissal be potentially fair if the target is an employee who, after a relevant transfer, refuses to accept changes in terms and conditions that the transferee wants in order to make economies or to standardize terms and conditions for all workers in his employment.[53] Under Regulation 5(5) it is stated that the automatic transfer is without prejudice to any right of an employee arising apart from the regulations to terminate his contract of employment without notice if a substantial change is made in his working conditions to his detriment. This is understood to preserve the right of the employee to complain of a constructive dismissal - and if he does so the dismissal will almost certainly be automatically unfair by reason of Regulation 8.

REMAINING PROBLEMS

The cases discussed above provide a sound basis for the argument that TUPE should be seen as applying to many instances of market testing, and there are already signs that this is being appreciated by the courts. However, the identification of a 'relevant transfer' in individual cases remains a matter of some mystery and concern. The Government has sought, by the production of guidance contained in a statement made by Mr William Waldegrave to the House of Commons on 11 March 1993, to provide some assistance. This guidance identifies a range of factors (type of undertaking, fate of assets, value of assets, fate of employees following transfer, fate of customers, degree of similarity between old and new operations) that are to be taken into account in deciding how to classify any particular contracting-out situation.[54] It must be doubtful, however, whether this is likely to provide much comfort in practice to those faced with having to make decisions and evaluate particular fact situations. Perhaps the Government's hope is that the courts will see the classification of transfers as raising mixed questions of fact and law, rather in the manner of classifications of contracts under which work is performed.[55] This might have the result of making courts unwilling to review decisions by tribunals at first instance, but there are so many important legal issues that turn on the outcome of classification (e.g. is a redundancy payment properly payable on dismissal; has continuity of employment been broken?) that such reticence seems unlikely.

The indications are that many challenges to purportedly non-TUPE transfers will continue to be mounted by workers in the future, using private law remedies such as actions seeking a declaration of contractual rights. There is also scope for using public law remedies on a wider scale, to challenge actions by public authorities that potentially infringe rights protected by TUPE. Thus, for example, it may be that judicial review can be used to prevent a move by a public authority to proceed with a contracting out, if it refuses to observe TUPE in circumstances where the regulations do in law apply.[56] Another interesting (and as yet untested) possibility is the use of judicial review to prevent the designing of tenders for market testing in ways designed to avoid the application of TUPE. The argument here might be on the grounds that such action would be inconsistent with the duty of the member state, arising under Article 5 of the EC Treaty, properly to give effect to the Directive within its law.[57]

Quite apart from developments in the future, there may also be scope for workers to pursue actions against employers (or former employers) in respect of past treatment, relying upon the directly effective[58] provisions of the Acquired Rights Directive. To the extent that individuals have suffered because TUPE has offered less protection than the Directive, such actions should be possible. Those dismissed, for example, from work in non-commercial organizations might form one such category. But a major constraint here will be that the principle of direct effect allows action to be taken only against employers who form part of the state or its emanation,[59] and typically the transferee employer will not fall within that category. To the extent that liability on the part of the transferor may be established, however, it may be possible to bring claims even though several years have elapsed since the offending act took place. It is an important principle of Community law that a state will not be able to rely on time limits as a defence to a claim brought against it on the basis of a directly effective Community right unless and until it has properly implemented the Directive in question.[60]

While there is thus considerable scope for using TUPE and/or Community law to protect workers' rights, the importance of this strategy should not, at the end of the day, be overestimated. In the first place, it is clear that the Government is determined to press ahead with market testing, notwithstanding the legal difficulties it faces. Second, there are two major limitations on the substantive protection that TUPE has to offer. The first limitation concerns the permanency of contractual terms. TUPE does not give any greater permanency to contractual rights than existed before the transfer took place. Thus it remains open, for example, for the transferee employer to seek variation of the contracts of employment of transferred staff, and thereby to secure conditions of employment that it desires. Variation of course requires agreement, but often the pressure an employer can bring to bear is decisive. It is also possible, in principle, for an employer to dismiss fairly staff who refuse to accept changes in employment terms,[61] although here the operation of Regulation 8(1) of TUPE should have a restraining effect on such oppressive behaviour.

The other major limitation of TUPE is that it probably has little impact on collective rights, despite the impassioned arguments of many academic writers to the contrary.[62] The obligation to consult unions representing workers affected by TUPE transfers arises only in respect of unions recognized for the purposes of collective bargaining,[63] and there is nothing in English law to prevent derecognition at the whim of the employer. In the words of a Government minister (Viscount Ullswater) speaking in the House of Lords, recognition is 'entirely at the option of the employer'.[64] Neither does TUPE offer any guarantee as to the continuation of collective agreements in circumstances where the transferee employer is minded not to carry on with these.

At the end of the day, perhaps the main contribution that Community law, acting through the medium of TUPE, will have to make to the protection of workers' rights in market testing situations will be by discouraging irresponsible and unreliable employers from taking part in the tendering process. There is an argument that only the larger, more well-organized and (perhaps) more responsible private-sector employer will feel confident about accepting the uncertainty that now, as a result of the fertile case law, applies in relation to obligations towards staff after transfers have occurred. The discouragement of the 'cowboy' employer from participation in market testing exercises, if it does result, will of course be a benefit worth having. Whether the courts, at domestic and Community level, will also be able to develop significant additional legal protections for individuals, based on the requirements of the Directive, remains to be seen.

NOTES

1. For a fuller study of the issues covered here, see the author's monograph, *Market Testing, Compulsory Competitive Tendering and Employment Rights* (Institute of Employment Rights, 1993). See too C. de Groot, The Council Directive on the safeguarding of employees' rights in the event of transfers of undertakings: an overview of the case law (1993) *Common Market Law Review* 331.

2. P. O'Higgins, International standards and British labour law. In R. Lewis (ed.), *Labour Law in Britain* (Oxford, 1986).

3. On this, see D. Brown and A. McColgan, UK employment law and the International Labour Organisation: the spirit of cooperation? (1992) 21 ILJ 265; K. D. Ewing, *Britain and ILO* (Institute of Employment Rights, 1989).

4. For a general account of the priority of Community law in this context, see Lord Wedderburn, *The Social Charter, European Company and Employment Rights* (Institute of Employment Rights, 1990), Chapter 1.

5. Case C 262/88, *Barber* v *Guardian Royal Exchange Assurance Group* [1991] 2 WLR 72.

6. Case 152/84, *Marshall* v *Southampton and South-West Hampshire Area Health Authority* [1986] QB 401.

7. EEC 75/129.

8. *R* v *British Coal Corporation and Secretary of State for Trade and Industry, ex parte Vardy* [1993] ICR 720.

9. For some idea of the general background and philosophy to market testing and CCT, see the White Paper, *Competing for Quality*, Cm 1730, 1991. On market testing in relation to local government law, see S. Cirell and J. Bennett, *Compulsory Competitive Tendering: Law and Practice* (loose-leaf, 1992); see too the Consultation Paper, Competing for quality: competition in the provision of local services (1992); *Tender Tactics: A Negotiator's Guide to Privatisation in the NHS* (NHS Privatisation Research Unit, 1991); *Privatisation: Disaster for Quality* (Public Services Privatisation Research Unit, March 1992).

10. See Public Competition and Purchasing Unit, Guidance Note 34, *Market Testing and Buying In* (HM Treasury, March 1992).

11. For the significance of this, and other differences between TUPE and the Acquired Rights Directive, see B. Hepple and A. Byre, *The Application of EEC Labour Law in the United Kingdom*, Report Prepared for the Commission of the European Communities (Directorate General Employment, Social Affairs, Education, 1988).

12. [1991] IRLR 156.

13. [1991] IRLR 368.

14. These and other decisions are considered by T. Linden, Service contracts and the transfer of business (1992) ILJ 293.

15. [1987] IRLR 98, CA.

16. E.g. Case 135/83, *Abels* [1985] ECR 469; Cases 144 and 145/87, *Berg* v *Besselsen* [1988] ECR 2559.

17. Case C-29/19, *Dr Sophie Redmond Stichting* v *Bartol* [1992] IRLR 366, ECJ.

18. Case 24/85, *Spijkers* v *Gebroeders Benedik Abattoir CV* [1986] ECR 1119, ECJ.

19. See below.

20. Case C-209/91, 12 November 1992, ECJ.

21. These are discussed in detail below.

22. [1985] IRLR 449.

23. Joined cases C-132/91, C-138/91 and C-139/91, Judgment of the Court, 16 December 1992.

24. Para. 32.

25. 'A relevant transfer shall not operate so as to terminate the contract of employment of any person employed by the transferor in the undertaking or part transferred but any such contract which would otherwise have been terminated by the transfer shall have effect after the transfer as if originally made between the person so employed and the transferor.'

26. *Premier Motors (Medway) Ltd* v *Total Oil Great Britain Ltd* [1984] ICR 58, 63 per Browne-Wilkinson J.

27. *Newns* v *British Airways plc* [1992] IRLR 575, CA; *Nokes* v *Doncaster Amalgamated Collieries Ltd* [1940] AC 1014.

28. *Litster* v *Forth Dry Dock & Engineering Co. Ltd* [1990] 1 AC 546, HL, per Lord Keith.

29. Strictly, it was not a decision of the Divisional Court but a submission to judgment. The Secretary of State agreed to the Court making an Order. This means that, technically, the content is not binding for the future in the way that a full decision would be.

30. Would TUPE itself apply to such statutory transferor function? The point was not argued in the *NATFHE* case. See, further, S. Corby, Industrial relations developments in NHS Trusts (1992) 14 *Employee Relations* 36.

31. E.g. Further and Higher Education Act 1992, s. 26; National Health Service and Community Care Act 1990, s. 6.

32. *Kenny* v *South Manchester College* [1993] IRLR 265, HC.

33. Commission Report to the Council on progress with regard to the implementation of Directive 77/187/EEC relating to the safeguarding of employees' rights in the event of transfers of undertakings, businesses or parts of businesses.

34. See above, note 11.

35. See now Trade Union Reform and Employment Rights Act 1993, s. 33(7).

36. Above, p. 133.

37. It follows that there will be no application of either TUPE or the Acquired Rights Directive when the employer remains the same. So TUPE will not apply to the situation where a successful in-house bid is made, and the employer does not change.

38. *Secretary of State for Employment* v *Spence* [1986] IRLR 248, per Balcombe LJ at 250.

39. F. Younson, *Employment Law and Business Transfers: A Practical Guide* (1989), p. 50. P. Davies and M. Freedland, *Transfer of Employment* (1982), annotation to TUPE, Regulation 5. In *Premier Motors (Medway) Ltd* v *Total Oil Great Britain Ltd* [1984] ICR 377, Browne-Wilkinson P (as he then was) said 'under the old [i.e. pre-TUPE] law, if an employer, A, transferred his business to another, B, the employees' contract of employment with A undoubtedly came to an end' (p. 380). But cf. the view of Lord Oliver in *Litster* v *Forth Estuary Engineering Co. Ltd* [1990] 1 AC 546: 'The reason why a contract of employment is said to "terminate" on a transfer of the employer's business is simply that such a transfer operates as a unilateral repudiation by the employer of his obligations under the contract and thus as a dismissal of the employee from his service.'

40. Cf. *Litster* v *Forth Estuary Engineering Co. Ltd*, *op. cit.*, per Lord Oliver.

41. H. Collins, Dismissals on transfer of a business [1986] 15 ILJ 244, 247.

42. [1992] IRLR 575, CA.

43. This is possible even when TUPE applies, because pensions are excluded, under Regulation 7, from the scope of Regulation 5. For the application of the implied duty of good faith in the context of pension schemes, see *Imperial Group Pension Trust Ltd* v *Imperial Tobacco Ltd* [1991] 1 WLR 589.

44. See above, p. 136.

45. It may be possible to challenge the maximum limit of £10,000 by reference to community law. See the Opinion of Advocate-General Van Gerven in Case C-271/91, *Marshall* v *Southampton and South-West Hampshire Area Health Authority*, 26 January 1993.

46. Cf. *Porter* v *Queen's Medical Centre (Nottingham University Hospital)* [1993] IRLR 486, HC.

47. *Walden Engineering Co. Ltd* v *Warrener* [1993] IRLR 420.

48. HL Debs, 30 March 1993, col. 746ff. (Lord Mottistone).

49. Regulation 8(1).

50. [1990] 1 AC 546.

51. Neither will it be fair. It will simply be a dismissal for a substantial reason, and its fairness or unfairness will be decided according to the ordinary rules of unfair dismissal law.

52. *Wheeler* v *Patel* [1987] ICR 631.

53. *Berriman* v *Delabole Slate* [1985] ICR 546, CA. It is not enough that there is a need to change the terms on which the workforce is employed; there must, for Regulation 8(2), be a need proceeding from a change in the workforce itself.

54. The use of these multiple factors is derived from the views of the European Court, expressed in *Spijkers* v *Gebroeders Benedik Abattoir CV* [1986] ECR 1119, ECJ, and often repeated subsequently.

55. Cf. *O'Kelly* v *Trusthouse Forte plc* [1984] QB 90.

56. This has in fact already occurred in substance: see the report concerning the South Glamorgan Health Authority, *Financial Times*, 16 March 1993.

57. Cf. Case 14/83, *Von Colson* v *Land Nordrhein-Westfalen* [1984] ECR 1891, ECJ. Interestingly, the Government has said (statement made by Mr William Waldegrave to House of Commons, 11 March 1993) that it would be inconsistent with policy so to arrange tenders as to *attract* TUPE.

58. Cf. *NATFHE* decision, discussed above.

59. Case 188/89, *Foster* v *British Gas plc* [1990] 2 CMLR 833.

60. *Emmott* v *Minister for Social Welfare and Attorney General* [1992] IRLR 474, ECJ; *Rankin* v *British Coal Corporation* [1993] IRLR 69.

61. Cf. *Chubb Fire Security Ltd* v *Harper* [1983] IRLR 311.

62. Cf. O'Higgins, *op. cit.*, p. 589; Lord Wedderburn, HL Debs, 30 March 1993, col. 728ff.

63. TUPE, Regulation 10(2).

64. HL Debs, 30 March 1993, col. 744.

7

The Bill of Rights Debate: Democracy or Juristocracy in Britain?

K. D. Ewing

INTRODUCTION

There is considerable pressure for the introduction of a Bill of Rights in Britain, or for the incorporation of the European Convention on Human Rights into domestic law. The campaign for an initiative of this kind, which is vigorously supported by groups such as Charter 88 and the Institute for Public Policy Research[1] (and in a modified form by Liberty[2]), has attracted widespread approval in the press and elsewhere.[3] It used to be claimed that there was no need for a Bill of Rights or anything of the sort to protect our freedoms, for the common law was just as effective. But these views, which have their origins in the work of Dicey,[4] cannot now be squared with contemporary reality, despite having been given an airing in the courts recently.[5] The common law is impotent in the face of strong executive government, with political freedom being too readily sacrificed on the altar of political expediency.[6] Yet although there may be a need to take steps to deal with the political threat to our liberties, it does not follow that a Bill of Rights is a justifiable or indeed an adequate response. It tends to be overlooked that what a Bill of Rights does above all else is to transfer sovereign power from Westminster to the Strand, from Parliament to the courts. The judges would thus be empowered to strike down not only administrative action but also legislation that is said by the courts to be inconsistent with the requirements of the Bill of Rights or the incorporated European Convention.[7] As is now the case in many other countries, all legislation would be subject to judicial review to determine whether it was consistent with some express, implied or imagined provision of the Bill of Rights. The courts would thus be empowered to say what the people through their elected representatives could or could not do on any particular question.

In this chapter I propose to consider some of the difficult problems of principle to which these proposals give rise. The central dilemma is easily stated, though not so easily resolved: how can we reconcile with the first principles of democratic self-government the transfer of sovereign power from an elected legislature to an unelected judiciary? In order to answer that question it is necessary first to seek to identify the first principles of democratic self-government, principles that are both prescriptive and normative (in the sense that they form a base-line that in practice is followed and applied to some extent by many countries in the Western liberal tradition).[8] Having identified these principles it is necessary secondly to demonstrate how the process of adjudication of disputes in a court of law is inconsistent with these principles, which in turn invites consideration of some of the different theoretical writings (of American scholars in particular) seeking to show, sometimes very persuasively, how the circle can be squared and how judicial review, rather than being seen as a device that destroys democracy, is, on the contrary, a device that reinforces and defends both the institutions of democracy and the democratic process itself. It is proposed to take here the work of John Hart Ely[9] as the basis for the discussion, not only because his work is the most accessible, lucid and elegant, but also because he makes the strongest and most authoritative case for a Bill of Rights.[10] The essay concludes with some consideration of reform of the judiciary, much needed and long overdue. The question here is the extent to which such reform might also help to reduce the democratic deficit which a Bill of Rights would help to create.

PRINCIPLES OF GOVERNMENT

The concept of democracy is controversial, though not as a basis for government, which cannot now be gainsaid. Rather, the controversy relates to its meaning, with the different forms of government in the Western liberal tradition bearing testimony to its uncertainty. For the purposes of this study, however, democracy is a method of government that does not guarantee any specific substantive outcomes. It is a means whereby people can make their own choices. Perhaps it does not necessarily mean rule by the majority. If it did then it might be difficult to identify several Western systems of government as being democratic. This would certainly be true of Britain, where few governments since the war have been elected on a majority of the popular vote; these do not include the Thatcher governments, which were unable to secure the endorsement of more than 43 per cent of those actually voting.[11] So at least in the British context the case against a Bill of Rights or against incorporation of the European Convention cannot be based entirely on arguments about its counter-majoritarian tendencies. These are arguments that have troubled American scholars seeking to come to terms with, and to justify, the power of the courts to strike down legislation passed by Congress and approved by the President. But they can hardly be serious concerns here given the fact that our governments typically represent a minority of the voting population and an even smaller minority of the total adult population. The position might be different were we to introduce a system of proportional representation so that in practice a government had to be drawn from representatives of at least a majority of the voting public. But unless we do, our system of government would tend to reinforce rather than undermine the case for incorporation of the Convention into domestic law or for introducing our own tailor-made Bill of Rights. It would be a means of protecting the majority from the tyranny of an elected minority.

In truth the American (and now Canadian) concerns about counter-majoritarianism miss the point, or at least are not the whole point, about the role of a Bill of Rights in a democratic system of government. For essential to such a system of government are three fundamental principles. The first of these is the principle of equal participation; that is to say, the right of us all to participate as equals in the policy-making institutions of government.[12] By this it is not denied that some adult citizens may be excluded on grounds of incapacity. But otherwise questions of intelligence, social status and professional standing would not be regarded as acceptable conditions of participation.[13] Each of these may be an advantage helping to secure more effective participation. But they would not now be regarded as a proper basis to qualify for participation. Democratic self-rule is now taken to mean government of the people by all of the people. C5s thus enjoy the same political status as Sir Clive Sinclair and in some respects even more than peers of the realm. We would not, for example, accept as a condition of the franchise a requirement that an individual should be identifiable as a member of a particular social class or a member of a particular occupational group.[14] And it would be absurd to say that the right to be an elected representative is too important to be extended to anyone other than university lecturers, or other than barristers, or other than judges. The legitimacy of our system of government presumes the right of everyone to participate equally as electors and to have the same right to stand for and hold political office.

The second of the three principles flows naturally from the first and relates to the fact that because of the sheer size of contemporary society it is not possible for us all to participate in the making of decisions, as it might be, say, in the case of a small community governed by a town meeting.[15] Policy-making must thus be undertaken by representatives of the population, though it does not follow that all decisions should be taken in this way and that some matters should not be reserved for plebiscite or referendum. But to the extent that representative government is a practical necessity, representatives must be chosen from among the community as a whole. This brings us to the second principle, which is simply that in a system of representative government, the representatives must be selected by the community they claim to represent. The representative is the medium through which the people govern; he or she is impressed with a political trust by the community he or she represents.[16] That trust can be created only by the decision of the people, not by the assumption of authority by the representative or by someone else delegating power to him or her. So no matter how benevolent and no matter how deeply loved and widely respected, neither a monarch nor a dictator satisfies our principle. Although they may seek to discover, articulate and implement the wishes of their subjects, whom they may thus claim to represent in an abstract sort of way, it is not the method of representation that is contemplated here. For this purpose the principle of representation is met only if the person or persons engaged in policy-making are selected by the community, which will be governed by its or their decisions. This is not to imply any particular form of selection, though it might be expected that the method chosen would underline and reinforce rather than undermine and defeat the purpose of the activity.

Just as this second principle flows naturally from the first, so the third flows naturally from the second. This is the principle that those who hold representative positions must in some sense be accountable to the people they represent for the decisions they purport to take on their behalf. This concept of accountability has at least two dimensions. In its weakest sense accountability involves explaining the reasons for a policy decision by communicating with those to whom the official is directly accountable. Although democracy does not appear necessarily to embrace the theory of the representative as delegate,[17] this does not absolve the representative of the duty to account to the represented the reasons why a particular decision may have been taken. Indeed, the acceptance of Burkean notions of representation strengthen rather than weaken the case for accountability in this sense.[18] That is to say, if the representative is acting contrary to the known wishes of those whom he or she represents, then there is an obligation on him or her to explain, justify and defend the position and if possible to persuade those whom he or she represents of the wisdom of his or her course of action. But what becomes desirable in principle is necessary in practice when consideration turns to the second, stronger, dimension of accountability. This reflects the view that it is not enough that the representative should account by way of explanation and information. While this is required, the second dimension insists that the community must have an opportunity to assess the work of its representative and if necessary to reject him or her by choosing a different representative, whose views on both community and broader issues may more closely reflect their own. Indeed the community must have the opportunity to change its representative for any reason it sees fit - good or bad. The incumbent may be doing a good job, but he or she may have become too arrogant, too remote or morally out of tune with the community. The composition or views and values of the community may have changed. Or none of these things may have happened: there may be someone else the community would rather have, for no obviously rational reason.

THE NATURE OF JUDICIAL REVIEW

If we take the first of the above requirements, the right of equal participation, it is clear that this is not something that can be met by a process of adjudication. Judicial office is closed to all but a very few members of the community, above all by the conditions of appointment laid down in legislation.[19] Different conditions apply in the case of different levels in the process, but in the case of the House of Lords, an eligible candidate must have been a judge in either the High Court or the Court of Appeal for at least two years, or have enjoyed rights of audience in the superior courts for at least fifteen,[20] though in practice no one is appointed to the most senior court without judicial experience, usually in the Court of Appeal. In the case of the Court of Appeal, a person is not qualified for appointment unless he has enjoyed rights of audience in the superior courts for at least ten years, unless he is a judge of the High Court. In the case of the High Court a person is not qualified for appointment unless he has enjoyed rights of audience in the superior court for at least ten years.[21] What this means in effect is that no more than twenty-eight people (excluding the *ex officio* members of the Court) are eligible or appointment to the House of Lords at any one time, that no more than eighty-six are eligible for appointment to the Court of Appeal at any one time and that no more than 5000 are eligible (in principle) for appointment to the High Court at any one time (though this figure could rise significantly under the Courts and Legal Services Act 1990 extending rights of audience to solicitors). In fact, appointment to the High Court is even more exclusive, being confined for the most part to those members of the Bar who have attained the rank of Queen's Counsel, the condition of appointment to which is that the individual in question should normally be of at least ten years' standing as a barrister and 'have reached an appropriate level of professional eminence and distinction'.[22] It has been suggested by Professor Griffith that when a High Court vacancy does arise, the number of genuinely eligible candidates ('experienced barristers between the ages of forty-five and sixty') may be as small as 'half a dozen'.[23]

Given the inherently political nature of adjudication under a Bill of Rights and the right of the judges to have the last say on political questions, these exclusive conditions of access to the process come close to creating the over-representation of people who have particular intellectual qualities. It is a political process, participation in which is confined to those who are trained to a high level of achievement in the law. Partly as a result it is also a process that at the present time is socially exclusive and in practice denies access to people from disadvantaged backgrounds. This leads to the second difficulty with political decision-making under a Bill of Rights, namely that the people who make these decisions - the people with ultimate authority to make political decisions for a community - are not in any sense representative of the community they serve. The concept of representation was discussed in the previous section with reference to a system whereby the members of a community choose from among their number someone who will represent them in government. The first problem with judicial review, however, is that political decisions are made by a small group of individuals who represent no one. Judges are not chosen by the community as a means through which the community may govern. Rather they are appointed by the Queen, on the advice of the Prime Minister and the Lord Chancellor. The community is thus denied the opportunity to select from among its number the very people who will hold the most powerful political positions in that community - that is to say the people who will determine what it is and what it is not that the community may do through its law-making institutions. At best the community is engaged only indirectly through the input of the Prime Minister and remotely through the Lord Chancellor, whom the Prime Minister has appointed. The Prime Minister is not politically accountable for these decisions in any meaningful way, while in the case of the Lord Chancellor there is not even the indirect accountability to particular, constituents or the nation at large in an election campaign, the Lord Chancellor being a member of the House of Lords.

It is possible to argue, perhaps, that the requirement of representation can be met by means other than direct representation through individuals chosen or selected by the community for this purpose. Thus, it might be argued that the requirement of representation would be met by a system of functional representation whereby all the principal interests and views in the community were to be found on the Bench.[24] Judges would not then represent the community but it might be said that they were at least representative of it. The difficulty, however, is that even if this were an acceptable substitute (itself highly controversial) it is far from being met in the British judicial system, which perhaps more than any other in the common law world is distinctive for its homogeneity. This is true whatever factor we take into account, whether it be gender, race, age or social origin, to the extent that the last can be determined (admittedly very imperfectly) by educational background.[25] If we look at the ten members of the House of Lords in 1991 (all but one of whom were appointed on the advice of Mrs Thatcher) we find that they are all men, that they are all white, that the youngest was born in 1926, that all but one was educated at a public school (with Marlborough, Winchester, Eton and Charterhouse all being represented) and that all but one was educated at either Oxford or Cambridge, the odd one out being Lord Bridge of Harwich, who does not record any university education at all (Table 7.1). For the record Cambridge had a 6:3 lead over Oxford. Matters may, of course, change in the future, but unless they do it would be hard to argue that the senior court is in any sense representative of the community. It is in any event open to question whether matters are likely to change significantly in the foreseeable future given the present composition of the High Court and the Court of Appeal from which members of the House of Lords are invariably drawn. At the time of writing, only three of the High Court judges are women, and none belongs to any of the minority communities.

Given the non-representative nature of at least the senior judiciary, the third requirement, that of accountability, perhaps assumes even more importance. It might be argued that the fact that the judiciary is not representative in any meaningful sense could be excused if it could also be shown that the judges as political actors were in some way accountable for what they did with the Bill of Rights. But it is difficult to see how this is met under present arrangements. It is true that the judiciary meets the first dimension of accountability – explaining the reasons for policy decisions – to which it might be added that the procedure is normally a public one so that the judge's

Table 7.1
The Members of the House of Lords 1991

Name	**Year of birth**	**Year of appointment**	**Secondary education**	**Tertiary education**
Lord Keith of Kinkel	1922	1977	Edinburgh Academy	Magdalen College, Oxford
Lord Bridge of Harwich	1917	1980	Marlborough	-
Lord Brandon of Oakbrook	1920	1981	Winchester	King's College, Cambridge
Lord Templeman	1920	1982	Southall Grammar	St John's College, Cambridge
Lord Griffiths	1923	1985	Charterhouse	St John's College, Cambridge
Lord Ackner	1920	1986	Highgate	Clare College, Cambridge
Lord Oliver of Aylmerton	1921	1986	Leys School, Cambridge	Trinity Hall, Cambridge
Lord Goff of Chieveley	1926	1986	Eton	New College, Oxford
Lord Jauncey of Tullichettle	1925	1988	Radley	Christ Church, Oxford
Lord Lowry of Crossgar	1919	1979	Royal Belfast Acad. Inst.	Jesus College, Cambridge

Source: Who's Who.

conduct - as well as the reasons for his or her decisions - is at least under some kind of spotlight.[26] In this way inappropriate conduct can be checked or decisions corrected by the process of appeal. Yet while publicity in the administration of justice should not be underestimated, there are important limits to the notion of publicity as accountability, in the sense that judges will never allow themselves to be questioned publicly about a decision and will only rarely give public insights into the personal political values that inform their decisions. So judges will rarely give press conferences about decided cases, and indeed until recently were actually discouraged - by the so-called Kilmuir rules - from appearing on radio and television, in this last case for reasons that seem designed to discourage or reduce the possibility of publicity as accountability.[27] For according to Lord Kilmuir: 'So long as a Judge keeps silent his reputation for wisdom and impartiality remains unassailable: but every utterance which he makes in public, except in the course of the actual performance of his judicial duties, must necessarily bring him within the focus of criticism.'[28] Judges do now from time to time appear on television to give interviews and lectures,[29] but these are wide-ranging and of a general nature only (though sometimes dealing with controversial issues), and rarely (if ever) touch upon the exercise of power in an individual case.

This trend towards greater publicity raises a number of difficulties. On the one hand it may be helpful to know that judges have prejudices and political views, as well as opinions on matters of contemporary public interest, just like the rest of us. But, on the other hand, their free expression merely serves to highlight the fact that perhaps alone of rule-makers, the judges have no obligation to account to the community. Yet the people at large may not share these opinions and may not approve of the way in which these opinions contribute to a decision in any particular case. This brings us obviously to our second dimension of accountability which is that the community must have an opportunity to assess the work of its rule-makers and, if it so chooses, replace them with others of their choice. As far as the judicial branch is concerned - which, it must again be repeated, would be the supreme rule-making body under a Bill of Rights - there is no such opportunity. It is true that junior judges - magistrates, circuit judges and recorders - may be removed from office on the grounds of incapacity or misbehaviour.[30] But this can be done only by the Lord Chancellor, who is answerable to no one for the way in which this power is exercised. More importantly, perhaps, this power does not extend to the senior judiciary - the High Court, the Court of Appeal and the House of Lords - the members of which hold office during good behaviour until death or retirement, subject to a resolution for their removal passed by both Houses of Parliament.[31] There is no known instance of a senior judge having been removed in modern times, and indeed the precise scope of the power for their removal remains controversial.[32] This is not to suggest that such powers should be used extensively or to deny that the independence of the judiciary is of immense importance in a liberal democracy.[33] But it could suggest that measures necessary to preserve judicial independence may be incompatible with the requirements of the second dimension of accountability, as discussed in the previous section. The consequences of this potential conflict between judicial independence and judicial accountability will be considered later.

JUDICIAL REVIEW AND THE ROLE OF INTERPRETATION

The process of resolving disputes by the courts fails to meet the criteria discussed in the second section, and perhaps it never could. Yet the effect of a Bill of Rights or an incorporated European Convention is to empower the judges to unsettle decisions made in the political arena by the people's representatives and thereby frustrate the democratic process. One possible way of squaring the circle would be to say that in applying the Bill of Rights the courts are not in fact imposing personal policy choices to restrain the freedom of the elected representatives of the people. On the contrary, the courts are merely interpreting the document, that is to say their duty is literally to apply the values of the community as laid down in the Bill of Rights to ensure that Parliament does not overstep a predetermined boundary. In other words, the courts are not using the document as a vehicle to impose their own views, but are simply reflecting and applying the wishes of the community at the time the document was drafted and approved. Yet although this approach, or perhaps a less simplified version of it, and perhaps in a more urgently prescriptive vein, enjoys some support in the United States,[34] it is one that becomes less credible to sustain as the document ages; and even more difficult to reconcile with the reality of what the Court actually does. So although the First Amendment states expressly that 'Congress shall make no law . . . abridging the freedom of speech', the Supreme Court has found it necessary to accept that some limits may be imposed by Congress, with different justifications for restriction, despite the literal requirements of the First Amendment, being developed at different times in the court's history.[35] On the other hand, there is no right to privacy in the Bill of Rights, but the court has been willing to read one in – hardly manifesting a desire literally to apply the text of the document.[36] According to Mr Justice Goldberg, the Court has never held that the Bill of Rights protects only those rights that the Constitution specifically mentions by name.[37]

It may be argued that the problems with the US Constitution would not inevitably arise here. The problems are related not only to its remarkably 'open-ended provisions' but also to its age. If the document is to be more than a cadaver it can be so only to the extent that the courts are prepared to breathe life into it in order to ensure that it relates to contemporary reality. In the case of a document that is more clearly drafted to reflect more accurately the wishes of the people, however, it might be possible for a court to take a more literal approach to construction. At the very least, it might be argued, the

US experience offers no guidance as to the legitimacy of a more literal approach where the governing document is more fully and generously drawn. If we take the European Convention on Human Rights – which would be likely to form the basis of a British Bill of Rights – it is indeed the case that the Convention is much wider in terms of the rights and freedoms that it purports expressly to guarantee. Although it covers much the same ground as the US Bill of Rights, the authors of the Convention often express concepts in wider terms. Thus, while the US First Amendment protects free speech, the Convention protects the right to freedom of expression. Moreover, the Convention applies to areas not expressly regulated by the US Bill of Rights and offers express guarantees on privacy and family life (Article 8); on conscience and religious freedom (Article 9); on association, including the right to form and join trade unions (Article 11); and on marriage and the right to start a family (Article 12). So much of the controversy of US constitutional theory may be avoided to the extent that some of the problem areas are much more obviously covered by the Convention than by the US Bill of Rights. The need and scope for judicial creativity, it may be argued, is also reduced by the fact that unlike many of the key provisions of the US Bill of Rights, the corresponding provisions of the Convention are not unqualified. This is true, for example, of the guarantee of freedom of expression in Article 10, which may be restricted by laws that are necessary in a democratic society for various purposes, which include the protection of national security and public safety, the prevention of disorder or crime, or the protection of health or morals.[38]

Although the scope for expansive judicial law-making is in one sense greatly reduced by the Convention, it is also the case that by painting a large canvass with a broad brush, the Convention (if incorporated) would thereby give judges extensive powers over a large area. It would legitimize judicial review of legislation (and administrative action) of a wide and varied kind and legitimize it more by addressing any latent judicial insecurity about the areas into which the judges might legitimately intrude. For it is necessary only to look at the Convention to appreciate just how unsustainable is any suggestion that the judges would simply interpret and literally apply its provisions. It too is drafted at times in question-begging terms. Indeed this problem arises in the first substantive article, namely Article 2, which provides that 'Everyone's life shall be protected by law.' What does 'everyone' mean here? Does it include the unborn? If so, what is the effect of Article 2 on laws authorizing abortion? And how does Article 2 connect with Article 8, which seeks to guarantee a right to respect for private and family life?[39] At other times the Convention is drafted in opaque and value laden terms.[40] Thus, what is the judge to make of the qualifications of the right to privacy in Article 8, the right to freedom of religion in Article 9, the right to freedom of expression in Article 10 and the right to freedom of assembly and association in Article 11? In all cases restrictions are permitted where these are 'prescribed by law' (itself not an uncontentious term[41]) and are shown to be necessary in a democratic society for a number of permitted reasons (including such ill-defined grounds as the protection of morals and the interests of national security). What is the literal meaning of the term democratic society in a treaty ratified by the governments of Malta, Sweden, Ireland and Liechtenstein, as well as Britain?

It is true that these qualifications of particular Convention-protected freedoms give domestic legislatures an important power to balance individual liberty against what the European Court of Human Rights has referred to as a pressing social need, such as the protection of national security and public safety, or the prevention of disorder or crime, or for the protection of health or morals.[42] The difficulty with this, however, is that the power of the legislative branch is retained only if the courts, having already found a violation, then agree that the legislation was necessary in a democratic society for any of the permitted purposes. So even if it could be argued that the guarantees laid down in the Convention could be applied literally, this is certainly not true of the provisos of the kind under discussion. As already suggested, there is no literal approach that can be devised to determine what is necessary in a democratic society for the protection of national security. These are concepts distinguished above all by their uncertainty, and, as Patrick Monahan has pointed out, they can only be operated by the courts devising 'some normative theory about the nature of freedom and of democracy'.[43] In writing about the similar task presented to the Canadian courts by the proviso contained in section 1 of the Charter of Rights and Freedoms, Monahan also pointed out that the trouble with this is that 'there is no fixed or uncontroversial "core meaning" to these concepts: they are "contested concepts", with a rich and sophisticated debate continuing within political theory over their content and application'.[44] The courts are thus not only invited, they are in fact required by the Convention to articulate a theory of democracy by which to judge the propriety of legislation.[45] Apart from the fact that the judges are thus empowered to second-guess the different but equally validly held perceptions of the wider community and its elected representatives, we are left to speculate from precisely where this theory is to emerge. From extensive reading and reflection? From the arguments of counsel? Or from the ill-informed and unreflective prejudices of the Senior Combination Room?[46]

MAINTAINING FUNDAMENTAL VALUES

Given that a literal and mechanical interpretation of the Convention appears to be impossible and in any event apparently not necessarily regarded as appropriate by the Court, we return to our dilemma. Thus, how do we reconcile with democratic principle the power of an unelected judiciary to strike down legislation passed by an (albeit imperfectly) elected and accountable legislature, particularly when the power to strike down legislation is on the basis of vague and open-ended measures such as those contained in the ECHR? In his important book *The Least Dangerous Branch*,[47] Alexander Bickel acknowledges that 'nothing can finally depreciate the central function that is assigned in democratic theory and practice to the electoral process; nor can it be denied that the policy-making power of representative institutions, born of the electoral process, is the distinguishing characteristic of the system. Judicial review runs counter to this characteristic.'[48] Nevertheless, he argues in defence of judicial review, starting from the premise that 'government should serve not only what we conceive from time to time to be our immediate material needs but also certain enduring values'.[49] Legislative assemblies often fail to uphold this 'second aspect of public questions', for 'when the pressure for immediate results is strong enough and emotions ride high enough, men will ordinarily prefer to act on expediency rather than take the long view'.[50] But while he concedes that, 'everything else being equal', legislators are 'possibly' as able as other people 'of following the path of principle', this is only where the path is 'clear or at any rate discernible'.[51] A further difficulty, however, is that the American system, 'like all secular systems, calls for the evolution of principle in novel circumstances, rather than only for its mechanical application'.[52] The proven weakness of legislatures related not only to their lack of respect for the rule of established principles but also to their failure with regard to 'the creative establishment and renewal of a coherent body of principled rules'.[53] The courts in contrast are well-suited to the task, having 'certain capacities for dealing with matters of principle' that are not shared with legislatures and executives. Thus, judges 'have, or should have, the leisure, the training, and the insulation to follow the ways of the scholar in pursuing the ends of government'.[54] This, claims Bickel, 'is crucial in sorting out the enduring values of a society, and it is not something that institutions can do well occasionally, while operating for the most part with a different set of gears. It calls for a habit of mind, and for undeviating institutional customs.'[55] Judicial review is thus justified as 'the principled process of enunciating and applying certain enduring values'.[56]

Questions of principle in fact arise at two quite distinct levels, though this tends to be obscured in the literature. The first is to determine which values and principles we should select to freeze in our constitutional text (textual principles); and the second is to determine which values and principles we should bring to the interpretation of that inevitably open-textured document (interpretive principles). As far as the first of these is concerned, this attracts little attention in the literature, unsurprising perhaps in view of the fact that most of the literature is American and that American scholars have a text to work with. But this is not to say that there are no difficulties with textual principles. Thus we might all agree that people should be nice to one another, that governments should be accountable, and that citizens should have the right to bear or bare arms. But which of these do we constitutionalize and why? As Bickel himself recognizes, admittedly in the context of interpretive principles, 'such values do not present themselves ready-made . . . they must be continally derived, enunciated, and seen in relevant application'.[57] But this is true not only with regard to the interpretive principles but also with regard to the textual principles by which a society is to be governed. So just as some interpretive principles must change and adapt, so some textual principles may cease to be relevant while others may grow in importance as the social nature of the community changes and develops. Yet under a system of constitutionalized principle, weeds will continue to grow and be nurtured in fertile soil, while new flowers will struggle for survival in barren terrain. The last point is perhaps best illustrated by the growth of the women's movement in the late twentieth century. The problems here may be illustrated by the US Constitution, which has nothing to say about women's rights, with the result that the enduring values promoted by the text of the document may be seen to frustrate rather than facilitate the emancipation of women.

A good example of this is presented by *American Booksellers' Association Inc.* v *Hudnet.*[58] Although it might be argued forcefully - and perhaps with some truth - that such a case could never happen here, it does bring the problem into sharp focus. At issue was an Indianapolis Ordinance that imposed restrictions on pornography, which was defined to mean the graphic, sexually explicit subordination of women, whether in pictures or in words, including among other things: (a) women being presented as sexual objects who enjoy pain or humiliation; (b) women being presented as sexual objects who experience sexual pleasure in being raped; and (c) women being presented as sexual objects tied up or cut up or mutilated or bruised or physically hurt, or as dismembered or truncated or fragmented or severed into body parts. Under the legislation it was unlawful to traffic in pornography, coerce others into performing pornographic acts or force pornography on anyone. Inevitably the legislation was challenged on First Amendment grounds and just as inevitably the challenge succeeded, despite the court accepting the premises of the legislation, namely that 'Depictions of subordination tend to perpetuate subordination. The subordinate status of women in turn leads to affront and lower pay at work, insult and injury at home, battery and rape on the street.' The legislation was designed to promote new and emerging principles that address the dignity and status of women, principles not recognized expressly by the Constitution but principles necessary if women are to play a full, active and confident part in the political life of the community the Constitution is designed to serve. But there is no room for these principles in the Constitution and certainly no question that they could compete on equal terms, far less trump the constitutionalized protection of freedom of speech. According to the District Court, the 'compelling state interest which [the] defendants claim gives constitutional life to their Ordinance' was not 'so fundamental an interest as to warrant a broad intrusion into otherwise free expression'.[59] So evidence of material depicting sexual torture, penetration of women by red-hot irons and the like is of no consequence; in the marketplace of ideas 'there is no such thing as a false idea'.[60]

Apart from difficulties relating to which principles and enduring values are appropriate for freezing in a constitutional text, there are also difficulties relating to the second-level principles discussed above, namely principles of an interpretive nature. The problem arises because of the open texture of the language used in constitutional texts. This is illustrated by the Canadian Charter of Rights, which provides a wide range of guarantees, often very loosely drafted. Section 7, for example, provides that everyone has the right to life, liberty and security of the person. This is a measure pregnant with ambiguity, capable of being interpreted as widely or as narrowly as the courts wish. But like many of the other provisions of the Charter, section 7 is subject to the overriding principles of section 1, which allows the legislatures to impose reasonable limits on Charter guaranteed freedoms if these can be demonstrably justified in a free and democratic society. This also leaves a lot of scope for the courts, which are required to confront what is reasonable, what is demonstrably justified and, harder still, what is a democratic society. As we have seen in the discussion of the European Convention, these measures require the courts 'to devise some normative theory about the nature of freedom and of democracy'.[61] But, as we have also seen, 'there is no fixed or uncontroversial "core meaning" to these concepts; they are "contested concepts", with a rich and sophisticated debate continuing within political theory over their content and application'.[62] Bickel would presumably answer that both the interpretive questions – the content of the right and the scope of permitted restrictions – are to be answered by the judge discovering and applying the enduring values of society. The difficulty with this, however, and the central weakness of Bickel's position, is that there is no consensus as to what these values are,[63] with the result that in practice a quite enormous power would be conceded to the judicial branch to apply principles essentially of its own making in order to authorize or curtail the activities of the legislative branch. Although judges might conscientiously seek to decide on the basis of principle and to discover the enduring values of society, it is difficult to see how that can be done without at least some personal values being brought to bear upon the process.[64]

A nice illustration of the problem is provided by the decision of the Supreme Court of Canada in *R* v *Morgentaler*,[65] where the defendant was charged with performing abortions otherwise than in a hospital approved for this purpose and otherwise than in accordance with the pre-abortion procedures laid down in the Criminal Code. In his defence Morgentaler argued that the restrictions on abortion in the Criminal Code violated section 7 of the Charter on the ground that the right to life, liberty and security of the person protected therein created an implied constitutional right to an abortion, although there was no express right to abortion. So the question before the court was whether section 7 could be interpreted to include a woman's right to abortion, with the result that the restrictions in the Criminal Code would be struck down unless they could be justified by section 1. There is some reason to believe that in answering this question the justices sought guidance in the fundamental values of Canadian society. But they were unable to agree in a case that highlights the fact that the values which a judge discovers will depend to a large extent on the point at which he or she chooses to begin his or her enquiry. One judge (McIntyre J) embarked on a historical enquiry 'to cast light on the underlying philosophies of [Canadian] society'.[66] In his view the evidence 'establishes that there has never been a general right to abortion in Canada. There has always been clear recognition of a public interest of the unborn and there has been no evidence or indication of any general acceptance of the concept of abortion at will in our society.'[67] But rather than adopt a historical approach another judge (Wilson J) based her search for community values in more abstract philosophical terms, referring to the need to protect personal autonomy over important decisions intimately affecting people's private lives. According to Wilson J the Charter erects around each individual an invisible fence over which the state will not be allowed to trespass. One right that she held to fall within this protected area was the right to reproduce or not reproduce, something 'properly perceived as an integral part of modern woman's struggle to assert *her* dignity and worth as a human being'.[68] It is not necessarily clear why the Charter's root in the notion of personal autonomy leads to this result - an essential part of the equation appears to be missing. Nevertheless, the judgment illustrates nicely that the judge's search for the fundamental values of the community will be determined partly by his or her starting point (for example, history or moral philosophy) but partly also by personal values and life experience.

REINFORCING DEMOCRATIC PRINCIPLES

A noble attempt to reconcile the practice of judicial review with the principles of representative government is to be found in the work of John Hart Ely. He rejects Bickel's conclusions, writing that 'When we search for an external source of values with which to fill in the Constitution's open-texture . . . one that will not simply end up constituting the Court a council of legislative revision - we search in vain.'[69] He also 'recognizes the unacceptability of the claim that appointed and life-tenured judges are better reflectors of conventional values than elected representatives'.[70] But this does not lead him to reject the Bill of Rights; it suggests the need for a rather different rationale for judicial review, a search for a role that judges are 'conspicuously well situated to fill'.[71] So while rejecting Bickel, Ely argues in favour of 'a participation-oriented, representation-reinforcing approach to judicial review',[72] an approach for which he draws inspiration from the history and the text of the US Bill of Rights itself, though it is not a justification or an approach to interpretation that need be confined to the particular circumstances of the United States. This approach to judicial review reserves to the court an avowedly secondary and supportive role, which, 'unlike its rival value-protecting approach, is not inconsistent with, but on the contrary . . . entirely supportive of . . . the underlying premises of . . . representative democracy'.[73] For if it were to adopt Ely's approach, the court would not be concerned with outcomes with which it disagreed, but would be justified in intervening to strike down legislation only where the democratic process itself is malfunctioning. This could arise in one of two ways: first, where the party in power takes steps to choke off the channels of political change; second, where 'representatives beholden to an effective majority are systematically disadvantaging some minority out of simple hostility or a prejudiced refusal to recognize commonalities of interest, and thereby denying that minority the protection afforded other groups by a representative system'.[74]

The first of these functions is fulfilled, first, by judicial scrutiny of impediments to free speech, publication and political association, with the courts being required to eliminate any 'inhibition of expression that is necessary to the promotion of a government interest'.[75] Second, the need to unblock 'stoppages in the democratic process' requires 'judicial activism in the voting area', for along with the freedom of expression, the right to vote is 'central to a right of participation in the democratic process'.[76] Ely thus justifies a number of important but controversial decisions of the Warren Court, which struck down a number of electoral malpractices. These decisions include *Reynolds* v *Sims*,[77] in which the court displayed a willingness to monitor electoral boundaries to ensure that they were fairly apportioned, and in the course of so doing the Chief Justice said: 'representative government is in essence self-government through the medium of elected representatives of the people, and each and every citizen has an inalienable right to full and effective participation in the political processes of his State's legislative bodies'.[78] Two years later, in *Harper* v *Virginia State Board of Elections*,[79] the Court struck down a poll tax, with Mr Justice Douglas writing:

> Wealth, like race, creed, or color, is not germane to one's ability to participate intelligently in the electoral process. Lines drawn on the basis of wealth or property, like those of race . . . are traditionally disfavored . . . To introduce wealth or payment of a fee as a measure of a voter's qualifications is to introduce a capricious or irrelevant factor.[80]

For Ely, such intervention could be easily justified as the cases involved rights 'essential to the democratic process' and vindicated his claim that the protection of such rights 'cannot safely be left to our elected representatives, who have an obvious vested interest in the status quo'.[81]

A representation-reinforcing approach is clearly more acceptable than what Ely refers to as a value-protecting approach. Yet despite the elegance and attraction of Ely's work, this particular theory also gives rise to major difficulties that seem impossible to resolve. Such an approach is no less controversial than Bickel's, of which Ely is rightly highly critical, for the harsh reality is that a representation-reinforcing function requires the courts to confront hard questions about the very system of democracy itself. In defending cases such as those referred to above, Ely condemned the practice of 'malapportionment' where 'one person's vote counts only a fraction (and sometimes it was a very small fraction) of another's'.[82] According to Ely, 'Half a vote is only half a vote, a sixth of a vote is scarcely better than no vote at all, and here again those in power have a vested interest keeping things the way they are.'[83] These are arguments developed in the context of cases concerned with gerrymandered electoral boundaries. But they are possible arguments in Britain in the rather different context of proportional representation.[84] The logic of Ely's arguments and the rhetoric and decisions of the court, which he applauds, would appear to point inexorably in the direction of some consideration of whether the simple majority voting system employed in the UK is subject to scrutiny by a court committed to unblocking stoppages in the democratic process.[85] The case for such intervention would be arguably much stronger under a document based on the ECHR rather than the US Bill of Rights, for the former unlike the latter at least recognizes the duty 'to hold free elections at reasonable intervals by secret ballot, under conditions which will ensure the free expression of the opinion of the people in the choice of the legislature'.[86] The European Commission of Human Rights has already held - in a case brought by the Liberal Party - that this provision does not require a country to adopt any particular system of voting.[87] But if we were to have our own Bill or Rights with a similar measure, and if the courts were to adopt a representation-reinforcing role this matter would have to be re-opened. It would then be for the courts to enter a political minefield to determine whether or not the simple majority system is an adequate implementation of the right to vote. Should they fail to deal with this inquiry they would thereby signal the irrelevance of Ely's theory for the British judicial process. We would then be back to the drawing board.

Ely's approach could thus require the courts to make an important value judgment about a fundamental question that sits at the very heart of our democratic process. Claims about the task being procedural and unconcerned with substantive outcomes cannot escape from the fact that it is highly controversial. Although the courts might be unconcerned with outcomes, by the power to intervene in structural questions of this kind, they have a very real power to determine what these outcomes would be. Yet this is a power that is not confined to the voting system, in the sense that it also arises in the power the courts would have to scrutinize legislation designed to regulate the way in which election campaigns are conducted. The problem here is often overlooked by proponents of Bills of Rights. It is the problem of private political power and the need for state intervention to control and regulate that power in an election campaign, to ensure that all candidates and parties have as far as possible an equal chance of securing election.[88] The principle has been recognized in Britain since 1883, when the Corrupt and Illegal Practices Act first introduced limits on the amount of money each candidate could spend in a campaign.[89] This was reinforced in 1918 by a restriction on so-called independent expenditures, that is to say expenditures by persons or organizations other than the candidate.[90] Since 1918 these expenditures have been unlawful unless they are authorized by a candidate, in which case they form part of his or her permitted maximum.[91] In other countries additional steps have been taken to equalize electoral opportunities and to prevent any such legislation being undermined by the unregulated campaigning of so-called third parties. In Canada, for example, legislation introduced in 1974 imposed limits not only on the maximum permitted expenditure of candidates in parliamentary elections, but also on the maximum permitted expenditure of the political parties as well.[92] It is sometimes argued that similar measures should be introduced in this country to restrain spiralling campaign costs and to control the financial advantage which the Conservatives enjoy over the other parties.[93] As originally introduced, the Canadian legislation provided that the parties could spend a total of 30 cents multiplied by the number of electors in each of the constituencies in which the party had a candidate. The 30 cents was index-linked, with the result that the maximum permitted expenditure by each party (with a candidate in every constituency) at the 1988 election was just over $8 million.[94]

Because of the absence of a Bill of Rights, measures of this kind are relatively free of judicial attention in Britain.[95] This, however, is not the case in Canada, where the legislation has been challenged and undermined as violating the 1982 Charter of Rights and Freedoms. In addition to the limits on party expenditures, the Canadian legislation also imposed restrictions on election expenditures by anyone other than a candidate or political party. In *National Citizens' Coalition Inc.* v *Attorney-General for Canada*[96] these latter restrictions were held to violate the freedom of expression guarantees of the Charter (section 2), and not to be justified under section 1, which as we have seen permits restrictions on Charter-protected freedoms where these can be demonstrably justified in a free and democratic society. In reaching this conclusion the Court was influenced to some extent by the landmark decision of the US Supreme Court in *Buckley* v *Valeo*.[97] There it was held that spending limits on both candidates and so-called third parties were unlawful as violating the First Amendment's guarantee of free speech. In so holding, the Court said in a remarkably explicit passage that 'the concept that government may restrict the speech of some elements of our society in order to enhance the relative voice of others is wholly foreign to the First Amendment'.[98] The Court continued by saying that the First Amendment's protection against governmental abridgement of free expression cannot properly be made to depend on a person's financial ability to engage in public discussion. In so holding, the justices thereby determined that the free speech guarantees of the First Amendment would serve to ensure that the political influence of economic power could not be regulated or controlled;[99] liberty was to take priority over equality in the political arena. While this may well be a perfectly respectable position, it is difficult to see why it is necessarily any more so than the reverse position that the legislation embraced, and it is also difficult to see why a community should not be free to make its own determination as to where its priorities lie and as to the nature of the democracy under which it wishes to be governed. To empower the court to make representation-reinforcing decisions in the Ely sense is thus to surrender to unelected and unaccountable officials the authority to determine the permitted influence of economic power and the nature and structure of the forms of government under which we live. That in a sense is more important than the power to control particular substantive outcomes, for it is a power to determine indirectly all substantive outcomes that vitally affect the economically enfranchised.[100]

FACILITATING THE REPRESENTATION OF MINORITIES

As part of his theory of judicial review as a means of policing the process of representation, Ely argues that the courts should be empowered to strike down legislation which discriminates against minorities. Thus, it is not enough that the court should keep open the process of representation if 'those with most of the votes are in a position to vote themselves advantages at the expense of the others, or otherwise to refuse to take their interests into account'.[101] His particular concern was with minority groups who are unable to help themselves politically, possibly because they are excluded from the process (as in the case of aliens) or because they have no effective voice in the process. Here Ely recognizes the weaknesses of classical pluralist political theory, which promised that 'any group whose members were not denied the franchise could protect itself by entering into the give and take of the political marketplace'.[102] As a result of more contemporary work, 'pluralism has come under powerful attack, as more stress has been placed on the undeniable concentrations of power, and inequalities among the various competing groups'.[103] Although these are problems that decisions like *Buckley* v *Valeo*[104] serve only to reinforce, it is argued nevertheless that the courts are appropriate bodies to protect any minority that for all practical purposes 'is barred from the pluralist's bazaar', and thus keeps finding itself on the wrong end of legislation.[105] In Ely's view it is the duty of the courts to intervene when 'representatives beholden to an effective majority are systematically disadvantaging some minority out of simple hostility or a prejudiced refusal to recognize commonalities of interest, and thereby denying that minority the protection afforded other groups by a representative system'.[106] Ely devotes the whole of Chapter 6 of his book to the task of determining who constitutes a minority for this purpose and although there is scope for disagreement as to the nature and form of the classification, this does not seriously detract from the strength of his overall approach, which draws inspiration from a famous footnote in Justice Stone's opinion in *US* v *Carolene Products Co.*,[107] where he referred to 'prejudice against discrete and insular minorities . . . which tends seriously to curtail the operation of those political processes ordinarily to be relied upon to protect minorities, and which may call for a correspondingly more searching judicial inquiry'.[108]

The possibility that a Bill of Rights might be a useful protection for persecuted minorities has attracted many supporters. In its recent document on a Bill of Rights for Britain, for example, the IPPR argues that 'enforcement of a Bill of Rights by the courts holds Parliament to a paramount commitment to protect basic freedoms, and protects minorities against the tyranny of the majority'.[109] This, however, may be to claim too much. It is already open to the courts to take steps to protect minorities from oppression by the majority. Yet it is only too often the case that under existing law in times of crisis and panic, judges are every bit as likely to be swept along by the same tide of emotion and prejudice as are the legislators. A classic example of this is provided by the detention in 1940 of Jack Perlzweig (alias Robert Liversidge) under the Defence (General) Regulations 1939.[110] These authorized the Home Secretary to detain any person whom he had reasonable cause to believe to be of hostile origins or associations or to have been recently concerned in acts prejudicial to the public safety or the defence of the realm. When Liversidge challenged his detention in the courts the question that arose was whether the legislation could be interpreted to mean that the Home Secretary need only think he had reasonable grounds for his belief or whether he must in fact have had such grounds. The House of Lords (by a majority) preferred the former and infinitely wider interpretation over the latter, which had been advocated by Liversidge to force the Home Secretary to disclose what were the reasons for his belief. This approach was adopted on the basis that it is necessary to adopt a more benevolent attitude to government in times of stress, a concern that led Lord MacMillan to concede that 'in a time of emergency . . . it may well be that a regulation for the defence of the realm may quite properly have a meaning which because of its drastic invasion of the liberty of the subject the courts would be slow to attribute to a peace time measure'.[111]

Given the attitudes in this and other cases,[112] it is difficult to see why a Bill of Rights would make a great deal of difference. In the USA the Constitution did not protect the Japanese Americans who were detained in concentration camps during the Second World War.[113] Nor did it prevent the persecution of Communist Party members during the Cold War under legislation that made it illegal to 'advocate, abet, advise, or teach the duty, necessity, desirability, or propriety of overthrowing or destroying any government in the United States by force or violence'.[114] After convictions based on little more than Communist Party doctrine, leading officials were imprisoned for three to five years and defence attorneys were cited for contempt, to be imprisoned and later disbarred.[115] It is true of course that in its most famous ever decision, *Brown* v *Board of Education*,[116] the Supreme Court held that segregated schools were unconstitutional. That case is rightly celebrated as an example of the potential of a Bill of Rights for the protection of minorities, in this case racial minorities.[117] But other groups have not done so well, including those discrete and insular minorities that Ely identified as being in particular need of constitutional protection. A recent illustration is *Bowers* v *Hardwick*,[118] concerning the rights of homosexual men. In that case the Court refused to declare unconstitutional the sodomy laws in the state of Georgia, whereby it was a criminal offence punishable by imprisonment for two consenting adult males to engage in homosexual activity in the privacy of their own bedroom. In a 5:4 decision that has been widely criticized, the Chief Justice drew inspiration for sustaining the law from the condemnation of homosexuality that he said was firmly rooted in Judaeo-Christian moral and ethical standards. In so doing he referred to Blackstone, who referred to 'the infamous crime against nature' as an offence of 'deeper malignity' than rape, a heinous act, 'the very mention of which is a disgrace to human nature' and 'a crime not fit to be named'.[119] The case is all the more remarkable for the fact that in a lecture to New York University law students, Justice Powell said that he 'probably made a mistake' in voting with the majority.[120] But by that time it was a bit late for second thoughts.

Apart from the fact that Bills of Rights thus appear unable to secure the protection for minorities which their proponents claim, a further difficulty often overlooked by such proponents is that the freedoms guaranteed are not restricted to minorities or disadvantaged groups. The paradox then is that a Bill of Rights has the potential to allow the judiciary to frustrate legislative initiatives designed to protect minorities insofar as they intrude upon the rights of the majority; it is as likely to hinder as it is to help minorities and disadvantaged groups. So while the First Amendment does not protect the right of the poor to beg on the New York subway,[121] the equivalent free speech guarantees of the Canadian Charter have been held to protect tobacco companies from restrictions on the advertising of their product.[122] Take the position of women. A major report commissioned by the Canadian Advisory Council on the Status of Women[123] on the equality guarantees in the Canadian Charter makes rather disturbing reading. After analysing the 591 decisions handed down by the courts at all levels during the first three years of the operation of the relevant section of the Charter, the authors were drawn to conclude that 'women are initiating few cases, and men are using the Charter to strike back at women's hard-won protections and benefits'.[124] This is not really very surprising.[125] For if, as the authors claim, women 'are severely oppressed',[126] it is perhaps inevitable that this oppression should be reflected in the legal system and the legal process. For not only is the personnel of the law predominantly male ('judges are white, middle-aged, middle-class men with no direct experiences of disadvantage')[127], access to the law is likely to be easier for men rather than women. Litigation as a strategy requires a deep pocket reflecting a measure of economic power which is precisely what women do not have. As a practical matter women's groups may thus find that their limited resources are being used defensively against attacks on rights won in the democratic system rather than offensively to change conditions of disadvantage by legal rather than political means.[128]

Turning from sex discrimination to the question of race, a good example of the dangers of a Bill of Rights for legislative measures designed for the protection of minorities is provided by the decision of the US Supreme Court in *RAV* v *St Paul*.[129] This case involved the prosecution of a number of youths for breach of a city ordinance that made it an offence for anyone to place on public or private property a symbol or object, including a burning cross or a Nazi swastika, which he or she knows or has reasonable grounds to know arouses anger, alarm or resentment in others on the basis of race, colour, creed, religion or gender. The ordinance would thus appear to serve the same function as the statutory offence of incitement to racial hatred in Britain,[130] a measure which successfully stood up to constitutional challenge (on the ground that it violated free speech) in an action brought by Colin Jordan.[131] As might be expected, the Divisional Court ruled on the ground of parliamentary sovereignty and the inability of the courts to question the validity of an Act of Parliament. In the St Paul case, in contrast, the ordinance was struck down as violating the First Amendment's free speech guarantees. It is true that the Court acknowledged that the First Amendment did not forbid some restrictions on speech which is 'of such slight social value as a step to truth that any benefit that may be derived from [it] is clearly outweighed by the social interest in order and morality'.[132] This, however, does not appear to have been such a case. The ordinance was invalidated on two grounds, the first being that it applied selectively only to certain 'ideas' - racial insults - and did not apply to expressions of hostility on the basis of political affiliation, union membership or homosexuality.[133] It was held to be unlawful secondly because the so-called fighting words that were proscribed would be usable by those arguing in favour of racial tolerance and equality but could not be used by the opponents of these speakers.[134] In the view of the Court the city of St Paul had no authority to license one side of a debate to fight freestyle while requiring the other to follow the Queensbury rules. Remarkably, a community may thus only restrict incitement to racial hatred if it is also prepared to restrict incitement to racial equality. The decision is all the more remarkable in view of the Court's endorsement in the same case of the claim that it is the responsibility and obligation of diverse communities to confront virulent notions of racial supremacy in whatever form they appear.[135]

REFORM OF THE JUDICIARY

There thus appear to be difficulties in reconciling the current proposals for a Bill of Rights with the current arrangements relating to the judiciary. It is fair to say, however, that many of those who propose the introduction of a Bill of Rights couple their proposal with some initiative for the 'reform of the judiciary'. One of the reforms that has been proposed for some time has been to end the barristers' monopoly of appointment to senior judicial positions. This has in fact been challenged to some extent by the Courts and Legal Services Act

1990, which for the first time raises the possibility of solicitors being appointed to the Bench, although there is still room for argument about the restrictive qualifying conditions, which may be prohibitive. A second possible reform relates to the need to broaden the racial background of the Bench and to ensure a greater representation of women. So while the first reform is designed to increase the right of participation the second is designed to ensure a more representative judiciary. The third possible reform relates to the method of appointment and begins to touch upon the essential requirement of accountability. There are proposals for a more open system of judicial appointment involving a wider range of people, in particular people who are not members of the executive branch of government. This more public and thus perhaps accountable system of appointment is sometimes coupled with proposals for greater accountability on the part of the appointed judges themselves, reflected perhaps in proposals for more effective judicial training. Before we consider each of these proposals, it ought to be said that while these initiatives and proposals are important and potentially very valuable, they do not begin to address the three very fundamental concerns that were raised in the previous sections of this chapter.

The Appointment of Solicitors

The first item on the agenda for reform has been the appointment of solicitors to senior judicial positions. This is an important initiative which could immediately increase the pool from which appointments are made from some 5000 to some 50,000. The Courts Act 1971 allowed for solicitors to be appointed as recorders and after due experience in that position to be appointed further as circuit judges. Additional pressure has opened the door still further, with the Courts and Legal Services Act 1990 facilitating in some circumstances the appointment of solicitors to the High Court and above.[136] This measure has its immediate origins in the Green Paper issued by the Lord Chancellor's Department in January 1989 on the Work and Organisation of the Legal Profession.[137] The original proposal was tied to proposed new arrangements relating to the right of audience before all the courts. Thus, qualification at the Bar or as a solicitor would no longer be enough to guarantee a right of audience. Anyone wishing to become an advocate would be required to obtain a further qualification as a certified advocate to be issued after a period of formal training.[138] The different treatment of the different branches of the profession would disappear, with rights of audience before particular courts depending only upon whether advocates could demonstrate that they had the appropriate education, training and qualifications, matters to be determined by the Lord Chancellor on the advice of an advisory committee appointed by him, and after consultations with the judiciary. It is from this pool of certified advocates that High Court judges would in future be appointed, with the Lord Chancellor doubting whether it could be right to limit eligibility to judicial office to one side of the profession or the other and that eligibility should be determined by reference to whether any individual practitioner has had the necessary experience as an advocate, with ten years' experience being suggested as a basis for eligibility for appointment to the High Court.[139]

It is an open question whether the government's proposals would have led to a significantly large number of solicitors obtaining advocacy certificates enabling them to be appointed direct to the High Court. The arrangements were, however, stillborn, attracting widespread condemnation from senior judges, which was partly responsible for the government bringing forward its new watered down proposals in the White Paper, *Legal Services: A Framework for the Future*, published in July 1989.[140] The hostility of the judges was expressed publicly in a Lords Debate on 7 April 1989, in which the Lord Chief Justice, the Master of the Rolls and several serving as well as former Law Lords participated.[141] The venom of the judges was directed not at the proposal that solicitors should have rights of audience, but at a range of other matters, particularly the fact that rights of audience were to be governed by the Lord Chancellor's Advisory Committee. This had previously been 'the province of the judges, acting in some instances through the intermediary of the Inns of Court'.[142] Under the new proposals, which were enacted in the Courts and Legal Services Act 1990, members of the Bar will continue to have rights of audience before all courts and tribunals,[143] but solicitors will have a right of audience only if they comply with standards and requirements laid down by the Law Society, with the relevant rules requiring the concurrence of the Lord Chancellor and the senior judges.[144] So the judges will retain their rights to determine who may appear before them. These new proposals for rights of audience also had implications for eligibility for appointment to the Bench, the government accepting that 'experience as an advocate in work of an appropriate range and complexity is required in order to preside effectively as a judge'.[145] So under the new arrangements, eligibility for appointment to the Bench is to be confined to barristers (of ten years' standing in the case of appointment to the High Court) and to solicitors who have rights of audience.[146] At the time of writing arrangements have yet to be made about the solicitors' rights of audience, so it is not possible to say at this stage just how deep the pool of selection will be. But it is clear that we are still a long way short of a regime that guarantees a right of audience to all solicitors.

The Question of Gender

Apart from a desire to open up access to the Bench (and with it the rights of participation) to legal professionals other than barristers, there is also concern to ensure that the composition of the Bench should be more representative of the community in terms of the race and gender of its members. Presumably, the idea is that within whatever categories of legal professionals are deemed eligible for judicial office, more members of the minority communities and more women should be chosen from among their ranks. There is much to be said for these proposals, which enjoy widespread support, for as noted earlier in this chapter, the British judiciary is notable for its homogeneity, perhaps especially for the fact that it is a body consisting almost exclusively of white men.[147] There are presently no women members of the House of Lords, though there is a lone female voice in the Court of Appeal, Dame Ann Elizabeth Butler-Sloss. What is remarkable, however, is that the legislation governing appointments to both the Court of Appeal and the House of Lords fails to anticipate the possibility that a woman might be appointed to either. Under the Supreme Court Act 1981 the ordinary judges of the Court of Appeal are to be styled 'Lords Justices of Appeal'.[148] So Ann Elizabeth Butler-Sloss becomes Lord Justice Butler-Sloss. The same masculinization of women would also have to take place were a woman to be appointed to the House of Lords. Under the governing legislation, qualified persons may be appointed to be 'Lords of Appeal in Ordinary' and as such shall be entitled to rank 'as a Baron by such style as Her Majesty may be pleased to appoint'.[149] So in the event of Dame Ann Elizabeth Butler-Sloss being elevated to the Lords, she would cease being Dame Ann Elizabeth Butler-Sloss, Lord Justice of Appeal, and would become Baroness Butler-Sloss, Lord of Appeal in Ordinary, and would presumably appear in the law reports as Lord Butler-Sloss.

The importance of women on the Bench has been clearly demonstrated by the work of Bertha Wilson, appointed in 1982 as the first justice of the Supreme Court of Canada. In a public lecture delivered at Osgoode Hall Law School in February 1990, which attracted much academic interest and media controversy, she asked, 'will women judges really make a difference?'[150] In answering this question, Wilson

J conceded that there are areas of the law - contract, property and corporations - where there is no distinctly feminine perspective (*sed quaere*?). But in some other areas, 'a distinctly male perspective is clearly discernible', referring in particular to some aspects of the criminal law, which she does not specifically identify, but which 'are based on presuppositions about the nature of women and women's sexuality that, in this day and age, are little short of ludicrous'. These views struck a chord in England and Wales when in 1991 lawyers and judges were still arguing whether a husband could rape his wife, with the courts in the late twentieth century still taking seriously and still applying a dictum of Sir Matthew Hale in 1736 to the effect that 'the husband cannot be guilty of a rape committed by himself upon his lawful wife, for by their mutual matrimonial consent and contract the wife hath given up herself in this kind unto her husband, which she cannot retract'.[151] Perhaps more than any other controversy in recent years, this debate reinforces the view that female judges would not only act as a valuable role-model for other women in the profession, but would 'have an impact . . . on the development of the substantive law'.[152] This may also be true in other areas - apart from those where women are the clear and unequivocal victims of male aggression and domination.[153] For as Wilson J asserts, 'women view the world and what goes on in it from a different perspective from men'.[154] By bringing that perspective to bear on the cases they hear, women judges 'can play a major role in introducing judicial neutrality and impartiality into the justice system', which in her view presently reflects predominantly male values and attitudes.[155]

The importance of a woman's voice in the court was in fact highlighted forcefully by Wilson J herself in several crucial cases. Perhaps the most important of these is *R* v *Morgantaler*,[156] which was concerned with whether restrictions on the right of women to secure an abortion were consistent with a number of provisions of the Canadian Charter of Rights, including section 7, which protects the right to life, liberty and security of the person. The Supreme Court, by a majority, struck down the restrictions whereby it was a criminal offence for anyone to perform an abortion without a certificate from a therapeutic abortion committee of an accredited or approved hospital, with such committees being empowered to certify the performing of an abortion on limited grounds only. The legislation was held to be unconstitutional on a number of grounds, but mainly for procedural reasons. For Wilson J, however, the substantive question could not be ignored and in answering the substantive question of whether abortion could be restricted under the Charter, she brought a perspective that has never been revealed in an English court. Thus, a woman's decision to terminate a pregnancy 'will have profound psychological, economic and social consequences for the pregnant woman. The circumstances giving rise to it can be complex and varied and there may be, and usually are, powerful considerations militating in opposite directions. It is a decision that deeply reflects the way the woman thinks about herself and her relationship to others and to society at large. It is not just a medical decision; it is a profound social and ethical one as well.'[157] But before allowing the retort that a man or a group of men could identify with this bundle of problems, at least vicariously, she responded by saying that '*It is probably impossible for a man to respond, even imaginatively, to such a dilemma not just because it is outside the realm of his personal experience (although this is, of course, the case) but because he can relate to it only by objectifying it, thereby eliminating the subjective elements of the female psyche which are at the heart of the dilemma*'[158] (emphasis added).

New Methods of Selection and Removal

The two items so far on the agenda will have the effect of increasing the number of people who will be eligible for appointment to the Bench and also of ensuring that the Bench is more representative of the community as a whole. A third item may help to ensure that judges are more accountable for what they do in the courts. Much concern has been expressed recently about the way in which judges are appointed. The procedures - formerly shrouded in mist - are now explained in a pamphlet issued by the Lord Chancellor's Department.[159] But although we may be reassured that the policy is to appoint persons best qualified to fill any vacant post, regardless of 'party, sex, religion or ethnic origin',[160] it is clear that consultations with judges and other senior members of the profession play a decisive part, albeit that 'no one person's view about a candidate, whether positive or negative, should be regarded as decisive in itself'.[161] Unsurprisingly, these arrangements have provoked criticism. The whole process is secret, 'conducted behind closed doors',[162] by members of the executive branch. To the extent that the judges have a key role in the process they have become a 'self-appointed oligarchy',[163] answerable to no one in the way in which they use their power to recommend. There is also a suspicion that the arrangements might be racially discriminatory, perhaps offering one explanation of why there are so few judges from Britain's ethnic minorities, and no black or Asian member of the High Court, the Court of Appeal or the House of Lords. The potentially racist nature of the procedures has been put forcefully by Geoffrey Bindman, a solicitor specializing in discrimination law, who asks whether the current arrangements not only violate the Commission for Racial Equality's Code of Practice on Discrimination in Employment but may also constitute unlawful indirect discrimination under the Race Relations Act 1976.[164]

One suggestion for reforming these procedures is to be found in the Institute for Public Policy Research's proposed new constitution for the UK.[165] Chapter 9 and Schedule 5 deal with the Judiciary and propose not only a new Supreme Court, but also new procedures for the appointment of judges. Appointment would be removed from the Lord Chancellor and his officials and transferred to the proposed new Minister of Justice, who would be required to appoint to vacancies for high office one of only two people whose names had been submitted to him for this purpose by the Judicial Services Commission. This would be a body of fifteen members: five judges (including the Master of the Rolls and the Lord Chief Justice); two senior practising lawyers; seven lay members, who would be 'broadly representative of the community'; and a lay President. These proposals are similar to those that had been made earlier by a council member of Charter 88, as expressed in a letter to the *Guardian* in July 1990.[166] Helena Kennedy argued that a judicial appointments committee should be established, 'composed of judges, lawyers, academics, and an equal number of lay members appointed by a select committee which would be answerable to Parliament'. In some respects this is better than the fuller proposals of the IPPR, which anticipates appointments to its Judicial Services Commission to be made by the Minister of Justice. Not only would there thus be no cross-party involvement in the appointments to the Commission, an important opportunity to control the abuse of the power of patronage would be lost. It is indeed open to question whether the adoption of the IPPR proposal would make much difference in practice to judicial appointments, notwithstanding the duty of the proposed Judicial Services Commission to adopt procedures to ensure that 'adequate numbers' of candidates of both sexes and from diverse racial, religious and social backgrounds are considered for appointment. The pool from which candidates would be selected would be largely the same as at present, that is to say practising lawyers, while judges would continue to have a key role in appointments, for their influence might well exceed their number if the opportunity was taken by a Minister of Justice to appoint lay people who are cautious, conservative and deferential.

Proposals of this kind are clearly not without merit. They may help to infuse a greater degree of participation of a wider range of people in the appointment process. But equally they are not to be exaggerated for they will not necessarily lead to different people being appointed to the Bench. Indeed, if the criterion for appointment remains the same ('the best qualified candidate') as at present and if the pool of eligible people remains largely the same ('members of the legal profession in England and Wales') we may notice very little difference. But even if these new arrangements were to lead to a marginally less unrepresentative judiciary, as it is possible they might, this does not deal with the question of accountability of judges as rule-makers. A different system of appointing different people does not make these appointed persons in any sense accountable, even to the people who appointed them, to say nothing of those who will be governed by their decisions. Perhaps more significant in this sense are the current proposals for the removal of judges, which at the present time can be done – at least in the case of senior judges – only by the Queen following a resolution passed by both Houses of Parliament.[167] If we again take the IPPR – if only because it is likely to be the most influential on the centre left – it is proposed that a judge could be removed from office on the grounds of 'serious judicial misconduct',[168] following a recommendation by a Judicial Conduct Tribunal composed of both judicial and lay members, which would deal with cases referred to it by the Judicial Services Commission. If the Tribunal recommends the removal of a judge from office, the Minister of Justice would then be required to lay a resolution for the removal from office of the judge before Parliament, the resolution to take effect on being passed by both Houses. It appears, however, that Parliament would lose any original power it presently has to move for the removal of a judge, with the power to commence proceedings being transferred to bodies directly (the Judicial Services Commission) and indirectly (the Judicial Conduct Tribunal) appointed by the executive.

CONCLUSION

There are, then, a number of important reforms of the judiciary presently being considered. Yet whether they will meet the concerns expressed earlier in this chapter remains to be assessed. But before we turn specifically to this question, it is important to bear in mind precisely what a Bill of Rights entails. The freedoms guaranteed by a Bill of Rights are not self-executing; nor are they usually self-explanatory. They can only be brought to life by the judges, who must give these freedoms a meaning in a case that comes before them, and then decide whether legislation passed by Parliament is consistent with the Bill of Rights as interpreted by the court. What this means in effect is that judges are given quite enormous power to strike down legislation as violating the terms of a document, the meaning of which they fully control. So unless the judiciary is in some way reformed, the operation of a Bill of Rights would run counter to the essential principles of democracy identified earlier in this chapter, for the effect would be to transfer power from an elected and accountable government to judges who are neither elected nor accountable. The question now is whether the present package of proposed reforms would overcome this fundamental objection. Will their implementation (a) open up the judiciary to a significantly wider category of people than is presently the case; (b) make the judiciary in any sense representative of the community it serves; and (c) make the judiciary in any sense more accountable than it is at present? If the answer to any, never mind all, of these questions is negative, then any proposal for a Bill of Rights must be stillborn, for the operation of such a device would be at variance with the first principles of democratic self-government.

Although many of the current proposals for reforming the judiciary are important, they do not begin to meet the preconditions that have been outlined. As far as the right of equal participation is concerned, it is difficult to see how this will be guaranteed by opening up the system to a few solicitors. The right of access to the supreme sovereign body would continue to depend on candidates having professional qualifications and practical experience in the law, which would in turn continue to place a premium on social background and educational pedigree. It should also be borne in mind that the solicitors who are likely to be appointed are those who hold senior positions with leading city firms in commercial practice. Although there appear to be some who think otherwise, it seems highly unlikely that the appointment of solicitors will open up the process to radicals engaged in what might be called 'people's law'. For if so-called radical barristers have been overlooked in the past, there is no reason to believe anything other than that radical solicitors would suffer the same fate, no matter how eminent and well-known they might be. The appointment of solicitors is thus likely to mean more of the same, though paradoxically, perhaps, it could mean an even less representative and appropriate body of adjudicators than at present if it means that we would have people who had spent all their working lives in the practice of commercial law servicing the needs of a handful of commercial clients. It is difficult to see what special skills such an individual can bring to cases involving migrants, prisoners or the poor, all of whom may be persuaded from time to time to rely on the Bill of Rights to promote their interests. It is less difficult to imagine how such an individual might identify with the corporation that wished to use freedom of expression to fight restrictions on advertising, to use freedom of religion to challenge Sunday trading laws and to use the right to liberty and security of the person or the right to privacy to resist the intrusive investigations of the tax inspectorate or agencies entrusted with the elimination of discrimination. It is also difficult to see why a trade union should have more faith in such people than in the present crop of judges, especially if the solicitor judges have spent all their lives working for the interests of management, without ever having a trade union client.

So the introduction of a few solicitors into the system will not greatly enhance the number of people who will be able to participate in this particular political process. Nor will it make the system any more representative, if we turn now to the second theme. Indeed, it could well make the system less rather than more representative of the community it appointment was to be confined to commercial types. On the other hand, however, there is no doubt that the greater introduction of women and members of the minority ethnic communities would be a very significant advance. But, again at the risk of spoiling the party, there are a number of qualifications to be made here too. First, the problems for women are not simply problems of direct discrimination against eligible applicants. The point is made lucidly, again by Helena Kennedy, who draws attention to the difficulties faced by women so that they are rarely able in practice to reach the starting gate. These include discrimination in selecting tenants, pressure to enter the low prestige areas of the law (family law and crime) and the lack of adequate maternity leave arrangements.[169] The problems are thus deep-rooted and need radical surgery before equal representation of men and women on the Bench becomes a reality. The Courts and Legal Services Act 1990,[170] which extends both the Sex Discrimination Act 1975 and the Race Relations Act 1976 to the legal profession, is a step in the right direction. But even if it is successful, and even if we are able to build a Bench that is more representative of the community, it does not follow that judges thereby represent the community. An appointed woman has no more authority to speak on behalf of other women than does an appointed man. There is no single women's perspective even on women's issues, whether it be abortion, prostitution or pornography, a point vividly highlighted in Canada in 1989 when the anti-feminist organization 'REAL Women of Canada' complained to the Canadian Judicial Council following Wilson J's lecture, which is referred to earlier.[171]

The implementation of the current package of proposed reforms may thus help to ensure that the judiciary is marginally more representative of the community, but it will not guarantee that the judiciary represents the community. By the same token, the present package of proposed reforms will do little to enhance the accountability of the judiciary. The IPPR's proposal for a Judicial Conduct Tribunal is a worthy idea that would allow for the development of a body of principle regulating the behaviour of judges.[172] It is flawed, however, by the proposal that decisions of the tribunal would be subject to judicial review, thereby allowing the senior judges to have the last say in determining what should be the principles that regulate their own performance. But that in a sense is a minor point, for the problem of accountability is not whether judges are removed from office when they overstep the mark of judicial propriety. To some extent judicial officers are already accountable in this way. Judges in the lower courts can be removed by the Lord Chancellor without the need for an address by each House of Parliament, and senior judges may find it expedient to resign when they overstep the mark. But the real question of accountability relates not to the removal of naughty judges, but to the way in which judges exercise powers that are properly assigned to them. At the present time judges may misinterpret a statute, but Parliament can always intervene to set the matter to rights. With a Bill of Rights that power of Parliament is, for all practical purposes, lost. The judiciary would have the power to strike down legislation by using the Bill of Rights, which they and they alone would be free to interpret as they wished. As someone once said about a Prime Minister, the Bill of Rights is putty waiting to be moulded. The courts would be under no duty to account to anyone with regard to the way in which this power - the ultimate sovereign power - was exercised.

What this means is that judges could make major political decisions - whether abortion is consistent with the right to life, whether Sunday trading laws are consistent with the right to freedom of religion, and whether pornography is protected by freedom of expression - without having to account for what they have done. It is not suggested that judges should be, or indeed could be, accountable to the community in the sense contemplated in this chapter. For it is accepted that as well as the accountability of political decision-makers, the independence of the judiciary is a valuable and indispensable principle of liberal democracy.[173] And it is accepted further that it is not possible to have both, for, as has been written in one treatise, 'it must be possible for a judge to decide a case without fear of reprisals'[174] from whatever quarter these may come. What this suggests is that if principle dictates that the ultimate sovereign power in a community should rest above all with decision-makers who are popularly accountable, the case for a Bill of Rights is simply unsustainable. The problems, admittedly, would be much less acute if the Bill of Rights (or an incorporated European Convention) were to be limited in its scope by operating simply as a guide to the interpretation of statutes and as a means of regulating executive discretion, but not also as a device for limiting the sovereign power of Parliament. A limited measure of this kind has in fact been adopted in New Zealand and appears to be anticipated by a Labour Member's Human Rights Bill, printed in 1992.[175] This may or may not offer a sensible way forward. But to go further would represent a monumental historic retreat, a step backwards from democracy to the creation of what could only be regarded as a juristocracy, a system of government predominantly by lawyers and judges, from participation in which the great bulk of the people would be permanently and irrevocably excluded.

NOTES

1. See A British Bill of Rights, Constitution Paper No 1 (1990).

2. A People's Charter. Liberty's Bill of Rights. A Consultation Document (1991). For the position of the Scottish Council for Civil Liberties (also in favour of Bill of Rights) see A. Miller, Why we need a Bill of Rights for Scotland, *Glasgow Herald*, 12 February 1992.

3. The proposal is strongly supported by the Liberal Democrats. See We, the people . . . towards a written constitution. Federal Green Paper No. 13. For a Conservative view, see J. Patten, *Political Culture, Conservatism and Rolling Constitutional Change* (Conservative Political Centre, 1991).

4. *An Introduction to the Study and Law of the Constitution* (10th edn, 1959). For a critique, see P. P. Craig, *Public Law and Democracy in the United Kingdom and the United States of America* (Oxford, 1990), especially Chapter 2.

5. 'You have to look long and hard before you can detect any difference between the English common law and the principles set out in the Convention': *R* v *Secretary of State for the Home Department, ex parte Brind* [1990] 2 WLR 787, at p. 797 (Lord Donaldson).

6. See K. D. Ewing and C. A. Gearty, *Freedom under Thatcher: Civil Liberties in Modern Britain* (Oxford, 1990).

7. It would be possible in principle to restrict the operation of the Bill of Rights to permit the review only of administrative action, but not also primary legislation. See, for example, the New Zealand Bill of Rights Act 1990. See also J. Jowell and A. Lester, Beyond *Wednesbury*: substantive principles of administrative law [1987] PL 368.

8. For an earlier treatment of these issues see K. D. Ewing and C. A. Gearty, *Democracy or a Bill of Rights* (Society of Labour Lawyers, 1991), especially Chapter 2.

9. John Hart Ely, *Democracy and Distrust: A Theory of Judicial Review* (Cambridge, MA, 1980).

10. This is not to say that Ely is without his critics, some of whom are devastating and convincing. For an account of Ely and references to further reading, see P. P. Craig, *Public Law and Democracy*, *op. cit.*, pp. 91–116.

11. See R. Brazier, *Constitutional Practice* (Oxford, 1988), p. 192.

12. On the right of equal participation generally, see Ely, *op. cit.*, pp. 75–7.

13. For a consideration of this issue, see A. H.Birch, *Representative and Responsible Government* (London, 1977), p. 62.

14. On the question whether intelligence or property ownership should entitle individuals to extra influence in the democratic process, see Birch, *ibid.* See further C. B. MacPherson, *The Life and Times of Liberal Democracy* (Oxford, 1977), esp. Chapter 2.

15. See A. Bickel, *The Least Dangerous Branch: The Supreme Court at the Bar of Politics* (New York, 1962), p. 17.

16. For judicial consideration of the role and function of the representative in the British system of government, see *Amalgamated Society of Railway Servants* v *Osborne* [1910] A C 87; and *Kemp* v *Glasgow Corporation* [1920] A C 836.

17. See *Amalgamated Society of Railway Servants* v *Osborne* [1910] A C 87 and *Kemp* v *Glasgow Corporation* [1920] A C 836.

18. See *Edmund Burke on Government, Politics and Society*, Selected and edited by B.W. Hill (Glasgow, 1975).

19. On judicial appointments, see R. Brazier, *Constitutional Practice* (Oxford, 1988), pp. 224–34.

20. Appellate Jurisdiction Act 1876, s. 6, as amended by Courts and Legal Services Act 1990, s. 71 and Schedule 10.

21. Supreme Court Act 1981 s. 10(3)(b) and (c) as amended by Courts and Legal Services Act 1990, s. 71(1). On rights of audience (which it is intended shall include solicitors), see s. 27.

22. Lord Chancellor's Department, Judicial Appointments (1986), pp. 7–8.

23. *The Politics of the Judiciary* (4th edn, 1991), p. 29.

24. On the idea of functional representation, see S. H. Beer, *Modern British Politics* (1969).

25. See Griffith, *op. cit.*, pp. 30–8.

26. This is not to deny that questions arise from time to time about the adequacy of these reasons. See, for example, *Re S* [1992] 3 WLR 806.

27. On the Kilmuir rules see R. Brazier, *Constitutional Practice* (Oxford, 1988), pp. 242–3.

28. The rules are reproduced in R. Brazier, *Constitutional Texts* (Oxford, 1990) pp. 595–6, from which this extract is drawn.

29. For an account of the rules, see A. W. Bradley, Judges and the media: the Kilmuir Rules [1986] PL 383.

30. E. C. S. Wade and A. W. Bradley, *Constitutional and Administrative Law* (11th edn by A. W. Bradley and K. D. Ewing, 1993), pp. 377–8.

31. *Ibid.*, p. 337.

32. *Ibid.*

33. 'What is of fundamental importance is that the judicial authorities of the state should be independent, so that their decisions are reached in accordance with law and not in submission to the wishes of government': C. Turpin, *British Government and the Constitution* (2nd edn, 1990), p. 65.

34. See R. Bork, Neutral principles and some First Amendment problems (1971) 47 *Indiana Law Journal* 1: 'The judge must stick close to the text and the history, and their fair implications, and not construct new rights' (p. 8).

35. For an account of this see Ely, *op. cit.*, pp. 105–16.

36. *Griswold* v *Connecticut*, 381 US 479 (1965).

37. *Ibid.*, at p. 486, note 1.

38. Article 10(2). See also articles 8(2), 9(2), and 11(2).

39. See K. D. Ewing and C. A. Gearty, Terminating abortion rights? (1992) 142 *New Law Journal* 1696.

40. See, for example, article 3, which protects against inhuman or degrading treatment or punishment. Is there a fixed and objective standard of inhumanity or degradation? If not, how do we give the words meaning? See *Ireland* v *UK* (1978) 2 EHRR 25; *Tyrer* v *UK* (1978) 2 EHRR 1; *Campbell* v *UK* (1982) 4 EHRR 293; and *Soering* v *UK* (1989) 11 EHRR 439.

41. See, for example, *Malone* v *UK* (1985) 7 EHRR 14.

42. See, for example, *Silver* v *UK* (1983) 5 EHRR 347.

43. P. Monahan, *Politics and the Constitution: The Charter, Federalism and the Supreme Court of Canada* (Toronto, 1987), p. 54.

44. *Ibid.*

45. *Ibid.*

46. Quite apart from textual difficulties which render difficult any literal solution to this problem, it is clear that judges in both Britain and Europe are no more willing to be constrained by such an approach than are their counterparts in North America. See respectively *Minister of Home Affairs* v *Fisher* [1980] AC 319, esp. per Lord Wilberforce at pp. 328–9 and *Young, James and Webster* v *UK* (1982) 4 EHRR 38. See M. Forde, The 'closed shop' case (1982) 11 ILJ 1.

47. A. Bickel, *The Least Dangerous Branch: The Supreme Court at the Bar of Politics* (New York, 1962).
48. *Ibid.*, p. 19.
49. *Ibid.*, p. 24.
50. *Ibid.*, p. 25.
51. *Ibid.*, p. 25.
52. *Ibid.*, p. 25.
53. *Ibid.*, p. 25.
54. *Ibid.*, pp. 25–6.
55. *Ibid.*, p. 26.
56. *Ibid.*, p. 58.
57. *Ibid.*, p. 24.
58. 771 F 2d 323 (1985).
59. 598 F Supp 1316 (1984), at p. 1336.
60. 771 F 2d 323 (1985), at p. 331. The Court was concerned that speech which portrayed women in a position of equality was lawful under the Ordinance, no matter how graphic its sexual content. This, said the court, was 'thought control'!
61. Monahan, *op. cit.*, p. 54.
62. *Ibid.*
63. The point is perhaps well made by Hoffman LJ in the rather different circumstances of the tragic Anthony Bland case. There he emphasized (at p. 352) that there is no morally correct solution that can be deduced from a single ethical principle. Perhaps unwittingly that passage is one of the most important judicial contributions to the Bill of Rights debate. *Airedale NHS Trust* v *Bland* [1993] 2 WLR 316.
64. See also Ely, *op. cit.*, pp. 43–72.
65. (1988) 44 DLR (4th) 385.
66. *Ibid.*, at p. 471.
67. *Ibid.*
68. *Ibid.*, p. 491.
69. Ely, *op. cit.*, p. 73.
70. *Ibid.*, p. 102.
71. *Ibid.*, p. 102.
72. *Ibid.*, p. 87.
73. *Ibid.*, p. 88.
74. *Ibid.*, p. 103.
75. *Ibid.*, p. 105.
76. *Ibid.*, p. 116.
77. 377 US 533 (1964).
78. *Ibid.*, at p. 565.
79. 383 US 663 (1966).
80. *Ibid.*, at p. 668.
81. Ely, *op. cit.*, p. 117.
82. *Ibid.*, p. 120.
83. *Ibid.*, p. 120.
84. For a consideration of this issue, see Turpin, *op. cit.*, pp. 523–34.
85. It might also have invited a more robust commitment to the principle of 'equal representation of all electors' by the Court of Appeal in *R* v *Boundary Commission for England, ex parte Foot* [1983] 1 Q B 600.
86. First Protocol to the Convention 1952, Cmd 9221, article 3.
87. For an account see H. F. Rawlings, *Law and the Electoral Process* (1988), pp. 61–2.
88. For a discussion, see K. D. Ewing, *Money, Politics, and Law: A Study of Electoral Campaign Finance Reform in Canada* (Oxford, 1992), Chapter 2.
89. This issue is considered in K. Ewing, *The Funding of Political Parties in Britain* (Cambridge, 1987), pp. 80–2.
90. Representation of the People Act 1918, s. 34.
91. The position is now governed by the Representation of the People Act 1983, s. 75.
92. For an account of the Canadian legislation, see K. D. Ewing, *op. cit.*

93. This issue is considered in K. Ewing, *The Funding of Political Parties in Britain*, *op. cit.*, Chapter 8.

94. See K. D. Ewing, *op. cit.*, note 88, p. 217.

95. But see *R* v *Tronoh Mines Ltd* [1952] 1 All ER 697.

96. (1985) 11 DLR (4th) 481.

97. 424 US 1 (1976). This case has spawned an enormous literature, quite properly in view of its great significance. Among the most powerful pieces are J. Skelly Wright, Politics and the Constitution: is money speech? (1976) 85 *Yale Law Journal* 1001, and J. Skelly Wright, Money and the pollution of politics: is the First Amendment an obstacle to political equality? (1982) 82 *Columbia Law Review* 609.

98. 424 US 1 (1976), pp. 48–9.

99. Nevertheless, the decision is very influential. Apart from its adoption in Canada it had a bearing on the outcome of the important decision of the High Court of Australia in *Australian Capital Television Pty Ltd* v *Commonwealth of Australia* (1992) 66 ALJR 695, in which the court implied a limited Bill of Rights into the Constitution of Australia and then used it to strike down broadcasting restrictions which operated during an election. It is interesting to note that the Australian (Federal) Minister for Administrative Services had written earlier to the *New York Times* (10 May 1991) to justify the legislation. He wrote in the context of the US First Amendment that 'the Australian government does not regard advertising as ''free'' speech, but very expensive purchased speech, available only to those who possess the financial means to buy it'. He also wrote that the Australian government had 'decided not to wait until influence buying or corruption becomes entrenched in our system, or until the day arrives when only millionaires can afford to run for office'. Unhappily for the minister these arguments were subsequently to cut little ice in his own country's High Court.

100. There is also the wider point that free speech guarantees cannot be confined to challenging restraints on political speech. Such guarantees are also a means of empowering corporate interests which find themselves subject to statutory regulation. For the possibility of the European Convention being used to emancipate and liberate corporate power, see *Barthold* v *Germany* (1985) 7 EHRR 383; *Markt Intern* v *Germany* (1990) 12 EHRR 161; *Autronic AG* v *Switzerland* (1990) 12 EHRR 485; *Groppera Radio AG* v *Switzerland* (1990) 12 EHRR 321.

101. Ely, *op. cit.*, p. 135.

102. *Ibid.*

103. *Ibid.*

104. 424 US 1 (1976).

105. Ely, *op. cit.*, p. 152.

106. *Ibid.*, p. 103.

107. 304 US 144 (1938).

108. *Ibid.*, pp. 152–3 (note 4)

109. Institute for Public Policy Research, *The Constitution of the United Kingdom* (1991), p. 13.

110. *Liversidge* v *Anderson* [1942] AC 206.

111. *Ibid.*, p. 251.

112. For a more recent example of the same see *R* v *Secretary of State for the Home Department, ex parte Cheblak* [1991] 1 WLR 890. This is the Gulf War deportations case in the course of which Lord Donaldson said that '"national security" and "civil liberties" are on the same side. In accepting, as we must, that to some extent the needs of national security must displace civil liberties, albeit to the least possible extent, it is not irrelevant to remember that the maintenance of national security underpins and is the foundation of all our civil liberties' (pp. 906–7). A strong critique of the Court of Appeal in that case is to be found in Hugo Young, Liberty lost in the fog of war, *Guardian*, 7 February 1991, in the course of which he wrote that 'By the standards of history, Donaldson's was an ignominious performance.'

113. *Korematsu* v *United States*, 323 US 214 (1944). For a full account of this episode see S. Walker, *In Defense of American Liberties: A History of the ACLU* (New York, 1990), Chapter 7.

114. *Dennis* v *United States*, 341 US 494 (1951).

115. For an account of this extraordinary episode see S. Walker, *op. cit.*, p. 186. A contemporary incident involving the intimidation of civil rights lawyers is reported in the *The Nation*, 7 December 1992.

116. 347 US 483 (1954).

117. Though it is not often enough realized that for 38 years after the Supreme Court's decision the matter remained unresolved, with the school board in question being told by a Federal appeals court in November 1992 'to come up with a plan to remedy unconstitutional racial imbalances that persist in the city's public schools': *New York Times*, 4 November 1992. For a sober reassessment of the Brown case, see M. Dudziak, Desegregation as a Cold War imperative (1988) 41 *Stanford Law Review* 61.

118. 478 US 186 (1986).

119. *Ibid.*, p. 197.

120. *New York Times*, 5 November 1990.

121. *Young* v *New York City Transit Authority, New York Times*, 27 November 1990.

122. *The Observer*, 24 November 1991 (letter from Jean-Louis Mercier, Chairman and Chief Executive Officer, Imperial Tobacco Ltd, Montreal). Unsurprisingly the case was the subject of an appeal. The Quebec Court of Appeal upheld the appeal: *Maclean's*, 25 January 1993.

123. G. Brodsky and S. Day, *Canadian Charter Equality Rights for Women: One Step Forward or Two Steps Back?* (Ottawa, 1989).

124. *Ibid.*, p. 3.

125. In the same vein, in an appraisal of the Charter's first ten years (*Toronto Star*, 11 April 1992) one woman law professor was quoted as saying that the Charter had been a resounding failure so far as women were concerned.

126. Brodsky and Day, *op. cit.*, p. 11.

127. *Ibid.*, p. 3.

128. The point is made in the ten year appraisal of the Charter in the *Toronto Star*, 11 April 1992. A particularly controversial example of this is the striking down of the so-called rape shield laws in *R* v *Seaboyer* (1991) 83 DLR (4th) 193. The legislation in question imposed restrictions on evidence for the accused in sexual assault cases which related to the sexual activity of the victim with any person other than the accused. The decision was strongly criticized by women's groups on the ground that it would discourage women from reporting sexual assaults to the police. See *Globe and Mail*, 24 August 1991. The federal minister for the status of women said the decision 'really was a surprise. Many of us working in this field thought it would not happen' (132 HC Debs 9518 (8 April 1992)). There are many in the UK who also seem determined to learn the hard way.

129. 120 L Ed 2d 305 (1992). In the same vein and equally controversial is *Collin* v *Smith*, 578 F 2d 1197 (1978) (the 'Skokie' case). See also *Dawson* v *Delaware*, *New York Times*, 10 March 1992, where the Court overturned a death sentence on the ground that the prosecution violated a convicted murderer's First Amendment rights by telling the jury that he was a member of a white racist prison gang called the Aryan Brotherhood.

130. Public Order Act 1986, ss. 17–25. This replaces earlier measures which had their origins in the Race Relations Act 1965, s. 6.

131. *R* v *Jordan* [1967] Crim LR 483.

132. *Chaplinsky* v *New Hamphire*, 315 US 568 (1941), cited at 120 L Ed 2d 305 (1992), p. 317 (Justice Scalia).

133. L Ed 2d 305 (1992), p. 323.

134. *Ibid.*, p. 323.

135. For a powerful critique see A. W. Bradley [1992] PL 357.

136. See especially Courts and Legal Services Act 1990, s. 71.

137. Lord Chancellor's Department, 'The work and organisation of the legal profession', Cm 570 (1989).

138. *Ibid.*, Chapter 5.

139. *Ibid.*, Chapter 10.

140. Cm 740 (1989).

141. 505 HL Debs 1307–1480 (7 April 1989).

142. *Ibid.*, col. 1331 (Lord Lane).

143. 1990 Act, ss. 32–3.

144. 1990 Act, ss. 32–3.

145. Cm 740 (1989), para. 15.5.

146. 1990 Act, s. 71.

147. According to a profile of the former Canadian Supreme Court Justice, Bertha Wilson,

she was told by a Lord of Appeal at a conference that 'no woman sat on Britain's high court [the House of Lords] because none is qualified' (*Toronto Star*, 13 September 1990).

148. Supreme Court Act 1981, s. 2(3).

149. Appellate Jurisdiction Act 1876, s. 6.

150. (1990) 28 *Osgoode Hall Law Journal* 507. Similar points were made by another female member of the Supreme Court of Canada, McLachlin J, who in a lecture to the Elizabeth Fry Society in Calgary in 1991 complained particularly of the failure of the criminal law to accord equality to women. She dealt in particular with prostitution laws (which continued to focus on the prostitute rather than the customer), abortion laws (insensitive to the plight of the unwed or impoverished woman facing the prospect of an unwanted pregnancy) and battered women (*Edmonton Journal*, 19 April 1991).

151. *R* v *R* [1992] 1 AC 599.

152. Wilson, *op. cit.*, p. 519.

153. *R* v *Thornton* [1992] 1 All ER 306, though compare *R* v *Ahluwalia* [1992] 4 All ER 889.

154. Wilson, *op. cit.*, p. 515.

155. *Ibid.*

156. (1988) 44 DLR (4th) 385.

157. *Ibid.*, p. 490.

158. *Ibid.*, p. 491.

159. Lord Chancellor's Department, Judicial Appointments (1986).

160. *Ibid.*, p. iv.

161. *Ibid.*, p. 3.

162. Helena Kennedy, letter to the Editor, *Guardian*, 20 July 1990.

163. *Ibid.*

164. G. Bindman, Is the system of judicial appointments illegal? (1991) (8) *Law Society Gazette* 24.

165. Institute for Public Policy Research, *op. cit.*

166. Letter to the Editor, *Guardian*, 20 July 1990.

167. See Wade and Bradley, *op. cit.*, p. 377.

168. Institute for Public Policy Research, *op. cit.*, Chapter 9, ss. 108–12.

169. H. Kennedy, Women at the Bar, *Counsel*, February 1991. The same point is made by Clare Dyer, Raw deal for sisters in law, *Guardian*, 15 May 1991.

170. 1990 Act, ss. 64–5.

171. *Toronto Star*, 15 February 1990. However, Wilson J enjoyed some support in the press. The *Toronto Star* welcomed her remarks in an editorial on 17 February 1991, which compared the lecture favourably with the performance in the previous week of a Quebec judge, who was reported as having said that 'Rules are like women, they are made to be violated.'

172. Institute for Public Policy Research, *op. cit.*, Chapter 9, s. 109.

173. Wade and Bradley, *op. cit.*, Chapter 18.

174. *Ibid.*, p. 375.

175. Human Rights Bill 1992 (introduced by Mr Graham Allen, 16 June 1992). See especially clause 4(2). But cf. his Human Rights (No. 3) Bill 1993, cl. 4(2).

8

Democracy and a Bill of Rights: Some Lessons from Ireland

C. A. Gearty

At times, judges proclaim that they are not making law but declaring what the law is. Rubbish! Every invocation of the Constitution means judge-made law. The Constitution means what the judges say it means.

Mr Justice McCarthy, Member of the Irish Supreme Court, 1982–92[1]

INTRODUCTION

In recent years, support for a bill of rights for Britain has been gathering momentum. The reform has long been favoured by those who occupy the centre ground in British politics, and it has regularly appeared in the programmes of the various parties that have at one time or another represented this interest.[2] These traditional protagonists have now been joined by many in the Labour Party; indeed the deep antipathy that that Party used to show towards such a reform has been supplanted by a keen enthusiasm for individual liberty,[3] and this has helped to push the question of a bill of rights high up the Party's internal agenda. Even the Conservative Government has sought to adopt the terminology of bills of rights, with the promulgation of a series of 'citizens' charters' being one of the central commitments of John Major's administration.[4] A similar broadening of support can be seen among the senior judges, where Lord Scarman's long but for many years lonely advocacy[5] has now been joined by such distinguished figures as Lord Bridge,[6] the new Lord Chief Justice Lord Taylor[7] and the recently appointed Master of the Rolls Sir Thomas Bingham.[8] The proposal enjoys wide support among public lawyers in academia[9] and at the bar.[10] The pressure groups are coalescing around the idea, with Charter 88's highly successful campaign[11] now being matched by Liberty's renewed commitment to its version of the same reform.[12] Indeed, reflecting this new consensus, the debate is increasingly about which bill of rights to adopt, what method of entrenchment to deploy and how much - or how little - power to give to the judges. The argument about substance is increasingly taken for granted. Even the obstacle of parliamentary sovereignty, once thought to be if not insuperable then at least enormously difficult,[13] is now dismissed with a wave of the hand and a casual reference to *Factortame*[14] or the judicial oath.[15]

There are three reasons in particular why the idea of a bill of rights has recently come to seem so attractive. First, for civil libertarians the 1980s provided an appalling demonstration of just how weak the British constitutional system was when faced with a strong government whose political agenda was clearly inimical to traditional concepts of liberty and freedom.[16] At its very least, a bill of rights appears to its advocates to offer a new judicial barrier against the repetition of such authoritarianism. Allied to this perspective is the view that the economic difficulties confronting Britain in the 1990s are directly linked to the failure of the nation's institutions and that their solution now requires a fresh start in constitutional as well as in political terms. For such reformers, a bill of rights would be valuable both in itself and as part of a wide-ranging package of radical change.[17] Second, there is an argument based on comparison between Britain and its main trading and political allies, most of whom have constitutional arrangements that explicitly protect human rights. In its weakened economic state, Britain is in no mood to be proud of its apparent isolation; what thirty years ago was proof of superiority is today further evidence of inefficient eccentricity.[18] Finally, there are the United Kingdom's various 'national questions', including in particular Northern Ireland, where support for a bill of rights has been expressed across the political divide,[19] but also Scotland and Wales, in the propitiation of each of whose separatist instincts a bill of rights may yet play a vital part.

In all this excitement about a bill of rights, little attention has been paid to what such a reform would be expected to achieve. There is a general sense that it would improve 'the culture of liberty'[20] in traditional civil libertarian areas such as expression, assembly, association and liberty. Whether this is true or not (and much would depend on how such a bill was phrased and on how it was interpreted by the judges), it is clear from the experience of other common law jurisdictions that judicially enforceable bills of rights have a habit of spreading their influence well beyond the realm of individual liberty. The best-known example of this came during the era of 'Lochnerism' in the United States, when a profoundly conservative federal Supreme Court used the Constitution's Fifth Amendment to block socially progressive legislation for over thirty years.[21] The experience of Canada with its recently entrenched Charter of Rights has also drawn attention to the dynamic dimension of a rights document, with dramatic decisions on such diverse issues as Sunday trading, abortion, cigarette advertising and sex equality demonstrating that bills of rights can quickly grow in directions not foreseen by their sponsors.[22]

The Republic of Ireland presents a third example of this general truth, but one that is much less well known in Britain. This is somewhat surprising, because Ireland's experience with its bill of rights is particularly relevant to the British debate. The Republic was part of the United Kingdom until 1922 and as a result its legal culture is closer to England's than that of perhaps any other jurisdiction (including Scotland). Ireland introduced its judicially enforceable bill of rights as part of a general constitutional settlement in 1937.[23] Its provisions were expressly designed to be superior to ordinary legislation and were imposed on an essentially British-style system combining common law and parliamentary sovereignty.[24] The judges who first interpreted the bill of rights were trained in English attitudes of deference to Parliament just as British judges (and to a lesser extent British students) still are today. So the fifty-six years of Ireland's experience with its bill of rights present the best available laboratory conditions as to what might happen in the UK. In this chapter, I am concerned with describing and assessing the impact of Ireland's bill of rights on the nation's industrial, economic and labour policies and on other areas of its public policy, including property ownership and education. I shall not be dealing with the more traditional areas of civil liberties, such as due process[25] or the freedoms of expression and assembly;[26] nor will I discuss those aspects of the Irish Constitution that reflect Ireland's overwhelmingly Catholic ethos.[27] The concern is with the unexpected rather than with the mainstream, but, as we shall see, it is the 'unexpected' in areas that might well be included in any bill of rights that is adopted in the United Kingdom.

THE EARLY CASES

The first case to raise the compatibility of a legislative provision with Ireland's brand new bill of rights was *The Pigs Marketing Board* v *Donnelly (Dublin) Ltd*,[28] decided on 30 March 1939. The plaintiffs were a statutory body corporate with responsibility for fixing the price of pigs. Pursuant to this power, the Board were entitled by legislation to levy charges on bacon manufacturers who paid less than a proper price (determined by the Board) for their produce. Acting under this provision, the Board launched legal proceedings against the defendant Company for the recovery of £14,712 3*s*. 7*d*. This very large sum relative to the Irish economy at the time shows the extent to which the Board's activities were distorting a very depressed market. The defendants raised many objections to the Board's planned course of action, including the argument that the legislation was inconsistent with the guarantee of the right to property contained in Ireland's new Constitution, then barely fifteen months in operation. At first glance this contention seemed solidly based. According to article 43, the 'State acknowledge[d] that man, in virtue of his rational being, [had] the natural right, antecedent to positive law, to the private ownership of external goods'[29] and that 'accordingly' the state guaranteed 'to pass no law attempting to abolish the right of private ownership or the general right to transfer, bequeath, and inherit property'.[30] The legislation in issue before the court empowered what was argued to be effectively a confiscation of the defendant's earned income.

This was not how the High Court judge who decided the case, Hanna J, saw the facts. Rejecting the defendant's constitutional submissions, he drew attention to the remaining clauses in article 43. These recognized that 'the exercise of the rights mentioned in the foregoing provisions of this Article ought, in civil society, to be regulated by the principles of social justice'[31] and that the state could 'as occasion requires delimit by law the exercise of the said rights with a view to reconciling their exercise with the exigencies of the common good'.[32] It is interesting to note that, as is so often the case with bills of rights in practice rather than in theory, the issue before Hanna J boiled down to one of judgment as to what was meant by such typically vague phrases as 'the principles of social justice' and 'the exigencies of the common good'. Hanna J refused even to countenance a judicial role in the matter. Noting that the pigs and bacon industry was 'of great importance, not only as providing a staple article of food in various forms for the citizens, but an industry which, both in home consumption and export [was] of considerable value,'[33] the judge went on to declare his firm 'opinion that the Oireachtas [the Irish Parliament] must be the judge of whatever limitation is to be enacted'[34] in the name of the common good in this area. As for the term 'social justice',

> I cannot define that phrase as a matter of law . . . As to the meaning of social justice, opinions will differ even more acutely than on the question of 'good government' [a phrase to be found in Ireland's earlier constitution]. I cannot conceive social justice

> as being a constant quality, either with individuals or in different States. What is social justice in one State may be the negation of what is considered social justice in another State. In a Court of law, it seems to me to be a nebulous phrase, involving no question of law for the Courts, but questions of ethics, morals, economics, and sociology, which are, in my opinion, beyond the determination of a Court of law, but which may be, in their various aspects, within the consideration of the Oireachtas, as representing the people, when framing the law.[35]

The judicial deference so clearly articulated here by Hanna J is generally believed to have epitomized the approach of the Irish courts in the first twenty-five years of the existence of the 1937 Constitution. The orthodoxy is that the atmosphere began to change in the early 1960s, in particular with the appointment of Cearbhall Ó'Dálaigh as Chief Justice, an event which in the words of one commentator heralded 'the beginning of a new era in Irish jurisprudence'.[36] In the second edition of his important work, *Fundamental Rights in Irish Law and Constitution*, published in 1967, Professor J. M. Kelly noted that, in his view, 'judicial interpretation of the Constitution has been becoming increasingly bold'[37] during the 1960s. There is a great deal of truth in these claims. During that decade, the Irish Supreme Court handed down a series of great constitutional decisions on such questions as extradition,[38] bail,[39] natural justice[40] and the admissibility of unlawfully obtained evidence.[41] There was a strong sense of the Court finally waking up to the enormous power that had been reposed in it by the bill of rights provisions of the by now well established Constitution. In contrast, the preceding decades had seen few constitutional cases and - in the context of this paucity - many examples of Hanna J style judicial reticence.[42] The contrast in approach and style was clear to all who perused the law reports.

While all this is true, there were three important and far-reaching decisions that bucked this trend. All of them dealt with deeply political issues and were highly controversial. In combination, they serve to undermine too ready an assumption that Hanna J's approach prevailed entirely in these early years, and that, in the words of one commentator, the judges always tended 'to tiptoe gingerly around judicial review because their English common law backgrounds lead them to distrust the discretionary power involved in it'.[43] Such reticence may have been frequent but it was not invariable. The first decision was *In the Matter of Article 26 of the Constitution and in the Matter of the School Attendance Bill 1942*,[44] so called because it arose as a result of a procedure provided for in Article 26 of the Constitution, which allows the President of the state to refer to the Supreme Court any bill that he or she judges might be constitutionally suspect. The Court is required to give a conclusive ruling on the constitutionality of any such measure within a certain time limit,[45] and if the decision is that the Bill (or any part of it) is repugnant to the Constitution, then the President is required to refuse to sign the Bill into law.

The School Attendance Bill 1942 was designed to secure the attendance of children at elementary school, by compelling 'parents to send their children within the prescribed age limits to one or other of the schools' provided for in the Bill.[46] There was a strong presumption that only by going to such schools could a child be 'receiving suitable education' as required by the Bill.[47] In particular, Clause 4(1) provided that a 'child shall not be deemed . . . to be receiving suitable education in a manner other than by attending a national school . . . unless such education and the manner in which such child is receiving it have been certified . . . by the Minister to be suitable.'[48] This emphasis on compulsory state education was particularly controversial in the Ireland of the 1940s, with its emphasis on family autonomy and the authority of the Catholic Church. Reflecting its cultural background, the Constitution placed a strong emphasis on the role of the family generally and on the family in education in particular. Article 41.1 declared, first, that the 'State recognises the Family as the natural primary and fundamental unit group of society, and as a moral institution possessing inalienable and imprescriptible rights, antecedent and superior to all positive law', and, second, that the state 'guarantees to protect the Family in its constitution and authority, as the necessary basis of social order and as indispensable to the welfare of the Nation and the State'. Combined with this article were the unequivocal statements in Article 42.1 that the 'primary and natural educator of the child is the family' and that it is 'the inalienable right and duty of parents to provide . . . for the religious and moral, intellectual, physical and social education of their children'. When the Bill was referred to the Supreme Court by President Hyde under the Article 26 procedure, however, the key constitutional argument centred on Article 42.3:

> 1 The State shall not oblige parents in violation of their conscience and lawful preference to send their children to schools established by the State, or to any particular type of school designated by the State.
> 2 The State shall, however, as guardian of the common good, require in view of actual conditions that the children receive a certain minimum education, moral, intellectual and social.

The Government's case was that whilst it respected the Constitution's enshrinement of family values, the Bill was doing no more than was permitted under Article 42.3.2. Once again, as in *Pigs Marketing Board*, the case hinged on the interpretation of rather vague formulae, in this instance the notion of the guardianship of 'the common good' and the provision of a 'certain minimum education'. It was on the basis of the Government's interpretation of these phrases that the legislation had been defended when its constitutionality had been challenged in Dáil Éireann. Responding to arguments that Clause 4(1) went beyond the requirement of a 'certain minimum education', the Minister for Education Thomas Derrig assured the House that he could not 'see any Minister for Education in the near future or – [he hoped] – in the distant future, interpreting this clause, if it becomes law, in anything other than a reasonable spirit.'[49] The Minister promised the Dáil that he would 'do what he considers himself in duty bound by the Constitution to achieve, that is, to ensure that all children attending such schools shall receive a basic minimum education'.[50] The Taoiseach, Éamon de Valera, who had been largely responsible for the enactment of the Constitution some five years before, intervened in the debate at the committee stage 'to bring to the attention of the House what is in the Constitution in regard to the matter'.[51] He then argued strongly that the measure was consistent with Articles 41 and 42.[52] Interestingly, neither Derrig nor de Valera seemed alive to the fact that it was not their interpretation of the Constitution but rather that of the Supreme Court that really mattered.

The justices in that Court were far less disposed than had been Mr Justice Hanna to defer to the judgment of the legislature or the executive. While 'the State, acting in its legislative capacity through the Oireachtas, [had] power to define' the phrase 'a certain minimum education', it should in the opinion of the Court 'be defined in such a way as to effectuate the general provisions of the clause without contravening any of the other provisions of the Constitution.'[53] Clause 4 went beyond this because under it, 'a Minister . . . might require a higher standard of education than could be properly prescribed as a minimum standard under Article 43.3.2'.[54] Furthermore, 'the standard contemplated by the section might vary from child to child, and, accordingly, it [was] not such a standard of general application as the Constitution contemplate[d].'[55] For these reasons, Clause 4 was repugnant to the Constitution and the whole Bill accordingly fell. When the President's message to this effect was given to Seanad Éireann by its Cathaoirleach (or Speaker), one Senator present, a Mr Foran, intervened to ask whether it was 'permissible to make any reference to the President's message'. The succinct answer from the Cathaoirleach was 'No'.[56]

This judicial reverse has an old-fashioned ring to modern ears, and Irish education has changed radically since the 1940s. But many commentators on education policy have noted what one writer has referred to as 'the paucity of educational legislation' in the Republic and the reliance of the system 'for its mode of operation on rules, memoranda and circulars issued on the authority of the Minister for Education'.[57] It has been suggested that this method, which is of doubtful legality, may have been adopted because of the anxiety of an overcautious department not to repeat the débâcle of 1943.[58] If this is true, then the decision has had the remarkable and totally unexpected effect of driving a vital area of public policy out of the traditional forums of democratic decision-making. A Committee set up to review the Constitution recommended in 1967 that the Constitution be amended 'to eliminate the difficulty posed by the Supreme Court decision'.[59]

The second major decision from the pre-Ó'Dálaigh era is *National Union of Railwaymen and Others* v *Sullivan and Others*.[60] The origins of the case lie in the enactment of a new Trade Union Act in 1941. The legislation was a reaction to the proliferation of trade unions in the 1930s and to the many 'evil effects of secession'[61] that flowed from this state of affairs. The Bill was intended to counter this process of fragmentation, as the Minister for Industry and Commerce, Mr Sean McEntee, explained to the Dáil when he presented the Bill to the House:

> Beyond question, therefore, the present unsatisfactory position of the trade union law tends not merely to disrupt the trade union movement and to destroy sound and enlightened leadership within it, but to encourage the fomentation of the disputes, strikes and general industrial unrest. So serious had the situation become in this regard that, in 1936, the then Minister for Industry and Commerce decided that an effort should be made to deal with the evil by executive action within the trade union movement itself. He made representations to the Irish Trades Union Congress, set the position, as he saw it, before them and said that, if the Congress was unable to deal with it, the Government, in the interests of the community as a whole, would be compelled to act.
>
> As a result of my predecessor's representations, the executive of the trade union movement called a special trade union conference in April, 1936. This conference set up a commission of inquiry to report upon the trade union movement, with the following terms of reference: –
>
> (1) the amalgamation or grouping of unions analogous to, or associated with, one another, within specific industries or occupations;

(2) to set up machinery . . . of a permanent arbitral character to decide on industrial demarcation and other inter-union disputes;
(3) to advise on rules to govern applications for affiliations by organisations to
(a) Irish Trade Union Congress and
(b) trades' or workers' councils.[62]

The Minister went on to explain to the House that the commission of inquiry had reported in November 1938, but that its members had been divided as to whether to embrace radical or moderate reforms. In view of this, the Government had intervened with this Bill, which was 'a sincere attempt to do for the movement what the movement knows must be done but has been powerless to do for itself, that is, to bring about its reorganisation upon an effective and rational basis'.[63] Part 3 of the Bill provided for the establishment of a trade union tribunal with power, on the application of any trade union claiming to have organized (for the purpose of negotiating as to wages or conditions of employment) a majority of the workers of a particular class, to grant or refuse, as the tribunal might consider proper in the public interest, a determination that such a union alone (or two or more specific unions alone) should have the right to organize workers of that class. A limited right of appeal from decisions of the tribunal to a special appeal board was provided. If a determination was made in favour of a particular union, and remained unrevoked, no other union could accept as a new member any worker of the class in question. In this way, the Minister hoped that the Bill would provide the machinery 'for settling those inevitable disputes which hitherto have been a source of strife and weakness . . . and the cause of grave and serious loss to the community in general',[64] but which machinery could never have been provided by the Irish Trades Union Congress, a body 'dependent for its existence upon the voluntary adherence of organised bodies, each with their own special interests to serve.'[65] The Bill was enacted after lengthy debate in both Houses of the Oireachtas,[66] during which the question of the constitutionality of the measure never occurred to any Deputy or Senator. After the Bill had passed through the Dáil and at the end of its second stage (or reading) in the Seanad, the Minister identified five main grounds of objection to his Bill that had emerged in debate, and none of these made any reference to the Constitution.[67]

Constitutional adjudication has a momentum of its own, however, generated by a combination of determined litigants and ingenious counsel. One of the biggest employers in Ireland in the 1940s was the semi-state passenger transport company, Córas Iompair Éireann (or

CIE as it is universally known). The exclusive right to organize its workforce under Part 3 of the 1941 Act was therefore a considerable prize, and after the Irish Transport and General Workers' Union (ITGWU) had submitted an application to this effect to the tribunal established by the Act, its British-based rival, the National Union of Railwaymen (NUR), launched High Court proceedings in which it sought a declaration that the whole procedure set out in Part 3 was constitutionally invalid. It relied on Article 40.6.1, which declared, *inter alia*, that the 'State guarantees liberty for the exercise . . . subject to public order and morality . . . of . . . the right of the citizens to form associations and unions'. For its part, the state drew attention to the acceptance in the same clause that laws 'may be enacted for the regulation and control in the public interest of the exercise of the foregoing right'. Gavan Duffy J was faced in the High Court with an inquiry, which as far as he was concerned far too closely resembled politics to be the subject matter of legal proceedings:

> I think the attack on the statute by the NUR is really intended to defeat a legislative policy which it mislikes, but this Court is concerned exclusively with the legal objections raised. Policy is emphatically within the legislative, as distinct from the judicial, domain. The ingenious method adopted by the Oireachtas, for strengthening the power of workmen (and the method applies to masters), by making the body representative of the majority of men in a class as effective as possible, seems in fact well calculated to achieve its purpose, but, if that method looked most unpromising, a Court of law would have no right to express any disapproval of the policy behind the plan. I am not concerned with the wisdom of the measure.[68]

As for the invitation to consider 'the public interest', Gavan Duffy J's response was similar to that of Hanna J in *Pigs Marketing Board*:

> Let us see what the Oireachtas has done. The Constitution declares that laws may be enacted for the regulation and control in the public interest of the exercise of the citizens' right to form associations and unions. In passing the Act of 1941, Parliament therefore had to consider the public interest and it proceeded, in relation to trade unions, to pass an Act to confer an organising privilege on the stronger union or unions, representing classes of workers and to create, *ad hoc*, a body qualified to adjudicate the monopoly to those who ought to have it; that is the regulation and control that commended itself to the Oireachtas in the public interest.[69]

Taking his cue from the legislature, Gavan Duffy J upheld the constitutionality of the Act. The Supreme Court, in a short single judgment[70] delivered by Murnaghan J, disagreed. The Court was unequivocal in the assertion of its own power:

> Constitutions frequently embody, within their framework, important principles of polity expressed in general language. In some Constitutions it is left to the Legislature to interpret the meaning of these principles, but in other types of Constitutions, of which ours is one, an authority is chosen which is clothed with the power and burdened with the duty of seeing that the Legislature shall not transgress the limits set upon its powers.[71]

In the exercise of their burdensome authority, the Court proceeded to strike down the whole of Part 3. 'Both logically and practically, to deprive a person of the choice of the persons with whom he will associate, is not a control of the exercise of the right of association, but a denial of the right altogether.'[72] Furthermore, it seemed 'impossible to harmonise' the 'emphatic' language of the Constitution on the question of freedom of association 'with a law which prohibit[ed] the forming of associations and unions, and allow[ed] the citizen only to join prescribed associations and unions'.[73] Whatever the legal merits of the Supreme Court's judgment, and it has been sharply criticized,[74] the decision was, in the words of the leading historian of the period, 'arguably contrary to any enlightened longer term concept of the national interest'[75] but was one to which the government 'had to adapt'.[76] In a similarly understated way, the former Chairman of the Labour Court, writing for publication in 1954, recalled that the powers given to the tribunal by the 1941 Act had not been 'arbitrary innovations' but had been 'effected in pursuance of a policy an important part of which . . . has been declared by the Supreme Court to be repugnant to the Constitution'.[77] Since it was decided, and in a way that resembles the earlier decision of the Court in *In re the School Attendance Bill 1942*, *NUR* v *Sullivan* has cast a debilitating shadow over trade union reform in Ireland, narrowing the options of policy-makers in a way that has no real connection with the contemporary public interest.[78]

The same is certainly true of our third and final decision from the supposedly quiescent era of Irish constitutional law, *Educational Company of Ireland Ltd and Others* v *Fitzpatrick and Others (No. 2)*.[79] Like *Sullivan*, the case is concerned with industrial relations and labour law, although the statute in issue, the Trade Disputes Act 1906, predated the 1937 Constitution and had been carried forward into the new legal regime. Fitzpatrick was the General Secretary of a trade union of which the other defendants (who were employees of the plaintiff company) were also members. The company had nine non-union employees on its books, all of whom had consistently refused the defendants' suggestion that they become members. The defendants sought to get the company to compel the nine to fall into line by threatening them with the sack if they continued their stand against membership. The company refused to do this, whereupon the defendants went on strike and began a picket of the plaintiff's premises. The company then sought an injunction restraining the picketing. In the High Court, it was accepted that the picketing was unlawful unless a trade dispute as defined in the 1906 Act existed, and that on the facts before the Court there was such a trade dispute. Matters would have ended there in the old Ireland of parliamentary sovereignty. But, as we have already seen in *Sullivan*, the union had to contend with Article 40.6.1's declaration that the state guarantees 'liberty for the exercise of the . . . right of the citizens to form associations and unions' subject to a proviso that laws 'may be enacted for the regulation and control in the public interest of the exercise of the foregoing right'.

On the basis of this Article, Budd J decided that to the extent that the provisions of the 1906 Act authorized a trade dispute to coerce persons to join a union against their will, the Act was void as being inconsistent with the 1937 Constitution. The judge took an expansive approach to the relevant words of Article 40:

> Taking the language of the Article quoted in its ordinary meaning it will be noted that what the State guarantees is 'liberty' for the exercise of the right of the citizens to form associations and unions. If it is a 'liberty' that is guaranteed, that means that the citizen is 'free' to form, and I think that must include join, such associations and unions, and, if he is free to do so, that obviously does not mean that he *must* form or join associations and unions but that he *may* if he so wills. Apart from authority, therefore, I would myself construe the words of the Article as meaning by implication that a citizen has the correlative right not to form or join associations or unions if he does not wish to do so, and it seems to me to follow that in the case of associations or unions already formed he is free to associate or not as he pleases.
>
> Fortunately I do not have to approach a construction of the relevant provisions of Article 40 of the Constitution *de novo*.[80]

The judge then turned to the *Sullivan* decision, from which he drew support for his interpretation. That he should have been anxious for judicial authority to be on his side is hardly surprising, given that he has applied a doubly creative touch to Article 40.6.1, reading in first a right to join as well as to form associations and then, having established this, manufacturing a further constitutional dimension to this already broadened provision in the form of a supposedly 'correlative right' not to join such bodies. But the power of precedent is as strong in constitutional adjudication as it is elsewhere in any common law system, and eccentric decisions on human rights can reverberate through the law reports for decades. Thus, towards the end of his judgment, Budd J laid down the law in the following way:

> I hold, therefore, in accordance as I believe with the views of the Supreme Court, that under the Constitution a citizen is free to join or not to join an association or union as he pleases. Further, that he cannot be deprived of the right to join or not to join such association or union as he pleases (subject always to the limitations in the Constitution, not relevant to this case) and that is tantamount to saying that he may not be compelled to join any association or union against his will.[81]

On appeal, the Supreme Court by a majority of three to two[82] upheld Budd J's decision to issue an injunction, with the majority asserting that the constitutional 'right of citizens not to join associations or unions if they did not so desire' existed by 'necessary implication'.[83] The three majority judgments emphasized the importance of *Sullivan*, which was 'most relevant, and very much in point, and [was] in support of the plaintiffs in this action'.[84] It was left to the two dissentients to point out that the case raised 'issues of far-reaching importance in the field of industrial relations in this country'[85] and that the decision of the majority threatened '[c]ollective bargaining between employers and employees', which was 'recognised as essential in the times we live in' and which through the 'organisations of capital and labour ha[d] done much to solve social and economic problems'.[86] In a very important passage in his dissenting judgment, the outgoing Chief Justice, Maguire CJ, drew attention to the gap that had developed between the purpose that lay behind Article 40.6.1 and how it had come to be interpreted by the judges:

> When our Constitution was enacted there can have been few voters who were unaware of the aims and objects of trade unions. It must have been well known to most intelligent voters that the trade unions had won recognition of their right, when engaged in collective bargaining, to use the weapon of the strike and the

right to picket in furtherance of a trade dispute . . . I must say that it came as a surprise to me that it should be contended that our Constitution had by implication withdrawn from the protection of [the 1906] Act a dispute of this nature to the extent that peaceful picketing could not be employed to further it.

Had the Constitution made no mention of trade unions I would find it difficult to accept the contention that it was the intention of the Dáil who framed the Constitution or of the people when enacting it that recognised trade union activity should be subject to any restraints to which they were not then subject. To my mind it would require clear and unambiguous language to bring about such a result. The Constitution, however, does mention trade unions. In my opinion, they were the main, if not the only, type of union contemplated in Article 40.6.iii. This sub-Article guarantees the right of the citizen to form associations or unions. When the Article goes on to say that 'Laws, however, may be enacted for the regulation and control in the public interest of the exercise of the foregoing right,' I have no doubt that it was trade unions which the framers of the Constitution and those who enacted it had principally in mind. Yet it is contended that in this sub-Article was concealed a provision which . . . deprives the trade unions of the right to use peaceful picketing in an effort to induce workers to join a particular union. This extraordinary result was achieved, it is submitted, by the force of the very provision of the Article which was designed to make clear that trade unions were accepted, and not alone accepted, but guaranteed protection.[87]

The majority decision was of course greeted with surprise and anger among trade unionists. In the ironical words of one dispassionate scholar, the Supreme Court had shown 'a rather surprising eagerness to second-guess the government as to when freedom of association is "in the public interest" '[88] and (the author went on) it was 'a pity that such judicial creativity should be spent in a field so unfruitful'.[89] Writing in the *Irish Jurist* a few years after the decision, J. B. McCartney reported that the case was 'so damaging to trade union interests that various remedies [had] been considered in trade union circles', but as the author ruefully noted, 'As this is a decision of the Supreme Court on a constitutional provision, only an amendment to article 40 can set it aside – and this requires a referendum', something which he believed was 'hardly in the realm of practical politics'.[90] After the decision, the Government consulted with the Irish Congress of Trade Unions and set up a working party to see how the right to picket to enforce union membership could be restored without being again struck down by the courts. A bill resulted from the working party's efforts, but it was never introduced.[91] Once again, as with *Sullivan*, there is a powerful sense of the Constitution closing off the options and restricting the field of policy debate in a highly artificial way. The judges' view of human rights, no matter how politically controversial it might be, sets the parameters within which the legislature must thereafter learn to act. What makes *Fitzpatrick* particularly extraordinary is the way in which the judges engaged in such creative analysis to achieve their ends. At very least, it can hardly be argued of this case (as it might be with, for example, *In re the School Attendance Bill 1942*) that the Constitution's words compelled the result. That Ireland's labour law is now dominated by its Constitution is well illustrated by the following comments from a leading scholar, made in the context of an article on a proposal to introduce a right to strike into Irish law:

> Just as after 1875 when the battleground shifted to the law of tort after the freedom to take industrial action had been insulated from the criminal law, so too today we run the risk of seeing the battleground shift to constitutional law after the right to strike and take industrial action has been insulated from the civil law. Here, in the event of any conflict between the statutory right and the constitutional rights of other persons - whether they be employers, other employees or innocent third parties - the statutory protection would have to submit.[92]

The author concludes that 'the right to strike must be enshrined in the Constitution',[93] though it may be that McCartney's comment in the context of *Fitzpatrick* that this is 'hardly in the realm of practical politics' applies here as well.

CONFIDENT JUDICIAL ACTIVISM

The Supreme Court decision in *Fitzpatrick* was handed down at exactly that moment in which the Court itself was in transition, with Maguire CJ about to make way for the new Chief Justice Céarbhall Ó'Dálaigh. Ó'Dálaigh's membership of the majority in that decision is a sharp reminder that the judicial activism for which he will be forever remembered could have negative consequences for the political left as well as for the better-known target of executive power. The case that more than any other has come to epitomize the judicial transformation of the 1960s, and that set down the foundations for the subsequent increasing confidence of the judges in the political sphere, is *Ryan* v *Attorney-General*.[94] The judicial creativity displayed by Kenny J in the High Court is reminiscent of Budd J's daring in *Fitzpatrick*. After extensive debate and study, and acting on the basis of recommendations in a report from the Fluorine Consultative Council, the Oireachtas had in 1960 enacted the Health (Fluoridation of Water Supplies) Act. The legislation set up a scheme for the fluoridation of water supplied to the public by sanitary authorities. A report by the Medical Research Council soon followed on the incidence of dental caries in the Dublin area and, after this was presented to the Oireachtas, the Fluoridation of Water Supplies (Dublin) Regulations 1962[95] were brought into force, introducing fluoridation into Dublin water for the first time. The plaintiff, a mother of five children, challenged the constitutionality of the relevant provisions of the 1960 Act. Her main argument was that the Act infringed Article 40.3 of the Constitution:

> 1 The State guarantees in its laws to respect, and, as far as practicable, by its laws to defend and vindicate the personal rights of the citizen.
> 2 The State shall, in particular, by its laws protect as best it may from unjust attack and, in the case of injustice done, vindicate the life, person, good name, and property rights of every citizen.[96]

Clearly there was nothing here specifically covering the risks of fluoridation. In the High Court, however, Kenny J considered that Article 40.3.1 related 'not only to the personal rights specified in [the rest of Article 40] but to those specified personal rights *and* other personal rights of the citizen which have to be formulated and defined by the High Court'.[97] These unenumerated rights included 'all those rights which result from the Christian and democratic nature of the State',[98] and these in turn included a 'right to bodily integrity' that could be applied to the facts before him. This did not, however, mean that the plaintiff was successful in her challenge to the legislation:

> None of the personal rights of the citizen are unlimited: their exercise may be regulated by the Oireachtas when the common good requires this. When dealing with controversial social, economic and medical matters on which it is notorious views change from generation to generation, the Oireachtas has to reconcile the exercise of personal rights with the claims of the

> common good and its decision on the reconciliation should prevail unless it was oppressive to all or some of the citizens or unless there is no reasonable proportion between the benefit which the legislation will confer on the citizens or a substantial body of them and the interference with the personal rights of the citizen.[99]

Both Kenny J's reasoning and the result which it led him to were upheld when the case reached the Supreme Court.[100] The deference that the judges were willing to accord to the Oireachtas was qualified by their insistence on having the last word where oppressiveness or the lack of reasonable proportionality (both as defined by themselves) were in issue. Thus, in this case, Kenny J rejected the Attorney-General's argument that he should not hear evidence on the dangers of fluoridation because the Oireachtas had already made a conclusive judgment on this point.[101] As a result, there were sixty-five days of argument in the High Court in which witnesses from as far afield as the United Kingdom, South Africa and Italy replayed for the benefit of Kenny J the arguments that had led to the enactment of the 1960 Act. Even before the Supreme Court hearing, the cost to the state of its successful defence of the action in the High Court was put at £28,000 by the Minister for Health, Mr McEntee.[102] The Minister emphasized that costs had been awarded against the plaintiff and that the Chief State Solicitor intended to seek recovery of the sums involved.[103] Some hint of the irritation felt in government circles at the action can be gleaned from a curious exchange in the Dáil in which a question from a Government backbencher about the extra costs (reputed to be a further £20,000) involved in the Supreme Court appeal was disallowed by the Ceann Comhairle as relating to a matter that was *sub judice*.[104] This prompted the opposition to condemn the question as a 'dirty device of a planted question to denigrate the courts',[105] which in turn provoked the Ceann Comhairle to declare that the 'courts are open to every member of the public to take a case.'[106] There can be little doubt that the civil service and the executive were at least aggravated at seeing the policies they had guided through the legislature being reopened in the judicial forum in such detail and at such a cost of time and money.

Of the many examples of judicial activism that have filled the Irish law reports since this and the other path-breaking decisions of the mid-1960s, three categories of case law in particular are relevant to our present inquiry, dealing as each of them does with public policies traditionally believed to be within the exclusive preserve of the legislature. These cases have had far-reaching implications for the state's policies on, respectively, taxation, rates and rent control. As regards taxation, the leading decision is *Murphy and Murphy* v *Attorney-General*.[107] The Irish income tax system discriminated against married couples: by restricting their allowances in comparison with two unmarried people; by causing them to reach higher tax thresholds more quickly than two unmarried people; and by causing them to start paying tax at a lower income level than two unmarried people.[108] The Supreme Court held that this system violated the Constitution's pledge that the state would 'guard with special care the institution of Marriage, on which the Family is founded' and furthermore that it would 'protect [the family] against attack'.[109] The Court recognized that the state conferred 'many revenue, social and other advantages and privileges on married couples and their children', but held that these did not compensate for or justify the 'breach of the pledge by the State to guard with special care the institution of marriage'.[110]

This judgment may be thought entirely fair and just, but it had two interesting consequences. First, the question of who else was to benefit from the decision became an immensely important and complicated one, the Court holding that though the relevant statutory provisions were void *ab initio*, the plaintiffs could recover tax refunds only from the tax year 1978–9, and other couples would only be able to recoup from the tax year 1980–1,[111] or an earlier year if they had commenced proceedings therein.[112] The logical problems in thus recognizing the effects of a void Act, or a 'zombie Act' as one writer has called it, have been drawn attention to by scholars,[113] and the Court's arguments about waiver and laches are not wholly convincing. (The Minister for Finance estimated in a written parliamentary answer that the cost to the exchequer would be in the region of £44 million if the decision were to apply generally for the two years 1978–9 and 1979–80.[114]) Second, the success of the Murphys led many other litigants to try their luck with the same sort of arguments, and the result was that for much of the following decade the state found itself regularly in court fighting analogous cases.[115] Although it is usually on the winning side, there is, as *Ryan* demonstrated, a cost to the state in terms of time and energy in even successful defences of constitutional challenges.

The second important area of judicial involvement, in the agricultural rating system, might also be thought to have produced an undeniably fair result. In *Brennan and Others* v *Attorney-General*,[116] the plaintiffs were members of an unincorporated association of Wexford farmers under the auspices of the Wexford branch of the Irish Farmers' Association (IFA). They were all holders of agricultural land and as such their property was subject to the poor law valuation (PLV). This valuation was of vital importance since it was on its basis that the plaintiffs were assessed for income tax, rates and other revenue obligations. The problem was with how the PLV for each property had been arrived at. It was the result of the Griffith Valuation, a massive bureaucratic exercise that had involved the valuation of the whole island's agricultural land and had taken fourteen years to complete, from 1852 to 1866. At the start of the valuation exercise, there had been a depression in Ireland, with the result that the valuations done during the early part of the fourteen year period had tended to be low. By the same token, the revival of agricultural prices in the 1860s saw an increase in the valuation of property covered at this point in the project. Add to this structural problem the inevitable fact that, despite all central control, different valuers applied their discretion in different ways, and it was obvious that almost before it was completed the Griffith Valuation was riddled with inequalities, oddities and discriminations. The Valuation Act 1852, on which the exercise was based, had envisaged a general re-evaluation from time to time,[117] but this had never occurred and the inequalities had simply been exacerbated with time.

All of this was uncontroversial and had been accepted by government and the civil service for many years. The Commissioner for Valuation in Ireland had admitted as early as May 1897 that the system was so out of date he could not defend it.[118] In 1902, the Royal Commission on Local Taxation had reported that 'the valuation ha[d] become quite out-of-date'[119] and had called for a general revision, adding that it was 'not easy to exaggerate the importance of "fair, uniform and accurate valuation as a preliminary to any just distribution of the burdens of local administration" '.[120] The PLV had few if any defenders, but equally there were few if any politicians or civil servants willing to grasp the issue and come up with a better scheme. So the unfair valuations survived decade after decade, more through the lethargy of central government than through any belief in their merit. The question before Barrington J in the High Court was not whether the system was 'shot through with unnecessary anomalies and inconsistencies'[121] – everyone agreed that it was – but whether it was also unconstitutional. The plaintiffs' principal arguments were that the system amounted to both an 'arbitrary and unjust discrimination' contrary to Article 40.1 and a violation of two elements of Article 40.3, namely its protection of property rights and its 'guarantee of basic fairness of procedures in legislation'.[122]

Evidence from farmers, an expert property valuer, soil scientists, a farm consultant, auctioneers and statisticians convinced the judge that 'the existing valuation system [did] not provide a uniform system for valuing lands throughout the State'; that 'there [was] no consistency between county and county or within individual counties'; and that 'the valuation system [had] failed to reflect changing patterns of agriculture with the result that land which modern agriculturalists would regard as good land often carrie[d] a low valuation while land which modern agriculturalists would regard as inferior often carrie[d] a higher valuation.'[123] While recognizing that the court 'should not enter on a consideration of the relative merits of different forms of taxation'[124] and that 'so far as revenue and fiscal statutes are concerned . . . the courts should be extremely slow to interfere',[125] Barrington J observed that this case was none the less concerned with problems that were 'simpler, and, perhaps more important: problems of measurement'.[126] The plaintiffs were legitimately able to complain that the effect of the statute was 'to freeze them in a situation of inequality'.[127] Furthermore, the legislation violated their property rights under Article 40.3. If such legislation were introduced today, linked in the same way to mid-Victorian values, then Barrington J had no doubt that it would be viewed as 'so eccentric and ludicrous that the courts would have . . . no difficulty in holding that it failed to respect the property rights of individual farmers'.[128] The Supreme Court upheld Barrington J's judgment on a different ground and restricted its decision to one based on Article 40.3. It is hard to resist the conclusion that in this case the courts took on the responsibility of compelling the Oireachtas to react to the recommendations of a Royal Commission which the courts felt justified in believing had been inappropriately ignored.

Much more controversial than either *Murphy* or *Brennan* were the cases falling within our third category of decisions with public policy implications, namely the judgments on rent control that were handed down by the courts at the start of the 1980s. With these decisions, members of the Oireachtas were left in no doubt as to where ultimate power resided in the Irish system of government. In *Blake and Others* v *Attorney-General*,[129] a challenge was mounted by aggrieved landlords to the constitutionality of rent restriction legislation that had originated in emergency measures taken during the First World War but that had remained a feature of Irish law in various legislative guises ever since. The legislation in issue was the Rent Restrictions Act 1960,[130] the principal provisions of which were described in the following terms by McWilliam J when the case came before him in the High Court:

> Part II of the Act restricts the amount of rent which may be charged to tenants of controlled dwellings, and Part IV restricts the right of a landlord of a controlled dwelling to recover possession of it on determination of a tenancy. Controlled dwellings include all dwellings other than those within the exceptions

> enumerated in s. 3 of the Act. Essentially, the Act now applies to various categories of dwellings having rateable valuations up to and including rateable valuations of £60, £40 and £30 respectively in Dublin and Dún Laoghaire, and up to and including rateable valuations of £40, £30 or £20 respectively elsewhere, which have been constructed before the 7th May 1941.[131]

The effect of the legislation was to fix rents by reference to the rents applicable in earlier generations, usually the 1940s, and to allow a tenant's family to retain possession of a property on the death of the tenant, while all the time retaining the landlord's traditional liability for repairs. In such a system, and it was estimated that some 45,000–50,000 dwellings were involved,[132] there were inevitable anomalies. McWilliam J drew attention to one property 'let at a controlled rent which, if normal repairs were carried out, would leave the landlord sustaining a net loss of £35 per annum'[133] and to another 'with tenants in occupation at rents which produce a reasonable return on the purchase price, although nothing like the return which could be obtained in the open market'.[134] The judge concluded that it was 'clear that, in certain circumstances, the effect of the provisions controlling rents and restricting the right of a landlord to obtain possession can have the effect of preventing a landlord from obtaining in the foreseeable future any benefit at all from his property; and that, in all the instances, it must prevent him from enjoying the normal benefits which he would have were there no restrictions'.[135] Turning to the constitutional question, the learned judge summarized the plaintiffs' claim as being that the legislation 'represents an unjust attack on . . . property right . . . that is not regulated by any principle of social justice, and is without any occasion now arising which requires that the exercise of their property rights be delimited with a view to reconciling their exercise with the exigencies of the common good'.[136] The judge acknowledged that he had been 'furnished with a number of the reports of commissions of one sort or another', which indicated that there was 'a considerable body of opinion to the effect that the controls imposed by the Rent Acts are not benefical for the provision of housing for the community generally', but that these did not appear . . . to be relevant to the present proceedings', which were 'confined to a consideration of the direct effects of the Act and its compliance or non-compliance with the provisions of the Constitution'.[137] A review of Irish and American case law led the judge to the conclusion that the legislation failed the constitutional test in that 'a group of citizens arbitrarily selected ha[d] been deprived of property for the benefit of another group of citizens without compensation, with no limitation on the period of deprivation, and with no indication of any occasion which necessitate[d] their selection for this purpose from amongst the general body of citizens.'[138] Both parts of the Act were accordingly struck down.

The case was immediately appealed to the Supreme Court by an Attorney-General acting on behalf of an anxious government. While it was proceeding, a private member's motion on the reform of rent control law was debated in Dáil Éireann,[139] during which the Deputy who had introduced the motion was interrupted by An Leas-Cheann Comhairle (the Deputy Speaker) when seeking to outline his proposals for reform of the law: 'I am sorry, but I am afraid the Deputy is getting into the area of the Supreme Court appeal. I would ask the Deputy to keep away from that subject. That is the understanding that we have.'[140] The Supreme Court decision shortly after this parliamentary ruling confirmed McWilliam J's judgment and held that both parts of the 1960 Act violated Article 40.3.2's guarantee to protect 'as best it may from unjust attack . . . [the] property rights of every citizen'. It was 'apparent that in this legislation rent control [was] applied only to some houses and dwellings and not to others; that the basis for the selection [was] not related to the needs of the tenants, to the financial or economic resources of the landlords, or to any established social necessity; and that, since the legislation [was] now not limited in duration, it [was] not associated with any particular temporary or emergency situation.'[141] In the opinion of the Court, the impugned provisions restricted 'the property rights of one group of citizens for the benefit of another group . . . without compensation and without regard to the financial capacity or the financial needs of either group' and without any time limit or other opportunity for reviewing the legislations; they were therefore unconstitutional, being both 'unfair and arbitrary'.[142]

In a concluding passage under the heading 'further observations', the Supreme Court considered the effect that its judgment would have:

> This decision has the effect that a statutory protection which many thousands of families relied on for the continuance of the existing tenancies in the dwellings in which they live is no longer available to them. A ruling of this nature on the constitutional validity of a particular statutory provision usually exhausts the functions of this Court. In this instance, however, because of the special features of the case and the consequences involved, the Court considers that some further observations are called for.
>
> The removal from the affected tenants of the degree of security of possession and of rent control which they hitherto enjoyed will

> leave a statutory void. The Court assumes that the situation thereby created will receive the immediate attention of the Oireachtas and that new legislation will be speedily enacted. Such legislation may be expected to provide for the determination of fair rents, for a degree of security of tenure and for other relevant social and economic factors. Pending the enactment of such legislation as may be decided upon, it may be possible in many cases for agreement to be reached between landlords and tenants. Where, however, such agreement is not possible, either because of the tenant's inability to pay the rent demanded or because of the landlord's determination to recover possession, considerable hardship would be caused in certain cases if possession were obtained by the ejectment of the tenant. This Court does not wish to pre-empt or prejudge any situation of litigation that may flow from this judgment. It desires to emphasise, however, that it is the duty of the Courts to have regard to the basic requirements of justice when exercising their jurisdiction. In this regard, in the reasonable expectation of new legislation, when a decree for possession is sought, the court should, where justice so warrants, in a case where the now condemned provisions of Part IV would have given a defence against the recovery of possession, either adjourn the case or grant a decree for possession with such stay as appears proper in the circumstances.[143]

The Oireachtas did not need this judicial hint to realize the extent of the crisis that the Court had precipitated. There was general agreement that legislation was now necessary, 'a statutory void having been torn in the legal system by its own judgment'.[144] Within three weeks, the Rent Restrictions (Temporary Provisions) Act had been enacted, passing through all its stages in the Dáil and the Seanad without amendment in a single day in each House.[145] The Minister of State at the Department of the Environment, Mr Fergus O'Brien, described the bill as 'an emergency measure designed to deal with an immediate and acute social problem within the confines set by the Supreme Court decision'.[146] The legislation was needed to protect the tenants exposed by the ruling, many of whom were 'elderly or otherwise among the poorer sections of the community'.[147] The opposition spokesman described the judgment as having 'the potential of being the single biggest element of social distress ever arising from a court decision'.[148] The emergency Act had a life-span of no more than six months, so the question of a more permanent response to the judgment remained. Later in the year, the Housing (Private Rented Dwellings) Bill was passed by both Houses.[149] The Bill implemented the change to market rents for previously controlled dwellings that the Supreme Court had insisted on, but sought to ameliorate the worst consequences of this by providing for a phasing-in period of five years, during which a rebate was to operate to allow the rent payable by tenants to reach the market level gradually. The Minister of State at the Department of the Environment, Mr Creed, explained to the Dáil that the 'advice to the Government [was] that the formula for fixing rents together with the rebate provisions [was] consistent with the Constitution and the Supreme Court decision'.[150] The Bill represented a 'balanced approach to a difficult legal area'.[151]

The rebate element led some deputies and commentators to believe that the Bill might still be constitutionally suspect, and so it proved when it was referred to the Supreme Court by the President under Article 26. In its judgment delivered on 19 February 1982, the Court declared the Bill repugnant to the Constitution.[152] The rebate system and five-year implementation period 'clearly constitute[d] an unjust attack upon [the landlords'] property rights',[153] since for this number of years the landlords were 'to receive an amount which will be substantially less than the just and proper rent payable in respect of their property'.[154] The Court recognized that 'hardship may be caused to some tenants' as a result of its ruling, but in an extraordinary and thinly veiled threat to the legislature the Court went on to say that on 'the assumption that undue hardship is likely to be caused in some instances, a question may arise whether such hardship would amount to an unjust attack upon the property rights of a tenant contrary to Article 40.3 of the Constitution, or would amount to an unjustifiable treatment of such tenant in contravention of Article 40.1 of the Constitution'.[155] While not considering the matter further, the Court noted that 'having regard to the obligation imposed on the State by the Constitution to act in accordance with the principles of social justice, the Court recognise[d] the presumption that any such hardship [would] be provided for adequately by the State'.[156] The judges might not have been actually writing the next financial budget for the Minister of Finance, but they were informing him of a large part of its content.

In Spring 1982, the issue was back in the Oireachtas, with the legislature 'faced once again with the urgent need to enact law to prevent the dire consequences, recognised by all, that would occur if the legislative vacuum that has been created is not filled'.[157] A fresh Housing (Private Rented Dwellings) Bill, tailored to suit the judges, was passed by both Houses and signed into law by the President without a further Article 26 reference to the Supreme Court. During the debate on the Bill in Dáil Éireann, a senior spokesman for the

Labour Party, Mr Ruari Quinn, declared 'on behalf of [his] Party' that 'members of the Supreme Court ha[d] disgraced themselves in so partially interpreting the Constitution.'[158] An interesting exchange then developed as Mr Quinn continued:

> We could be coming back to the House day after day with different Bills trying to get around the Constitution. As long as we have Supreme Court judges so biased in their defence of property rights and in defence of people who own property we will always end up with this kind of situation.
>
> The nub of the problem is not the legislative inventiveness of the civil servants, the Opposition or the members of the Government. The nub of the problem is not even our Constitution but the bias in the property interpretations of members of the Supreme Court interpreting the Constitution . . .
>
> *An Leas-Cheann Comhairle*: The deputy will appreciate that I have allowed him a certain latitude. We must not challenge the decisions of the courts in the House.
>
> *Mr Quinn*: Maybe it is about time we did.[159]

Mr Quinn was alone in his effort to focus attention on the Court. His remarks drew strong criticism from all sides of the House and were implicitly disowned by his own Party leader, Mr Dick Spring, who assured the House of his belief that the Article 26 judgment was 'soundly on the basis of law'.[160] The cost to the exchequer of covering the increase to tenants who were judged to be worthy of the receipt of allowances to help them pay was estimated by the Minister for the Environment to be in the region of £6 million,[161] but he later assured Senators that 'the Government [would] provide whatever funds [were] needed to finance the allowance schemes'.[162]

CONCLUSION

It would be churlish to deny that the Irish Constitution as it has been interpreted by the country's judges has achieved great improvement in many areas of civil liberties. But in order properly to evaluate the impact on Irish society of the bill of rights provisions in the 1937 document, it is important to take into account the whole picture. This chapter has sought to show that such a picture necessarily includes important but unexpected judicial forays into the economic, social and industrial arenas. It would not be appropriate to explain away such decisions as unique to Ireland or as peculiar to a bill of rights that it alone has adopted. While it is true that certain of the clauses in the 1937 document, in particular those on the family and Christian values, are rooted in a very particular society at a particular time, the provisions that have given rise to the litigation discussed here have a uniformly contemporary ring. Thus Articles 40.3 and 43 on property rights mirror the guarantee to be found in the First Article of the First Protocol to the European Convention on Human Rights and Fundamental Freedoms:

> Every natural or legal person is entitled to the peaceful enjoyment of his possessions. No one shall be deprived of his possessions except in the public interest and subject to the conditions provided for by law and by the general principles of international law.
>
> The preceding provisions shall not, however, impair the right of a State to enforce such laws as it deems necessary to control the use of property in accordance with the general interest or to secure the payment of taxes or other contributions or penalties.[163]

In a way that brings the *School Attendance Bill 1942* case sharply to mind, the First Protocol also declares that 'No person shall be denied the right to education' and that in the 'exercise of any functions which it assumes in relation to education and teaching, the State shall respect the right of parents to ensure such education and teaching in conformity with their own religious and philosophical convictions'.[164] This clause has led many commentators in Britain to the view that public policy on private education has been narrowly circumscribed by its terms.[165] Similarly, Article 11 of the Convention proper guarantees freedom of association and this has led the European Court of Human Rights to produce its own version of *Fitzpatrick*.[166] Even if there were not such uncanny resemblances between the two documents, the Irish bill of rights would stand for a more general truth, namely that such documents are dynamic instruments whose meaning cannot of their very nature be pinned down or delimited in advance.

Three further points on the Irish experience may be made by way of conclusion. First, while it is true that 'very few enactments of any significance have been struck down',[167] it is the case that in the important decisions that we have examined here, there has been a pronounced antipathy, informed by the provisions of the bill of rights, towards collectivism or indeed any form of communal enterprise perceived by the judges to be at the expense of the individual. This is hardly surprising given that by definition a bill of rights on the liberal model is based on the assumption that the individual needs to be defended against state action. In this sense a bill of rights is nothing more or less than traditional anti-state liberalism written in constitutional stone and handed to the judges for protection. In many ways more interesting than the cases that have been litigated are the pieces of legislation that have not been enacted or have been enacted differently on account of a fear of litigation. It has long been believed that the property guarantees in the Constitution have had a baleful influence on planning and land-use law, and a former Secretary to the Department of Finance, who is also a retired Governor of the Central Bank, Mr T. K. Whitaker, wondered aloud in a Seanad debate on the Constitution in 1981 whether the 'Constitutional protection of private property also needs review . . . so that, for instance, effective restraints may be placed on the inordinate private profit that can be made out of land required for housing and other community needs.'[168]

Second, because the vindication of these liberal interests takes place in court and is achieved through the language of human rights, it often follows that close attention is not paid to the economic and social costs that flow from such decisions. It seems crass and ill-mannered to talk of the 'cost' of protecting 'human rights', and judges – at least in Ireland[169] – rarely if ever do. Thus, in the cases discussed here, including in particular *Murphy*, *Brennan* and *Blake*, the courts displayed no knowledge of, or even interest in, the cost to the exchequer of its decisions. It may be correct to observe, as one commentator has of the rent restriction cases, that it 'should have been borne more strongly in mind by the Courts . . . that many landlords of controlled dwellings had purchased these premises subsequent to the coming into operation of the rent restrictions regime and the price paid reflected this fact'.[170] Rights adjudication tends to reach the moral high ground, but at the expense of the full policy picture.

Finally, it is said in the courts' defence that they are merely filling gaps left open by the inability of the legislature to deal adequately with many policy issues. As Professor Casey has remarked, it 'is a matter for regret that the imperfect functioning of our political system requires the courts to play so positive a role; but that until the system is altered, that role appears to be essential'.[171] There is a lot to be said for this argument. Certainly it is hard to argue with the justice of the outcome of at least the *Murphy* and *Brennan* cases. But it begs an important question as to who is stimulating this gap-filling. There are lots of deficiencies everywhere one looks in all systems of government and that overseen by the Oireachtas is no exception. The question of which gaps to fill and when is itself a political issue, the resolution of which has much to do with the imposition of politicial muscle and the bringing to bear of effective pressure for change. The judicial stimulation of the Oireachtas to fill certain legislative gaps is in some ways a hijacking of the political agenda of gap-filling. Why should such a power be made to depend on the vagaries of litigation, particularly when the effect of this is further to favour the deep pockets and articulate power of those groups already favoured by the democratic process? It is not accidental that the chief beneficaries of this judicially stimulated 'gap-filling' should have been employers, farmers and landlords. Furthermore, relying on the courts in this way can have a stultifying impact on a legislature, providing what Professor Casey has called 'an excuse for inertia'[172] and what Mr Justice Keane has described as the 'all purpose justification' offered by 'the more inert section of our public service' to the unsuitably reform-minded politician, namely that 'we could run into trouble with the Constitution, Minister'.[173] But perhaps the most disturbing aspect of all is the silence that surrounds the judicial law-making that we have encountered in this article. From the inability of Senator Foran to comment on the Supreme Court decision in the *School Attendance Bill* case right through to Mr Quinn's failure to focus attention on the judges after the rent control decisions, the story is one of judicial aloofness secured and protected by parliamentary deference, of courts insulated by convention from any recognition that their decisions are simply part of the political process. It took one of their own number, the late Mr Justice McCarthy to destroy this silencing myth of legality, when he pithily uttered the declaration with which this chapter began: 'The Constitution means what the judges say it means.'[174]

NOTES

1. To do a great right, do a little wrong (1987) 6 *Journal of the Irish Society for Labour Law* 1, at p. 1.
2. See most recently Liberal Democratic Party, *'We the People . . .' – Towards a Written Constitution* (Federal Green Paper No. 13, 1990).
3. Labour Party, *The Charter of Rights: Guaranteeing Individual Liberty in a Free Society* (1991). The Party did not commit itself to a judicially enforceable bill of rights in the period before the 1992 General Election, partly at least because of the hostility to the idea shown by its then deputy leader Roy Hattersley: see Hattersley, A fatally flawed approach to protecting fundamental liberties, *Independent*, 4 May 1989.
4. *The Citizen's Charter* (Cm 1599, 1991).
5. See in particular Sir Leslie Scarman, *English Law: The New Dimension* (1974).

6. See his dissenting speech in the first *Spycatcher* case, *Attorney-General* v *Guardian Newspaper Ltd* [1987] 3 All ER 316.

7. Lord Taylor declared his support for a bill of rights in the course of his Dimbleby Lecture, broadcast on BBC 1 on 30 November 1992. For a full report, see *Guardian*, 1 December 1992.

8. Sir Thomas Bingham's point of view emerged in the course of a debate on a bill of rights for Britain held at the Annual Conference of the Bar in September 1992: see *Guardian*, 28 September 1992.

9. The literature is surveyed in D. Oliver, *Government in the United Kingdom: The Search for Accountability, Effectiveness and Citizenship* (Milton Keynes, 1991), Chapter 9. For a dissenting view see K. D. Ewing and C. A. Gearty, *Freedom under Thatcher: Civil Liberties in Modern Britain* (Oxford, 1990), Chapter 8.

10. A. Lester, Fundamental rights: the United Kingdom isolated [1984] PL 46.

11. Charter 88, *New Statesman and Society*, 2 December 1988.

12. Liberty, *A People's Charter* (1991).

13. *Report of the House of Lords Select Committee on a Bill of Rights* (HL 176).

14. *R* v *Transport Secretary, ex parte Factortame (No. 1)* [1989] 2 WLR 997; *R* v *Transport Secretary, ex parte Factortame (No. 2)* [1990] 3 WLR 818.

15. H. W. Wade, *Constitutional Fundamentals* (1980).

16. See G. Robertson, *Freedom, the Individual and the Law* (6th edn, earlier editions by Harry Street, Harmondsworth, 1989); P. Thornton, *Decade of Decline: Civil Liberties in the Thatcher Years* (1989); Ewing and Gearty, *op. cit.*

17. Institute of Public Policy Research, *The Constitution of the United Kingdom* (1991).

18. A. Lester, *op. cit.*

19. See the annual reports of the Standing Advisory Commission on Human Rights, most recently the Seventeenth Report, for 1991–2 (1992). See, in particular, Standing Advisory Commission on Human Rights, *The Protection of Human Rights by Law in Northern Ireland* (Cmnd 7009, 1977).

20. See R. Dworkin, *A Bill of Rights for Britain* (1990).

21. The story is well told in A. Cox, *The Court and the Constitution* (Boston, 1987), Chapters 6–9.

22. See generally M. Mandel, *The Charter of Rights and the Legalization of Politics in Canada* (Toronto, 1989).

23. For the background, see D. Keogh, The constitutional revolution: an analysis of the making of the constitution, in F. Litton (ed.), *The Constitution of Ireland 1937–1987* (Dublin, 1987), pp. 4–84.

24. For the failure of the 1922 Constitution of the Irish Free State to function as a Constitution in anything other than name, see J. P. Casey, *Constitutional Law in Ireland* (1987), Chapter 1.

25. See Casey, *op. cit.*, Chapter 14.

26. There is a very good general survey of this ground in R. F. V. Heuston, Personal rights under the Irish Constitution (1976) 11 *Irish Jurist* (n.s.) 205.

27. G. W. Hogan, Law and religion: church–state relations in Ireland from independence to the present day (1987) 35 *American Journal of Comparative Law* 47.

28. [1939] IR 413. *In re P.C., G.C. and C.C. Arranging Debtors* [1939] IR 306 appears before *Pigs Marketing Board* in the law reports for 1939, but judgment was handed down on 26 April.

29. Article 43.1.1.

30. Article 43.1.2.

31. Article 43.2.1.

32. Article 43.2.2.

33. *Op. cit.*, pp. 418–19.

34. *Ibid.*, p. 422.

35. *Ibid.*, p. 418.

36. G. Hogan, Irish nationalism as a legal ideology (1986) 75 *Studies* 528, at p. 532, quoted with approval by B. Chubb, *The Politics of the Irish Constitution* (Dublin, 1991), p. 65.

37. J. M. Kelly, *Fundamental Rights in the Irish Law and Constitution* (2nd edn, Dublin, 1967), p. 25.

38. *The State (Quinn)* v *Ryan* [1965] IR 70.

39. *The People (Attorney-General)* v *O'Callaghan* [1966] IR 501.

40. *McDonald* v *Bord na gCon* [1965] IR 217.
41. *The People (Attorney-General)* v *O'Brien* [1965] IR 142.
42. See e.g. *Fisher* v *Irish Land Commission and the Attorney-General* [1948] IR 3; *Comyn* v *Attorney-General* [1950] IR 142; *The State (Crowley)* v *Irish Land Commission and the Lay Commissioners* [1951] IR 250; *Foley* v *Irish Land Commission and the Attorney-General* [1952] IR 118. In 1952, the anonymous reviewer of two new works by O. Hood Phillips on the United Kingdom's constitutional law had 'the greatest confidence in recommending them to the profession in Ireland': 17 *Irish Jurist* 59, at p. 60.
43. L. Beth, *The Development of Judicial Review in Ireland 1937–66* (Dublin, 1967), p. 3.
44. [1943] IR 334.
45. The Court must give its decision in a single judgment within sixty days of the reference.
46. [1943] IR 334, at p. 342 *per* Sullivan CJ giving the judgment of the Court.
47. Clause 4(1).
48. *Ibid.* Clause 4(2) set out the provisions relating to the issuance of ministerial certificates under clause 4(1).
49. Dáil Éireann Parliamentary Debates, vol. 88, col. 2119 (18 November 1942).
50. *Ibid.*
51. *Ibid.*, col. 2120.
52. *Ibid.*
53. [1943] IR 334, at p. 345, *per* Sullivan CJ giving the judgment of the Court.
54. *Ibid.*
55. *Ibid.*
56. The exchange is at Seanad Éireann Parliamentary Debates, vol. 27, col. 1845 (20 April 1943).
57. J. C. Coolahan, *Irish Education: Its History and Structure* (Dublin, 1981), at p. 159, quoted in Casey, *op. cit.*, at p. 521.
58. W. N. Osborough, Education in the Irish law and constitution (1978) 13 *Irish Jurist* (n.s.) 145, at p. 174.
59. Report of the Committee on the Constitution (Dublin, Pr. 9817), para. 133.
60. [1947] IR 77.
61. Dáil Éireann Parliamentary Debates, vol. 83, col. 1539 (4 June 1941). Mr McEntee.
62. *Ibid.*, cols 1540–1.
63. *Ibid.*, col. 1548.
64. *Ibid.*
65. *Ibid.*
66. The second stage of the Bill is at: Dáil Éireann Parliamentary Debates, vol. 83, cols 1535–68 (4 June 1941); 1584–683 (5 June 1941). The Bill was debated in committee in Dáil Éireann on 24 June, 25 June (two sittings), 26 June, 1 July, 2 July (two sittings), 3 July (two sittings), 4 July and 8 July 1941. The debate on the final stages is at vol. 84, cols 1562–707 (15 July 1941) and cols 2114–79 (22 July 1941). The nine-hour debate on the second stage of the Bill in Seanad Éireann is at Seanad Éireann Parliamentary Debates, vol. 25, cols 2257–401 (7 August 1941). The committee proceedings in the second chamber are at *ibid.*, cols 2484–528 (13 August 1941) and 2531–624 (14 August 1941). The debate on the final stages of the Bill are at *ibid.*, cols 2646–719 (20 August 1941).
67. Seanad Éireann Parliamentary Debates, vol. 25, col. 2384 (7 August 1941). There was one prophetic note of dissent from this consensus: a leading article in the *Irish Law Times and Solicitors' Journal* queried the constitutionality of Part 3 of the Bill: see (1942) 76 ILTSJ 15.
68. [1947] IR 77, at p. 86.
69. Ibid., p. 90. See the same judge's further elaboration of this theme of judicial deference in *Fisher* v *Irish Land Commission and the Attorney-General*, *op. cit.* See also G. M. Golding, *George Gavan Duffy (1882–1951)* (Naas, 1982), Chapter 11.
70. Under Article 34.4.5 of the Constitution, Supreme Court decisions on the validity of legislation enacted after the introduction of the Constitution must contain only a single judgment.
71. [1947] IR 77, at p. 99.
72. *Ibid.*, p. 102.

73. *Ibid.* Cf. *Tierney* v *Amalgamated Society of Woodworkers* [1959] IR 254.

74. Casey, *op. cit.*, p. 474; G. Whyte, Industrial relations and the Irish constitution (1981) 16 *Irish Jurist* (n.s.) 35.

75. J. J. Lee, *Ireland 1912–85: Politics and Society* (Cambridge, 1989), p. 290.

76. *Ibid.*

77. R. J. P. Mortished, Irish trade union law, in R. King (ed.), *Public Administration in Ireland* (vol. 3, Dublin, Civics Institute of Ireland, 1954), p. 176.

78. See J. P. Casey, Reform of collective bargaining law: some constitutional implications (1972) 7 *Irish Jurist* (n.s.) 1; G. Whyte, *op. cit.*

79. [1961] IR 345. The High Court decision was handed down on 17 June 1960. The Supreme Court gave its decision on 13 December 1961. For a precursor of the decision see *Brendan Dunne Ltd* v *W. J. Fitzpatrick and Others* [1958] IR 29. For subsequent cases, see *Murtagh Properties Ltd* v *Cleary* [1972] IR 330; *Meskell* v *CIE* [1973] IR 121.

80. *Ibid.*, p. 362. Italics in the original.

81. *Ibid.*, p. 365.

82. The statute in question having been passed before the adoption of the 1937 Constitution, the requirement of a single judgment decision did not apply.

83. [1961] IR 345, at p. 395 *per* Kingsmill Moore J.

84. *Ibid.*, p. 405 *per* Haugh J.

85. *Ibid.*, p. 376 *per* Maguire CJ.

86. *Ibid.*, p. 384 *per* Lavery J.

87. *Ibid.*, pp. 379–80.

88. Beth, *op. cit.*, p. 57.

89. *Ibid.*, p. 59.

90. J. B. McCartney, Strike law and the constitution (1964) 30 *Irish Jurist* 54, at p. 60.

91. *Report of the Committee on the Constitution*, *op. cit.*, para. 120.

92. A. Kerr, Industrial action: rights or immunities (1986) 5 *Journal of the Irish Society for Labour Law* 7, at p. 18.

93. *Ibid.*

94. [1965] IR 294. The High Court decision in the case was handed down on 31 June 1963, with the Supreme Court decision following on 3 July 1964.

95. SI no. 75 of 1962.

96. Mrs Ryan also claimed that the Act infringed the authority of the family guaranteed by Article 41 and the family's right to the physical education of its children under Article 42. Both these contentions were rejected in the High Court and the Supreme Court.

97. [1965] IR 294, at p. 311. Italics in the original.

98. *Ibid.*, p. 312.

99. *Ibid.*, pp. 312–13.

100. See in particular *ibid.*, pp. 344–5.

101. *Ibid.*, p. 314.

102. Dáil Éireann Parliamentary Debates, vol. 205, col. 1221 (12 November 1963).

103. *Ibid.*, cols 1221–2.

104. *Ibid.*, col. 1222.

105. *Ibid.*

106. *Ibid.*

107. [1982] IR 241.

108. The latter anomaly had been rectified by the Finance Act 1978.

109. Article 41.3.1.

110. [1982] IR 241, at p. 287 *per* Kenny J giving the judgment of the Court.

111. The Supreme Court judgment was handed down on 25 January 1980.

112. *Ibid.*

113. See Casey, *op. cit.*, p. 291, whose phrase it is.

114. Dáil Éireann Parliamentary Debates, vol. 322, col. 2318 (26 June 1990). Mr O'Kennedy.

115. *H* v *Eastern Health Board* [1988] IR 747; *Hyland* v *Minister for Social Welfare and the Attorney-General* [1989] IR 624; *MacMathuna* v *Ireland and the Attorney-General* [1989] IR 504; *Greene* v *Minister for Agriculture and Others* [1990] 2 IR 17; *Browne* v *Attorney-General* [1991] 2 IR 58.

116. [1983] ILRM 449 HC; [1984] ILRM 355 SC.

117. Section 34.
118. [1983] ILRM 449, at p. 470, *per* Barrington J.
119. *Ibid.*, p. 454.
120. *Ibid.*, quoting from the Report of the Royal Commission.
121. *Ibid.*, p. 469.
122. *Ibid.*, p. 456.
123. *Ibid.*, p. 469.
142. *Ibid.*, p. 478.
125. *Ibid.*
126. *Ibid.*
127. *Ibid.*, p. 483.
128. *Ibid.*, p. 486.
129. [1982] IR 117. For the background to the case and an excellent general treatment of this area, see G. McCormack, Blake-Madigan and its aftermath (1983) 5 DULJ (n.s.) 205.
130. As amended by the Rent Restrictions (Amendment) Act 1967 and the Landlord and Tenant (Amendment) Act 1971.
131. [1982] IR 117, p. 120.
132. *Ibid.*, p. 127 *per* O'Higgins CJ giving the judgment of the Supreme Court.
133. *Ibid.*, p. 120.
134. *Ibid.*
135. *Ibid.*, p. 122.
136. *Ibid.*, p. 123.
137. *Ibid.*
138. *Ibid.*, p. 126.
139. Dáil Éireann Parliamentary Debates, vol. 328, cols 2691–725 (12 May 1981); 2848–78 (13 May 1981).
140. *Ibid.*, col. 2701.
141. [1982] IR 117, p. 138 *per* O'Higgins CJ giving the judgment of the Court.
142. *Ibid.*, pp. 139–40.
143. *Ibid.*, pp. 141–2.
144. Dáil Éireann Parliamentary Debates, vol. 329, col. 394 (9 July 1981). Mr John Kelly, TD, Minister for Industry, Commerce and Tourism.
145. The Dáil debates are at: Dáil Éireann Parliamentary Debates, vol. 329, cols 376–409; 451–3 (9 July 1981). The Seanad debates are at Seanad Éireann Parliamentary Debates, vol. 95, cols 2263–92 (16 July 1981).
146. Dáil Éireann Parliamentary Debates, vol. 329, col. 377 (9 July 1981).
147. *Ibid.*, col. 378.
148. *Ibid.*, col. 380. Mr Raphael Burke.
149. The Dáil debates are at: Dáil Éireann Parliamentary Debates, vol. 331, cols 1373–414; 1484–511 (9 December 1981) [second stage]; *ibid.*, cols 2036–9 (15 December 1981) [committee and final stages]. The Seanad debates are at Seanad Éireann Parliamentary Debates, vol. 96, cols 160–73 (17 December 1981). The Bill was passed without amendment in either House.
150. Dáil Éireann Parliamentary Debates, *ibid.*, col. 1379 (9 December 1981).
151. *Ibid.*, col. 1380.
152. *In the Matter of Article 26 of the Constitution and in the Matter of the Housing (Private Rented Dwellings) Bill* [1983] IR 181.
153. *Ibid.*, p. 191 *per* O'Higgins CJ giving the judgment of the Court.
154. *Ibid.*
155. *Ibid.*
156. *Ibid.*, p. 192.
157. Dáil Éireann Parliamentary Debates, vol. 333, col. 1119 (31 March 1982). Mr Raphael Burke, Minister for the Environment.
158. *Ibid.*, col. 1130.
159. *Ibid.*, col. 1131.
160. *Ibid.*, col. 1246 (1 April 1982).
161. *Ibid.*, col. 1268. Mr Raphael Burke.
162. Seanad Éireann Parliamentary Debates, vol. 97, col. 502 (6 April 1982).

163. For examples of what are usually unsuccessful attempts to raise this clause, see *James* v *United Kingdom* (1986) 8 EHRR 329; *Allgemeine Gold- und Silberscheideanstalt* v *United Kingdom* (1986) 9 EHRR 1; *Gillow* v *United Kingdom* (1986) 11 EHRR 335; *Mellacher* v *Austria* (1989) 12 EHRR 391; *Hakansson and Sturesson* v *Sweden* (1990) 13 EHRR 1; *Pine Valley Developments Ltd* v *Ireland* (1991) 14 EHRR 319. Cf. *Darby* v *Sweden* (1991) 13 EHRR 774.

164. Article 2.

165. See e.g. Independent Schools Information Service, *Independent Schools: The Legal Case* (a joint opinion by Anthony Lester QC and David Pannick, with a foreword by Lord Scarman, ISIS, 1991).

166. *Young, James and Webster* v *United Kingdom* (1981) 4 EHRR 38.

167. Mr Justice Keane, Property in the constitution and in the courts, in B. Farrell (ed.), *De Valera's Constitution and Ours* (Dublin, 1988), 137, at p. 145. The author was referring specifically to property decisions but the point is equally valid for social and economic legislation.

168. Seanad Éireann Parliamentary Debates, vol. 96, col. 174 (9 October 1981). For an interesting critique of the property provisions of the Constitution, see Mr Justice Keane, Land use, compensation and the community (1983) 18 *Irish Jurist* (n.s.) 23. Note, however, that recent decisions indicate that in exceptional circumstances, compensation may not be required for the taking of land: *Dreher* v *Irish Land Commission* [1984] ILRM 94; *ESB* v *Gormley* [1985] IR 129; *O'Callaghan* v *Commissioner for Public Works* [1985] ILRM 364.

169. The US Supreme Court permits the filing of 'Brandeis briefs' dealing with the anticipated consequences of its decisions in constitutional adjudication.

170. G. McCormack, *op. cit.*, p. 214.

171. J. Casey, The development of constitutional law under Chief Justice O'Higgins (1986) 21 *Irish Jurist* (n.s.) 7, at p. 34.

172. J. Casey, Government and polities in the Irish Republic: judicial activism and executive inertia, in B. Hadfield (ed.), *Northern Ireland: Politics and the Constitution* (Buckingham, 1992), 165, at p. 169.

173. Mr Justice Keane, The constitution and public administration: accountability and the public service, administrative law and planning law, in Litton (ed.), *op. cit.*, 128, at p. 141.

174. Mr Justice N. McCarthy, *op. cit.*

9

Who Can Remedy Human Rights Abuses? The 'State Action' Question

Michael Forde

When foreign lawyers who take an interest in constitutional law matters visit Ireland, one of the first questions they ask is our position regarding the 'state action' issue. If they are German or Austrian, or are familiar with constitutional affairs in those countries, they probably describe it as the *Drittwirkung* question. How this matter has been dealt with by the Irish courts is indeed interesting because the issue is one which arises in every state that adopts a Constitution providing for human rights protection enforceable through the courts.

'STATE ACTION'

The traditional view of constitutional rights and obligations is as follows. A constitution is a form of social contract that binds together the community. Under this contract, all agree to accept majority rule provided that several institutional safeguards are adhered to. For instance, there must be periodic general elections, a fair electoral system, independent courts and laws that are of general application and ordinarily apply prospectively. In modern times many constitutions go further than this. As well as laying down a structure through which persons are to be governed, they go on to proclaim certain human rights. The characterization of those rights varies: they may be called 'civil rights', 'human rights', 'civil liberties' or 'fundamental rights', as they are in the Irish Constitution.[1]

What these rights are designed principally, if not exclusively, to achieve is to protect the individual against the state. *Habeas corpus* ensures that one is not unlawfully locked up in a prison, police station or mental institution.[2] Freedom of expression provides some protection against state censorship and the persecution of individuals expressing views that are unpopular with government. Private property rights ensure that the state or local authorities do not take away property except for some justifiable public purpose and, ordinarily, on payment of reasonable compensation. Accordingly, one of the fundamental conditions of the Irish social contract or Constitution is the acceptance of majority rule on condition that this majority respects the various fundamental rights set out in Articles 40 to 44 of the Constitution.

The classic state action doctrine holds that the duty to respect these rights is an obligation on the state - and *only* on the state. That is to say, the various fundamental rights do not impose obligations on private individuals and organizations. As far as they are concerned, once they comply with the common law and statutory requirements, they have done all that the law can expect of them. But they are not directly bound by the Constitution, which binds only government, including local government and all other public or governmental agencies. Under this view of constitutional obligation, to cite a few examples:

- A Jew goes to buy land but the owner will not sell on account of the intending buyer's religion. Despite the principle of religious freedom,[3] the Constitution does not prevent the landowner from discriminating among potential purchasers of land on account of their religious beliefs or affiliations, though discrimination along these lines might be proscribed by legislation.[4]
- A woman goes to join a golf club but is refused admission, being informed that she should try the 'lady membership system'. Despite the guarantee of equality before the law,[5] the state action principle holds that her constitutional right to equality is not infringed - unless the golf club was owned by Dublin or Cork Corporation or some other public body.
- A person with very strong political views who vigorously expresses them loses his job on account of his opinions. Again, under the state action principle, the Constitution does not provide him with any redress. He is left to whatever claim might arise under the law of wrongful or unfair dismissal. But if the employer is a public agency, it must respect his political views within reasonable bounds. Presumably it is for this reason that most statutes dealing with public sector bodies provide that the body's employees shall take and be entitled to time off if they are elected to the Oireachtas or the European Parliament.[6]

The German word *Drittwirkung* means third-party effect. In the constitutional law context, it means the effect of the Constitution on third parties, meaning private individuals, and, in particular, whether private individuals and organizations have obligations under the

German Basic Law. Undoubtedly, private individuals and bodies have rights under that law - that is the very purpose of fundamental rights. But does the Basic Law go further and also impose Constitutional duties on individuals? Before I attempt to answer that question and address the position under the Irish Constitution, it is instructive to consider briefly the position in the United States.

THE US CONSTITUTION

In the United States, the state action question has generated a vast case law and an enormous academic literature.[7] As a recent commentator observed about another matter, this scholarly output, if shredded, would provide abundant confetti for a dozen royal weddings.[8] Even though the Irish Constitution is far from being identical to the US Constitution, it is always enlightening to see how Americans deal with any constitutional problem; for they have very able judges and the standard of legal analysis and abstract discussion is extremely high in the United States. While some might disagree with the conclusions in several of Chief Justice Rehnquist's decisions, one cannot deny his formidable mastery of the English language and ability to argue his corner most forcibly and eloquently. American constitutional practices have been influential in the evolution of Irish constitutional law and the constitutional law in many other jurisdictions. For instance, if one looks at the Irish Reports in the 1940s and 1950s, at the main constitutional cases, there is extensive citation of American decisions in the arguments of counsel and also in the judgments.

How the Americans deal with the state action question is very simple: the Constitution places duties only on the state and all public authorities, not on private individuals and bodies. This was the net issue in the famous *Civil Rights Cases*,[9] where the question to be decided was the impact of the recently enacted Fourteenth Amendment. That Amendment says: 'No state shall make or enforce any law which shall abridge the privileges or immunities of citizens . . . ; nor shall any state deprive any person of life, liberty, or property without due process of law; nor deny any person . . . the equal protection of the law.' According to Mr Justice Bradley in the *Civil Rights Cases*,

> It is state action of a particular character that is prohibited. Individual invasion of individual rights is not the subject matter of the amendment. It nullifies and makes void all state legislation and state action of any kind, which impairs the privileges and

> immunities of citizens . . . or which injures them in life, liberty or property without due process of law, or which denies to any of them the equal protection of the laws.[10]

Under this analysis, public agencies of any kind may not discriminate on the grounds of race or religion, and more recently on the grounds of sex or gender. But as far as the US Constitution is concerned, private or non-governmental racism or sexism is of no direct relevance. For instance, in 1956 when black railway workers challenged the 'whites only' membership policy of the trade union, arguing that they were being denied the equal protection of the law, the courts would not give them any redress.[11] The discrimination was being practised by a private body; it was not state action. For the very same reason, in 1972 the US Supreme Court would not intervene against the 'whites only' membership policy of the Moose Lodge.[12]

A perennial problem, of course, is drawing the line between what is state action and what is mere private or non-governmental action. This is the issue in almost all the reported cases on the topic. For instance, in 1974 the US Supreme Court was asked to decide whether the Metropolitan Edison Company, which is the privately owned and publicly regulated electricity monopoly in the New York region, was carrying out state action.[13] The Court's answer was no.

The American attitude on state action is followed in many countries that have similar constitutions. And when new Constitutions are being drafted, a major concern is whether their obligations should ever extend beyond state action. Ten years ago a charter of rights and freedoms was incorporated into the Canadian Constitution. Then in 1987 the question arose, in a case involving picketing by the retail workers' trade union, whether those guarantees applied to the actions of private sector employers and trade unions. The Canadian Supreme Court's answer was that they applied only to governmental action, in much the same way as the US Constitution applies.[14]

THE GERMAN BASIC LAW

The 'Basic Rights' provisions of the Constitution of the Federal Republic of Germany[15] have much in common with the US Constitution in that the substantive guarantees are confined to the traditional civil liberties type of rights, and the Federal Constitutional Court is empowered to invalidate any law that contravenes those guarantees. However, whereas it is accepted as axiomatic that the US Bill of Rights does not lay down standards for private conduct, this very issue has been the source of considerable dispute in the Federal Republic, and has spawned an enormous literature under what has become known as the *Drittwirkung* debate.[16]

Certain of the Basic Rights provisions suggest that the enumerated guarantees may be invoked only against governmental action of one form or another; thus, for example, Article 1(3) states that 'The following basic rights shall be binding as directly valid law on legislation, administration and judiciary', and the concluding provision, Article 19(4), that 'Should any person's rights be infringed by a public authority, he may appeal to the courts.' On the other hand, the way some of the specific rights are formulated suggests that they apply *vis-à-vis* private conduct too, most notably the trade union freedom guarantee, Article 8(3): 'The right to form associations to safeguard and improve working and economic conditions shall be guaranteed to everyone and to all professions. Agreements which seek to restrict or hinder this right shall be null and void; measures directed to this end shall be illegal.'

The formulation of certain other guarantees is capable of being construed as applying or as not applying to private conduct, for instance Article 3(2) that 'Men and women shall have equal rights.' This could be read as proscribing private discrimination; but against this, the term rights may connote legal entitlements conferred on persons by the state. It is possible, however, to find a compromise position in the Basic Law's very first clause, that 'The dignity of man shall be inviolable. To respect and protect it shall be the duty of all State authority.' Assuming that the enumerated rights are all aspects of the 'dignity of man', this provision could be interpreted as meaning that where private interferences with these rights happen without an adequate legal remedy being available to the victims, then the state is in breach of its constitutional obligations. Indeed, this argument could be extended further by saying that where such a situation is allowed to continue, the private actors may he regarded as agents of the state, which is aware of and is tolerating their activities.

Influential academic writings on the *Drittwirkung* question are divided into two major camps. There are those who contend that the guarantees – such as to sexual equality, freedom of expression, etc. – apply directly to private conduct, i.e. that private interference with these freedoms is a direct violation of the Basic Law's provisions. The opposing view, which is supported by the majority of writers, is that these provisions do not place obligations directly on individuals, but do so indirectly by filling out the general clauses of the Civil Code – most notably Article 826, which states that 'A person who wilfully causes damage to another in a manner contrary to good morals [*güte Sitten*] is obliged to compensate the other for the damage', and Article 138, which provides that 'A juristic act that is contrary to good morals is void'. Thus, to take a person excluded from a private association on account of his or her race or sex: once damage (which need not be financial) is established, this could be regarded as a wrong contrary to *güte Sitten*, the anti-discrimination provision of the Basic Law giving precise content to the 'good morals' standard. Similarly, expelling someone from an organization because of his or her religious or political opinions could, if authorized by that body's rules, be regarded as enforcing contract provisions that are against good morals. The Federal Constitutional Court and the Administrative Court have come down on the side of 'indirect' application in this way. At one time the Labour Court preferred the 'direct' approach, but more recently it has adopted the 'indirect' approach; the Federal Supreme Court in some instances has 'indirectly' applied the Basic Law, but in other cases has taken an ambiguous stance.

EUROPEAN LAW

A similar problem arises today in European Community law. This is the question of who is in effect bound by EC Directives that member states have not actually implemented into law. It has been held that neither the state nor public agencies would be allowed to, in effect, hide behind the non-implementation of a directive.[17] But as far as private individuals and bodies are concerned, an unimplemented Directive does not place any duties on their shoulders until an Act is passed or a statutory instrument is adopted to implement the Directive. For this purpose the question then arises of what is public and what is private.

The answer can be found in the leading case, *Foster* v *British Gas*,[18] which concerned the applicability of the EC Equal Treatment Directive to a Government-owned public utility, which has since passed into private ownership. In accordance with the practice in Article 177 references, the European Court of Justice did not decide that particular dispute between the parties; that is a matter for the national court, which referred the question, in the light of the answer given by the Luxembourg Court. The governing principle is that

> any body, whatever its legal form, which has been made responsible, pursuant to a measure adopted by the State, for providing

> a public service under the control of the State and has for that purpose special powers beyond those which result from the normal rules applicable in relation between individuals is included among the bodies against which the provisions of a directive capable of having direct effect may be relied upon.[19]

In the light of this principle, it was subsequently held that British Gas plc was a public body for these purposes.[20]

The issue also arises under the European Convention on Human Rights. This Convention's obligations are imposed on the several state parties, i.e. the governments that have ratified the Convention. Where then does state action end and non-governmental action begin for the purpose of state responsibility under this Convention?[21] One of the early cases is a little-known application that came from Ireland in 1970, concerning the activities of the Electricity Supply Board,[22] a publicly owned electricity-producing monopoly. The complaint concerned a trade union with which the Board would not negotiate; the Board was being accused by the applicant of wrongly discriminating against his union. In the event, it was held that the Board's policy on trade union matters did not directly implicate the Irish Government and, accordingly, the merits of the complaint could not even be considered by the Human Rights Commission.

The state action question engendered considerable debate in the substantive labour law cases decided by the Human Rights Court.[23] In the *Swedish Engine Drivers' Union* case,[24] which concerned a claim by a minority trade union to be a party to a collective agreement with the state agency that employed its members, the argument for a state action gloss on Article 11 was put eloquently by Mr Danelius, agent for the Swedish Government, and an eminent authority on the European Convention:

> Clearly this Article prevents the Government . . . from interfering with the activities of a trade union whose policy is not agreeable to the Government [and] prevents the Parliament . . . from adopting a law which prohibits trade union activities [etc.] and it also prohibits interference with trade union activities by way of judicial decisions.
>
> But does Article 11 go further than that? Does it put an obligation on the State to ensure that employers do not improperly take action which is detrimental to trade unions? Does it impose . . . an obligation to enact legislation in the field of labour law, which adequately protects trade unions against certain acts by employers or employers' associations and which protects

> employers' associations against certain acts by trade unions? Does Article 11 perhaps even cover other aspects of relations between organizations and private individuals in the labour market, for instance the relations between trade unions and their members?[25]

To take an example of particular relevance to the UK: assuming that a state party is in violation of the article where the government refuses to employ persons on account of their trade union, political or religious affiliations,[26] is the UK then in violation of the article because private employers are allowed thus to discriminate at the point of hiring?

Danelius's answer was that as regards the rights enumerated in Articles 8, 9, 10 and 11 of the Convention,

> States may be required to ensure by appropriate means that these freedoms can in fact be exercised without risk of physical harm or violent action of some kind; [but] this does not mean that State is obliged . . . to regulate various sorts of contractual relations or other private law relations between individuals. [For the] history of these rights shows that their purpose was to guarantee that the State did not, by means of legislation or otherwise, suppress or restrict the freedom of expression, the freedom of religion and the other freedoms concerned.[27]

This was their 'overriding purpose' and 'primary aim'. In support of this view, he contrasts the International Convention on the Elimination of All Forms of Racial Discrimination,[28] which by express terms reaches certain forms of private discrimination,[29] with Article 14 of the European Convention, which contains no indication of its application to relations between individuals. He then focuses on the other right referred to in Article 11, freedom of assembly, which is

> basically a right to non-interference by the public authorities. It means that no legislation may be enacted to forbid peaceful meetings or to restrict them. It also means that public authorities such as the police must not break up meetings or interfere with them in any other way. It does not, however, affect any private law relations which may exist, any agreements which may be concluded between landlord and tenant, between employer and employee and which may restrict the right to hold public gatherings in certain private premises, or, for instance, during working hours.[30]

Mr Danelius goes on to reject the conclusions *a contrario* that may be drawn from the references in Articles 8 and 10 of the European Convention to interferences by 'public authority'.[31] Those references 'may be seen merely as a clarification of the meaning of that Article, a clarification which was natural in the context but which does not justify the conclusion that the other freedom-rights . . . should also be understood as rights vis à vis private individuals.'[32] Having pointed out that reference to the *travaux préparatoires* of the UN Covenants was inconclusive on the position under the European Convention, he concluded by warning the Court of the undesirable consequences that could ensure if Article 11 was applied to private conduct; this could require that the court construct a single labour relations code for the diverse industrial relations systems in the state parties to the European Convention.

The response of the European Commission on Human Rights to these points was based mainly on the principle that treaties must be construed in the light of their objects and purposes, and that the European Convention must be interpreted in a way that makes the protection of the individual effective. Thus, in respect of Article 11,

> if unions are to achieve their purpose . . . it would be compatible with the text to provide them with some kind of protection against certain types of interference not only by the State but also by employers in which case protection would have to be ensured by legislation. . . . It is true that the Convention fundamentally guarantees traditional 'liberal' rights in relation to the State as a holder of public power. This does not, however, imply that the State may not be obliged to protect individuals through appropriate measures taken against some forms of interference by other individuals, groups, or organizations. While they themselves cannot, under the Convention, be held responsible for any such acts which are in breach of the Convention, the State may, under certain circumstances, be responsible for them. This consideration should in particular apply to Article 11 which combines the aspects of a traditional liberal right or a civil liberty and an economic right . . . Social and economic rights . . . may correspond to a duty to enact legislation to govern 'private' relations.[33]

During the oral hearings in the *Swedish Engine Drivers' Union* case the late Professor Fawcett, the Commission's principal delegate, cited the example of a trade union denying admission to applicants on the grounds of race. In his view, Article 14, the non-discrimination provision, 'would immediately come into the issue and if the state allowed this situation to continue, there would be a breach of the Convention'.[34] In the event, the Court declined to pronounce authoritatively on the state action question, given that the complaint concerned policies of the Swedish public service bargain agency and that these did not violate Article 11.

The issue was raised again in the *Young, James and Webster*, or 'closed shop', case,[35] which has close parallels with state action controversies under US constitutional law.[36] Essentially the same arguments as were made by Mr Danelius and Professor Fawcett respectively in the *Swedish Engine Drivers' Union* case were repeated before the Commission and the Court in this case. A significant twist in the case was that by the time it came before the court the pro-closed shop Labour administration had been replaced by the Conservatives, who came into office with dogmatic anti-closed shop pledges. The British representatives before the Court conceded that Britain should be held responsible under the Convention if it was shown that the applicants' dismissal constituted a 'relevant interference' with their Article 11 rights that was a 'direct consequence of' the then trade union legislation. The Court found that there was such a causal relationship and, consequently, did not have to examine the broader question. As the majority judgment put it,

> Under Article 1 of the Convention, each Contracting State shall secure to everyone within [its] jurisdiction the rights and freedoms defined in [the] Convention; hence, if a violation of one of those rights and freedoms is the result of non-observance of that obligation in the enactment of domestic legislation, the responsibility of the State for that violation is engaged. Although the proximate cause of the events giving rise to this case was the 1975 agreement between British Rail and the railway unions, it was the domestic law in force at the relevant time that made lawful the treatment of which the applicants complained. The responsibility of the respondent State for any resultant breach of the Convention is thus engaged on this basis. Accordingly, there is no call to examine whether . . . the State might also be responsible on the ground that it should be regarded as employer or that British Rail was under its control.[37]

THE POSITION OF IRELAND

What is the situation in Ireland as regards this very important constitutional law question?[38] It is fair to say that there is no leading case. There is no shortage of dicta and there are several assertions but there is no at least reported instance where this question was argued extensively and then squarely addressed by the Supreme Court, with convincing reasons given for the conclusions reached.

Nevertheless, this was a critical issue in the series of abortion or 'right to life' cases decided in recent years: *Open Door Counselling*,[39] concerning advice and referrals abroad; *Grogan*,[40] involving the UCD and Trinity students; and the '*X*' case,[41] where the Attorney-General sought an injunction to prevent a young girl from going to England for an abortion. In all those cases the defendants were private entities: a registered company, a group of students and a pregnant juvenile, respectively. What exactly does the relevant Constitutional provision, Article 40.3.3, say? The text is as follows: '*The State* acknowledges the right to life of the unborn and, with due regard to the equal right to life of the mother, guarantees *in its laws* to respect and, as far as practical, *by its laws* to defend and vindicate that right' (emphasis added). It was held by the Supreme Court that this guarantee bound private individuals and organizations an well as the state.

If any of those three cases were brought in the United States or Canada under identical wording, there can be little doubt that the defendants would have a cast iron defence. They would say, look at the wording of this clause: '*The State* acknowledges . . . and guarantees *by its laws* . . .'. We are not the state. What we are doing – disseminating information or travelling to England – cannot conceivably be regarded as a form of state activity. Mr Attorney-General (the plaintiff in the '*X*' case) or Messrs SPUC (the plaintiff in the other two cases), you have got the wrong defendants here. The constitutional duty clearly is on the state and is on it to introduce appropriate laws to protect the unborn. We are a private company or mere students or a fourteen-year-old girl, respectively, and have no real say at all in what laws can be enacted. Why then sue us? The position might be different if Article 40.3.3 said, 'Everyone shall have due respect for the unborn.' That could possibly be interpreted as imposing constitutional obligations on us as well as on the state. But when the amendment was so carefully drafted – remember the agonizing in 1983 about the wording – how could a provision that puts such emphasis on protection *by laws* impose duties on private individuals?

During the '*X*' case this argument seems to have been raised in the

Supreme Court, which at the very beginning ruled that the entire proceedings should be heard *in camera* because it involved the welfare of a child. There is no verbatim record of the arguments, let alone any written submissions as one would get in appeals to the House of Lords or the United States Supreme Court. A summary of the principal submissions made has been published[42] and the argument being considered in this chapter is recorded as follows:

> *John Rogers SC*: Referring to the eighth amendment. The eighth amendment calls on the State not to make laws authorising abortion except where the life of the mother is affected. Going beyond this, the laws must be laws of the Oireachtas, which are generally applied. I will refer to Article 13 of the United Nations Declaration on Human Rights on the right to travel. This right may be trammelled by laws which are 'prescribed'. Surely this is the hallmark of a civilised democratic system of law? Standards are prescribed by law. Fourth protocol to the European Convention on Human Rights of 16th September 1963. Again I would refer to the right to travel. Again the right is trammelled by reference to restrictions prescribed by law, for example, legislation.
>
> *Finlay CJ*: This court and a number of decisions said that legislation to protect constitutional rights is not strictly necessary – for example *Open Door Counselling* case in particular.[43]

So has this point already been decided? The previous abortion case was *Grogan*, concerning the UCD and Trinity students; the law report shows no indication of this issue being dealt with in argument or in the judgment. So back to the *Open Door Counselling* case. There is just one judgment given by the Chief Justice; the other four judges simply agreed with him. This judgment contains no reference at all, not even by oblique inference, to the state action question. The law report contains no summary of what was argued before the Supreme Court, except for a list of the various cases referred to by counsel. None of these seem to have any relevance to the state action issue. It therefore would seem that this vital question has not yet been decided in a proper manner by the Supreme Court, meaning after hearing a full legal argument on this very matter and giving a reasoned decision on the point.

There is one Supreme Court case where this very point was raised, although only one of the five judges chose to deal with the issue. In *McGrath and O'Rourke* v *Maynooth College*[44] the plaintiffs were professors in Maynooth College who were dismissed because they refused to adopt certain practices dictated by the religious nature of their employer. Maynooth is a Catholic seminary and pontifical university. They argued that they were being discriminated against on religious grounds, which is proscribed by the Constitution. Mr Justice Kenny's answer was that the guarantee of religious freedom binds only the state and does not place obligations on private bodies, not even if they obtain some state funding for their activities.[45]

So it seems that if the Supreme Court had previously decided on the state action question, it was in this case, which favoured the restrictive American approach. If that analysis had been followed in the several abortion cases it might have saved the courts a lot of trouble and placed the matter where the very words of Article 40.3.3 indicate it belongs - with the legislature, to introduce appropriate laws. Whether those laws would then be sufficient to protect the unborn could be adjudicated on by the courts, taking account of the mother's equal right to life. There would then have been no injunctions against these private individuals and bodies. *Open Door Counselling* would never have gone to Strasbourg to ventilate its grievances at the international level,[46] nor would the students in *Grogan* have brought their case to Luxembourg.[47] The Attorney-General would not have started the '*X*' case. Indeed, if there was a big abortion case, it would have been brought against the state, represented by the Attorney, the plaintiffs questioning why in the ten years since this amendment was passed no laws were ever introduced to protect the right to life of the unborn, which is stated to be so fundamental. In his judgment in the '*X*' case, the late Mr Justice Niall McCarthy's remarks about legislation were very much an understatement. He observed that

> In the context of the eight years that have passed since the Amendment was adopted and the two years since Grogan's case the failure by the legislature to enact the appropriate legislation is no longer just unfortunate; it is inexcusable. What are pregnant women to do? What are the parents of a pregnant girl under age to do? What are the medical profession to do? They have no guidelines save what may be gleaned from the judgments in this case. What additional considerations are there? . . . The Amendment, born of public disquiet, historically divisive of our people, guaranteeing in its laws to respect and by its laws to defend the right to life of the unborn, remains bare of legislative direction.[48]

During the 1970s, many Supreme Courts across the world had to address the abortion question.[49] One of these was the Austrian

Supreme Court. This is what it had to say on the state action issue in connection with abortion:

> Such a right to life [for the unborn] could, according to the provisions contained in the Constitution for protecting the rights it incorporates, only have the effect of protecting the individual against attacks on his life by the State. However, the provisions of paragraphs 96 and 97 of the Penal Code [which were being challenged in that case] do not concern an interference with life by the State.[50]

There are, however, several dicta in cases decided previously by the Irish courts which suggest that the American (and Austrian and Canadian) state action doctrine would not be followed in Ireland. There is Mr Justice Budd's statement in the *Educational Company (No. 2)* case.[51] But that case clearly involved state action – picketing which ordinarily would have been unlawful but for s. 2 of the Trade Disputes Act 1906, and was expressly legitimated by legislation. There are then the remarks of Mr Justice Walsh in the *Meskell* case.[52] But the defendant in that case was not a private individual or body; it was the state-owned public transport monopoly, Córas Iompair Éireann. A reasonable conclusion from this part of the discussion, I suggest, is that the assertion during the argument in the '*X*' case that a state action defence had already been rejected by the Supreme Court greatly exaggerates the position. At least it seems that the merits of that defence have never been fully debated in that Court and remain to be finally decided.

THE SOLUTION?

What stance should the Court take on this question? To begin with, the near-universal adoption of a state action principle in constitutional law strongly suggests that Irish courts should follow suit. The argument to the contrary would go something as follows. The Constitution recognizes and incorporates certain human rights. Those are entitlements that individuals have that must be universally respected. Those are inalienable and imprescriptable rights and it is an entirely artificial exercise to differentiate between their infringement by the state and private infringements. This is the point Mr Justice Walsh made in his remarks in the *Meskell* case: 'If the Oireachtas cannot validly seek to compel a person to forego a constitutional right, can such a power be effectively exercised by some lower body or by some individual employer?'[54] An answer to this is that, practical considerations aside, there is a huge qualitative difference between interferences with rights by public agencies and by private bodies. That case concerned the dismissal of a man who refused to remain a member of a trade union. If, under the Constitution, a public agency could dismiss persons for that reason, then as a matter of law the whole public service (about 30 per cent of the entire workforce) could be conscripted into one particular trade union. And individuals who object to that kind of practice would see their taxes being spent in maintaining it and, at the furthest theoretical extreme, could be conscripted to fight a war to defend that practice. By contrast, if one private-sector employer wants to maintain a closed shop, that is entirely his business if he can get away with it. There are enough other private employers around who are prepared to hire non-trade unionists.

Another argument against a state action principle is summed up in what Budd J said in the *Educational Company (No. 2)* case:

> If an established right in law exists the citizen has the right to assert it and it is the duty of the courts to aid and assist him in the assertion in his right. The court will, therefore, assist and uphold a citizen's Constitutional rights. Obedience to the law is required of every citizen, and it follows that if one citizen has a right under the Constitution there exists a correlative duty on the part of other citizens to respect that right and not to interfere with it. To say otherwise would be tantamount to saying that a citizen can set the constitution at nought and that a right solemnly given by our fundamental law is valueless. It follows that the courts will not so act as to permit any body of the citizens to deprive another of his Constitutional rights and will in any proceedings before them see that these rights are protected, whether they be assailed under the guise of statutory right or otherwise.[55]

An answer to this piece of logic is that to say that, under a state action principle, a 'citizen can set the constitution at nought' and that 'a right solemnly given by our fundamental law is made valueless' simply begs the question. If the right is indeed one that exists against the state and government only, how can it be devalued by not applying it against private individuals and bodies? If that right is fully applied within public authority, how can one say that it is a valueless right? Most likely after some time, when the state gets accustomed to respecting that right, it will introduce legislation to ensure that private bodies also act consistently with that right.

Another argument still is that the courts are part of the state, so that when a court upholds or condemns some practice, for instance abortion in one or other manifestation, there is state action present. That is the view expressed by the learned President of the High Court at first instance in the *Open Door Counselling* case:

> Under the Constitution . . . the State's powers of government are exercised in their respective spheres by the legislative, executive and judicial organs established under the Constitution and the courts will act and protect the rights of individuals and the provisions of the Constitution . . . the judicial organ of government is obliged to lend support to the enforcement of the right to life of the unborn, to defend and vindicate that right and if there is a threat to that right from whatever source, to protect that right from such a threat if its support is sought.[56]

An answer to this reasoning is threefold. First, as with Mr Justice Budd's statement, this surely begs the question. For if the right to life is only against public action that threatens an unborn's life the courts have no business pursuing private individuals and bodies who may pose a threat to that right. Second, if the courts are really only another arm of the state, is there not some paradox in them adjudicating disputes between individuals and the state? If the courts are part of the state, how can individuals suing the state expect to get an entirely unbiased hearing? At least the old doctrine of sovereign immunity was an entirely honest one. The courts were the King's courts so there was no point in even pretending that an individual who wanted to sue the Crown could get justice in his courts; accordingly, the sovereign could not be sued. Third, when we look at the actual wording of the abortion article in the Constitution, does it say that 'the state by its judges' shall vindicate the right to life? No, it says the very opposite; that the state 'by its laws', etc. In fact, the word 'laws' is repeated in that short article, so it must have been put in for some reason. Who knows, when the records of the Society for the Protection of the Unborn Child (the main protagonist for amending the Constitution to condemn abortion) are eventually open to the public we may very well discover that the word 'laws' was carefully chosen by their draftsman in order to ensure that Article 40.3.3 would be enforced by laws, anticipating that the legislature would then perform its constitutional duty by enacting appropriate laws – as has happened in nearly every country where the abortion question has engendered constitutional controversy.

There are also very important practical difficulties with abandoning a state action restriction on constitutional obligation. It introduces enormous uncertainty into the law. We live under it system of the rule of law, where individuals expect their legal obligations to be laid down in clear and precise laws. Obligations deriving from some vague constitutional provision are the very opposite of the rule of law. On account of the enormously powerful position the state is in, and the even greater power the state can assume for itself if it disregards accepted political conventions, it is essential that state power be constrained by constitutional guarantees. And those guarantees by their very nature must be in general terms and somewhat imprecise. But there is no great need to regulate the affairs of private individuals and bodies by way of some sweeping constitutional prescription. Laws can be enacted for that purpose. Take, for example, the question of sex discrimination, including special protection for maternity. This is a highly complex matter and in Ireland the subject of three quite lengthy pieces of legislation, along with a short measure enacted in 1919. It would be completely unacceptable to let this question be regulated entirely by the courts simply applying Article 40.1.1 (the equality guarantee) of the Constitution. Think of the unfortunate employer or employee who simply wants to know what exactly is required and will do just that for a quiet life if for no other reason.

It has never been suggested by the courts that the constitutional guarantee of equality applies to private as well as public action. But the case for such an application is far stronger. For unlike the abortion article, the equality clause in not expressed in terms of 'the state shall'; nor does it place any emphasis at all on the state dealing with the equality or non-discrimination question through 'laws'. If there is to be consistency in constitutional law, then sex discrimination throughout the private sector would seem to be unconstitutional and rules that purport to exclude women from a variety of bodies and associations are null and void, and perhaps even actionable torts. Can we now expect the Attorney-General and the courts to vindicate the right to equality, for instance, whenever a liquor license application is being heard or planning permission is being sought by a 'men only' body? Or will a state action principle be applied to the equality article. And if that is done, why should the abortion article be any different?

NOTES

1. Articles 40 *et seq.* of Constitution of Ireland. See, generally, M. Forde, *Constitutional Law of Ireland* (1987) and J.M. Kelly, *The Irish Constitution* (2nd edn, 1984).

2. Article 40.4. This procedure can also be invoked against private or non-governmental defendants since the Habeas Corpus Acts 1781 and 1816.

3. Article 44.1.
4. No such law has been enacted in the Republic.
5. Article 40.1.
6. For example, Postal and Telecommunications Services Act 1983, s. 38.
7. See, generally, L. H. Tribe, *American Constitutional Law* (2nd edn, 1988), Chapter 18.
8. Note in [1992] Cam LJ 15.
9. (1883) 109 US 3.
10. *Ibid.*, p. 11.
11. *Oliphant* v *Brotherhood of Locomotive, Firemen and Engineermen*, 262 F 2d 359; 359 US 935 (1959).
12. *Moose Lodge No. 107* v *Irvis*, 407 US 163 (1972).
13. *Jackson* v *Metropolitan Edison Co.*, 419 US 345 (1947); compare Case 188/89, *Foster* v *British Gas plc* [1990] 2 CMLR 833.
14. *Retail, Wholesale & Dept Store Union* v *Dolphin Delivery Ltd* (1986) 33 DLR. (4th) 174.
15. In S. E. Finer (ed), *Five Constitutions* (1979) pp. 195 *et seq.*
16. See, generally, K. M. Lewan, The significance of constitutional rights for private law, (1968) 17 ICLQ 571.
17. Case 152/84, *Marshall* v *Southampton and South-West Hampshire Area Health Authority* [1986] ECR 723.
18. Case 188/89, [1990] 2 CMLR 833.
19. *Ibid.*, p. 857. See, generally, D. Curtin, The province of government: delimiting the direct effect of directives in the common law context, (1990) 15 *Eur. L. Rev.* 195.
20. [1991] 2 AC 306. Contrast the *Metropolitan Edison* case, note 13.
21. See, generally, M. Forde, Non-governmental interferences with human rights, (1985) 56 BYIL 253.
22. *X* v *Ireland*, Decision of 24 July 1970 (partial) and 1 February 1971 (final); [1971] 14 YB, ECHR 188.
23. For an account of the main issues in these cases see, generally, M. Forde, The European conventions on human rights and labour law, (1983) 31 *American Journal of Comparative Law* 301.
24. [1976] 1 EHRR 617.
25. Series B, no. 18, at p. 146.
26. Cf. *City of Birmingham District Council* v *Beyer* [1978] 1 All ER 910.
27. See note 25.
28. In I. Brownlie, *Basic Documents on Human Rights* (2nd edn, 1981) pp. 150–63, Article 2(d).
29. Similarly, Article 2(e) of the UN Convention on the Elimination of All Forms of Discrimination against Women.
30. *Op. cit.*, note 25, p. 165. (But see now *Lingens* v *Austria* (1986) 8 EHRR 407.)
31. *Ibid.*, p. 165.
32. *Ibid.*, p. 166.
33. *Ibid.*, pp. 41–2.
34. *Ibid.*, p. 199.
35. (1982) 4 EHRR 38.
36. See, generally, D. H. Topol, Union shops, state action and the National Labor Relations Act (1992) 101 *Yale Law Journal* 1135.
37. *Op. cit.*, note 35, para. 49.
38. See, generally, M. Forde, *Constitutional Law of Ireland* (1987), Chapter 26.
39. [1988] IR 593.
40. [1989] IR 593.
41. [1992] 1 IR 1.
42. As part of the law report, [1991] 1 IR 1, pp. 16–41.
43. At p. 28.
44. [1979] ILRM 166.
45. *Ibid.*, p. 214.
46. (1993) EHRR 244.
47. Case C-159/60, [1991] 3 CMLR 849. See, generally, D. R. Phelan, Right to life of the unborn v promotion of trade in services: the European Court of Justice and the normative shaping of the European Union (1992) 55 MLR 670.

48. [1992] 1 IR, at p. 82.
49. See, generally, M. Cappelletti and W. Cohen, *Comparative Constitutional Law* (1979) Chapter 12.
50. Decision of 11 October 1974.
51. *Educational Co. of Ireland Ltd* v *Fitzpatrick (No. 2)* [1961] IR 345, at p. 368, quoted below.
52. *Meskell* v *CIE* [1973] IR 121, at p. 135, quoted below.
53. For example, *Murtagh Properties Ltd* v *Cleary* [1972] IR 330.
54. [1973] IR at p. 135.
55. [1961] IR at p. 368.
56. [1988] IR at p. 599.
57. In defence of the 'state action' limitation in Canadian constitutional law, see P. W. Hogg, *Constitutional Law of Canada* (3rd edn, 1992), pp. 849–50. See also P. C. Weiler, The Constitution at work: reflections on the constitutionalising of labour and employment law, 40 *U. Toronto L.J.* 117 (1990), pp. 152–5.

10

Taking on the Individual Trade Unionist: A New Emphasis in Legal Intervention

Sonia McKay

INTRODUCTION

When the Conservatives took office in 1979 the economy was in crisis. A confidential Treasury economic projection, leaked in October of that year,[1] predicted a steep decline in manufacturing over the next four years, with falls in motor vehicle production of 21 per cent by 1983 and in mechanical engineering of 23 per cent. Ministers warned that the economic outlook was bleak, at least in the short term, with national output set to fall by at least 2 per cent in the following year. For a recovery to take place a shake-up was inevitable. The government's manifesto issued a clear threat to jobs. 'Too much emphasis', it said, 'has been placed on attempts to preserve existing jobs.' Weak firms would have to go to the wall and inevitably unemployment would rise. To assist competition with other major economies, in particular that of Germany, wages would have to fall.

Union militancy was perceived as a potential opponent to such measures. Conservative party leader Margaret Thatcher, at a rally in April of that year, spoke of strikers and secondary pickets as 'wreckers', adding, 'some of these wreckers even have the law on their side and we cannot get at them'. Trade union membership had grown in the 1970s. And trade unionists had mobilized, not just out of self-interest, but in defence of other groups of workers. There were, however, obstacles to legal intervention. The Conservatives' experiences in the Government of 1970–4, with its unsuccessful attempts to reform employment law at a stroke, had convinced them of the need for what was called a 'step by step' approach. The legislative agenda would therefore proceed slowly, with its impact reviewed at each stage before further progress would be envisaged.

Since 1979 the immunities for action taken in contemplation or furtherance of a trade dispute have been greatly reduced. The purposes for which strike action may be taken have been limited by the redefinition of a trade dispute. The tactics that may be employed in the course of a dispute have been restricted in particular by the gradual withdrawal of immunity for various forms of secondary action. By the introduction of mandatory strike ballots, new procedural obligations have been imposed before industrial action may be called. Having thus restricted the immunities in respect of the circumstances in which industrial action may be taken, the government also removed the institutional immunity of trade unions from liability in tort. If industrial action takes place without the protection of the immunities the unions themselves may be restrained by injunction and their funds may be liable for (limited) damages. But more importantly, perhaps, union funds are also liable to sequestration in the event of a court order not being complied with.[2]

While the unions bore the brunt of this legal onslaught, individual workers have not escaped attention. Section 9 of the Employment Act 1982 amended section 62 of the Employment Protection (Consolidation) Act 1978, making it easier for employers selectively to dismiss workers on strike or engaged in industrial action.[3] The employer could retain immunity from unfair dismissal liability by dismissing only those workers on strike at the date of dismissal. In effect those workers who stayed out and were dismissed after an employer had issued an ultimatum would have no remedy in unfair dismissal. The 1982 amendments also permitted the selective rehiring of dismissed strikers, while further amendments introduced by the Employment Act 1990 enable the employer selectively to dismiss so-called 'unofficial' strikers whose conduct has been repudiated by their trade union.[4] Apart from this increased vulnerability to dismissal, individual strikers were affected by changes to social security rights with the passing of section 6 of the Social Security (No. 2) Act 1980 permitting deductions to be made from the benefit entitlements of the dependants of strikers.[4a]

THE IMPACT OF THE LAW

A cursory examination of the legislative changes since 1979 could suggest that they have had an impact on levels of industrial action. Strike figures have declined. Since 1980 the number of stoppages of work due to a trade dispute has fallen. Department of Employment (DE) statistics, published monthly in the Department of Employment Gazette, record 10,987 stoppages between 1980 and 1989, compared to 26,176 in the previous decade. Whether the strike fall is linked to the statutory changes is still the subject of much debate. According to a *Labour Research* survey of union representatives, just a fifth (23 per cent) had called off industrial action because of the law, although a larger proportion (62 per cent) said that the law had an impact on decisions on whether or not to strike.[5] Those representatives surveyed had a relatively high experience of industrial action, with more than half (53 per cent) having taken some form of action in the previous three years. But overall this survey found that it was at an earlier stage, when negotiations were still under way, that the legislation was most powerful as an influence on union action. In all, 42 per cent of employers had referred to the existence of the law during negotiations and 32 per cent had threatened to use it.

In a review of recent research, Edwards finds some evidence of the impact of legislation on strike activity.[6] He cites evidence from Canada to suggest that compulsory strike votes there had tended to reduce the incidence of strikes. He also cites research by Metcalf to suggest that in the UK the number of strikes was 13 per cent lower than it would have been had it not been for the legislative changes. Preliminary findings by Elgar and Simpson,[7] however, suggest that other factors may influence strike frequency. They point to the influence of the law as 'part of a continuing process of strengthening legal input into industrial relations', which they locate in a period commencing with the 1970s. Looking specifically at the post-1979 legislation, they single out the ballot as having had the greatest influence on industrial action. The only other prominent influence they point to is the employers' general exercise of a right, founded in contract, to make pay deductions in cases of industrial action.

To date two factors may have blunted the edge of the government's legislative attack. The first is that, in general, employers have shown themselves less than enthusiastic about using the law. Evans, in his analysis of the use of injunctions, found only 80 examples of employer use of the law over a three-year period.[8] Later surveys suggest that, if anything, recourse by employers to the law has receded.[9] While to some extent this parallels the decline in strike action itself, it does not tell the whole story. Although the number of stoppages has fallen, it is still the case that many do take place outside the protection of the immunities. As we have seen, to remain within their protection, unions must ballot. Yet it seems that much strike action is not preceded by a ballot. ACAS, whose statistics are admittedly not complete, has records of just 1122 ballots between 1985 and 1989, in a period in which 4407 stoppages took place. In other words, perhaps as many as three out of every four strikes went ahead without the protection of a ballot.

Why employers have not exhibited a greater willingness to use the law is a complex question. It may be that they fear the consequences of such action or that they have been concerned that, in a confrontation with the union, positions would actually harden, making the dispute more difficult to resolve. Or it could be that while profits were rising, they had greater scope for flexibility. But the response of the unions themselves is equally of interest. Fearing the impact of the law, unions have sought to protect themselves. Attention to legal detail is much more in evidence. Unions are now more likely to consult lawyers before taking strike action. Union rules have been amended to take account of the legislative change and, significantly, they may have begun looking at more imaginative forms of action, in attempts to avoid the impact of new laws.

In terms of the impact of the legislation, the evidence so far is thus rather inconclusive. There has been a decline in strike activity, but it cannot safely be said that this is mainly due to statutory developments since 1979. It is perhaps not insignificant to note that over the same period strike levels fell in most EC states, including the UK's main competitors, Germany, France and Italy, even though the legal systems in these countries are not necessarily hostile to industrial action. It may also be noted that, contrary to government expectations, while unions may have been encouraged to adopt new agendas, the legal changes were not accompanied by a fall in wage demands. Indeed the reverse happened. OECD figures show that the growth in earnings between 1980 and 1989 was 27 per cent in the UK, compared to 0.6 per cent in Germany and −0.2 per cent in France. Exactly why pay continued to rise is still open to debate, but the fact that it did may itself have contributed to the fall in strikes. While stoppages over all issues declined in the 1980s, it was over pay that they fell the most. In the 1970s, 54 per cent of all stoppages were over pay. By contrast, in the 1980s the proportion of stoppages over pay fell to 38 per cent.[10] According to the 1991 ACAS annual report, 41 per cent of disputes where collective conciliation was sought were over pay compared to 59 per cent in 1979.

ACTION SHORT OF A STRIKE

Neither the DE nor ACAS publishes statistics on action short of a strike. ACAS, in its annual reports, does supply information on the extent to which its collective conciliation services are used. The 1991 report pointed out that while 'the decline in the number of reported stoppages continued', the demand for collective conciliation rose for the third consecutive year. Table 10.1 gives the figures for stoppages and demands for collective conciliation throughout the decade. What the figures show is that while disputes culminating in stoppages of work fell by nearly three-quarters between the beginning and end of the decade, the incidence of disputes, as measured by requests for collective conciliation, did not fall by anything like the same proportion. In 1991 ACAS handled only just over a third fewer requests than it had in 1980.

The 1992 Workplace Industrial Relations Survey (WIRS) found that of non-manual workers the highest proportion (36 per cent) took non-strike action over staffing and work allocation, while only 7 per cent took strike action.[11] The WIRS found that the switch to non-strike action, particularly among non-manuals, 'may reflect a shift of tactics by the public sector unions' and is also the result of an increase in the proportion of workplaces 'with unions which were more likely to opt for non-strike action'. The WIRS also found that non-strike action lasted longer, with 56 per cent of non-manuals taking this form of action for six or more days compared to 45 per cent when taking strike action. For manual workers the divide was even greater, at 65 per cent for non-strike action, compared to 21 per cent where involved in a strike. Finally, the WIRS found an increase in the amount of unofficial non-strike action, rising from 8 per cent in 1984 to 26 per cent for non-manuals. Manual workers were even more likely to take unofficial non-strike action, with 69 per cent of establishments reporting it.

Table 10.1
Stoppages and demands for collective conciliation

Year	Number of recorded stoppages	ACAS collective conciliation
1991	354	1386
1990	630	1260
1989	701	1164
1988	781	1163
1987	899	1302
1986	1074	1457
1985	903	1475
1984	1154	1569
1983	1255	1789
1982	1528	1865
1981	1344	1958
1980	1348	2091

If action short of a stoppage, including overtime bans, working to rule and withdrawal of goodwill, has assumed a more significant role, particularly in public sector employment, then the legal issues it raises are of more general interest. And the measures taken by employers to counter such action, often in the form of deductions from pay, are more significant. Under the Truck Acts 1831–1940 protection from arbitrary deductions by the employer was presumed not to cover deductions arising from industrial action. In *Bird* v *British Celanese Ltd*[12] the employee was suspended from work owing to a breach of the terms of his contract. His claim that the non-payment was an unlawful deduction under the Truck Acts was rejected because in the view of the court there was no contractual entitlement to wages from which a deduction could be made.

The Wages Act 1986, which repealed and replaced the Truck Acts, provided that no deduction may be made from a worker's wages, unless either required or permitted by a statutory or contractual provision or where prior written consent to the deduction has been given.[13] 'Deductions' are deemed by s. 8(3) to include any failure to pay the amount properly due on the date due, and sums 'properly payable', that is, wages, are defined in s. 7(1)(a) as any 'fee, bonus, commission, holiday pay or other emolument referable to . . . employment'. However, the Act specifically excludes deductions made from a worker's wages for taking part in a strike or other industrial action (s. 1(5)(e)). In making any such deduction, employers are not constrained by the provisions of the Act. There is neither a requirement for statutory authority nor one for prior written consent from the employee. There is therefore no statutory bar to such deductions. The justification for the exclusion of strike action from the protection of the 1986 Act was said to be one of avoiding industrial tribunals having to deal with disputes in circumstances 'where tempers flare'.

It does not follow, however, from the non-application of the Wages Act 1986 in these situations that the workers involved are without a remedy, at least in principle. If in withholding pay or a portion thereof, the employer has no contractual authority to do so, then it would be open to the workers in question to seek to recover the money in the county court. It is generally accepted by trade unionists that they will have no entitlement to be paid while on strike. But if a dispute does not involve a stoppage, for example where a work to rule is in force, there is more likely to be an expectation that pay will be maintained. Indeed, in 1983 one leading textbook claimed that 'In practice, wages are normally paid during most forms of industrial action, other than strikes and lockouts.'[14] One impact of the statutory changes of the 1980s may well have been to push workers and unions into different forms of industrial action as a way of pursuing their claims, and this, as the WIRS study shows (see above), is particularly true of non-manual public sector workers. However, the belief that in doing so they would escape legal liability turned out to be untenable.

COMMON LAW LIABILITY FOR INDUSTRIAL ACTION SHORT OF A STRIKE

Industrial Action and Breach of Contract

The 1980s saw an acceptance of the notion that even limited forms of industrial action always involve a breach of contract. This has occurred as a consequence of the employer's response to employees taking forms of non-strike action, a response that has centred on the question of whether the employer is empowered to withhold pay, and if so how much. Industrial action that involves a stoppage of work will almost certainly amount to a repudiatory breach of the striker's contract of employment, entitling the employer to dismiss without notice. Where industrial action is limited to conduct short of a stoppage, it too is likely to be seen as a breach of contract. So in *Cresswell* v *Board of Inland Revenue*[15] the High Court held that the refusal to cooperate with a transfer to computer-generated work was a repudiatory breach of contract. Similarly, in *Sim* v *Rotherham Metropolitan Borough Council*[16] the court identified a central obligation on the part of teachers to comply with a headteacher's reasonable directions and held that a refusal to cover for absent teachers was therefore a breach of that obligation and in *Miles* v *Wakefield Metropolitan District Council*[17] Lord Templeman declared unequivocally that 'any form of industrial action by a worker is a breach of contract which entitled the employer at common law to dismiss the worker, because no employer is contractually bound to retain a worker who is intentionally causing harm to the employer's business'.

Possible Employer Responses to Limited Forms of Industrial Action

Traditionally an employer faced with industrial action short of a strike could respond in one of two ways, quite apart from dismissing those involved. In the first place, employers could send employees home if they demonstrated an unwillingness to work as instructed. In *Cresswell* v *Board of Inland Revenue*,[18] as a consequence of a dispute employees were refusing to cooperate in a transfer to new technology. Both the employees and the union believed that their position was unchallengeable. They were ready to report for work as normal, carrying out the tasks and duties they had always undertaken. It was their belief that this willingness to work to the strict terms of their contracts avoided any potential legal challenge. But Walton J made short shrift of the argument. The move to new working practices, in circumstances where their old methods of working were no longer required, were within their existing contractual obligations. In refusing to transfer they had breached their contracts of employment. According to Walton J employers had the right to respond to a refusal to adopt changed working practices by sending home those involved without pay.

Misconduct by an employee that is sufficient to amount to a breach of contract will also entitle an employer to bring a claim for damages for any loss suffered as a result. The measure of damages could be the value of the lost output, less the expense that would have occurred in obtaining it. But inevitably there are difficulties in trying to assess this loss, particularly if the employee is only one of many and more so where the employee's productive output cannot be directly assessed. One early attempt to assess the extent of recoverable damages for breach of contract was in *Ebbw Vale Steel, Iron and Coal Co.* v *Tew.*[19] There the employees had ceased work owing to a fatal accident. The company brought in action for damages against employees and succeeded in obtaining a county court judgment in its favour, which assessed damages to reflect a share of certain overhead expenses, regardless of whether or not they would have been fully recouped had the employees actually performed their contracts. The employees appealed, stating that damages should be limited to the possible net profit on the coal they would have raised. Roche LJ, delivering his judgment, rejected both attempts to determine how damages should be assessed. In his view they could only be arrived at by ascertaining the worker's probable output, finding its selling value and deducting expenses that would have occurred had the contract been performed. The balance represented the damages. Overhead expenses, which occurred whether or not workers performed their duties, should not be deducted.

This complex attempt to arrive at the value of labour was not followed in the later case *National Coal Board* v *Galley*,[20] where the Court of Appeal had to deal with an employer's claim for damages for lost production. Galley, a pit deputy, had participated in an overtime ban, effectively bringing to a halt productive work in the mines on the days affected by the ban. After two months the employers brought in substitute workers and at the same time brought an action for damages for breach of contract. The Court of Appeal determined that the National Coal Board could claim damages, but confined them to the loss caused by the individual breach of contract, namely the cost of paying wages to a replacement. Yet if Galley was not being paid during his absence, it is difficult to see how even this could have been recoverable. If the employer was paying the equivalent of Galley's wages to a third party, there was no loss. But this may be a small price to pay for a decision which holds that the employers could not claim their loss of production. The outcome of *Galley* at the time effectively put paid to any similar action in the future, though as will be seen below the possibility of workers being held liable for damages on the *Galley* principles has recently been revived.

DEDUCTIONS FROM PAY

Apart from dismissal, or the other options available to the employer already discussed, recent case law has dealt in some detail with the circumstances in which an employer may deduct wages to reflect the portion of the contract that he or she alleges is not being properly performed.

The Royle Case

In a campaign against cuts in the education services, teachers were instructed by their unions 'to continue to operate the same work patterns as have operated this term'. This meant that when class sizes were enlarged to make up for fewer teachers, they were to refuse to teach in excess of the numbers of pupils previously in the class. The education authority responded with a threat 'not to pay teachers for the periods of time which they refuse to teach' but at the same time said that 'such staff may remain on the school premises as they wish'. In effect, for a period of some six months, while the industrial action continued, a number of pupils were sent home. Nevertheless, the teachers continued to present themselves for work, teach up to the previous pupil numbers and perform additional duties when not in the classroom. Did the authority thereby have the right to refuse to pay their wages or to make a deduction?

Perhaps remarkably, in the light of the later decisions, the court did not give the employer an unrestricted right to deduct. Park J began by reviewing the events that led to the deductions. He turned to

Secretary of State for Employment v *Aslef (No. 2)*,[21] where Lord Denning had stated that an individual wilfully obstructing an employer's business breaches 'an implied term not wilfully to prevent the carrying out of the contract'. It was this 'wilful disruption' that was the breach of contract giving the employers the right to refuse payment. Lord Denning had summed it up in the following words: 'wages are to be paid for services rendered, not for producing deliberate chaos'. However, Park J believed that there were differences between the *Aslef (No. 2) case* and that of *Royle*, who had not 'been shown to have broken his contract of employment in a way that goes to the very root of consideration'. While the action was intended to bring about a change in policy, it was 'not directed to rendering it impossible for the defendants to discharge their statutory duty. It seems to me that on the evidence the worst that can be said is that their acts made the discharge of that duty difficult and resulted in many children being deprived of a full-time education to which they were entitled.' The fact that the teachers had continued to work meant that this work could not have been of no effect. Nor was the action carried out 'with such complete irresponsibility as to bring education within the defendant's area virtually to a standstill'.

There was a problem, however. The Court of Appeal in *Henthorn* v *Central Electricity Generating Board*[22] had upheld the employers' right to withhold pay in full. Park J distinguished this by suggesting that *Henthorn* was authority only on the issue of the burden of proof. It was therefore no more than 'authority for the proposition that in a claim for unpaid salary or wages the burden of proof is upon the plaintiff to establish that he is entitled to be paid for work done under the contract of employment'. He was also able to distinguish the plaintiff's position from an earlier case, *Bowes and Partners Ltd* v *Press*,[23] where, as part of a campaign of action, union members had refused to travel in the same lift shaft as non-members. On each day of their refusal they were sent home and not paid. The non-payment was upheld by the Court of Appeal. *Royle*, however, according to Park J, was different. Here the education authority could have refused to allow the plaintiff to teach, unless he agreed to take the larger class size. In other words it could have adopted the position the employers had taken in *Press*, but it did not. Instead it accepted the imperfect performance of the contract and impliedly affirmed it. It was therefore under a duty to pay.

Having got this far, Park J faced a dilemma. Having distinguished all previous authorities on the power to deduct wages he was in danger of ending up with the proposition that teachers had to be paid in full during their campaign of action. This clearly would be politically unacceptable. His solution was simple and advanced without any real argument to support it. Since the plaintiff taught only 31 of the 36 children he was instructed to teach, he should have 5/36ths of his wages deducted to reflect this shortfall. To support this ruling a recently reported case, *Miles* v *Wakefield Metropolitan District Council*,[24] came to the aid of the court. But in citing it Park J also cautioned for the future. He made it clear that his decision was influenced by the fact that the respondents had not suffered any financial loss. No additional teachers had been employed. Had they been, Park J hinted that 'they might well have succeeded in recovering the cost of such employment', citing *NCB* v *Galley* in support. *Galley* thus lives on.

Subsequent Developments

Teachers and industrial action short of a strike were back before the courts within two years of *Royle*. The circumstances were somewhat similar. In *Sim* v *Rotherham Metropolitan Borough Council*[25] the industrial action involved a refusal to cover for absent teachers. The teachers concerned argued that their action was not in breach of contract, since their contracts did not provide a breakdown to determine how their working day would be distributed. They argued that 'free' periods, when they did not teach, were part of their contractual entitlement, with a corresponding right to refuse to cover. The employer's response had been to advise the teachers in advance that a deduction would be made from the salary of any teacher refusing to cover. When this happened the employees sued for recovery.

According to Scott J the deductions were valid only if the refusal to cover was a breach of contract. The first task was therefore to establish whether or not the teachers had a contractual duty to comply with cover arrangements. The resulting decision appears to have been particularly influenced by the notion of teacher professionalism. Scott J held that there was a professional obligation on each teacher to cooperate in running the school during school hours, in accordance with the timetable and other administrative regulations. This professional obligation in turn became part of their contractual obligation. Scott J did not believe, however, that the teachers' action would have permitted the authority to withhold all monies due, since it was clear that the contract of employment persisted.

Here too the court was faced with a problem as to how much could be deducted. The calculations used in *Royle* were not very helpful. A simple mathematical formula could not come to the aid of the court. The employers had to be doing more than claiming nominal damages, the damages had to be related to the severity of the breach. Scott J looked at the common law principles of abatement and quantum meruit but decided that they were not appropriate and instead opted for the doctrine of equitable set-off. This did not 'depend on the size of the damages or on the severity of the breach of contract. It depends on the nature of the breach relative to the nature of the contractual claim.' The deductions, amounting to a proportion of each teacher's monthly salary, were no greater than the amount the employer could have claimed in damages, and were therefore equitable set-offs.

By the time that the House of Lords had heard *Miles* v *Wakefield Metropolitan District Council*[26] the legally complex justifications advanced in *Sim* had been all but abandoned. The Law Lords were less concerned with the need to establish whether the right to withhold pay was based on principles of equitable set-off or abatement or indeed quantum meruit. It was, they said, unnecessary to consider the law relating to damages and unnecessary for the employer to rely on the defence of abatement or equitable set-off. What the Law Lords advanced instead was a simple doctrine: 'so far as wages are concerned, the worker can only claim if he is willing to work'. Mr Miles was a superintendent registrar of births, deaths and marriages. As part of a campaign of industrial action he refused to perform weddings on a Saturday morning. The local authority said that if he was not prepared to perform his full range of duties he would neither be required to attend work nor be paid. Nevertheless, he worked normally from Monday to Friday and on Saturday performed all duties save weddings.

Lord Bridge accepted that if an employee refused to perform the full duties that could be required of him under his contract of service, the employer was entitled to refuse any partial employment. Lord Brightman took this a stage further. The principle at stake meant that, in such cases, the employee was not entitled to any remuneration for his unwanted services, even if they were performed. The Law Lords were accepting not just the right to deduct a proportion to reflect the duties not performed, but that the employer could withhold all payment. Having advanced this interpretation they then appeared to wish to draw back from its consequences. Since the employers had limited themselves to making a partial deduction, representing that portion of wages payable for the Saturday, and since 'the value of lost services cannot be less than the value attributable to the lost hours of work', this was acceptable. But as Miles had not shown himself to be ready and willing to work the full range of his duties on the Saturday he had no right to payment for that day under his contract. However, the case did raise very seriously the possibility that an employer faced with partial performance of the contract could in fact respond by refusing to make any payment. These fears were soon realized by the important decision of the Court of Appeal in *Wiluszynski* v *London Borough of Tower Hamlets*.

Withholding All Pay

If employees, by taking industrial action, breach their contractual obligations, they now may forfeit all right to be paid. An early example of this is *Henthorn* v *Central Electricity Generating Board.*[27] The plaintiffs were in dispute with their employer and operating a 'work to rule'. They reported for work each day and followed their supervisor's instructions. The employer withheld their pay for the whole period of the dispute on the grounds both that the industrial action was unofficial and that it was contrary to their employment contracts. The plaintiffs brought an action in the county court for recovery of their lost wages, seeking arbitration under s. 92 of the County Courts Act 1959. At arbitration the plaintiffs' action had been upheld. The burden of proof was said to rest with the employer, whose obligation it was to satisfy the court that the employees were unwilling to work. But on the employer's appeal to the Court of Appeal these decisions were reversed. Using examples from breach of marriage claims, Lawton LJ held that 'when a plaintiff claims that he is entitled to be paid money under a contract which he alleges the defendant has broken, he must prove that he was ready and willing to perform the contract'. Thus the burden of proof rested on the plaintiffs and never shifted. Since the plaintiffs had been unable to meet the test of proof, their claim inevitably had to fall.

In *Wiluszynski* v *London Borough of Tower Hamlets*,[28] which followed *Miles* v *Wakefield Metropolitan District Council*, the employers withheld all pay and the Court of Appeal in examining the earlier decision viewed it as establishing that an employee cannot be entitled to remuneration unless he is willing to perform the contract. In *Wiluszynski* the employee's industrial action had involved a boycott of certain defined work. This lasted some six weeks. Although other than on the boycotted work the plaintiff had worked normally, the court agreed that he could be made to forgo his full entitlement to pay for the whole period. No longer as in *Miles* was the court attempting to apportion pay to duties properly worked; instead it agreed that the employer was under no contractual obligation to pay wages at all. This had been anticipated by *MacPherson* v *London Borough of Lambeth*,[29] where Vinelott J upheld the employer's right to refuse payment. The case involved employees affected by the introduction of new technology, over which union agreement had not been concluded. The union instructed its members not to cooperate with the new equipment and the employer refused to accept any other work. Vinelott J held that the employees could not perform fully and effectively all the duties they were contractually called upon to perform without using the new computer. In turn the employer could not be asked to pay for something significantly less than full and efficient performance.

Returning to Work after a Strike

The 1992 Court of Appeal decision in *Ticehurst* v *British Telecommunications plc*[30] goes a considerable step further than the cases already discussed, for in *Ticehurst* the plaintiffs, having taken a day's strike action, returned to work. They were then asked to sign a no-strike clause and refused. As a result the employer sent them home without pay, despite their willingness to work normally. The employer's justification for doing this was that a union campaign for a withdrawal of goodwill continued and the plaintiffs supported it in principle even if they might not be called upon to act on it.

The Court of Appeal followed *Miles* in ruling that where an employee was willing only to perform part of his or her duties, with the intention of damaging an employer's business, then even if the duties remaining unperformed were minimal, the employer could refuse all payment. Second, it affirmed that a withdrawal of goodwill could amount to a breach of an implied term to serve an employer faithfully. By supporting the union, the plaintiffs were deemed to be intending to break their obligation to serve their employers faithfully. It was not the plaintiffs' intention possibly to strike in the future that defeated the claim to payment. Their refusal to sign the no-strike undertaking on return was not significant. The court was clear that there was no right to refuse an employee work on the basis of a potential future withdrawal of labour. But by returning to work on the same basis as when they had left, that is, by continuing to support the union campaign for a withdrawal of goodwill, they could be refused work. The ruling clearly located the burden of proof as resting on the employee, who, according to *Ticehurst*, must prove a readiness and willingness to work in accordance with the contract.

CONCLUSION

This contribution has recorded some of the legislative and case law consequences of a long-term shift in government thinking away from the consensual view perhaps best expressed by Grunfeld in the 1960s, who described the trade union movement as 'one of the pillars of the unwritten British constitution'.[32] Over the past decade, unions and, in particular, their more active members have come increasingly to be viewed and dealt with by government and now the courts as 'the enemy within'. Attempts to counter the cohesion of organized workers, while occurring within the framework of that unwritten constitution, are reaching a point at which human rights are in danger of being infringed.

It is of course difficult to predict what the effects of the case law developments of the 1980s might be. But when they seek to advise their members about to embark on industrial action, particularly where the action is intended to be short of a full stoppage, it will now be necessary for unions to consider the consequences for the payment of wages of taking of such action. The sword may, however, be doubled-edged. While the risk of losing all pay may deter some groups from taking action, it may serve to encourage others to push for all-out strike action. If the consequences in terms of earnings are the same to the individual then there must be a strong argument for inflicting equal pain on the employer through loss of full production or service. An increase in the overall strike figures may therefore be an unexpected consequence of the judicial imaginativeness of the 1980s.

Although the legislative changes contained in the various Employment Acts of the 1980s appear to take account of action short of a strike, in reality the legislation has been of little value in dealing with this particular form of industrial action. In general, employers have not used the legislative opportunities offered by the legal changes, either in dealing with strike action, where relatively few injunctive actions have been taken, or for lesser forms of industrial action. This does not imply that employers have ignored the possibility of using law to their advantage. Particularly in public sector employment, they have been ready to respond to industrial action through semi-disciplinary means aimed at the employee's right to be paid. But the consequences of these attacks have been that it is no longer clear what the limits are of this right to withhold wages. The case law of the 1980s appears to give *carte blanche* to whatever penalty the employer may choose to impose, provided that a breach of contract can be inferred.

Whether the recent rulings are equally applicable to wider groups of workers taking limited forms of industrial action is not yet certain. There is at least a suggestion in some of the cases that the judges may have been influenced by the status of the employees on whom they were required to adjudicate. In *Ticehurst* it was apparent that employees with a managerial status were viewed as being bound by higher standards of behaviour, and in some of the earlier cases the professional or managerial nature of posts seems to have played a part in their judgments. But there is nothing within the rulings to demand that they only cover specific groups of workers. Instead, what the cases point to is a willingness on the part of the judiciary to expand the common law almost as required to deal with new situations. The result is less than satisfactory for the workers affected, who no longer can predict the likely penalty that will flow from their actions. As Wedderburn points out, 'It is rather unsatisfactory that case law should offer no better guidance to workers who have committed a partial breach of their contracts (perhaps in a work to rule) and wish to recover wages stopped by an employer than that he may be obliged to pay them in full, or nothing, or a fraction, as appears just to the judge whom they happen to be allocated.'[31]

NOTES

1. *Financial Times*, 29 October 1979.
2. For a full account of the restrictions on the trade dispute immunities, see S. Auerbach, *Legislating for Conflict* (1991).
3. For an account of this change, see P. Wallington, The Employment Act 1982: Section 9 - A recipe for victimisation (1983) 46 MLR 310.
4. See H. Carty, The Employment Act 1990: still fighting the industrial cold war (1991) 20 ILJ 1. See now Trade Union and Labour Relations (Consolidation) Act 1992, s. 237.

4a. See now Social Security Contributions and Benefits Act 1992, s. 126.

5. *Labour Research*, September 1990 (Are the anti-strike laws working?).
6. P. K. Edwards, Industrial conflict: themes and issues in recent research (1992) 30 BJIR 361.
7. J. Elgar and B. Simpson, The impact of law on industrial disputes in the 1980s (CEP Discussion Paper, 1992).
8. S. Evans, The use of injunctions in industrial disputes, May 1984–April 1987 (1987) 25 BJIR 419.
9. See *Labour Research*, September 1988, October 1989 and October 1991. These trace in all 163 cases, of which 117 were applications for injunctions.
10. *Labour Research*, June 1992 (New workers retain strike weapon).
11. N. Millward *et al.*, *Workplace Industrial Relations in Transition* (1992).
12. [1945] 1 All ER 488.
13. Wages Act 1986, s. 1(1).
14. R.W. Rideout, *Principles of Labour Law* (4th edn, with J. Dyson, 1983).
15. [1984] ICR 508.
16. [1986] ICR 897.

17. [1987] 1 AC 539.
18. [1984] ICR 508.
19. (1935) Sol. Jo. 593.
20. [1958] 1 WLR 16.
21. [1972] ICR 19.
22. *Henthorn* v *Central Electricity Generating Board* [1980] IRLR 361.
23. (1894) QBD 202.
24. [1987] 1 AC 539.
25. [1986] ICR 897.
26. [1987] 1 AC 539.
27. [1980] IRLR 361.
28. [1989] IRLR 259.
29. [1988] IRLR 470.
30. [1992] IRLR 219.
31. Wedderburn, *The Worker and the Law* (3rd edn, 1986), p. 198.
32. C. Grunfeld, *Modern Trade Union Law* (1966), p. 1.

11

The Strike and Breach of Contract: A Reassessment

Patrick Elias

The question of whether strike action involves a breach of the contract of employment is one of fundamental importance.[1] If it does, then not only does this confer various contractual remedies on the employer but - and in practice this is more important - it means that at common law those organizing the strike are liable in tort for inducing a breach of contract. In certain circumstances immunity is conferred by statute against such liability,[2] but under the current statutory regime one of the preconditions is that there should have been a ballot of the relevant workers, and that they should have voted in favour.[3] If strike action does not involve a breach of contract, no common law liability is likely to arise and therefore no ballot is required to provide protection against legal action by the employer.[4]

The orthodox view is that strike action does involve a breach of contract by the workers participating unless they lawfully terminate their contracts of employment on notice.[5] This conventional wisdom is supported by certain comments of Lord Templeman in *Miles* v *Wakefield Metropolitan District Council.*[6] In the course of his judgment, he said this: 'Industrial action is unique in that in order to be effective the action must involve a repudiatory breach of contract designed to harm the employer.'[7] And again: 'Any form of industrial action by a worker is a breach of contract which entitled the employer at common law to dismiss the worker because no employer is contractually bound to retain a worker who is intentionally causing harm to the employer's business.'[8] The purpose of this chapter is to suggest that this conventional analysis is too sweeping; that provided certain conditions are met, workers can lawfully participate in strike action against their employer where their action is a defensive response to a continuing actual or anticipatory breach of contract by the employer; that such action will not constitute a breach of contract; and that accordingly no tort liability based on breach of contract or the inducement of such a breach can arise from such industrial action.

TWO ROUTES TO LEGALITY

It is suggested that there are two routes by which such industrial action can be rendered lawful. The first depends upon the workers involved terminating their contracts; under the second they do not terminate their contracts but rather keep them alive while refusing to perform their contracts until the employer undertakes to honour his obligations. The first involves what might be termed 'strike by concerted constructive dismissals' and the second involves the invocation of the principle 'no pay, no work'. I will consider the legality of each in turn.

Strike by Concerted Constructive Dismissals

It is now generally accepted that employees can lawfully take strike action without acting in breach of contract if they make it clear that they are lawfully terminating their contracts. English law even flirted with the idea that a notice to strike of equivalent length to the notice required to terminate the contract would in law suspend the contract without involving breach.[9] But that argument has been decisively rejected;[10] it was always fraught with difficulties.[11]

No doubt in most cases where employees give notice of intention to strike, they do not wish that notice to be construed as notice to terminate; they want the contract to stay on foot. But there is no rule of law that employees cannot effect a lawful strike in any circumstances by lawfully terminating their contracts. As Saville J observed in *Boxfoldia Ltd* v *The National Graphical Association*,[12] it is not inconsistent to terminate the contract while wanting the relationship to continue:

> in any given case the employees (or their union) may consider that by actually terminating the contracts on due notice, greater or more effective pressure can be put upon the employers. . . . Furthermore, . . . there is a distinction to be drawn between wanting to continue with the existing but improved contracts of employment and wanting to continue (but with new contracts) the relationship of employer and employee.[13]

In effect, striking by giving concerted notice to terminate is no different from the employer dismissing his employees and offering to re-engage them on new contracts with fresh terms. In each case the parties are seeking to achieve certain objectives without breaking the contracts of employment.

In practice, employees very rarely give notice to terminate. The reason is that by so doing they are highly vulnerable. Having voluntarily resigned from their employment, they have no protection against the employer. They have no claim in wrongful dismissal and lose even such protection as is afforded by unfair dismissal,[14] since they are not dismissed within the statutory definition at all. Moreover, there are often practical difficulties involved. Employees must resign on giving contractual notice, which may vary from individual to individual; that notice must be clear and unambiguous; and, as Saville J held in the *Boxfoldia* case,[15] in the absence of some clear authority vested in the union to act on behalf of its members, each employee will have to give appropriate strike notice.

Most of these problems are eliminated, however, where the strike is in response to a breach of contract by the employer, at least where that breach is repudiatory. In such circumstances the employees can lawfully terminate their contracts in response to the repudiatory breach. They may do this by giving no notice or such other notice as is considered desirable, even if this falls short of their contractual notice period. Technically, they are giving notice that they accept the repudiation by the employer, not giving lawful notice to terminate. The strike is initiated not by concerted lawful resignation but rather by concerted constructive dismissals, by repudiations in response to the repudiatory breach.

This distinction between a strike being triggered by mass constructive dismissals rather than by mass resignations is of fundamental importance. The former greatly improves the bargaining position of the union, for if ultimately the grievances are not settled and the employees reinstated, the employees will have claims for wrongful dismissal. Furthermore, although this is more contentious, it is submitted that their rights to unfair dismissal are also preserved. Under section 238 of the Trade Union and Labour Relations (Consolidation) Act 1992 those rights are removed if certain conditions are met. One of these is that at the date of dismissal the employee should have been taking part in a strike or other industrial action. In *Heath* v *J. F. Longman (Meat Salesman) Ltd*,[16] the National Industrial Relations Court held that this requirement meant that the relevant employees actually had to be taking part in the industrial action at the moment of dismissal. Unless the concerted giving of notice is itself treated as industrial action, it must follow that the dismissals are effected prior to the strike commencing. The dismissals initiate or trigger the industrial action; they do not constitute part of that action. Moreover, it would be highly artificial to say that a collective giving of notice of itself constitutes industrial action. It would mean that if employees all gave, say, two days' notice to strike, they would in law be deemed to be taking industrial action during the two days when they were working normally.

If the employees take strike action by terminating their contracts, yet preserving the right to claim for wrongful and unfair dismissal, the pressure on the employer to revert to the original terms and honour the contract will be considerable. Even if he fails to do so, it is possible that an industrial tribunal would consider the dismissals to be unfair[17] and might even award reinstatement of workers found to be unfairly dismissed. Such a finding, which would involve reimposing the original terms, must be a real possibility where the dismissal is the result of repudiatory conduct by the employer, particularly if the only objection to their continued employment is that they are unwilling to accept less favourable employment terms.

Obviously, if this strategy is to work the employees must in taking the industrial action comply with the conditions necessary to constitute a constructive dismissal.[18] For example, they must not by their conduct have affirmed the contract, and the resignations must be in response to the repudiatory breach. But in practice these requirements will readily be met in a strike context. Moreover, as indicated above, there is no need to give contractual or any notice since the essence of constructive dismissal is that the employee can summarily terminate the contract in response to the repudiatory breach, although some notice could be given.

This does not eliminate all the practical difficulties. As indicated above, in the *Boxfoldia* case Saville J held that in the absence of express authority given to the union, employees will individually have to give notice stating that they are terminating the contract because of the employer's breach of contract; and this might be difficult to organize where a large number of workers are involved. Union rules could in theory vest the union with the requisite authority, but in practice they do not do so.

It is submitted that there is no authority that would deprive employees of the right to initiate strike action in this way. Indeed, in *Thompson* v *Eaton Ltd*,[19] Phillips J foreshadowed the argument. He suggested that a repudiatory breach by the employer could itself constitute a termination of the contract so that any strike in response would be after the dismissal. This was wrong as a matter of law since it has never been the law that any repudiatory breach would automatically terminate the contract; possibly it does so where the breach takes the form of a wrongful dismissal, but even that is uncertain.[20] Where, however, the employee accepts the breach and terminates the contract, that does effectively bring the contract to an end. It is true that in *Wilkins* v *Cantrell and Cochrane (GB) Ltd*,[21] the Employment Appeal

Tribunal (Kilner Brown J presiding) held that going on strike could not of itself be treated as an acceptance of the repudiatory breach, and no doubt that is right. But insofar as that case suggests that an employee is not in law entitled as part of a concerted campaign to terminate his contract in response to a repudiatory breach, it is inconsistent with both general legal principle and the *Boxfoldia* case. As to the former, it cannot conceivably successfully be contended that the termination is in some sense a nullity merely because it is done in concert with others. That would not only treat the fact of combination as rendering unlawful what would otherwise be lawful,[22] it would be going further in treating what in terms is an unequivocal termination as a notice to break the contract. As to the latter, if employees can strike after lawfully terminating the contract on notice, they must equally be entitled to do so where they act lawfully by terminating summarily (or possibly on short notice) in response to the repudiatory breach by the employer.

No Pay, No Work

Paradoxically the starting point for this alternative basis for asserting that strikes may be undertaken consistently with the contract of employment, and not as a breach, is the case of *Miles* v *Wakefield Metropolitan District Council* itself, the case in which Lord Templeman suggested that all strikes would constitute a breach. In that case the plaintiff was superintendent registrar of births, marriages and deaths. Along with other superintendent registrars, and at the behest of his trade union, he took industrial action that involved, *inter alia*, refusing to conduct weddings on Saturdays. Although he attended work on Saturdays for other purposes, the Council made it clear that while registration officers were not prepared to undertake their full range of duties on Saturdays they were not required to attend for work and would not be paid. In view of the position adopted by the Council, the House of Lords considered that the plaintiff should be treated in effect as if he had refused to work on Saturdays and was voluntarily absent on that day.[23] The question, therefore, was whether he was entitled to be paid while not working. The plaintiff argued that he was entitled to be paid. He contended that an employer can respond to the breach in one of two ways: if the breach is sufficiently serious he can accept it as repudiatory and terminate the contract; alternatively he may affirm the contract and sue for damages (and in that context can, by way of counterclaim or set-off, withhold such wages or salary as he can demonstrate is justified by the damage actually suffered). Their

Lordships rejected this analysis. They held that the employer had a third option: if the employee refuses to work in accordance with his contract then the employer can opt to maintain the contract. Lord Templeman summed it up as follows: 'In a contract of employment wages and work go together. *If the employer declines to pay*, the worker need not work. If the worker declines to work, the employer need not pay' (emphasis added).[24]

As the words emphasized indicate, notwithstanding the extravagant language employed earlier in his judgment, which suggested that there is no right to strike without breaking the employment contract, Lord Templeman saw the 'no work, no pay' principle as capable of being relied upon by the employee under the guise 'no pay, no work'. What is sauce for the employer goose must be sauce for the employee gander. Furthermore, just as the principle may be invoked by the employer where the employee is in fact willing to carry out some, but not all, of his duties under the contract, as in the *Miles* case itself, so can it be relied upon by the employee if the employer is willing to provide some, but not all, of the pay to which he is entitled.

In this context it is clear that 'pay' in the maxim 'no work, no pay' (or 'no pay, no work') is not limited to financial reward, but means the whole of the consideration that the employer is obliged to provide pursuant to the contract of employment. Not only is that dictated by the logic of the principle underpinning the *Miles* decision, it is also supported by authority. In *Miles* itself, Lord Bridge held that the relevant principle was that 'if the employee refuses to perform the full duties required of him under his contract of service, the employer is entitled to refuse to accept any partial performance'.[25] Similarly, the employee must be entitled to refuse to work if the employer declines to perform the full duties required by him under the contract. In short, the principle is that if one party is not willing to perform, the other may withhold performance while keeping the contract alive.

Once this principle is accepted in respect of any single employee, it can make no difference that the employees are acting in concert. A lawful act by one cannot become unlawful because it is carried out by a combination unless the purpose is to injure the plaintiff, in which case the tort of simple conspiracy is committed. Here, of course, the purpose is to advance the legitimate self-interest of the workers. This is not to deny that there are certain limits to this principle. First, the employees or their representatives must make it clear that any strike will only take place unless and until the employer indicates that he is willing to honour the contract. It is not a weapon that can be used to remedy past grievances; and it cannot be carried on to punish an employer once he has given an unequivocal undertaking to honour the contract in future. Second, it probably cannot be employed in response to an anticipatory breach since the doctrine appears to be limited to a response to non-performance, not a response to future breach.

COMPARING THE TWO FORMS OF DEFENSIVE STRIKES

If the above analysis is correct, employees may be able to take strike action in response to a repudiatory breach by the employer in one of two ways. Either they may be able to withhold their labour until the employer is willing to perform his part of the contract; or they might be able to give notice to terminate their contracts in response to the repudiatory breach. However, the scope of the two possible responses is not identical. The former can continue only while the employer continues to act in breach of contract. For example, if he unilaterally reduces the salary, but later reinstates it, the employees cannot invoke the 'no pay, no work' dictum to justify striking after the reinstatement of the original terms even if the employer refuses to pay the full rate for the intervening period during which he was willing to pay only the reduced rate. By contrast, any refusal to pay the contractual wage will almost inevitably constitute a repudiatory breach of contract, and employees can strike by accepting that breach even though at the time of dismissal the employer is willing to honour the contract in the future. To that extent, therefore, the potential scope of the strike effected by a notice to terminate is greater.

However, the weakness is, as indicated, that in practice notice of termination will have to be given individually where the latter form of strike is adopted, since the union will not have the requisite authority. In contrast, where the employee is merely going on strike to compel the employer to honour the contract in future, it is submitted that in normal circumstances the union will have the authority to act on his behalf in notifying the employer that the strike would last only until the employer undertook to respect his contractual obligations. It could not, in other words, reasonably be inferred that by taking strike action the employee was intending to break his contract if the union had notified the employer of the conditions under which the action would take place, and these indicated that no breach would occur. The inference must be that the individual will strike in accordance with, and pursuant to, the instructions issued by his union and notified to the employer.

INDUSTRIAL ACTION SHORT OF A STRIKE

It is important to recognize that neither doctrine can render lawful industrial action short of a strike (although exceptionally, such as where that action takes the form of a ban on voluntary overtime, there may be no breach in any event). The strike based upon the 'no pay, no work' principle rests upon a right of non-performance, not an entitlement to partial performance. The strike initiated by notice of termination obviously presupposes the ending of the contract, and it would be inconsistent with any such notice to perform any of the duties under the contract.

CONCLUSION

Ultimately, whether or not a strike involves a breach of the contract of employment must depend upon the terms of that contract. In theory an employer could expressly confer such a right. Alternatively it might be possible to imply the right. It has been suggested, for example, that a provision in a collective agreement restricting a right to strike until procedures are exhausted could be treated as implying such a right once procedures are exhausted.[26] The purpose of this chapter is to suggest that, independently of particular contractual provisions, employees may be entitled to take strike action of a defensive kind in order to compel the employer to honour the terms of the contract, without thereby infringing their contracts of employment.

This analysis suggests that there will, after all, be some significance in the distinction between disputes of right and disputes of interest, at least insofar as the rights in dispute are in fact secured by contract. Defensive strikes to protect such rights will be lawful, not because Parliament has provided any special protection to such action, but because such action will not constitute a breach of contract or any other unlawful act, at least provided unions take pains to ensure that the action meets the relevant conditions referred to above. Ironically it is the developing principles of the common law - so often assumed to be hostile to the interests of workers - that, albeit in a restricted field, will have carved out a right to strike. Moreover, while the scope for lawful action clearly is limited, it is particularly important in a time of recession when employers are frequently seeking unilaterally to vary the contract of employment in a manner adverse to employees. In addition, if lawful action is to be taken, it has the very significant practical advantage that it can be mounted swiftly in response to the employer's conduct. This is not possible where the union has to rely upon a ballot to establish the legality of the action. Indeed, under the Trade Union Reform and Employment Rights Act 1993, there are further procedural restrictions imposed on the carrying out of union ballots, which will make it difficult for any strike pursuant to a ballot to be implemented much within three weeks of the decision to hold the ballot.[27] The reason is that the union has to give a week's notice to the employer of the ballot, then carry out a postal ballot, and then, having established the result, give another week's notice of the intention to strike.

Given these procedural difficulties, the attraction of taking action that does not give rise to a breach of contract, and is therefore unlikely to involve those participating or organizing the strike in any tort liability, is obvious. The potential protection for strike action is not based on any novel doctrine of law, merely the application of developing principles that have overtaken the orthodox analysis. Moreover, it would be wrong to assume that these developments will be thwarted by a hostile judiciary. It is distinctly possible that in the changed climate of relations, the courts will be sympathetic to employees who are merely striking in response to a breach of contract by the employer, and will be receptive to the idea that employees should be permitted to strike when they are doing so to preserve rights the employer is contractually bound to honour.

NOTES

I am grateful to Philip Sales for provoking and discussing some of the thoughts in this chapter.

1. Paul O'Higgins demonstrated the great variety of union practices in his article. 'Strike notices: another approach' (1973) 2 ILJ 152.
2. Trade Union and Labour Relations (Consolidation) Act 1992, s. 219.
3. *Ibid.*, ss. 226ff.
4. The failure to hold a ballot even where no breach is committed may still create difficulties for the union, however. The reason is that a member of a trade union who claims that members of the trade union, including himself, have been induced to take part in industrial action without the support of ballot may apply to the court to restrain industrial action whether or not the alleged inducement is unlawful, i.e. whether or not the workers are acting in breach of contract by taking the strike action: see section 62 of the 1992 Act.
5. See e.g. Professor K.D. Ewing, *The Right to Strike* (Oxford, 1991), p. 141: 'A strike, for whatever reason, is a breach of contract'; Lord Wedderburn, *The Worker and the Law* (3rd edn, Harmondsworth, 1986), pp. 190–3; Sweet & Maxwell's *Encyclopaedia of Employment Law*, para 1.8403: 'A strike, which involves a complete cessation of work, will always constitute a breach of contract. Whether giving notice of a strike changes the position depends on the

terms of that notice; *Harvey on Industrial Relations and Employment Law*, Part N, para. 1887, is a little more reticent: 'in the current climate of judicial opinion, the courts will almost inevitably say that industrial action on the part of workers is a breach of contract'.

6. [1987] 1 AC 539.
7. *Ibid.*, pp. 561–2.
8. *Ibid.*, p. 559A.
9. See *Morgan* v *Fry* [1968] 2 QB 710 *per* Lord Denning.
10. *Simmons* v *Hoover Ltd* [1977] ICR 61.
11. Many of the difficulties were described in the report of the *Royal Commission on Trade Unions and Employers' Association* (1965–1968). Chairman: Lord Donovan, Cmnd 3623 (1968), para. 943.
12. [1988] ICR 753.
13. *Ibid.*, p. 756.
14. See the Trade Union and Labour Relations (Consolidation) Act 1992, s. 238.
15. [1988] ICR 752, 758.
16. [1973] ICR 407.
17. Sometimes a dismissal will be fair notwithstanding that it results from a desire by the employer adversely to vary the terms of the contract of employment. See the discussion in Harvey, *op. cit.*, Div. 2, para. 1024ff.
18. See Harvey, *op. cit.*, Div. 2, para. 271ff.
19. [1976] ICR 336.
20. See generally Harvey, *op. cit.*, Div. A, para. 886ff.
21. [1978] IRLR 483.
22. The House of Lords has recently affirmed that liability for simple conspiracy (i.e. in the absence of unlawful means) will only arise if the predominant motive or purpose is to injure the plaintiff, and not if it is to promote the self-interest of the defendants: *Lonrho plc* v *Fayed* [1992] AC 448.
23. See the judgment of Lord Oliver, [1987] 1 AC 539 at 568.
24. *Ibid.*, p. 561.
25. *Ibid.*, p. 551.
26. Wedderburn, *op. cit.*, pp. 341 and 622.
27. See Trade Union Reform and Employment Rights Act 1993, ss. 17–21.

12

Criminal Law and the Development of Labour Relations in Nineteenth-Century Ireland

J. McEldowney

INTRODUCTION

The significance of the criminal law in the development of Irish trade unionism is largely neglected by legal writers, and contemporary textbooks of Irish labour law focus on modern developments, largely ignoring history.[1] This is perhaps surprising, for during the nineteenth century Irish labour faced the exceptional problems of de-industrialization long before most other European countries had industrialized. Trade unions were agreed that repeal of the union with England was essential for economic survival, as the only means of securing economic sovereignty over their own affairs. Irish nationalism provided a platform for workers' grievances and a rallying point for common causes.

The main characteristics of the development of labour organizations may be briefly outlined. In Ireland the early process of combination began in the 1670s in Dublin and by the beginning of the eighteenth century in the provinces. The evidence suggests that Irish trade union activity was more widespread and better organized than its equivalent in England.[2] The purpose of the early combinations, composed mainly of journeyman workers, was to defend wages, hours and conditions of work. Evidently they were successful in their endeavours, because employers obtained a series of Acts making combinations of masters or employees illegal. Dependent on local enforcement, these laws proved ineffective, as regular combinations of skilled workmen were formed under the guise of friendly societies. Employers who combined had little to fear, as prosecutions were rare and the magistracy was composed of local employers. The Dublin societies of employees flourished and were tolerated by employers who were often magistrates and were particularly well organized and effective in petitioning Parliament for reform. In the 1780s in Belfast regular wage negotiations between cotton workers and employers became a traditional means of wage settlement.

Records of strikes in Belfast and Cork during the second half of the eighteenth century show high support for trade unionism, which included unskilled workers taking part in general strikes during the early 1800s. A more serious threat was the covert style adopted by many Irish combinations. Collective action for political and economic reasons united Irish workers to various agrarian or peasant societies formed out of the poor economic conditions caused by an inadequate land system and famine. From the middle of the eighteenth century and throughout the famine years in the 1840s various secret tenant societies helped to create a broadly based trade union movement. Concerned with a general range of social and political issues, bounded by secret oaths and allegiances, Irish nationalism ensured that the Irish trade union movement would remain distinctive throughout the nineteenth century, only in 1900 joining the British trade union movement.

Significantly, towards the end of the nineteenth century accompanying demands from British trade unions for greater rights included demands for reform of the magistracy, the jury system and the system of prosecutions. Such reform demands became a common theme of the Trades Union Congress in the 1880s, which sought uniform laws for England, Scotland and Ireland in the 'belief that nothing can be calculated more to promote content among the Irish workmen than the voluntary extension of liberties to Ireland similar to England and Wales'.

The focus of this chapter is pertinent to the O'Higgins analysis of Irish legal history, with its emphasis on studying problems in Irish law as helpful to an understanding of how English legal principles actually worked when tested by the conflicts and pressures in Ireland.[3] Perceptions about law are more acute when examined in the context of conflicts and tensions inherent in Irish problems. The chapter is divided into three sections. The first section is a historical overview of the early use of criminal law in the regulation of master and servant relations from the seventeenth century. The second section deals with the trade union movement in nineteenth-century Ireland. The removal of the prohibition against combinations and the passage of the Master and Servant Act 1867 followed by the Employers and Workmen Act 1875 are explained in the context of their effects on trade unions in Ireland. The third section elaborates the principal argument of the chapter, that the impact and severity of the criminal law on trade union activity in Ireland may have served to strengthen the link between trade union activities and secret agrarian societies in Ireland. In the context of the broader political, social and economic issues of the day, such as the Home Rule movement and Irish land law reform, Irish trade unions were overwhelmed by the broader political agenda rather than the ideological conflict between capital and labour. After 1922, and the creation of Northern Ireland separate from the Irish Republic, trade unions remain weak, an enduring legacy of the historical development of labour relations in Ireland.

THE CRIMINAL LAW IN THE EARLY DEVELOPMENT OF TRADE UNIONS IN IRELAND

Two sources of law are evident from the early history of Irish law. Before 1800, legislation passed for Ireland consisted primarily of Acts of the English Parliament applied to Ireland. In addition, the Irish Parliament passed enactments, very often similar to the laws in operation in England. An important theme, common in both Irish and English enactments, was the use of both wage regulation *and* criminal sanctions in the relationship between master and servant.[4]

Statutory Wage Regulation

In England, the earliest use of statute law to enforce criminal sanctions in the relationship between master and servant may be traced to the fourteenth century.[5] The Ordinance of Labourers 1349 (23 Edw. III, c. 1) was an English statute that also applied as a result of Poyning's law in Ireland. It required compulsion as a key element in the general duty owed by a labourer to his master. Two years afterwards it was superseded by the Statute of Labourers 1351 (25 Edw. 3, st. 1), which fixed certain wages of workmen in specific crafts, imposing penalties where workmen failed or refused to work at set wages. Wage regulation may also be seen in the Statute of Artificers 1563 (5 Eliz. 1, c. 4), which also applied in Ireland. Under this Act Justices of the Peace acted as 'regulators' of the pay of masters, journeymen and apprentices.[6] Such powers were extended well into the seventeenth century.

English statutes in 1603 and 1640 extended the magistrates' jurisdiction over workmen and their wages. Earlier statutes of Henry VIII (1542: 33 Henry VIII, c. 9) and Elizabeth (1569: Eliz., c. 5, sess. i) authorized magistrates to fix maximum wages twice yearly.[7] By the early nineteenth century these statutes had fallen into disuse, though Citrine records that 'as late as 1801 and even in 1811 an attempt was made by certain Kent millers to enforce' an earlier statute by ordering justices to hear and make an assessment of wages.[8] Also significant were the eighteenth-century English statutes (1 Geo. I, st. 2, c. 15, 1715; 3 Geo. II, c. 14, 1729; 17 Geo. II, c. 8, 1743) for the judicial recovery of unpaid wages, which required that wages should be paid in full, an earlier version of the later nineteenth-century Truck Acts.[9] A miscellaneous number of eighteenth-century Acts applied to specific trades. For example, in 1780 an Act fixed wages and hours for tailors and shipwrights in Dublin.[10]

Statutory Restrictions on Trade Unions

The extensive wage regulation jurisdiction granted to magistrates was accompanied by criminal law sanctions, also applied through the jurisdiction of magistrates. Criminal law provisions prohibited various agreements or combinations to alter wages or conditions of labour from the fourteenth century. At first such legislation applied to particular trades but later the statutory provisions had a more general application and applied widely. Orth notes that the term 'combination' first entered the statute book in 1721 (7 Geo. I, st. 1, c. 13: Tailors Combination Act Ireland) and later statutes referred loosely to 'conspiracies' or 'confederacies'.[11] The use of criminal conspiracy law, a common law crime, was sufficiently flexible to cover an agreement to commit a statutory crime.[12] At the beginning of the eighteenth century cases abound of prosecutions for conspiracy to increase wages.[13]

In Ireland, a number of Acts of the Irish Parliament were passed, specifically intended to outlaw combinations of workmen. At first these Acts were specific in nature, applicable to a particular trade. Gradually the Acts were extended to apply to all workmen and all forms of trade. The majority of Acts passed in the eighteenth century applicable to combinations were enacted by the Irish Parliament. But the English Parliament enacted general laws for England, some of which were applicable in Ireland. Importation of English statute law into Irish law was gradual, spasmodic and on a case-by-case basis. An example of the early English legislation and the first applicable in Ireland was the Weavers' Combination Act 1726 (12 Geo. I, c. 39), which applied to the woollen industry. The Act might be said to have limited use in Ireland since earlier legislation in 1699 had suppressed the Irish woollen industry. The 1726 English legislation was not applied to Ireland until 1817 when it was put into effect with limited use because the Irish industry had declined. The 1726 Act empowered two justices to collect overdue money wages by distress and sale and when unsuccessful the master weaver could be subject to imprisonment for six months. Appeals against conviction fell under the jurisdiction of Quarter Sessions. Combinations of weavers were illegal and a conviction could result in three months' imprisonment.

GENERAL RESTRICTIONS ON COMBINATION

In England, towards the middle of the eighteenth century, English Acts were passed that applied criminal provisions to all workmen. This approach, favouring regulation through the general use of the criminal law, began with an omnibus Combination Act 1749 (22 Geo. II, c. 27) which was eventually applied in Ireland in 1817. This was as a result of the rising fortunes of the Irish weavers in their ability to combine. The 1749 Act was the forerunner of future general legislation applying to the master and servant relationship. A long list of trades was drawn up in the 1749 legislation and the Act intended to make provision 'for more effectual preventing of Frauds and Abuses' arising from activities of servants. One of the earliest cases heard under the 1749 Act, *Rex* v *Hammond and Webb*,[14] established important evidential rules concerning proof of common law conspiracy. The judge admitted into evidence the rule of the journeymen shoemakers' association, which had been published some years previously. This left the prosecution with the relatively easy job of proving the existence of an agreement. The case is also interesting because it raised the possibility that conspiracy might potentially apply to masters where they agreed to interfere with wage settlements set by legislation, by altering wages. There is little evidence to show that this possibility was widely exploited.

In Ireland, statutes of general application to all workmen were enacted by the Irish Parliament, earlier than in England. It is unclear if the English provisions discussed above had been influenced by the earlier Irish law. It is clear, however, that the Irish law was intended to distinguish between the lawful combination of workmen to petition Parliament for redress of grievances and the illegal activities of such combinations. There were three significant Acts passed in Ireland applicable to workmen generally. In 1729, 3 Geo. II, c. 14, an Irish Act of Parliament, prohibited combinations of workmen and their contracts, and agreements of 'such unlawful clubs were null and void'. The 1729 Act also contained provisions that the employer must pay full wages and make no deductions. It is doubtful if such obligations on masters were ever enforced. Clarkson concluded that the Act proved 'ineffectual and was notoriously evaded' by employers.[15]

The growth in the organization of labour during this period took many forms. Clubs and societies began to provide for the regulation of apprentices and servants and it was suggested that the existence of such organizations was a 'threat to trade and manufacturers'.[16] As a result the Irish 1729 legislation was supplemented in 1731 by an English Act (5 Geo. II, c. 4), which made any journeyman who assaulted another to stop him working for an employer or who assaulted an employer for employing a person of his choice subject to a fine of forty shillings or in cases of default three months' imprisonment. This Act seemed equally ineffective in preventing the continued organization of labour in Ireland.[17]

The second Irish Act, passed in 1743 (17 Geo. II, c. 8), addressed the question 'of great disorders and riots' that might result from the activities of combinations defined as 'assemblies of three or more persons'. The 1743 Act, Clarkson believed, was intended to place legal controls over any public meetings or houses where meetings were held and, by treating such meetings as 'public nuisances', to bring their existence within the criminal law. In common with previous statutory provisions, obligations were also placed on employers to pay the full amount of wages subject to a penalty.[18] Evidence given before the Irish House of Commons in 1749,[19] however, heard that this Act was ineffective. Wages were unregulated in practice and great dissatisfaction existed with the hours of work. An attempt was made to prove that the loss of output from manufacturing was influenced by the conditions of work.

A third general Irish Act of 1780 (19 and 20 Geo. III, c. 19) declared that 'all combinations, whether among masters or journeymen', were to be 'public nuisances'. Many activities were prescribed, such as quitting work or departing before the end of service. A wide variety of evidence could be used to support a conviction. Park noted that 'On the face of it, the Act was directed against all trade unions . . . but it is submitted that, in fact the Act was directed only against combinations of workmen, as distinct from combinations of masters.'[20] Clarkson's analysis[21] is that the 1780 Act was passed because of the effectiveness of a petition presented by various Protestant employers and was aimed at the Catholic workers and employers who threatened the establishment and Protestant ascendancy.[22] This might explain why the legislation appeared to address both masters and servants.

RESTRICTIONS ON PARTICULAR TRADES

In addition to the general legislation outlawing trade combinations, legislation was passed in Ireland to prohibit combinations in particular trades. The most notable Acts applied to linen, cotton and bakery trades. Legislation was also enacted for specific cities such as Cork and Dublin.[23] Legislation in Ireland was also related to local circumstances. Belfast, Dublin and Cork often received specific attention in legislation intended to cope with local problems, such as the existence of a particular trade combination. McDowell observes that 'Dublin journeyman seem to have been largely responsible for the legislation directed against combinations'.[24] In 1772, a measure was passed (11 and 12 Geo. III, c. 33) that persons in Dublin who allowed their houses to be used as meeting places for journeymen clubs were to be fined. This was followed by an Act some years later strengthening the law in this area (19 and 20 Geo. III, c. 9). This legislation was also intended to regulate wages, and make provision to prevent the rise in agitation that was threatened from the activities of the workers' combinations operating in Dublin and Cork.

The evidence is patchy as to how often such laws were applied.[25] However, the legislation was proof of the perceived fears that the organization of labour created in the minds of the government. The passage of such draconian legislation coincided with heightened fears of revolution in Ireland leading up to the 1798 rebellion and the influence of the French Revolution. Undoubtedly Ireland's main industries, wool, silk, cotton and hosiery, were ideally suited to the organization of trade combinations.[26] Industrial pressure and market competition were seen as a direct threat to industries and trades in England. This question became acute in the period leading up to the Act of Union in 1800. McCarthy suggests that perhaps tighter restrictions on the Irish workforce had an effect on the competitiveness of Irish industries, leading to strikes and poor industrial relations. It is arguable that the economic hardship of Irish industries may have promoted English interests.[27]

Irish economic growth in the eighteenth century and at the beginning of the nineteenth century was considerable, but population increase had steadily eroded any improvement.[28] Activities in the Irish brewing and distilling industries led to the development of factories in Belfast, Dublin and Cork. Industrialization, especially in the flax industry, gave rise to a thriving linen trade. The master and servant relationship became a crucial element in the development and future prosperity of these key industries.

The miscellaneous Irish Acts passed at the end of the eighteenth century are discussed in detail by Park.[29] The common form adopted was to attempt to curtail trade unions or associations. The scope of the enactments varied according to the trade to be regulated and the enactments were sufficiently wide-ranging to cover the lamplighters of Dublin, bakery workers and the butter trade.

Significantly, in addition to the legislation intended to penalize workers' combinations, legislation was also passed in Ireland aimed at employers. Park has identified five Acts enacted by the Irish Parliament aimed at certain combinations of employers. The main function of these Acts was to create criminal offences that were aimed at deterring employers from combining to raise the price of their goods. Legislation applied to a wide range of goods, including necessities such as coal and bread. It was also common to apply such legislation to a particular city, such as Cork or Dublin.

THE COMBINATION ACTS OF 1799 AND 1800

In England, similar provisions to the Irish law applied in Acts passed by the British Parliament in 1799 and 1800 but not directly applicable to Ireland until 1803, when a special Act was passed for Ireland by the United Kingdom Parliament, applying the English law. The English Combination Act of 1800 (39 and 40 Geo. III, c. 106) declared illegal all combinations of workmen to regulate the conditions of their work. The scope and extent of these prohibitions may be summarized as follows: 'All contracts, covenants, and agreements for obtaining an advance in wages, altering the hours of work or decreasing the quantity of work, preventing workmen hiring themselves or attempting to induce them to leave work were declared illegal; so also was attending any meeting held for any of these purposes.'[30] In common with most of the legislation of this type, the effectiveness of the Act was open to doubt. Hedges and Winterbottom have suggested the Acts were not rigorously applied.[31] Other writers have emphasized continuity as a principle of the 1800 Act, as the Act provided a codification into a single generalized statute of the miscellaneous enactments of the eighteenth century.[32]

In Ireland the application of the English Combination Act of 1800 took place in 1803 (43 Geo. III, c. 86), but this resulted in heavier penalties for various offences as compared to the English law. A unique feature of the English law, namely its provision for arbitration between master and servants over wages and work, did not apply in Ireland. In Ireland the 1803 Act was confined to artisans and section 7, making the employment of a man already employed by another master a criminal offence, applied to masters in Ireland for the first time. Clarkson noted that section 12 of the 1803 Act uniquely provided for Ireland a provision that no master in the trade of the servant involved in legal proceedings could act as a justice in any proceedings heard under the combination law. Little is known as to whether this important provision was ever put into practical operation. The significance of the 1800 Act and its subsequent application in Ireland may be seen in the recognition that Parliament had decided against trade combinations of every kind. Dicey explained the legal position succinctly: 'Any artisan who organised a strike or joined a trade union was a criminal and liable on conviction to imprisonment; the strike was a crime, the trade union was an unlawful association.'[33] He attributed the severity of the Act to the sentiment of 'public opinion as influenced by the French revolution' combined with the 'tradition of paternal government', which, Dicey reasoned, supported the conviction that 'it was the duty of labourers to work for reasonable, that is to say for customary, wages'.

In theory the eighteenth-century combination laws were intended to act as a check on the activities of combinations, in particular those that involved oath-taking or attempting to dissuade workers from working at an agreed price.[34] In practice the laws may have contributed to the culture of forming secret societies and alliances beyond the reach of the authorities.[35] The use of informants and paid spies was rampant as the authorities attempted to infiltrate union organizations.[36]

THE CRIMINAL LAW IN THE DEVELOPMENT OF TRADE UNIONS IN THE NINETEENTH CENTURY

The great famine from 1845 to 1851 provides a useful dividing line in the development of the criminal law and trade unions in Ireland during the nineteenth century. Two distinct periods may be noted. The first period to 1850 includes the development of trade unions, illegal under the various Combination Acts prior to June 1824, but made lawful subject to the criminal regulation of the master and servant relationship. During the first half of the nineteenth century trade unions found common cause with supporters of repeal of the Treaty of Union as the only effective way to protect indigenous work. Ireland's de-industrialization and economic condition left unions vulnerable. Irish unions recognized long before their English counterparts that economic and political sovereignty were interrelated. Self-government might achieve better employment levels, wages and conditions of work. Taking care not to become too closely identified with active revolution, trade unions found common cause with many secret societies but continued to operate on the fringes of legality.

The second period from 1850 to the close of the century covers the period when trade unions came to terms with post-famine Ireland.

Depopulation through emigration and famine made Ireland one of the poorest countries in Europe, gradually giving way to increased urbanization and prosperity through new economic growth focused on a largely unskilled work force. The predominance of industry in the northern part of Ireland was significant and Belfast grew in importance, largely with heavy industry and shipbuilding. Political issues dominated questions relating to the future of Ireland, especially Ireland under some form of Home Rule Parliament. Trade unions were never united. At the end of the nineteenth century Irish trade unions came to terms with the decline in the traditional craft activities and the growth in new industrial processes, where Irish trade union interests were more clearly linked to the British labour movement.

Trade Unions from 1800 to 1850

In Ireland much of the legislation passed by the Irish Parliament to regulate wages and trade combinations continued in force. The Act of Union 1800, having created legislative responsibility for Ireland at Westminster, abolished the Irish Parliament. As a result Irish law was supplemented by English statutes applicable to Ireland. In the context of the development of trade unions the use of the criminal law served two functions. First, it sought to regulate the relations between individual masters and servants. This involved granting an extensive criminal jurisdiction to magistrates to enforce the law, which remained a characteristic of the law for the greater part of the nineteenth century. Second, the criminal law up until 1824 continued to apply to trade combinations in much the same way that it had developed from the eighteenth century. Legalization of trade unions in Ireland came about after serious doubts about the efficiency of enforcing the law led to the existence of the law itself being questioned.[37]

THE MASTER AND SERVANT LAWS

In carrying out its first function, the criminal law in both England and Ireland was consolidated and codified by the Master and Servant Act 1823. Described by the Webbs as 'intolerable oppression', the 1823 Act maintained the principle that any breach of an employment contract by a servant was a summary offence. The 1823 Act also considerably extended the jurisdiction and powers of magistrates.[38] Magistrates were granted additional powers of arrest by warrant whenever 'deemed necessary'. In any action by the employer, magistrates had powers to forfeit the worker's wages and grant damages to the employer. This power was in addition to the power to fine or imprison. It retained as offences any absence from service, failure to enter into the work contracted, neglect or misconduct. Such offences could be punished by up to three months' hard labour. The 1823 Act also added the use of violence, threats, intimidation, molestation or obstruction as offences that might be committed in the course of a combination.

Additional disciplinary powers given to magistrates included the power of arrest without warrant should the magistrate deem it appropriate. Magistrates had not only the power to fine or imprison, but also the power to make an order to abate a worker's wages, in the cases where employers claimed damages. The substantial powers granted to masters against servants to enforce the criminal law under the 1823 Act filled any gap left by the later repeal of the Combination Acts in 1824 and 1825. In fact, as Daphne Simon has pointed out, prosecutions of workmen for breach of contract were almost all made under the 1823 Act.[39] The breadth of section 3 of the Act allowed for prosecution for breach of contract, the master complaining upon oath to a Justice of the Peace, who could issue a warrant for the servant's arrest. If imprisonment followed, the servant could lose his wages during the time he was in prison and the amount was not recovered. Masters were not required to re-employ servants in such circumstances. Various statutory enactments maintained the inequality between master and servant.

In general, the use of the criminal law to regulate individual relations between master and servant was one-sided. The servant in England and Wales or Scotland could not invoke the criminal law against his master on the ground of a mere breach of contract. The three forms of breach of contract open to servants were activated in civil law through the county courts. Cruelty, dismissal of the servant before the end of the term of his employment or with inadequate notice, and failure to pay wages were the main grounds for a civil action. Servants who wished to pursue such an action had difficulty in proving any breach of contract. Viewed from the perspective of the servant such litigation seemed unattractive. Economic and social problems such as illiteracy or ignorance militated against giving evidence that might satisfy a court. In many cases this might prove to be an insurmountable hurdle to overcome. Some protection was afforded to employees by the Truck Act 1831, which was later amended and consolidated in 1887 and then extended to Ireland. This made it a criminal offence in certain trades to make payment of wages in goods other than ordinary currency. In England, servants, with the exception of domestic servants, could summons their masters for wages not exceeding £10 in the case of farm workers and £5 in other cases. Warrants were issued if the master did not appear after summons, and in cases of non-payment the amount due might be levied by distress, but only on default was there the possibility of imprisonment for a period not exceeding three months.

In Ireland the law of master and servant followed a similar pattern to England and Wales. The criminal jurisdiction of Justices included the law regarding servants who absented themselves, neglected to perform their contracts or were guilty of any misconduct or misdemeanour. Punishment included a fine not exceeding £5, enforceable by imprisonment not exceeding three months. The petty sessions courts in Ireland had power to punish cases of wilful damage by servants provided the value of the damage was under £5. Compensation or a fine not exceeding 40 per cent or imprisonment not exceeding one month were penalties available to the court. The civil jurisdiction of Justices extended to all claims for wages to any apprentice or labourer to the amount of £10. However, masters in Ireland, unlike in England, could be punished by fine not exceeding forty shillings for 'ill usage of their apprentice'. Cases were heard in the Petty Sessions Courts before two or more Justices. The origins of the criminal jurisdiction over masters came from a unique Irish 1819 statute (59 Geo. III, c. 92, ss. 5 and 6). But masters were rarely prosecuted and the anomalous right to prosecute the employer in Irish law seems to have gone largely unnoticed. The operation of criminal sanctions in Ireland was harsher and more extensive than in England, partly because the magistrates' jurisdiction in Ireland was more extensive than under English law. In Ireland, the magistrates' jurisdiction extended to all claims for wages for any apprentice, labourer or servant for amounts up to £10. Magistrates had jurisdiction over servants who absented themselves from work or were negligent and could impose a fine of up to £5 enforceable by imprisonment not exceeding three months. The procedure in Ireland was by use of a summons or warrant and the cases were heard by one or more justices.

THE REPEAL OF THE COMBINATION ACTS

The criminal law, in its second function to control trade combinations, gradually shifted to a regulatory structure to regulate combinations, which during the eighteenth century had been extensively prohibited in both England and Ireland. This shift of emphasis was caused by recognition of the difficulty of enforcing the law. It has already been noted that in Ireland the penalties and operation of the law had been harsher than in England. Irish opposition to the combination laws had intensified from 1800. Some commentators believe that the continued existence of criminal law regulation over the master and servant relationship made possible the repeal of the combination laws. But this view in not necessarily widely shared.[40]

Demands for repeal in both England and Ireland were regularly made.[41] More recent research[42] has concluded that their repeal may have come about because of 'how numerous and extensive early trade combinations or trade clubs had become', questioning the effectiveness of the law. In Ireland the evidence of widespread union membership scattered in trade clubs and associations was convincing proof that the combination laws could be ignored. Boyd recalls how the Chief Constable of the Dublin Police had estimated that 'every one of the sixteen trades in the city had its own club or trade union'.[43]

In Ireland different reasons for the abolition of criminal sanctions against trade combinations were advanced. The most compelling reason for abolition arose because a more potent threat posed by the criminalization of trade combinations was identified in evidence to the 1824 Select Committee on Artisans and Machinery:[44] the illegality of trade combinations encouraged their secrecy, and evidence given to the Select Committee suggested that the combination laws had not been effective. Secret societies posed a serious threat to the maintenance of law and order.[45] The fear was that the combination laws would drive workers further into the network of illegal secret societies, thereby further undermining Irish society.[46]

In both jurisdictions, the repeal of the Combination Acts in 1824 and 1825 was achieved virtually at the same time as the consolidation of the master and servant law in 1823. The Combination Laws Repeal Act 1824 (5 Geo. IV, c. 95) was passed and applied to any part of the United Kingdom of Great Britain and Ireland. The Act expressly repealed many of the earlier Irish statutes and in a general provision by implication repealed any statute that was not mentioned in the Act but that made trade union activity illegal *per se*. A noticeable feature of the 1824 Act was the inclusion of an exemption from punishment for masters who engaged in any combination.[47]

Repeal of the Combination Acts in Ireland resulted in the recognition of trade unions in Ireland. Early labour activities in pre-famine Ireland may be calculated from the 1841 census. The census identified over two million males aged fifteen and above with farm labouring accounting for over half the adult male population. The remainder were employed in the clothing trade; almost half were weavers and 158,000 were engaged in furniture, building and machinery activities. The census also showed that the female workforce numbered over one million. A large proportion were engaged in the clothing industry;

over 400,000 were spinners. A large number, over 200,000, were in domestic service. O'Connor has noted that 'Unskilled unionism therefore operated among 1.2 million labourers, who to contemporary eyes were the poor; craft unionism accounted for 240,000 artisans in apprenticed trades. At one extremity of labour organisation were 1.1 million agricultural workers; at the other were 26,000 Dublin artisans.'[48]

Craft unions were a significant feature of trade union activity in the south of Ireland. Mainly urban and centred on Dublin, the craft unions were able to take advantage of the largely unskilled labour force and this was reflected in poor working conditions. Relative to English wages, Irish craft wages were lower, though claims made by employers that Irish labour costs were higher were used successfully to defeat union attempts to restore average wages to their full value after they dropped significantly during periods of economic decline. During the period from 1840 to 1844 wages decreased by 27 per cent, an indication of the economic severity of the famine in Ireland at that period.

Irish trade union activity may also be estimated from the Friendly Societies Act 1829, which revised the original 1797 legislation. There were 281 craft societies registered, with 119 in Dublin. The remainder were scattered throughout Ireland, with clusters of union activity in Belfast, Cork and Derry. Irish trade unions were strongly identified with specific demands, such as improved working conditions and adequate wages. Evidence from the various Select Committees is inconclusive but consistent with an overall perception that Irish workers' 'demands were similar to their equivalent workers' in England.[49] Apprentices were regularly hired on a weekly or a daily basis as a 'means to reduce wages'. A common complaint was the low payment of wages, especially in circumstances where English workers would obtain higher wages.[50] In particular trades, such as printing, common complaints were of poor wages and the excessive use of apprentices. Generally the formation of Irish unions seemed to correspond to the formation and existence of trade unions in Great Britain, which reinforces the perception of similar demands.[51] Certain specific trades began to form their own interest groups or guilds, often known as associations. Examples of such trades are painters, bricklayers, cabinet makers, carpenters and saddlers. Occasionally masters approved of such organizations, as they provided a useful means of controlling the workforce.[52] Masters would insist on hiring someone drawn from a particular trade or guild. In 1838 trade guilds were formed by bookbinders, printers, plasterers and shipwrights. The Webbs identified the Dublin trades as 'the best organised in the Kingdom';[53] they ruthlessly enforced the regulation of their various industries. Estimates of trade union membership in the 1820s suggested that about 10,000 organized artisans combined in trade associations in Dublin.[54] The scope for further internal regulation and thereby monopoly came from the 1838 trade societies formed in Dublin. Even before then, the link between trade union and pressure group was established.

TRADE UNIONS AND POLITICAL ACTIVITIES

Trade union members became a regular source of support for popular political causes. Demand for Catholic emancipation intensified as initial scepticism about the Union gave rise to demands for its repeal. The campaign for Catholic emancipation achieved success in 1829 but this only served to increase popular political awareness. Particularly alarming to the British authorities was the continued rise in support for secret societies. The 1825 Select Committee on the State of Ireland[55] heard evidence about Irish unrest and the threat to the Union. Concern was expressed that such violence and intimidation might make the workforce disaffected and ineffective in Dublin, Cork and Belfast. The predominantly agricultural nature of Irish employment had been supplemented by the linen mills and shipyards of Belfast. Dublin had developed breweries and distilleries with a large market in biscuit and bread manufacturing. High unemployment in rural Ireland, with skilled labour and manufacturing confined to only a few centres such as Dublin, Belfast and Cork, left Irish labour under considerable economic pressure. Emigration from Ireland to England was significant and moved the employment of Irish labour to the centre of British politics, making it an intrinsic part of British employment relations.[56]

The impact of the famine on labour relations was significant in agricultural communities, which made up a sizeable proportion of the Irish labour force. Oliver MacDonagh believes that 'the era of comparative prosperity (18th century) had been built on insecure foundations. Tillage was labour-intensive, and the necessary labour had been supplied by early marriages and high birth rates.'[57] The potato failures in seven successive seasons led to famine; the most serious famine occurred from 1845 to 1851.[58] A general collapse in Irish rural society occurred, the population fell by one-fifth and over two million people either died from hunger or emigrated. Evidence from the Select Committee of the House of Commons in 1824 on Combinations[59] showed the violent nature of many agricultural labourers when combined in secret societies. As land holdings were inadequate to sustain the basic necessities of tenant farmers, unskilled farm labourers were displaced by tenant farmers and throughout the century Ireland experienced unrest; the threat of the Union collapsing was ever-present. Agrarian secret societies were the focal point of labour opposition to oppressive laws.[60] Most active in the counties of Leinster, Munster and the midland regions of Southern Ireland, such societies operated under different names, such as Whiteboys, Ribbonmen and Defenders.[61] Even in the towns and cities equivalent organizations appeared in the 1830s. Accompanying economic demands for changes in the land law, Catholic emancipation was finally granted in 1829. Political agitation was perceived to be effective and popular awareness among all the social classes was raised.

Aside from agrarian violence, violence caused from strikes, lockouts or wage disputes was also heavily regulated by the criminal law. Prosecutions might be brought under the master and servant legislation, for breach of contract, for riot, assault or common law conspiracy. In Ireland the crime of conspiracy was very broadly defined.[62] Prosecutions could also be taken under a number of eighteenth-century statutes, which were retained and further consolidated in 1843 (6 and 7 Vict., c. 40). Occasionally Parliament added additional measures, responding to the requirements of the time. Orth notes that from 1828 to 1861 an 1828 Act was in force, which recognized a separate crime of 'assault committed in pursuance of any conspiracy to raise the rate of wages'.[63] In Ireland prosecutions were made under the 1823 Act, many such prosecutions coinciding with periods of political agitation. Park has noted that

> it may be observed that the majority of the Combination Acts were enacted at a time of crisis for England, and most of them fit within the following periods, viz 1740–48 (War of Austrian Succession), 1756–63 (Seven Years' War), 1775–83 (American Revolution), 1793–1815 (Napoleonic War). For example, the repressive laws against combination in the linen and cotton trades were passed when the Seven Years' War was in progress. The 1780 Act was enacted when England was at war in America, and the 1803 Act was passed after Ireland had witnessed rebellions in 1798 and 1803.[64]

However, in analysing the importance of the criminal law to the development of trade union activity, Park fails to take account of the importance of the legislation affecting master and servant, which was potentially as severe on combination as the combination laws themselves.

Evidence received before the Select Committee on Combinations of Workmen in 1838 told of large numbers of outrages and associated problems among the workforce attributed to the existence of combinations. Evidence also given to the 1838 Select Committee explained the loss of shipbuilding from Dublin as attributable to the 'oppressive ship-carpenters' union'.[65] As William Hall, a solicitor, had argued in 1824, trade had left Dublin because of disputes between masters and servants.

TRADE UNIONISM AND THE CRIMINAL LAW

Criminal prosecutions were possible under the Combination Laws Repeal Act 1824. It has been noted above how the 1824 Act was intended to abolish all combination laws, but it preserved under sections 5 and 6 specific offences that might be committed but only by individuals, not by groups or organizations. However, soon after the 1824 Act was put into operation, a number of defects became the apparent. First, as Hedges and Winterbottom observed, the Act did not 'deal with coercive measures taken by masters and [its] terms did not cover the whole ground in enumerating instances in which threats, violence or other coercive measures might be used by workmen'.[66] Second, doubts existed as to whether the 1824 Act could be construed as overriding existing common law, which rendered a combination to induce a breach of contract itself a criminal offence. This point was reconsidered in *R* v *Bunn*,[67] which admitted the possibility that criminal sanctions might be invoked in certain circumstances for a conspiracy to break a contract.

More significant than both of these defects was the policy question of where the 1824 Act fitted into the social, economic and political needs of the period. Sections 5 and 6 of the Act maintained specific offences which were considered inadequate to deal with industrial stoppages, violence and public unrest. In 1825 the question of the effectiveness of the criminal law was once more considered by a Select Committee. The repeal of the combination laws had coincided with an increase in workers' activity, the organization of mass demonstrations and strike action. There was also a perception that the 1824 legislation had gone too far in favour of workers' rights. The outcome was fresh legislation for England, Wales, Ireland and Scotland in a new Act. The 1825 Act repealed the 1824 Act and introduced new sections that were more carefully constructed than the previous law. These sections allowed for the prosecution of specified illegal activities. In contrast to the broader sections in the 1824 Act, sections 4 and 5 expressly defined combinations that were not to be criminal in a narrow way.

In general terms the construction placed upon sections 4 and 5 by the courts accepted that collective bargaining over wages and hours was legal. Doubts existed as to the legal right to resort to strike or lockouts to enforce collective decisions. The assumption was made that a strike for the sole purpose of raising wages or altering hours was not criminal if pursued as part of an agreement. Court cases such as *Duffield*[68] and *Rowlands*[69] upheld the view that it was illegal for workmen to combine to induce men to leave their work as an obstruction to the master, both under section 7 of the 1825 Act and at common law. Instances of the use of the criminal law appear from accounts of various trials in Ireland. O'Connor notes that in 1826 strikers at a printer's works in Carrickfergus were imprisoned under the 1825 Act. Two years later in Clonmel five men were sentenced to the treadmill after a dispute over wages. At least seven men were transported between 1825 and 1834 from Ireland for the most serious offences arising out of unrest over wages and conditions.[70]

An important aspect of section 3 of the 1825 Act was that it stipulated various criminal offences that could be committed by a single individual. The section was difficult to interpret because by their nature combinations involved more than one individual. It was difficult for the prosecuting authorities to establish among a group of persons sufficient evidence to prove a common purpose within the definition of the individual offences defined in the Act. A significant factor in any combination was the idea of coercion common to all the activities undertaken. Another factor was how to identify the various activities, such as 'obstruction', 'threats', 'force', 'intimidation' and 'molestation', in terms of their effect, namely to prevent someone from working or returning to work. Such difficulties in the interpretation of the law added to the complexity of deciding whether or not to prosecute. Conspiracy prosecutions taken against workmen involved jury trial, which left the jury to determine whether on the facts proven the defendant had used coercion.[71] This left a further element of uncertainty as to the success of prosecutions.[72] As Hedges and Winterbottom pointed out, 'It was a regrettable blunder on the part of the legislature in 1825 to have left those combinations which it desired to be criminal to the vagueness of the common law.'[73]

In Ireland the power of union membership was a barometer of food prices and economic activity. A severe economic slump from 1839 to 1842 severely depressed trade union activity among the traditional craft and industrial sectors of the economy. Revival came in 1844 among industrial workers in the cities of Dublin and Belfast. The famine left the agricultural sector so firmly depressed that labour activity found a political force in Daniel O'Connell's popular repeal movement. Irish trade unionism seemed firmly distracted from issues of class and labour by the nationalist cause. This never achieved a political agenda for the unions in Ireland. O'Connell's distrust of union activities came from a number of concerns. He distrusted union support for activities in restraint of trade and resisted union activities that bordered on the illegal. Trade union support for secret societies that favoured violence threatened the repeal cause. In O'Connell's mind the tension between the repeal movement and trade unions appears to arise from the stigma attached to breaches of the criminal law that O'Connell opposed. Tactically, O'Connell distanced himself from the various trade union combinations showing that many of the rules were illegal. Originally, in the 1820s, O'Connell had called for the repeal of the trade union combination laws and an inquiry into trade union activities. He later chaired such an inquiry in 1837–8, which never produced a final report but provided evidence of the violent nature of some trade union activities in Ireland.

Trade Unions from 1850 to 1900

During the first half of the nineteenth century, Irish trade unions had organized and taken shape despite the strict laws by which they were regulated. Throughout the second half of the nineteenth century, Irish trade union activities were inexorably linked to the economic and political state of the country. Post-famine Ireland underwent considerable change. Emigration and death reduced its population size and economic progress was rapid, especially in the industrialized areas in the north of Ireland, particularly Belfast. Urbanization was a major factor in economic and social change. By 1911, Belfast had experienced a phenomenal growth in size to 387,000 from only 37,000 in 1821. This new industrialization focused on textiles and a massive expansion in the metals trade engaged in shipbuilding, such as turners, boilermakers, machine makers and iron manufacturers. Significantly, this led to the development of a sectarian workforce as the vast majority of workers in employment were Protestant.

Irish trade unions were fragmented although numerous and widespread, and, as the century progressed, increasing in sophistication. A noticeable trend was the development of links with the British trade union movement. By 1898 the Chief Registrar of Friendly Societies noted that 'the great majority of organised workers in Ireland were associated with British societies'.[74] Partly this was a reflection of the need for organizational change among the Irish unions and partly recognition of the political force in the United Kingdom to bring about an amelioration in the conditions of work. Linked to the question of relations between workers and employers, current issues of the day were debated at trade union meetings. The Annual British Trades Union Congress (TUC) met in Dublin in September 1880 and in Belfast in 1893. In its Thirteenth Report, Irish land laws, reform of the jury law and the extension of the Summary Jurisdiction Acts were discussed, indicating the breadth and scope of the matters that fell to discussion by the TUC in Ireland. Reforms in public health, sanitation, education and local government were adopted in Ireland, assisted by British trade union pressure. The assimilation of Irish law with the law in England, Wales and Scotland was seen as a fundamental principle for working men and encouraged the relationship between trade unions in Britain.

Irish trade union activities operated for the remainder of the nineteenth century at the fringes of illegality as membership embraced secret societies and the more usual form of trade organization. In fact, internal organization of union activities prospered with the formation of trade associations, formed from Dublin craftsmen, which by 1863 had become a United Trades' Association with regular meetings in Cork and Dublin. In 1868 the formation of the British Trades Union Congress provided an opportunity for the development of a larger organization. It was suggested that an 'amalgamation of trades' might be formed throughout Great Britain and Ireland. Instances of such relations between British and Irish trade union activities may be found in a number of examples. In 1880 the annual meeting of the TUC was held in Dublin. Clarkson calculated that out of the twenty-three Dublin trades societies represented, eleven were branches of amalgamated unions.[75] A noticeable feature of the business transacted by the Irish unions was their emphasis and concern for nationalist issues. Issues of wide contemporary significance were discussed at the meeting of Congress, including land law reform, home rule, codification of the criminal law and the use of coercion in enforcing the law in Ireland.[76]

The British trade union movement could form itself into an effective lobby for reforms. Parliamentary intervention included the Molestation of Workmen Act 1859, which amended the law to allow workmen to enter agreements and claim better wages or hours with legal immunity. Later the Trade Union Act 1871 explicitly recognized this right.[77] The criminal law could be used to protect trade unionists as well as restrict their activities. The Bakehouse (Regulations) Act 1863 outlawed night work for journeymen workers in bakeries and granted the power of inspection to inspectors to visit bakeries. The consolidation of smaller trade unions caused some organizational changes in 1851 with the Irish equivalent of the Amalgamated Society of Engineers being formed to consolidate the Irish engineering unions. In 1866 the Amalgamated Society of Carpenters and Joiners was formed six years after its English counterpart. Two years later there were twelve English trades associations with branches in Ireland. The United Trades Association was formed in 1863 to protect the rights of labour and encourage cooperation. An attempt was made a year later to unify all trade associations in Ireland into one grand general union. The Dublin United Trades Association undertook to form what it regarded as a 'useful and respectable' organization in Ireland. Thirty Irish unions were formed between 1889 and 1891, and many comprised unskilled workers.[78] Significant legislative change came about with the introduction of the Master and Servant Act 1867. Events leading up to the passage of the Master and Servant Act 1867 may be shortly told. Because of the legal restraints trade unions continued to operate under, there was an increasing trend towards general campaigns to motivate support for trade unions. A national conference in May 1865 attended by many delegates led to a political campaign to reform the law of master and servant. The result was the Master and Servant Act 1867, which followed soon after a Select Committee on the operation of master and servant law, appointed in 1866, had reported. The 1867 Act made significant concessions to workers.

Workers were entitled to give evidence on their own behalf, and summonses were to be issued rather than arrests made when the defendant failed to appear at court. The power to abate wages remained, as did the power to impose a fine, not exceeding £20, and in default to commit the offender to gaol for up to three months. The 1867 Act still preserved imprisonment for aggravated misconduct concerning 'injury to person and property, misconduct, misdemeanour, or ill-treatment'.[79] Magistrates retained discretion in cases of 'misconduct'. Criminal prosecution in England and Wales continued to be taken and remained a characteristic of the law after 1867. In Ireland the 1867 Act also applied. It operated, as in England and Wales, with a number of prosecutions taken against workmen and the law was regarded as 'oppressive and harsh' in its application. Nevertheless, despite the availability of the criminal laws used, most notably for breach of contract or in neglecting work or leaving service, trade unions continued to survive and flourish.[80]

Earlier Irish law recognized a number of additional offences codified in the Summary Jurisdiction (Ireland) Act 1851,[81] preserved from the earlier centuries. An example was the power of one Justice to punish servants and labourers guilty of ill-behaviour during work, by imprisonment not exceeding one month of hard labour. The use of the criminal law in both England and Ireland was reviewed by a Royal

Commission of Inquiry in 1867. Registration of trade unions under the Friendly Societies Act 1855 had taken place on the assumption that trade unions were not unlawful. This assumption was questioned in *Hornby* v *Close*,[82] where it was held that trade unions were acting 'in restraint of trade'. Following the Report of the Royal Commission and further lobbying, the Trade Union Act 1871 clarified the legal status of registered trade unions. The passing of the Criminal Law Amendment (Violence, etc.) Act 1871 and the Conspiracy and Protection of Property Act 1875 further modified the use of special criminal legislation relating to trade unions. Finally, the Employers and Workmen Act 1875 abolished the old law of master and servant. Employer and employee became 'equal' under the law of contract. The application of the 1875 Act to Ireland appeared as a result of the efforts of the Trades Union Congress.

Despite these changes, which appeared to remove the widespread use of the criminal law, in Ireland a residual criminal jurisdiction remained. This arose because the civil jurisdiction of magistrates under the Petty Session (Ireland) Act 1852 survived. Default of any payment or debt could result in a term of imprisonment not exceeding six weeks or until the sum of money was paid. One further peculiarity was the law relating to domestic servants. In England the law treated domestic servants differently from in Ireland. In England no criminal offence applied to domestic servants for breaches of contract. In Ireland the criminal jurisdiction of the courts applied. An additional source of criminal proscription appears from the early Linen and Hempen Manufacturers Ireland Acts 1835. This legislation was retained in force by annual renewal and provided that breach of contract by linen weavers was a criminal offence. Some parts of the 1835 Act relating to embezzling and purloining material gradually ceased to have any use as linen mills came to replace the work of weavers. Offences were retained up to the end of the nineteenth century, but gradually ceased to be prosecuted.[83] Despite the passage of the 1875 legislation these laws were retained and attempts to make them permanent after 1875 were resisted by the TUC.

Vaughan estimates that Irish masters and servants used the courts frequently to gain convictions for criminal offences.[84] For example, in 1854 and 1855 'almost one-third of the UK's convictions for breach of contract were in Ireland'. After 1867 convictions continued and between 1868 and 1872 Ireland continued to have one-third of the convictions. One example was in 1873 at the petty sessions in Lisnaskea, when a hired servant was 'insubordinate, disobedient, and refused to work'.[85] He was sentenced to one month's imprisonment. The use of criminal sanctions continued to dominate relations between master and servant in both England and Ireland.[86] In Ireland the harsher criminal jurisdiction maintained the use of oppressive laws to regulate Irish offences. Despite the use of criminal sanctions, trade associations developed and workers combined. In the scale of national affairs, Irish nationalism and politics had a higher priority than workers' rights and popular support for home rule appeared to overshadow any development of labour in Ireland. That legacy remains today. As a reflection of the economic state of Ireland as well as the attitude to labour relations, the criminal roots in the relationship between master and servant remain influential.

Irish immigration and patterns of settlement also had an impact on the trade union movement in Britain. Hunt has estimated that 'The famine influx raised the number of Irish-born in Britain to approaching three-quarters of a million, about 3.5% of the population. . . . By 1911 the number of Irish-born had fallen to 550,000 or about 1.3% of the population.'[87] However, these figures are deceptive as to their impact on the trade union movement in England. One distortion in the figures is the fact that there were more males than females and most were usually of working age. Many born of Irish parents in Britain were brought up in well-defined immigrant communities but were not recorded in the statistics as being born in Ireland. Hunt believes that, from the 1840s to the First World War, the 'overall Irish contribution to the British labour force must have been between 4 [and] 6% of the total'.[88] There is considerable debate about the exact importance of Irish labour to the British economy. Some historians regard Irish labour as indispensable to industrial growth in England while others regard this as an exaggeration of the importance of the Irish labourer. Also controversial is the question of the link between Irish workers and political movements in England. Some historical evidence points to a clear link between the Irish workforce and the Chartist movement in the 1840s.[89] Certainly the fear of public violence and disorder linked to Ireland may explain the suspicion of the authorities of Irish involvement in British labour unions.[90] The use of railways brought a new labour force in the 1850s. Rising wage prospects in Britain and substantial employment possibilities increased the demand for Irish labour in England. The 1870s marked a period when the Irish economy and social structure became interlinked with Britain,[91] while the 1840s was a period when industrialization in Britain had little impact on Ireland.

CONCLUSION

Criminal prosecutions taken against servants by masters were an important element in the historical development of trade union relations in both England and Ireland.[92] It has generally been concluded that criminal sanctions were ineffective against the rise in combinations.[93] In Ireland the early and fragmented development of trade associations and combinations, often in secret societies and within a nationalist culture, may have been due to the harsh effects of the criminal law. Indirectly this made labour organizations in Ireland less effective as a unifying force. Despite its harshness the criminal law appears no more effective in Ireland in preventing the formation of trade unions than in England.

Ireland's trade union relations were linked to the nationalist cause and the political agitation for home rule in the 1870s and 1880s. The use of coercive powers to enforce the ordinary law reinforced the harshness of criminal sanctions against trade unions and combinations. Ireland never fully unionized its workforce and the absence of a strong manufacturing base may have been a major factor in the development of trade union politics. Among the skilled activities, such as printing and linen making, trade unions flourished. Despite the presence of harsh combination laws until 1825, the development of trade combinations does not appear to have been unduly inhibited. Ireland's establishment of its own Trades Union Congress came later, in 1894. By 1902 it consisted of 70,000 affiliated members, a figure that remained static for years after. Ireland's economic and industrial activities were centred on Cork, Dublin and Belfast, and major industrial activities were confined to those cities.

Irish workers were mainly unskilled. Only a small proportion of the workforce had a skill, and in the 1880s, skills were confined to the main city industries of shipbuilding, printing and, for example, the gas industry. Political issues of the day overshadowed the development of active trade union activities, which survived on a narrow base of workers. By the turn of the century Belfast came to dominate trade unionism and labour politics in Ireland amid the growing conflict between the nationalist and unionist causes. In conclusion, Ireland's experience of the development of the criminal law in the master and servant relationship only served to confirm the oppressive nature of law in Ireland. The legacy of the early history remains. A largely unskilled workforce within the context of a low-wage economy was a symptom of the unequal relations between master and servant, with its origins in the eighteenth and nineteenth centuries.

NOTES

I am grateful to Professor Ishida, Faculty of Law, Nagoya University, Japan, for help and advice in my thinking about this subject. Errors are my own responsibility.

1. A. Kerr and G. Whyte, *Irish Trade Union Law* (1985); F. von Prondynski, *Employment Law in Ireland* (1991).
2. E. O'Connor, *A Labour History of Ireland 1824-1960* (Dublin, 1992).
3. P. O'Higgins, English law and the Irish question (1966) 1 *Irish Jurist* 59.
4. J. V. Orth, *Trade Union Combinations and Conspiracy: A Legal History of Trade Unionism 1721-1906* (1991), pp. 5–59.
5. R. Y. Hedges and A. Winterbottom, *The Legal History of Trade Unionism* (1930).
6. H. Smythe, *The Office of Justice of the Peace in Ireland* (Dublin, 1861).
7. J. Boyle, *The Irish Labor Movement in the Nineteenth Century* (1988), p. 7.
8. N. A. Citrine, *Trade Union Law* (3rd edn, 1967); P. O'Higgins, *A Bibliography of Irish Trials and Other Legal Proceedings* (1986), para. 3.130.
9. P. Park, The Combination Acts in Ireland, 1727–1825 (1979) 14 *Irish Jurist* (n.s.) 340.
10. J. D. Clarkson, *Labour and Nationalism in Ireland* (New York, 1925).
11. Orth, *op. cit.*, p. 5.
12. A. V. Dicey, The combination laws as illustrating the relation between law and opinion in England during the nineteenth century (1903–4) 17 *Harvard Law Review* 511; W. Erle, *The Law Relating to Trade Unions* (1869); Royal Commission on Trade Unions (1868–9), Session paper XXXI (20).
13. Orth, *op. cit.*, pp. 5–59.
14. 2 Esp. 719, 170 Eng Rep 508.
15. Clarkson, *op cit.*
16. Clarkson, *op. cit.*
17. Park, *op. cit.*
18. J. E. Davis, *The Master and Servant Act 1867* (1868).
19. Park, *op. cit.*
20. Park, *op. cit.*
21. Clarkson, *op. cit.*
22. D. Bleakley, Trade union beginnings in Belfast and district with special reference to the period 1881–1900, MA thesis, Belfast, 1955.
23. Boyle, *op. cit.*, pp. 15–25.
24. R. B. McDowell, *Public Opinion and Government Policy in Ireland 1801–1846* (1952).
25. Boyle, *op. cit.*
26. O. MacDonagh, The economy and society, in W. E. Vaughan (ed.), *A New History of Ireland*, vol. V, *1801–1870* (Oxford, 1989), pp. 222–6.
27. C. McCarthy, *Trade Unions in Ireland 1894–1960* (Dublin, 1977).
28. MacDonagh, *op. cit.*
29. Park, *op. cit.*, pp. 345–55.
30. Orth, *op. cit.*, p. 50.
31. Hedges and Winterbottom, *op. cit.*, p. 34.
32. B. Bercusson, One hundred years of conspiracy and protection of property: time for a change (1977) 40 MLR 268.
33. A. V. Dicey, *Lectures on the Relation between Law and Public Opinion in England during the Nineteenth Century* (2nd edn, 1914), p. 99.
34. P. L. R. Horn, The National Agricultural Labourers' Union in Ireland, 1873–9 (1971) 107 *Irish Historical Studies*, March; T. O'Nolan, The origin and development of guilds and trade unions (1912) *Irish Ecclesiastical Review*.
35. O'Connor, *op. cit.*, pp. 3–24.
36. J. F. McEldowney, Legal aspects of the Irish secret service fund, 1793–1833 (1986) 25 *Irish Historical Studies* 129, at pp. 132–4.

37. E. Strauss, *Irish Nationalism and British Democracy* (1951).
38. H. L. Humphreys, *Justice of the Peace for Ireland* (9th edn, Dublin, 1897).
39. D. Simon, Master and servant, in J. Saville (ed.), *Democracy and the Labour Movement* (London, 1954), pp. 195–200.
40. Bercusson, *op. cit.*; A. E. Musson, *British Trade Unions 1800–1875* (1976); F. B. Sayre, Criminal conspiracy (1921–2) 35 *Harvard Law Review* 393; Simon, *op. cit.*
41. M. A. Clegg, A. Fox and A. F. Thompson, *A History of British Trade Unions since 1889* (Oxford, 1962); M. D. George, The combination laws (1935–6) 6 *Economic History Review* First Series, 172; S. Webb and B. Webb, *The History of Trade Unionism* (1907).
42. Musson, *op. cit.*
43. A. Boyd, *The Rise of the Irish Trade Unions* (Dublin, 1972), pp. 34–5.
44. First Report from the Select Committee to inquire into the state of the law regarding artisans and machinery (1824) HC 51.
45. M. R. Beames, *Peasants and Power: The Whiteboy Movements and Their Control in Pre-famine Ireland* (1983).
46. Clark and Donelly (eds), *Irish Peasants: Violence and Political Unrest 1780–1914* (1983), p. 66.
47. B. W. Haines, English labour law and the separation from contract (1980) 1 *Journal of Legal History* 262; M. J. Klarman, The judges versus the unions: the development of British labor law, 1867–1913 (1989) 75 *Virginia Law Review* 1487; Musson, *op. cit.*
48. O'Connor, *op. cit.*, pp. 7–8.
49. First and Second Reports from the Select Committee on combinations of workmen (1837–8), Minutes of Evidence, HC 488, viii.
50. Boyle, *op. cit.*
51. McCarthy, *op. cit.*
52. Horn, *op. cit.*
53. Webb and Webb, *op. cit.*
54. O'Connor, *op. cit.*, p. 10.
55. Report from the Select Committee appointed to inquire into the effects of 5 Geo. IV, c. 95, in respect of the conduct of workmen and others in the United Kingdom, and how far it may be necessary to repeal and amend the same Act (1825) Minutes of Evidence, HC 417, 437.
56. W. N. Hancock, Law reforms which have been successfully advocated by the Trades Union Congress and the further law reforms which they now seek (1880) 8 *Journal of the Statistical and Social Inquiry Society of Ireland* 170.
57. MacDonagh, *op. cit.*, pp. 218–24.
58. McDowell, *op. cit.*
59. First Report from the Select Committee 1824 (see note 44).
60. P. Roberts, Caravats and Shanavests: Whiteboyism and faction fighting in East Munster, in Clark and Donelly (eds), *Irish Peasants: Violence and Political Unrest 1780–1914* (1983), p. 66.
61. Clark and Donelly, *op. cit.*
62. O'Higgins, *op. cit.* (1986), para. 3.153.
63. Orth, *op. cit.*, p. 165.
64. Park, *op. cit.*, p. 358.
65. First and Second Reports from the Select Committee 1837–8 (see note 49).
66. Hedges and Winterbottom, *op. cit.*
67. (1872) 12 Cox CC 316.
68. (1851) 5 Cox CC 592.
69. (1851) 5 Cox CC 436.
70. O'Connor, *op. cit.*, p. 16.
71. R. S. Wright, *Law of Criminal Conspiracies and Agreements* (1873).
72. L. M. Hill, The two-witness rule in English treason: some comments on the emergence of procedural law (1968) 12 *American Journal of Legal History* 95; G. W. Hilton, *The Truck System: Including a History of the British Truck Acts, 1465–1960* (Cambridge, 1960).
73. Hedges and Winterbottom, *op. cit.*, p. 59.
74. Boyd, *op. cit.*, p. 69.
75. Clarkson, *op. cit.*, p. 178.
76. Clarkson, *op. cit.*, p. 183.

77. B. Hepple and P. O'Higgins, *Employment Law* (4th edn, 1981), p. 61; Kerr and Whyte, *op. cit.*; von Prondynski, *op. cit.*

78. O'Connor, *op. cit.*, p. 47.

79. P. H. J. H. Gosden, *The Friendly Societies in England, 1815-1875* (Manchester, 1961); G. Himmelfarb, The politics of democracy: the English Reform Act of 1867 (1966-7) 6 *Journal of British Studies* 97; Simon, *op. cit.*

80. W. R. Cornish and G. de N. Clark, *Law and Society in England 1750-1950* (1989), pp. 205, 311-12; R. B. Haldane, The labourer and the law (1903) 83 *Contemporary Review* 362; J. R. Hicks, The early industrial conciliation in England (1930) 10 *Economica* 25.

81. 14 and 15 Vic., c. 92, s. 16(4).

82. (1867) 2 QB 153.

83. Humphreys, *op. cit.*, p. 318.

84. W. E. Vaughan, Ireland *c.* 1870, in Vaughan (ed.), *A New History of Ireland*, vol. V, *1801-1870* (Oxford, 1989), p. 755.

85. *Ibid.*

86. H. Crompton, *Our Criminal Justice* (1881).

87. E. H. Hunt, *British Labour History 1815-1914* (1991), p. 158.

88. *Ibid.*

89. R. O'Higgins, The Irish influence in the Chartist movement (1961) 20 *Past and Present* 83.

90. H. W. McCready, British labours' lobby, 1867-75 (1956) 22 *Canadian Journal of Economic and Political Science* 22.

91. C. T. E. Leslie, Trades unions and combinations in 1853 (1853) 3 *Transactions of the Dublin Statistical Society*, 6th session.

92. W. H. Coates, Benthamism, *laissez-faire* and collectivism (1950) 11 *Journal of the History of Ideas* 357.

93. A. L. Haslam, *The Law Relating to Trade Combinations* (1931); E. J. Hobsbawm, *Labouring Men* (1964); Musson, *op. cit.*

13

Change and Continuity: British Social Security Law in the 1990s

Julian Fulbrook

Social security law determines questions of income maintenance by the state. It is therefore principally concerned with poverty. In Britain it is the primary means of support for a sizeable percentage of the population who would otherwise be destitute, and an important component of the domestic budget of many others. The context of the law is therefore centred on the elderly, the unemployed and the infirm, for these are the main client groups.

It is scarcely surprising that the subject has not been at the forefront of legal debate and analysis. First, the sums involved are minuscule. For example, the new Disability Living Allowance, introduced in April 1992, which is intended for people with severe disabilities and attempts to ensure that they remain in the community rather than become hospitalized, started at a rate of £11.55 extra a week for the care component. Its predecessor benefit, the Attendance Allowance, spawned a vast quantity of administrative adjudication and litigation, and the likelihood is that the new allowance will follow this path. However, two points can be made about the financial implications: first, the saving to the Exchequer of keeping such an individual out of hospital is enormous; second, the marginal gain to the individual claimant, perhaps a young adult on basic Income Support of £33.60 a week, would be correspondingly very significant.

A second reason for the relegation of social security law in the legal edifice is that much of its litigation is in the twilight world of administrative tribunals. Until comparatively recently, these tribunals were not just out of sight, veiled by the long-standing bar on observers, they were largely out of mind because of the Dicey legacy of a refusal to countenance the concept of administrative justice. Despite their often baffling intricacy, social security questions were not generally thought of as legal questions. Recognition of the essentially legal nature of dispute resolution came slowly in the 1970s. For example, Professor Street, who had given the pathbreaking Hamlyn law lectures on Justice in the Welfare State in 1968, could still write in 1974 that

Supplementary Benefit Appeal Tribunals 'are not so much tribunals as an extension of social work'.[1]

However, much has changed in social security law in the past two decades. A good deal of the metamorphosis has derived from Paul O'Higgins, who with his scholarship and cheerful support of the endeavours of others has provided a considerable impetus. Not only was his Cambridge course on social security law one of the first in Britain, its graduates have provided a steady stream of theorists and practitioners. One by-product was this author's volume in Studies in Labour and Social Law,[2] but Professor O'Higgins's inveterate bibliographic skills have also produced the basic reference tools for research. An additional inspiration has been his work in the European Institute of Social Security, cross-fertilizing ideas between countries with widely disparate views on the scope and nature of social security law.

The formal retirement of Professor O'Higgins is not only a suitable occasion to celebrate a rite of passage for him, but also a suitable point to take stock of the development of a subject to which he has contributed so much. This short tribute to him examines four persistent themes of British welfare law, from the old Poor Law to the current milestone of the fiftieth anniversary of the Beveridge Report, with Sir Otto Kahn-Freund's wise proviso that social security law is 'not only complex [but] extraordinarily kaleidoscopic, so that everything said today may very well have lost its validity tomorrow'.[3]

LEGALISM AND VOLUNTARISM

Perhaps the greatest change in recent years has been an acknowledgement on all sides that social security law is very properly a concern of lawyers and not simply a minor branch of social administration. Historically, there seems to have been an ebb and flow in the involvement of lawyers in the welfare process. The recent experiment of the Social Fund, much embattled at its birth,[4] perhaps signals yet another attempt to 'keep the lawyers out', but it so far remains an exception to a general trend.

Interestingly, the foundations of the British national welfare system in the Poor Relief Act 1601 were very much in the legal domain, with a formula whose essential rating base remained until the advent of the poll tax. Previously, the care of the poor had been very much a matter for voluntary effort, particularly in private charity funnelled through the church. Although a series of statutes in the sixteenth century had attempted to regularize these church welfare institutions, the 1601 Act broke with the voluntary mode. Inevitably perhaps, given the widespread corruption of the time, the existing charitable structure was open to criticism; as Professor Rimlinger points out, these imperfections were largely because the system had a tendency towards indiscriminate giving, because the principal motivation was the salvation of the donor.[5] Siren voices are again to be heard for 'voluntarization' of both central and local services, and similar arguments are being rehearsed that 'dependency and vulnerability are endemic features of the human condition and the question then is how these dependencies are to be handled, whether through the state or more through private charity and voluntary sector provision'.[6] Although the spectre of corruption is perhaps not such an acute problem to be faced in the 1990s, the related element of public accountability is still a factor to be wrestled with.

The legal structure of the 1601 Act was very definitely a state enterprise system. A compulsory poor rate was levied on the occupiers of property within each parish, and there was no longer the pretence of a 1536 statute, which urged that 'Every preacher, parson, vicar and curate, as well as in their sermons, collections, bidding of the beads as in the time of confession and making of wills, is to exhort, move, stir, and provoke people to be liberal for the relief of the impotent.'[7] Following compulsory taxation, the 1601 Act then laid down a battery of legal guidelines for the distribution of benefits, which were to be carried out by the Overseer appointed by local justices to administer the poor rate fund. A right of appeal from a decision of the Overseer to the Justices was entrenched from the start, and indeed many claimants petitioned directly to the Justices before a decision had been made on their benefits.[8] In 1722, this legal right of appeal was statutorily modified so that no claimant could petition the Justices until they had been refused benefit by the Overseer. This has remained the basic structure of the 'statutory authorities' mode ever since, with an appeal from the decision of an Adjudication Officer to the independent Social Security Appeal Tribunal.

The fury unleashed when it was proposed that there be no such right in Social Fund cases suggests a deeply embedded principle. The short but swingeing criticisms of the Council on Tribunals in their unprecedented Special Report, and their follow-up visits to Ministers, was a vital matter in causing a reformulation; yet the membership list of the Council at the time does not suggest revolutionary tendencies.[9] The back-tracking, with a mollifying second tier appeal from the discretion of the local social security staff to a Social Fund Inspector, was a rare defeat for the Government view. However, the early signals are rather predictably that this half-baked alternative is not working satisfactorily,[10] and no doubt further changes will be in prospect. Certainly, the history suggests that, although a multiplicity of tribunals are spawned with new benefits, they tend to coalesce.

At the start of the statutory welfare system, one radical concept of the 1601 Act was not simply to give immediate cash handouts or benefits in kind such as clothing or groceries, but to compel the Overseer to buy raw materials 'to set the poor to work'. Certainly, in its theoretical form the Act was highly progressive for its time, and a significant change from the penal provisions of earlier legislation dealing with the poor; for example, the 1536 statute had as sanctions for being a 'sturdy vagabond' a sliding scale for three offences of voluntary unemployment, which were whipping, ear cropping and summary execution. However, Professor Jordan's historian's view that the 1601 Act was a 'brilliantly conceived system of administration in which the remotest parish was linked with Westminster; and the whole realm was declared to be a single community of responsibility for the relief of poverty'[11] seems a trifle too complimentary. By contrast, the perspective of a leading American welfare lawyer, Professor ten Brock, is that the 1601 statute 'is better characterized as rambling, imprecise and inartistic'.[12] Such a viewpoint would certainly seem to be more par for the course for British welfare legislation.

As ever, theory and practice were not wholly related in the subsequent administration of the 1601 Act. Sidney and Beatrice Webb, in their monumental history of the Poor Law, stated that 'between the statute book and the actual administration of the parish officers there was normally only a casual connection'.[13] However pathbreaking the concepts of the 1601 Act, its ideals were largely lost in the swirls of local corruption.

A critical reappraisal by Parliament in 1723, commonly known as Sir Edward Knatchbull's Act, attempted a restriction on the legal powers of magistrates, which were mainly thought to be responsible for the abuse. The 1723 Act is also important for authorizing the establishment of 'workhouses', in an endeavour to fulfil the 1601 principle of 'setting the poor to work'; this remains a prime historical example of a charitable model transmogrifying into a nationalized institution. The first workhouse had been established in Bristol in 1697 by a philanthropist, John Carey, with the aim of encouraging the unemployed through the provision of paid work until suitable alternative employment could be found for them. It was therefore originally a classic illustration of the 'Workfare' concept, currently the 'flavour of the month' with political commentators of all ideological perspectives in the United States, and perhaps ready for import into Britain. The workhouses of course became in time a monumental bureaucratic tyranny. And the fall-out, particularly from the Victorian workhouse era, still casts a pall over hospitals and elderly persons' homes to the present day.[14] Indeed, despite the triumphalism of the abolition in 1948 of the Poor Law, it is clear that many of the structures as well as the concepts lingered on. In a memorable phrase, Gill Burke states that the 1948 Act took the Poor Law relieving duties and 'bifurcated them'. '"Out Door Relief" became "National Assistance" and "In Door", or residential, relief became the responsibility of local authority Welfare (later Social Services) Departments.'[15] Undoubtedly, the aura of the Poor Law has lingered on even more obviously in the local authority housing context, and 'Indeed, for at least fifteen years after the passing of the 1948 Act most homeless family accommodation was situated in what had previously been workhouses.'[16]

With Knatchbull's Act another charitable model also moved into the state sector; Parliament gave a power to the Justices to build houses for the poor by funding from the poor rate rather than the previous construction of almshouses from sporadic charitable funding. Part of the aim was to kick-start construction work in the economy, but another aim was to settle itinerant vagrants. This policing or settling function is a further well-worn theme of welfare law. Although the first 'council homes' were not built until the 1890s, 1723 was the start of public sector housing. It led to emancipation for millions from the degradation of the worst sectors of private housing, but also to all the attendant travails of housing administration, such as waiting lists, repairs, rent collection and arrears. Above all, it led to the vexed legal and political conundrum of 'homelessness' as a trigger for accommodation provision.

The 1723 Act therefore set in train many activities in the public domain. Indeed, public housing and institutional care for the elderly have only in recent years become questioned as routine functions of local government in Britain. Whereas the workhouse was technically abolished in 1948, the actual buildings live on in many guises in the health service or in the local authority realm. And in public housing, there was of course a huge increase in council dwellings in the 1950s and 1960s. Already in the late 1970s there had been a slowing down of public-sector building starts, but with the advent of the Thatcher years the whole concept of public housing was placed at the centre of political debate. Similarly, the other Knatchbull relic of institutional care for the elderly is now under severe pressure; this is partly because of a sea-change in current thinking, similar to the winding up of children's homes in the 1970s, but principally because of demographic changes resulting in a sizeable population of senior citizens and the increasing reluctance of the Government to support the necessary financial expenditure either through the National Health Service or through local authorities.

The Knatchbull concepts were at the forefront of public administration until comparatively recently. And although the Government has gone into reverse on some of the later developments, it is interesting to note that in all the changes there appears to be one continuity. The statistical analysis of Gregory King's *Tables*, which gives us a snapshot of the eighteenth century, shows that at the time of Knatchbull's Act over one million people were in occasional receipt of alms from the Poor Law.[17] This amounted to one-fifth of the population. The proportion of those in receipt of Supplementary Benefit in its last year of operation was a not dissimilar 19 per cent of the population, although it included 21 per cent of British children.[18]

THE CONCEPT OF PLACE

Perhaps the most deeply rooted principle of the Poor Law was an individual's lifelong attachment to his or her birthplace. The whole evolution of a welfare system in Britain has to be seen against the backdrop of a legally enforced place of settlement. The modern echoes of this policy may seem muted or subtle, but they are nevertheless a vital factor in British social policy. Increasingly these residency regulations have looked archaic, particularly when viewed against the demands of European Community law.

From Chaucer and other medieval sources we know that the feudal system signally failed to prevent the wanderings of beggars, war cripples and 'lewed knaves'. The common legislative font for both British labour law and social security law, the Statute of Labourers 1350, was an attempt by Parliament to bind wandering labourers to their 'place of settlement'.[19] Under the general supervision of the Privy Council, Justices were to fix wages and conditions of employment at pre-plague rates. But as well as this embryonic Wages Council strategy, the 'welfare' aspect was the policing of 'sturdy beggars', who were legally defined as 'all persons able to labour and without other means of support'. Over 600 years later, the rather more detailed and infamous Form UB671, on the concept of 'available for work', amounts to the same point.[20] Fortunately, despite the continuity, there have been other very significant changes in British society in the meantime. Currently if a claimant falls foul of the availability test he or she risks a disqualification from benefit. The 1350 statute prescribed as sanctions a rising scale of whipping, branding, mutilation, solitary confinement, slavery and execution.

On the employment side, the 1350 statute was never capable of fulfilling its role of fixing wages and conditions in the face of relentless economic and social pressures, assisted by repeated bouts of the plague. But on the welfare law side, the statute crucially evolved into the complex code known as the Laws of Settlement and Removal.

The main focus of these laws was that each parish was required to support its own poor. This might have been acceptable in agrarian circumstances when few migrations occurred. But inevitably with the coming of an industrial economy, a worker might move to a town in periods of boom. When slump came, the law compelled the worker to be 'removed' to his place of settlement. The origin of the law is obscure. Certainly a return to a birthplace for various purposes, such as the biblical return to Bethlehem for a Roman census, seems to be customary in many cultures. In Britain, it seems once again to have been a custom eventually translated into statute; Professor Marshall gives as other illustrations of this transition from parochial initiative the Poor Law practice of 'badging' paupers by insignias on their clothing and the authorizing certificates that eventually legalized 'tramping'.[21]

Removal was normally a peaceful process, despite the hostility often shown to those returning to be a charge on the local rates. However, when persuasion failed, an Act of 1530 empowered Justices to order that a 'vagrant . . . be beaten with whips through the town until the body be bloody, and then to go to the place of birth'.[22] Later statutes dropped the sadism, although the laws were extended from applying simply to beggars. In time, removal applied to all manual workers, and in a diluted form the laws continued into the twentieth century, until their formal abolition by the National Assistance Act 1948. Even in 1909, when perhaps many would consider the laws to be obsolete, removals were still running at the rate of 12,000 a year.[23] Interestingly, when considering modern parallels, the Laws of Settlement and Removal operated a contingency fee system, where half the sum collected for the parish became the lawyer's fee. The description of this system by Professor Rodgers as 'a lawyer's paradise'[24] seems not too exaggerated, particularly when looking at the voluminous body of case law on such esoteric points as 'double derivative', 'the age of nurture' and 'settlement by estoppel'.[25]

The Settlement and Removal Laws became otiose as soon as there was a national social security system. If this is now to be subject to further fragmentation, as with local budgets with ceilings for the Social Fund, then the same technical problems will arise. Indeed, there are already many modern echoes elsewhere in social policy. First, there is the largely unexplored frontier of transnational social security law. International cooperation has been a developing theme in social security, and a critical factor has been an increase in the mobility of workers.[26] At the macro-level there is the Universal Declaration of Human Rights, giving an individual right to 'security in the event of unemployment, sickness, disability, widowhood, old age or other lack of livelihood in circumstances beyond his control'.[27] At a more concrete level, the International Labour Organisation, founded in 1919 but reformulated under the aegis of the United Nations in 1946, has produced a number of conventions in the social security field laying down minimum standards on these general themes. For most purposes, these conventions are of such a lowest common denominator value that they have not had a considerable impact in Britain. However, this work led to the formulation by the Council of Europe of the European Social Charter in 1961, with an exhortation in Article 12 to raise standards to a higher level.[28] Shortly afterwards in 1964 came the European Code of Social Security, with twelve principles, which has been ratified by the United Kingdom.[29] How far these treaties are likely to have an impact on British law is still debatable, as so far the minimum standards agreed are relatively minimal, so that agreement by governments of widely varying hues and circumstances can be achieved.

On the adjacent questions of conflict of laws, an attempt has been made to deal with practical questions by a maze of bilateral reciprocal treaties in social security. With increasing migration of labour, the extension of multinational concerns and the twentieth-century phenomenon of retirement to a different country, many legal problems of 'portability' have been thrown up. The pathbreaking agreement was with the Irish Republic[30] but there are currently over thirty reciprocal arrangements.[31]

However, with Britain's accession to the European Community, a much more potent lever has been Article 3(c) of the Treaty of Rome, stipulating the 'abolition . . . of obstacles to freedom of movement for persons'.[32] Although the principles underlying this have been extrapolated to mean equal treatment for all workers of member states, the 'aggregation' of insurance periods while working in different member states and the exporting of benefits, there have been many difficulties in practice. This is further compounded for the British situation because of course the United Kingdom was not admitted to the

Community until 1973 and no account was taken of the widely varying legal formulations in member states. Perhaps this explains the continuing surprise for the British authorities of decisions of the European Court of Justice; for example, the recent decision of *Newton*,[33] holding that the Mobility Allowance was exportable, which is also likely to apply to Attendance Allowance and Disability Living Allowance.

The next hurdle will be harmonization. The bewildering diversity of systems, contributions, benefits, disqualifications and adjudication in social security law has been a fertile field for comment.[34] Doing anything about harmonization has proved harder; in the leading British text, Professors Ogus and Barendt comment that 'progress in this field has been almost non-existent'.[35]

Multi-jurisdictional dissonance is familiar in many welfare systems – the United States is a classic illustration. Indeed, a famous Supreme Court decision, *Edwards* v *California*,[36] struck down a Californian statute, one of many examples, which made it a criminal offence to bring a non-resident into the state knowing him to be a poor person. Such a residency requirement was held to be an unconstitutional barrier to interstate commerce, but a majority also held that it was a right of national citizenship to enter any state. Such matters have been unfamiliar in British social security since nationalization in 1948.

The coordination of national systems in the European Community is likely to remain a formidable task,[37] but it is important to note that the relics of Settlement and Removal laws have been retained in many other areas of social policy following the 'break-up' of the Poor Law. They are particularly important in the byzantine recoupment regulations for health and education migrants in Britain. Until recently, with comparatively large regional health authorities and, in Inner London, a largish local education authority, these rules were tiresome but could be tolerated. But with the advent of smaller structures in both health and education, squeezed budgets and particularly the increasing fragmentation caused by 'opt outs' of trust status for hospitals and grant maintained status for schools, these issues of cross-border traffic have become vitally important.[38] Just as in the Poor Law a problem can sometimes be dealt with by 'exporting' it; the old parish relieving records contain many examples of small sums given to pregnant women to move quickly to another parish so that the child can be a charge elsewhere. In similar fashion, the operation of an internal market in both health and education is throwing up similar situations, or indeed throwing out patients from general practitioner lists and excluding pupils from schools to be a problem elsewhere.

The 'On yer bike' philosophy enunciated by a senior Conservative Minister had relatively little to do with social security law when there was a national system before the introduction of local Social Fund budgets. However, there were some occasions for enforced mobility; for example, there was the somewhat unusual case of a 22-year-old unmarried labourer in the Shetland Islands who had been unemployed for seven months and who was exported to Bletchley, 750 miles away, on pain of disqualification from unemployment benefit,[39] and certainly there was much anecdotal evidence of one-way ticket offers to foreign nationals.[40] But the 'Dick Whittington' phenomenon was a relatively minor matter in social security, left principally to be dealt with by market forces, lack of housing and a longing for home. The Social Fund changes, the byzantine rules for 16- and 17-year-olds in an endeavour to keep them in the parental home and the much-publicized 'turfing out' of claimants who are participating in summer music festivals or who are alleged to be part of a 'Costa del Dole' syndrome suggest that there are now other forces at work.

So far, residency rules in British social security law have remained fairly simple, because they apply to Britain as an entity. It is likely that increasing fragmentation internally will throw up more complications, whereas on the international front the moves towards a larger European Community and perhaps some harmonization will simplify other questions. Currently, the jurisdictional questions on residency are similar to those in tax or employment law; they revolve around the concept of where the claimant is 'ordinarily resident'.[41] The Benefits Agency has interpreted this to mean 'ordinarily resident' for three years, and so far this has been a relatively trouble-free gloss. However, the Draconian general principle is that disqualification from benefit occurs when a claimant is absent from Britain,[42] and inevitably there is an increasing number of exceptions. Litigation such as the *Akbar* case,[43] where Hodgson J determined that 'temporarily' could include 'indefinitely', so long as the absence concerned was not permanent, is likely to proliferate.

It is curious that just as on the one hand there is a clear trend towards international reciprocity, coordination and perhaps even harmonization, internally in Britain there appears to be a movement towards localization and fragmentation.

THE DOUBLE-DECKER SYSTEM

An enduring characteristic of twentieth-century social security law has been the cleavage between National Insurance and the supplementary welfare scheme. The latter has had various appellations in the retreat from the Poor Law: a hybrid limbo of Unemployment Assistance in 1934; National Assistance in 1948; Supplementary Benefits in 1966; and the latest garb of Income Support, introduced in 1986 and put into effect in 1988. Despite the complexity of the detail, overall the transformations have had surprisingly little effect on the basic structure of this second line, 'long stop' welfare system. In particular, there is no prospect of Income Support becoming a residual scheme for a declining minority, as propounded by the Beveridge Report in 1942.

Perhaps inevitably there had to be a 'double decker' system in social security from the moment that the concept of insurance was embraced in 1911. Although Beveridge in his various roles as parent of the 1911 Act, as dictator of the Unemployment Insurance Statutory Committee in the inter-war years and as prophet in the 1942 report, devoutly hoped that the assistance function would 'wither away', this was never likely, particularly not when there was a gulf between Beveridge Propounded and Beveridge Legislated. Just as in 1911, governments of every complexion have baulked at the full cost. The leading historian of the 1911 watershed, Professor Gilbert, states bluntly that, contrary to many other views,

> it would be untrue to say that social insurance grew out of the reform ideology of the Edwardian period . . . The immediate impulse came from . . . the inevitable extension of old age pensions. Invalidity and widows' pensions could not be borne by existing taxation. The cost would be too huge. In some way they would have to be financed by the beneficiaries of the system.[44]

Overshadowing all else in the welfare debate has been this question of expense.

As the academic Beveridge industry cranked itself in readiness for the fiftieth anniversary of the publication of *Social Insurance and Allied Services*, the apologists could argue with some justification that the full Beveridge programme has never been tried. For despite the assertion by Clement Attlee that the subsequent legislation was 'founded on the Beveridge Report',[45] there were critical distinctions. Foremost was the jettisoning of Beveridge's proposal that insurance benefits should continue as long as need lasted, subject only to attendance at a training centre and the usual disqualification controls.[46]

Even at the time, the cost of the full Beveridge scheme attracted criticism.[47] But in recent years there has been a crescendo of reproach. For example, a broadside from the Institute for Fiscal Studies launched in with the view that

> the Beveridge concept of social insurance has proved inadequate as a basis for the British social security system and that it has in fact been substantially abandoned, partly by modifications within the structure of the national insurance scheme itself and partly by the development of an increasingly extensive network of benefits outside it . . . One reason is that a comprehensive network of social insurance benefits is simply too expensive. The second is that the principle is insufficiently flexible to meet the variety of individual needs and changing economic circumstances.[48]

Spurred on by a mixture of such scholarly concern, budgetary considerations and quasi-Hayekian prejudice, the Government since 1979 has set about the Beveridge system with gusto. Some of its supporters may not have been satisfied,[49] and some of the changes have had unintended effects,[50] but no one can doubt that the structure is starting to fray around the edges.

What has proved difficult to shift is the basic concept of social insurance itself. As Professor Atkinson has pointed out, this 'is one of those comfortable short-hand expressions which people tend to use without close examination of its precise content', but his analysis is that the 'key elements in social insurance are that it is compulsory and that it does not involve, as such, a test of means'.[51] Both elements have been vociferously attacked. The beginning of the end of 'voluntarism' as an approach to unemployment has been traced to the Unemployed Workmen Act 1905,[52] but for many the wheel is turning full circle as it would appear currently that 'British social policy is based upon the principle that the unregulated operation of the market is the best means of maintaining and improving social standards'.[53] However, perhaps there is even here a bridge too far. The argument that unemployment benefit should be 'privatized', an American theoretical import but with its vociferous British protagonists,[54] seems to have foundered. Not least this is because of the futile attempt to see social insurance as a form of actuarial insurance, rather than as a taxation transfer. Indeed, it is difficult to see a way round the very powerful arguments advanced by Nicholas Barr that, for technical reasons, 'unemployment is an uninsurable risk'.[55]

Social insurance therefore appears to have become wedged as a landmark in social security systems, open to attack from different ideological perspectives but unlikely to disappear. An interesting point is that, in Britain in the inter-war period, the crass application of the 1911 principles led to disaster for the insurance system and near bankruptcy for the nation. Indeed, the slough of 'extended' or 'uncovenanted' benefits that afflicted Britain shortly after the First

World War was a matter of heated debate in the United States in the midst of recession during the election year of 1992. Paupers never had the vote, but faced with the prospect of putting ex-servicemen and civilian war workers on to the Poor Law, British governments saw merit in extending 'temporary' arrangements to keep claimants on National Insurance benefits, just as various national and state initiatives are attempting a similar manoeuvre in America to keep the unemployed on the top deck of the welfare system.

In Britain, this bowing to pressure led to over thirty amending statutes altering the Insurance Act 1920 before the recommendation of the May Committee in 1931 to abolish transitional benefits under national insurance and to substitute 'transitional payments' administered by Public Assistance Committees. Although the May Report may have 'grossly exaggerated the real dangers of the situation',[56] its recommendation that there be a saving of £66 million on unemployment benefit was unacceptable to the majority of Ramsey MacDonald's Labour Government, leading him to break with the party he had helped to build and form a National Government.[57] The tangled web of legislative enactments in the inter-war period clearly bear the stamp of being 'in the nature of emergency readjustments',[58] and, somewhat ironically given the turmoil in the United States in the election year of 1992, a contemporary American observer in the 1930s suggested that in reality 'insurance' had become 'a dignified name for a form of poor relief'.[59]

While it would not be appropriate to see too many parallels between the recession of the 1990s and the Depression years, there is certainly a growing problem of financing unemployment benefits in North America and Western Europe, particularly if the latter now can be taken to include the former East German state. A critical factor to note is that, with a double-decker system, only a minority of the unemployed are likely to draw from social insurance. For example, in 1989–90, it was anticipated that National Insurance payments only supported 28 per cent of unemployed people; the rest were solely dependent on Income Support and many of those on National Insurance were legally entitled to 'top up' payments from Income Support, although characteristically there is a take-up problem of claiming full rights here.[60] Attempts to cut National Insurance benefits, either in the time-honoured way by failing to take full account of inflation or by more subtle legislative means, will do little to reduce total expenditure in the current economic climate.

THE 'LESS ELIGIBILITY' PRINCIPLE

The notion that state-provided security for the poor should be unpleasant is the most venerable of administrative devices. As Professor Burns pointed out, 'public welfare systems which stand between the incomeless individual and starvation have always given assistance as grudgingly and unpleasantly as possible'.[61]

In the 1980s there were two wide-ranging reforms of the British public assistance system, in 1980 and 1988. It is therefore depressing that recent Bradford University/Family Service Unit studies of the post-1988 benefits regime report that 'the current system still fails, in many ways, to assist the very people it was set up to help'.[62] Although the 1988 changes were allegedly designed to simplify benefits, this major report suggests 'continuing difficulties in coping with social security administration, and in knowing what [individuals are] entitled to. For some, an internalised sense of stigma attached to being on benefit was exacerbated by stigmatising treatment from officialdom.'[63]

Partly these problems are to do with administrative failure, but they are also rooted in the legislative mechanisms of welfare. Despite the loudly heralded reforms, little of the underlying welfare structure changed. For example, a principal inheritance from the Poor Law has been the household means test, used for enforcing family contributions. It has had various offshoots, such as the cohabitation disqualification and the liable relative rules, but essentially it is an insistence on financial interdependence and thereby a reduction of charge on the state. This mechanism is undoubtedly supported by public opinion, although not always in its extreme manifestations. It is perhaps inevitable in some form in a needs-based public welfare system, and has certainly been entrenched in the law since 1601. The most controversial usage was the monthly investigation of the homes of all recipients of Unemployment Assistance in the 1930s, when claimants were 'hauled' before tribunals and 'charged with malingering'.[64] Its operation in this era led to Professor Robson's description of the household means test 'as the most hated expression in the entire vocabulary of social administration'.[65]

Although 'less eligibility' was a central principle of the Old Poor Law, it became a talisman in the New Poor Law of 1834. The picture painted of the system by the famous Royal Commission, and in particular of children in workhouses, is graphic in the extreme.[66] No doubt there was a great deal of abuse, but the conclusion of the Report was that the 'disease' to be eradicated was 'pauperism', defined as an 'unwarranted dependence on the poor rate'. Such a simplistic diagnosis naturally suggested its own remedy, and the remainder of the nineteenth century passed, as Professor Mendelsohn puts it, in a futile attempt to 'discourage the poor from their poverty'.[67] It is likely that the report was 'wildly unhistorical',[68] but as a study of social philosophy on welfare matters the Report is without parallel. All the stock twentieth-century clichés on malingering and abuse seem to have been derived from its pages, and it had a prodigious success in stirring public opinion and Parliament.

Two characteristics of the 1834 reforms are very much with us. As Professor Cranston points out,

> First, poor relief after 1834 was at the barest of standards because of the principle of less eligibility – that no-one should be better off on poor relief than at work – and that relief might be conditioned upon a person entering a workhouse. Secondly, poor law authorities had wide discretion under the legislation as to when and in what form they should provide relief.[69]

These policy instruments have diverse manifestations, and are also interrelated, but two particular areas in National Insurance need to be explored. The first is a unique change in Britain to the original 1911 Beveridge disqualification period of six weeks, and the second is a speculative reduction of the 'Beveridge as Implemented' one-year period on National Insurance unemployment benefits; when this expires the claimant tumbles to the lower deck.

Most of the changes to unemployment benefit have probably had as their main motivation the 'massaging' of the numbers of the 'unemployed', but the particularly important change to the disqualification period is more likely to have had financial as well as ideological motivation. This was an extraordinary increase of disqualification for voluntary unemployment from the original six weeks to the current six months.[70] These section 28 controls form the main bulk of the litigation in Social Security Appeal Tribunals and revolve around concepts such as 'misconduct' and 'voluntary leaving . . . without just cause', originally laid down in 1911. The phrases were drafted by Beveridge's colleague at Toynbee Hall and at the Board of Trade, Sir Hubert Llewellyn Smith, who felt it was 'absolutely necessary in the public interest' to exclude such claims.[71] At the time perhaps they were something of an advance on the stated views of the chief poverty lobby campaigner, Sir Charles Loch, the Secretary of the Charity Organisation Society, who believed that 'want of employment in nine cases out of ten in which the plea is used, is not the cause of distress. It is, as often as not, drink'.[72]

In more recent times, it has been questioned whether these disqualifications actually serve a purpose.[73] Perhaps they fulfil some deep psychological need elsewhere in the population, steeped as it is in the mythology of 'scrounging'. The change to 26 weeks as from April 1988 came after a short 18-month interregnum with a disqualification period of 13 weeks; this could hardly be regarded as an adequate trial period, and indeed all the evidence suggests that few of the 'voluntary unemployed' have anything but the haziest idea of technical details such as disqualification periods. It should be remembered that the section 28 disqualification has a reach well beyond National Insurance, as Income Support is reduced by either 40 or 20 per cent for the 26-week period.[74] Even in its earlier six-week form there could be legitimate criticisms of the harsh operation of the law.[75] But the law is now positively Draconian and it is difficult to avoid the conclusion that this and similar 'changes to the eligibility rules for Unemployment Benefit can all be traced back to the ideological premises of Thatcherism'.[76]

The second major change to the Beveridge scheme as implemented in 1946 is perhaps speculative. It is clear that cuts in social security benefits are being prepared currently by the Government. One option being studied by Peter Lilley, the Secretary of State for Social Security and perhaps the remaining Thatcherite in the Cabinet, is to cut unemployment benefit from one year to six months in duration. Other options, particularly 'working for benefits'', based on the system of Workfare in the United States, are also being considered to restrain the rise in social security payments caused by the recession. The introduction of such a Workfare system, and the correlative withholding of benefits from individuals who refuse offers of jobs or training, is known to be favoured by members of the Cabinet. To some extent it is already present in the section 28 controls of 'without good cause' refusing or failing to apply for a job, or neglecting to 'avail' oneself of a 'reasonable opportunity of employment', or refusing or failing to apply for a place on an 'approved training scheme'.[77] The shift would therefore appear to be what might constitute 'jobs' or 'training' to fulfil the requirements.

Despite these very significant possible changes, compulsory state insurance would, so far, appear to have been a concept that has escaped the main thrust of the Thatcherite critique, although it is clearly damaged around the edges. However, no reliance can be made on its fairly lengthy pedigree; the first statute appears to have been that of 1757, which made insurance against sickness and attached risks compulsory for coalheavers in London.[78] But it is the extension of this limited scheme by the National Insurance Act 1911 that remains the most innovative alteration to the British welfare system. With familiarity it is perhaps difficult to envisage how, to Beveridge, 'the project seemed then and was, a daring adventure'.[79] However, even in 1911 there was no uniformity of view that the model he created was the best. A National Insurance League had in fact been formed as early as 1882, to propagate the ideas of Canon Blackley, although he had no belief in compulsory insurance in his advocacy of a state-run scheme.[80] A Victorian opponent to Blackley stated, in language that has a contemporary ring, 'nothing in the nature of insurance warranted its removal from the healthy influence of private enterprise'.[81]

The Beveridge principles remain, but only just and perhaps not for much longer. Following a year when the fiftieth anniversary of his Report saw copious acknowledgment of his role as a source for many welfare systems, it is perhaps a little ironic that the Beveridge edifice is teetering in Britain. And it is certainly disheartening when it is clear that 'the policy of the British government inevitably puts it in conflict with the basic assumptions which have lain behind international social policy and continue to lie behind the social policy of most western European countries'.[82]

NOTES

1. H. Street, Judicial review refused (1974) *Legal Action Group Bulletin*, p. 128. SBATs had just one short paragraph devoted to them in J. A. G. Griffith and H. Street, *Principles of Administrative Law* (1973), pp. 161–2.
2. J. Fulbrook, *Administrative Justice and the Unemployed* (1978).
3. O. Kahn-Freund, in E. Stein and T. L. Nicholson (eds), *American Enterprise in the European Common Market* (1960), p. 298.
4. See in particular the protests by the Social Security Advisory Committee in their Fourth Report (1985), p. 83, and, more generally, R. Lister and B. Lakhani, *A Great Retreat in Fairness: A Critique of the Draft Social Fund Manual* (1987).
5. G. V. Rimlinger, *Welfare Policy and Industrialization in Europe, America and Russia* (1971), p. 19.
6. R. Plant, The New Right and social policy: a critique, in *Social Policy Review 1989–1990* (1990).
7. 27 Henry VIII, c. 25 (1536).
8. B. Rodgers, *The Battle against Poverty: From Pauperism to Human Rights* (1969), p. 14.
9. Council on Tribunals, *Social Security: Abolition of Independent Appeals under the proposed Social Fund*, Cmnd 9722 (1986).
10. See, for an analysis of the Social Fund procedure in action, G. Dalley and R. Berthoud, *Challenging Discretion* (1992).
11. W.K. Jordan, *Philanthropy in England 1480–1660* (1959), p. 126.
12. J. ten Brock, *Family Law and the Poor* (1971), p. 9.
13. S. Webb and B. Webb, *English Poor Law History* (1927), vol. 1, p. 149.
14. See generally N. Longmate, *The Workhouse* (1974).
15. G. Burke, *Housing and Social Justice* (1981), p. 64.

16. Burke, *op. cit.*, p. 65. The three former workhouses closest to the London School of Economics are still hostels for homeless men. The modern change has been the presence, until recently, of over 200 homeless men sleeping rough in Lincoln's Inn Fields nearby.

17. Printed in Charles Davenant's *Works* (1771), vol. II, p. 184.

18. 10,200,000 were on or below the level of Supplementary Benefit, including 2,490,000 children.

19. 25 Edw. III, c. 12 (1350–1), preceded by the Ordinance of Labourers, 23 Edw. III, c. 1–8 (1349).

20. Social Security Contributions and Benefits Act 1992, s. 57(1)(a).

21. D. Marshall, *The English Poor in the Eighteenth Century* (1926), pp. 9, 104.

22. 22 Henry VIII, c. 12 (1530).

23. *Final Report of the Royal Commission on the Poor Laws* (1909) Cd 4499, p. 402, and see generally Chapter IX.

24. B. Rodgers, *op. cit.*, pp. 16–17.

25. See generally A.F. Vulliamy, *The Law of Settlement and Removal of Paupers* (1895); E.J. Lidbetter, *Settlement and Removal* (1932).

26. See generally International Labour Organisation, *Social Security for Migrant Workers* (1977).

27. United Nations Doc. A/811, article 25 (1948).

28. See generally Holloway, *Social Policy Harmonisation in the European Community* (1981). See also, for an analysis of the developments in labour law, Wedderburn of Charlton, The social charter in Britain: labour law and labour courts? (1991) 54 MLR 1.

29. European Treaty Series, No. 48.

30. Irish Free State (Consequential Provisions) Act 1922, s. 6(1)(c).

31. See Social Security Administration Act 1992, s. 179; codifying Social Security Act 1975, s. 143, as amended by Social Security Act 1981, s. 6(1)(c).

32. The precise formulation for social security law is in Article 51, with implementation by Reg 3/58.

33. Case C-356/89. See also *Hughes* v *Chief Adjudication Officer*, European Court of Justice (16 July 1992).

34. See J. Fulbrook, Landesbericht für Grossbritannien, in H. F. Zacher (ed.), *Die Rolle des Beitrags in der sozialen Sicherung* (1980); and, more generally, P.R. Kaim-Caudle, *Comparative Social Policy and Social Security* (1973).

35. A.I. Ogus, E.M. Barendt, T.G. Buck and T. Lynes, *The Law of Social Security* (1988) 3rd edn, p. 598.

36. 314 US 160 (1941).

37. See, generally, P. Watson, *Social Security Law of the European Communities* (1980).

38. See, for example, the Education (Areas to which Pupils and Students Belong) Regulations 1989 (SI 1990/2037), made under the Education Act 1980 and the Education (No. 2) Act 1986, operative from 1 April 1990. See also, for the latest emanation of the Greenwich/Lewisham border dispute, *R* v *Bromley London Borough Council, ex parte C, The Times*, 6 June 1991, which determined that a local education authority cannot favour children within its own borough. This case is currently on appeal to the House of Lords.

39. R(U) 34/58.

40. The Irish Centre in North London has a special charity fund to help assist families back to the Republic after a futile search for work.

41. See, for example, R(P) 1/78, R(G)2/51.

42. Social Security Contributions and Benefits Act 1992, ss. 113(a) and 146.

43. *R* v *Social Security Commissioner, ex parte Akbar, The Times*, 6 November 1991.

44. B. B. Gilbert, *David Lloyd George* (1987), vol. 1, p. 429. See also Gilbert, *The Evolution of National Insurance in Great Britain* (1966), *Britain since 1918* (1967) and *British Social Policy 1914–1939* (1970).

45. HC Debs, 7 February 1946, col. 1896.

46. See further on the distinctions between 'Beveridge as implemented and Beveridge as intended', Brian Abel-Smith, Beveridge: another viewpoint, *New Society*, 1 (28 February 1963), p. 7.

47. See, for example, H.W. Singer, *Can We Afford Beveridge?* (1943).

48. A.W. Dilnot, J.A. Kay and C.N. Morris, *The Reform of Social Security* (1984), p. 1.

49. H. Parker, *The Moral Hazard of Social Security Benefits* (Institute for Economic Affairs, 1982).
50. See generally for a summary of changes, K. Andrews and J. Jacobs, *Punishing the Poor: Poverty under Thatcher* (1989).
51. A. B. Atkinson, *Social Insurance* (STICERD, 1991), pp. 1–2.
52. See J. Harris, *Unemployment and Politics* (1973).
53. P. O'Higgins, European social policy at the crossroads: British and European social policy, *Social Security and Europe 1992* (1990), p. 110.
54. See in particular M. Beenstock and V. Brasse, *Insurance for Unemployment* (1986).
55. N. Barr, *The Mirage of Private Unemployment Insurance* (STICERD, 1988).
56. G. D. H. Cole, *The Intelligent Man's Guide through World Chaos* (1932), p. 98.
57. See generally R. Skidelsky, *Politicians and the Slump* (1967).
58. R. C. Davison, *British Unemployment Policy* (1938), p. 9.
59. E. Wight Bakke, *Insurance or Dole?* (1935), p. 106.
60. *The Government's Expenditure Plans 1990/91 to 1992/93*, Cm 1001–1021 (1990).
61. E. M. Burns, *Towards Social Security* (1936), p. 139.
62. R. Cohen, J. Coxall, G. Craig and A. Sadiq-Sangster, *Hardship Britain: Being Poor in the 1990s* (1992).
63. *Ibid.*, p. 106.
64. See in particular W. Hannington, *Ten Lean Years* (1940), p. 15. A chapter on administrative injustices contains a very bitter account of suicides and wrecked families; *ibid.*, pp. 245 *et seq.*
65. W. A. Robson, *Social Security* (1943), p. 14.
66. *Report of the Royal Commission on the Poor Laws* (1834). See in particular Appendix A. See also S. G. and E. O. A. Checkland (eds), *The Poor Law Report of 1934* (1974).
67. R. Mendelsohn, *Social Security in the British Commonwealth* (1954), p. 23.
68. R. H. Tawney, *Religion and the Rise of Capitalism* (1926), p. 242.
69. R. Cranston, *Legal Foundations of the Welfare State* (1985), p. 203.
70. Social Security Contributions and Benefits Act 1992, s. 28.
71. Sir H. Llewellyn Smith, (1910) 20 *Economic Journal* 513.
72. Quoted in St J. Ervine, *God's Soldier: General William Booth* (1934), p. 708. See generally on the highly influential COS, C. L. Mowat, *The Charity Organisation Society* (1961).
73. See R. Hasson, Displine and punishment in the law of unemployment insurance – a critical view of disqualifications and disentitlement, (1987) 25 *Osgoode Hall Law Journal* 615.
74. See J. Fulbrook, Dismissals and the 40 per cent rule, (1980) 9 ILJ 129.
75. D. Lewis, Losing benefit through misconduct: time to stop punishing the unemployed? [1985] *Journal of Social Welfare Law* 145.
76. N. Wikeley, Unemployment benefit, the state and the labour market [1989] *Journal of Law and Society* 304.
77. There were significant changes to the law in 1989 on the training aspect. See, for a useful commentary, N. Wikeley, *Current Law Statutes Annotated*, 4(28), 4–39.
78. See generally Sir F. Eden, *The State of the Poor* (1797, reprint 1928), vol. I, p. 605.
79. Sir W. Beveridge, *The Past and Present of Unemployment Insurance* (1930), p. 3.
80. The original Blackley article was: National insurance, in *Nineteenth Century*, reprinted in M. J. J. Blackley, *Thrift and National Insurance as a Security against Pauperism* (1906), p. 44 *et seq.*
81. T. Mackay, *Working-class Insurance* (1890), p. v.
82. P. O'Higgins, European social policy at the crossroads, *op. cit.*, p. 102.

14

The Evolution of Administrative Justice in England: The Case of Social Security

Martin Partington

INTRODUCTION

Over the past twenty to thirty years, the English legal system has been in a state of almost continuous flux. The criminal justice system has been radically restructured, and the civil justice system has similarly been the subject of profound change. In the area of administrative justice there has also been significant change: the transformation of the role of the Divisional Court and the development of judicial review; institutional innovations, such as a range of ombudsmen, both statutory and private; and the creation of new tribunals. But the system of administrative justice as a whole has not been the subject of review.

There are signs that this could change. At least one powerful voice has been raised urging that consideration be given to the creation of an administrative division of the High Court.[1] His recent elevation to the House of Lords may mean that he is able to push these ideas more openly than might otherwise have been the case. In a number of other common law countries, there have been significant programmes of reform of administrative justice systems[2] or official initiatives which suggest that major programmes of change might be introduced.[3] Here, the Law Commission is now engaged on a detailed study of the *remedies* appropriate for administrative law.[4] While there has, as yet, been no official public discussion about reform of the *structure* of administrative law, pressure for such a debate could develop. This is, therefore, an opportune moment to begin a serious discussion about the possible structure of administrative justice into the twenty-first century. This chapter is presented as a preliminary contribution to such a debate.

The intention of the chapter is to look at the development of administrative justice in the context of social security from the first years of this century until the present in order to see what lessons this might have for those who may be responsible for generating ideas for further change and reform.[5]

THE YEARS OF DIVERSITY: 1908–1932

Three preliminary points need to be stressed in relation to the early years of the development of adjudication policy in social security programmes. First, there was widespread agreement that the 'Workmen's Compensation Act model', whereby disputes were taken to the county court, was not to be extended; this model did not work effectively because it clogged up the court machinery. Second, despite consensus on this last point, there was less agreement on what the appropriate alternative models of adjudication should be. This lack of consensus was in part a consequence of the considerable diversity of administrative responsibility for the development of the early social security programmes. There was no single social security ministry; different policies developed from different ministries. Third, in those early years there were no agreed sets of principles of administrative justice against which models of adjudication could be evaluated; indeed principles, such as those enunciated by the Donoughmore Committee of 1932 or the Franks Committee of 1957, only emerged from the experience of what was done in those early years.

The Old Age Pensions Acts 1908–1924 and the Blind Persons Act 1920

The first adjudicative model in relation to what would now be described as the social security system was created by section 7 of the Old Age Pensions Act 1908. This provided that claims for old age pensions and questions relating to the fulfilment of the statutory conditions upon which pensions were to be granted were to be referred to a *Local Pension Committee*. These committees comprised persons appointed by the relevant county, borough or urban district council. The Pension Officer was to inquire into any claim or question and report thereon to the Committee. But it was the Committee itself that came to the decision.

Appeals could be taken either by the Pension Officer or by any person aggrieved to the 'central pension authority'. This was initially defined in section 8(3) as the Local Government Board. This was amended later, so as to refer to the Minister of Health; he was empowered to act through such committee, person or persons appointed as he thought fit.

Details of the procedure on appeals to the Minister as they subsequently developed can be found in Articles 18 and 19 of the Old Age Pensions Consolidated Regulations 1922.[6] Under Article 19 the Minister was to cause such inquiries to be held, and other steps to be taken, as he thought necessary for the determination of the matters in question.[7] These procedures were also incorporated into the Blind Persons Act 1920.

Two points may be noted in relation to these procedures. First, decision-taking in relation to these benefits was not initially the direct responsibility of any central government department, though the Minister did take over appeals later. Second, these procedures involve one of the earliest examples of a Minister being given power to arrange for the holding of an inquiry for the resolution of a dispute, rather than relying on a tribunal procedure.

The National Insurance Act 1911: Unemployment Insurance

There is little doubt of the importance of the Act of 1911 in the overall development of social security law in Britain; many of the ground rules including those relating to adjudication were laid down there. However, one feature of the 1911 Act must not be forgotten. It introduced two separate forms of provision: unemployment insurance and health insurance. Quite different structures were created to administer these two schemes; adjudication under the two schemes was also quite differently organized.

The provisions relating to the Unemployment Insurance scheme were found in Part II of that Act. The starting point is section 88, which provided that:

> (1) All claims for unemployment benefit under this Part of this Act, and all questions whether the statutory conditions are fulfilled in the case of any workman claiming such benefit . . . shall be determined by one of the officers appointed under this Part of this Act . . .
>
> Provided that –
>
> > (a) in any case where unemployment benefit is refused or is stopped . . . the workman may require the insurance officer to report the matter to a court of referees . . . If the insurance officer disagrees with any . . . recommendation [of the court of referees], he shall, if so requested by the court of referees, refer the recommendation, with his reasons for disagreement, to the umpire appointed under this Part of this Act, whose decision shall be final and conclusive;
> >
> > (b) the insurance officer in any case in which he considers it expedient to do so may instead of himself determining the

> claim or question, refer it to a court of referees, who shall in such case determine the question, and the decision of the court of referees shall be final and conclusive.[8]

By contrast with the Old Age Pensions Act, the responsibility for adjudication was placed directly on insurance officers,[9] the Court of Referees and Umpires. The work of the Court of Referees was organized by dividing the country initially into 82 districts; this number was later reduced to 78.[10] In each of these districts, a panel of employers' representatives and a panel of workmen's representatives was prepared. The third member was an 'impartial' member appointed by the Board of Trade, generally possessing some legal qualification. He acted as chairman of the same court throughout the year, so that his was a permanent appointment; the representatives changed from week to week.[11]

Although chairmen were described as 'neutral', this neutrality should not be regarded as equivalent to the modern concept of 'independence'; the formal position was that the chairmen were appointed by the Board of Trade, who were themselves responsible for developing the policy and running the administrative machinery connected with the payment of unemployment benefit.[12] Indeed in the early days of unemployment insurance, the Courts of Referees were seen as little more than extensions of the Board of Trade.

Although the primary route for appeals was to the Court of Referees, there was in defined circumstances a further right of appeal or reference to the Umpire. The importance of the Umpire's jurisdiction was stressed in debate in the Standing Committee on the National Insurance Bill,[13] where it was argued that it would be very desirable for there to be a single person who, especially at the beginning of the scheme, could bring 'uniformity of administration, uniformity of decision and uniformity of treatment'.[14] The objective of ensuring that the Umpire's decisions influenced the administration of the legislation was to be achieved by the publication of his decisions, weekly, in the *Board of Trade Journal* and, monthly, in the *Board of Trade Gazette*.

The early work of the Court of Referees and the Umpire is described in the *First Report of Proceedings of the Board of Trade under Part II of the National Insurance Act 1911*.[15] This shows that, of the first 33,250 cases that were disallowed, 2907 (8.75 per cent) were taken on to the Courts of Referees. Of these about 45 per cent were decided in favour of the workman. Part of the explanation for this high figure was that claims were disallowed if there was a prima facie case against the workman, it being felt that more detailed enquiries were more appropriately conducted before the Court of Referees. It was also felt that many decisions would have gone the same way at the initial decision-taking stage if the Insurance Officer had the same information as the Court had.[16] The vast majority of the cases were about disqualification for misconduct or employment left without just cause (i.e. matters similar to those now determined by Social Security Appeal Tribunals). A very small number of cases were taken on to the Umpire: by 12 July 1913, only 105 in all.[17]

National Insurance Act 1911: National Health Insurance

Part I of the National Insurance Act 1911, dealing with National Health Insurance, provided that

> (a) questions whether any employment or any class of employment is or will be employment within the meaning of this Part of the Act or whether a person is entitled to become a voluntary contributor;
> (b) questions as to the rates of contributions payable by or in respect of any insured person; or
> (c) as to the rates of contributions payable in respect of an employed contributor by the employer and the contributor respectively

were to be determined by Insurance Commissioners[18] in accordance with regulations made by them for the purpose. If any person felt aggrieved by a decision under (a), he could appeal to the county court, with a further right of appeal to a High Court judge selected by the Lord Chancellor, whose decision would be final. In the case of decisions under (b), the regulations could provide that in the case of a person who was or was about to become a member of an approved society, the rules of the society itself could determine the matter.[19]

More generally, the Insurance Commissioners might, if they thought fit, refer any question as to whether any employment was or would be employment within the meaning of this Part of the Act for decision to the High Court. This was to be done in such summary manner as, subject to the rules of court, might be directed by the court. The court, after hearing the parties and taking such evidence (if any) as it thought just would take the decision, which was final.[20] These issues are similar to the kinds of issues that now go direct to the Secretary of State; but at this stage it was Insurance Commissioners, *not* the Minister, who was charged with the taking of these decisions.[21] We also see here the forerunner of the special High Court jurisdiction to determine certain categories of appeal.

The Unemployment Insurance Act 1920

The Unemployment Insurance Act 1920 transferred responsibility for Unemployment Insurance from the Board of Trade to the Ministry of Labour. As presented to Parliament in December 1919, Clause 8 of the draft Bill provided that:

> All claims for unemployment benefit under this Act and all questions whether the statutory conditions are fulfilled in the case of any person claiming such benefit or whether these conditions continue to be fulfilled . . . or whether a person is disqualified . . . or otherwise arising in connection with such claims, shall be determined by an Insurance Officer.

This was followed by provisions for appeals or references to the Court of Referees, who would give advice to the Insurance Officer.[22] Thus, as first presented, the adjudicative structure was to remain much as it had done under the 1911 Act (as amended by an amending Act of 1914).

However, a new version of the Bill was presented to the House in February 1920, prior to the second reading debate; clause 8 became clause 11 and a new clause 10 was introduced, which provided:

> (1) If any question arises -
>
> (a) as to whether any employment or any class of employment is or will be such employment as to make the person engaged therein an employed person within the meaning of this Act or whether a person is or was an employed person within the meaning of this Act; or
>
> (b) whether a person or class of persons is or is not a person or class of persons to whom a special or supplementary scheme under this Act applies; or
>
> (c) as to who is the employer of any employed person; or
>
> (d) as to the rate of contribution payable under or in pursuance of this Act by or in respect of any person or class of persons or as to the rates of contribution payable in respect of any employed person by the employer and that person respectively;
>
> the question shall be decided by the Minister.

The Explanatory Memorandum that accompanied the Bill as presented for second reading explained that this new clause was based on section 66 of the National Insurance Act 1911. It further noted that 'the object of substituting the Minister for the Umpire in this matter is to ensure uniformity of decisions in questions of industrial demarcation which concern not only unemployment insurance, but also the administration of trade boards and of the proposed legislation with regard to hours and wages'. It was further provided that there would be an appeal from the Minister to a single judge, whose decision would be final.[23] The court chosen was the High Court, rather than the county court, again for reasons of consistency of decision-making.[24] When these clauses were considered in Committee, they were agreed to without any debate whatsoever.

Within a short time, Ministers' decisions began to be issued,[25] and between 1920 and 1934, five large volumes of such decisions were produced together with a volume of High Court judgments.[26] However, these formal decisions were merely the tip of the iceberg. Between November 1920 and July 1923, the number of questions referred to the headquarters of the Department was about 120,000, and at least double that number was dealt with locally. Partly this work load was the result of settling into the new scheme, but even by July 1923, inquiries were coming to the Ministry's headquarters at the rate of 1250 a week.[27] Since many inquiries as to insurability affected both the Health and Unemployment Insurance schemes, there was close cooperation between the officers of the two departments, and on occasion out-door staff of the Health Insurance department would conduct inquiries that seemed necessary.[28]

National Health Insurance Acts 1924 to 1928

Information about the jurisdiction of the Minister of Health under the National Health Insurance Acts 1924–8 is given in the evidence of the Ministry of Health to the Donoughmore committee.[29] There is an interesting section on the powers of the Minister to determine questions of 'insurability' under section 89 of the Act of 1924. The Ministry's note of evidence states that 'this jurisdiction . . . is substantially the same as that conferred on the Insurance Commissioners by the [Act of 1911, s. 66]'. It is noted that the original right of appeal to the county court was abolished by amending legislation in 1920. The regulations for formally determining questions arising under the provisions were found in the Decision of Questions Regulations 1924.[30] When necessary, e.g. where there was a serious conflict of evidence, there would be a hearing held by a member of the legal staff of the Department. In practice hearings were not often required.[31]

Since the inception of the Health Insurance scheme, the evidence noted that 962 formal decisions were given by the Insurance Commissioners or the Minister under these provisions, or their predecessors. Details of 500 of those decisions had been published and were available to the general public for guidance. Notwithstanding these formal procedures, the evidence also notes that the vast majority of questions were determined informally, thus reflecting similar practice in the Ministry of Labour as regards Unemployment Insurance.

Widows', Orphans' and Old Age Contributory Pensions Act 1925

Under these provisions, any person dissatisfied by an award or a decision of the Minister of Health or Department of Health for Scotland in respect of any pension could have the question referred to a referee or referees selected from a panel of barristers and solicitors appointed by the National Health Insurance Joint Committee. No officer of the Department could be a member of the panel. The decision of the referee was final and conclusive, except that a case might be stated on a point of law for the High Court, or Court of Session. In either case the Court might order them so to do.[32]

1932: TAKING STOCK, ESTABLISHING INDEPENDENCE

For the first twenty or so years of social security provision, there was no single approach to adjudication. Some issues were decided centrally, others locally; some went to courts, others to specialist tribunals; in some the Minister was directly involved, in others he was kept at arm's length. In 1932, two reports were published that related to aspects of social security adjudication: the first specifically related to Unemployment Insurance, the second was of much more general import.

Report of the Royal Commission on Unemployment Insurance, 1932

Although it was only of secondary importance to the overall work of the Royal Commission, some evidence on adjudication was presented to this Commission. In particular, the Ministry of Labour argued that as a result of the major changes that had taken place in relation to the Unemployment Insurance scheme since 1920, there were by 1930 two main problems facing the then system of appeals: the umpire was too legalistic; he was also too overburdened with work.[33] A major reason why so many cases came to the Umpire (with correspondingly larger numbers coming to the Court of Referees), was that until 1930 *only* the Court of Referees had the power, with limited exceptions, to disallow claims to unemployment benefit. If they recommended a disallowance, or if they recommended an allowance and the Insurance Officer disputed this recommendation, there was a right of appeal to the Umpire.

Although the system changed in 1930, it was not in such a way as substantially to reduce the load on the Court of Referees and thus the Umpires. Indeed the number of cases going to the Umpire in 1931 was over 22,000.[34] This led to the suggestion from the Ministry that an intermediate tribunal, between the Umpire and the Court of Referees, should be established. The policy of having (from 1930) an Umpire with seven deputy Umpires was not thought to be a satisfactory solution.

However the Commission itself found that, generally, things were working well, and had no major alterations to suggest.[35] They did note that

> As the result of the Insurance Officer's inability to disallow claims other than those arising from trade disputes the Courts of Referees have had to deal with a large number of cases in which the question for decision is one of fact rather than of the motive or reason for the state of unemployment; the questions so referred include for example: –
> 1 whether the claimant has paid the required number of contributions to qualify for benefit;
> 2 whether he is following a subsidiary employment from which he receives more than 3s 4d per day

The Royal Commission made a number of points about details of the adjudicative process. One general statement of principle may also be recalled:

It should, however, be realised that one of the chief features of the scheme is that the decisions on individual claims are given by independent statutory authorities by a judicial process and it is not within the power of the Minister of Labour to question these decisions. We consider that it is essential to maintain this position and to protect the Minister from political or other influences in the day to day administration of a scheme providing monetary payments to a large number of individuals.[36]

The Donoughmore Committee on Ministers' Powers, 1932

By 1932, a rather more general debate had also been started concerning the implications of increasing state intervention in the lives of the citizen. Professor Robson, in the first edition of his book, *Justice and Administrative Law*, had put forward nineteen principles that he argued should be adhered to if public confidence in the newly emerging system of administrative justice was to be achieved. More dramatically, Lord Hewart, in *The New Despotism*, had, among other things, complained that the constitutional position of the judiciary - with their responsibilities for administering the law of the land - was being undermined by the creation of new adjudicative forums. He noted that public officials had been given the power to decide questions of a judicial nature:[37]

> To ally the terms administrative 'law' and administrative 'justice' to such a system is really grotesque. The exercise of arbitrary power is neither law nor justice, administrative or at all. The very conception of 'law' is a conception of something involving the application of known rules and principles, and a regular course of procedure.

These and other influences led to the creation of the Committee on Ministers' Powers. The Report of the Committee, when it appeared, made a number of points relating to social security adjudication.

From the first section of this chapter it will be realized that by the time of the establishment of the Donoughmore Committee there was a wide variety of adjudicative procedures available for what would now be called social security benefits. To a large extent, this variety can be explained by the range of Government Ministries engaged in the development of policy in relation to the administration and adjudication of these benefits. This diversity of responsibility inevitably resulted in what would now be regarded as a lack of principle. Another explanation was that with new administrative tasks to be undertaken, it was necessary to try out a number of adjudicative mechanisms. It would be unrealistic to have expected a single ideal model to have emerged right from the earliest days of the establishment of the National Insurance and related schemes.

However, there were those who took a more principled approach. For example, the Treasury Solicitor in a memorandum addressed to the Donoughmore Committee made a strong plea that wherever possible there should be internal decision-making procedures, particularly where technical knowledge was useful and had to be applied. He put the case largely in terms of the work being done by *departmental* tribunals, rather than individual officers. He suggested that the advantages of these tribunals were that they saved expense, they were accessible and free from technicality, they were expeditious, they had the technical knowledge, and their decisions were uniform and coordinated: 'it is my firm belief that the existence of departmental tribunals has been both fair and just'.[38]

Section III of the Committee's Report deals with judicial and quasi-judicial powers. The committee suggested that a judicial decision was one that presupposed an existing dispute between two or more parties, and then involved four requisites: the presentation of a case (not necessarily orally) by the parties to the dispute; the ascertainment of facts, where these were in dispute; the submission of legal argument where there was a question of law; and a decision disposing of the whole matter, including a finding of fact, an application of the law and where necessary a ruling on the law.[39]

They noted that a decision could still be 'judicial' even though the decision-taker was a Minister, citing decisions under the Unemployment Insurance Acts 1920–30, where any question arising as to whether any employment or class of employment was such employment as to make the person engaged therein an employed person within the meaning of the Act, as an example.[40] It was claimed that:

> The judicial character of the Minister's decision, when he gives the decision himself is recognised and illustrated by the provision in the Acts that any person aggrieved by the decision of the Minister may appeal to the High Court and by the further provision that the Minister shall have regard to decisions given by the Umpire by whom such questions were determined under the earlier Unemployment legislation.[41]

The Committee then discussed in more detail the significance of the notion of 'natural justice' in the context of judicial decision-taking.

The first element in this was that a person should not be judge in his own cause. They remarked: 'Parliament would do well [when considering assigning judicial functions to Ministers] to provide that the Minister himself should not be the judge, but that the case should be decided by an independent tribunal.'[42]

The Committee also stressed that the same principles of natural justice should ensure that a person know in good time the case he has to meet; possibly, that he should know the reason for any decision; and that the report of any inquiry should normally be made available at least to the parties.[43]

The Committee then turned to look at some examples of specific powers and procedures. They noted that in some circumstances there were specialized courts of law appointed to deal with judicial and quasi-judicial matters (none of these is relevant here); second, they pointed to ministerial tribunals, where the adjudicative structure used for Unemployment Insurance of the Insurance Officer appointed by the Minister of Labour, with appeal to the Court of Referees (consisting of members from representatives of employers and insured contributors with the chairman appointed by the Minister) and appeal thence to the Umpire appointed by the Crown was cited as an example;[44] thirdly they noted that certain judicial and quasi-judicial decisions were taken by Ministers themselves: the example of those decisions arising under s. 89 of the National Health Insurance Act were particularly mentioned.[45]

At the end of their description of the various categories of procedure they had identified, the Committee sought to draw some conclusions. They stated that where truly judicial issues had to be resolved 'then *prima facie* that part of the task should be separated from the rest, and reserved for decision by a Court of Law, whether ordinary or specialised, as in the circumstances Parliament may think right'.[46] Nevertheless, the Committee was reluctant to criticize directly situations which appeared to depart from this principle. For example, they said that 'on very exceptional grounds [it may] be necessary to leave certain judicial decisions to a Minister or other administrative authority'.[47] As regards Ministerial Tribunals they thought they could be used in exceptional circumstances, though they felt that judicial functions should normally be left to the Courts of Law. In those cases where work was given to tribunals, adherence to the principles of natural justice was stated to be very important.

The importance of the Donoughmore Committee's report is not to be measured in the number of actual legislative changes that occurred in its wake; in fact very little resulted directly from the report. Nonetheless, the Report is of considerable importance in that it provided the first official attempt to set down criteria for determining the principles which should govern adjudication. There is no doubt that the report has had great influence on thinking about these matters over the years since it was published.

For example, when the Pension Appeals Tribunals (PATs) were established in 1943 under the Pension Appeals Tribunals Act 1943 to deal with the claims of ex-servicemen injured on active service, all chairmen and members[48] were appointed by the Lord Chancellor who also provided the staff for the tribunal. The tribunals are organized on a Presidential basis and hear cases in London and other regional centres. They operate under rules of procedure which many might regard as being particularly favourable to the appellant.[49]

THE BEVERIDGE REPORT AND THE POST-WAR LEGISLATION

The next important stage in the historical development of social security adjudication policy is the report of the Beveridge committee. The main significance of this report, in terms of the development of social security policy, was his emphasis on the need to see the social security system as a whole, and not in the fragmented fashion that had been the hallmark of developments up to that time. Despite the fragmentation of adjudication, already noted, he actually had very little to say in his report on adjudication save for commenting that appeals on benefits should be subject to appeal to independent local tribunals analogous to the existing Courts of Referees, with a further right of appeal to an Umpire, appointed by the Crown, whose decision would be final.

What actually emerged were two separate adjudicative structures: one for the bulk of National Insurance benefits, the other for Industrial Injuries benefits. In addition there was a separate tribunal to hear National Assistance appeals, and appeal to a Referee in family allowance cases. A specialist channel for adjudicating medical matters – medical boards and the medical appeal tribunal – was also set in place.

As regards appeals on contributions, the report stated:

> Determination by or on behalf of the Minister as to liability to contribution, including the class in which contribution shall be made, will similarly be subject to appeals to local tribunals consisting of Chairmen of the Courts of Referees with further appeal

> to the Umpire. The problem of the relation between decisions of the Umpire and the ordinary Courts of Law is a matter for further examination.[50]

This robust approach did not survive the White Paper that followed publication of the Beveridge report. Indeed the White Paper proposed that the Minister should decide not only contribution questions but pension issues as well, though this latter proposal was dropped from the Bill.[51] The official summary of the 1946 National Insurance Bill[52] stated that 'claims to benefit will generally be determined by independent statutory authorities . . . [but] other questions arising under the Act . . . will be decided by the Minister. Appeals on points of law will be to the High Court. The Minister, instead of deciding a question himself, may refer it, on a point of law, to the High Court.'

When the Bill was debated in Parliament, the specific issue of Ministers' questions was not touched on at all in the House of Commons. It was raised briefly in the House of Lords in the context of a number of amendments proposed by Lord Meston,[53] but there was no real discussion of the issue, and certainly no consideration as to why and how the original Beveridge proposal had been dropped.

When the National Insurance Advisory Committee considered the Determination of Claims and Questions Regulations in 1948,[54] they did not press the view that there should be a requirement to give reasons in all cases. They did argue that applicants should have a right to a statement of reasons if they asked for them. They also suggested that the most important decisions should, as a matter of practice, be published. But again there was no debate about the principle of the Ministerial inquiry nor any reference back to the original Beveridge proposals.

An internal Departmental review of Adjudication under the National Insurance Act, prepared in 1955,[55] stated that the Beveridge proposal 'would have subjected the adjudication machinery to severe strain, and the risk of complete breakdown, without guaranteeing the necessary uniformity of decision and expert knowledge essential in determining these questions, and was not adopted'.

THE FRANKS COMMITTEE REPORT, 1957

The next public review of powers of adjudication in Social Security law came in evidence of the then Ministry of Pensions and National Insurance to the Franks Committee.[56] The 'tone' of the evidence is quite matter-of-fact, merely providing a description of the jurisdiction rather than any major justification of the jurisdiction or any link with theories of administrative justice.

The report of the Franks Committee itself was published in 1957.[57] Unlike the Donoughmore Committee, it had little to say specifically on social security. The report noted that 'The system [for adjudicating National Insurance and Industrial Injuries claims] is generally considered to have operated smoothly for many years, and we are satisfied that no structural changes are called for.'[58] They made a number of detailed recommendations for changes in procedure - some of which seem today quite surprising - reinforcing the point already made that tribunals and other adjudicative models are continually evolving. They did also recommend the abolition of the use of the Family Allowances Referees and the transfer of their jurisdiction to the National Insurance Local Tribunals.[59]

On the use of inquiries, the Committee stated that the vast bulk of evidence received related to inquiries regarding land.[60] They stated: 'The intention of the legislature in providing for an inquiry or hearing in certain circumstances appears to have been twofold: to ensure that the interests of the citizens closely affected should be protected by the grant to them of a statutory right to be heard in support of their objections, and to ensure that thereby the Minister should be better informed of the facts of the case.'[61] They went on: 'The consideration of objections thus involves the testing of an issue, though it must be remembered that it may only be a part of the issue which the Minister will ultimately have to determine.'[62] 'Our general conclusion is that these procedures cannot be classified as purely administrative or purely judicial.'[63]

The Committee therefore resisted coming down on one side rather than the other but stated that the general principles of openness, fairness and impartiality should be applied to inquiries as far as possible, though the last of these could not be applied without qualification.[64]

One specific recommendation they made was that 'the right course is to publish the inspector's report . . . we think it should be insisted upon wherever possible . . . the publication of the report seems to flow naturally from the fact that the inquiry itself is held in public.'[65] Further, they recommended that full reasons for decisions be set out in any decision letter.[66] Finally, they recommended the publication of certain decisions.[67] But apart from these general points the evidence about the use of inquiries in the social security field went undiscussed.

Reaction to Franks

The Franks Committee's report had a major impact on administrative justice in many areas of government. It led directly to the enactment of the Tribunals and Inquiries Act 1958 and the establishment of the Council on Tribunals. In that sense, it was more effective than the Donoughmore Committee's report.

However, given the more or less complete lack of comment from the Franks Committee on the adjudication structure of the Ministry of Pensions and National Insurance, it was not surprising that in this area there was little public policy change consequent upon the publication of the report, notwithstanding the fragmentation of adjudication. The main items of significance were the integration of appeals on Family Allowances into the main adjudicative structure in the National Insurance Act 1959; in 1966 the separate appeal tribunals for National Insurance and Industrial Injuries were merged, and the Supplementary Benefits Appeal Tribunals were created; and in 1970, when attendance allowance was introduced, a separate Attendance Allowance Board was established to adjudicate claims to that benefit.

DEVELOPMENTS FROM THE 1960s TO THE 1980s

Notwithstanding the conclusions of the Franks Committee that, broadly, all was well with social security adjudication, the 1960s and more especially the 1970s saw increasingly critical attention being focused on social security adjudication. A number of studies were conducted into the work of social security appeal tribunals, particularly those relating to supplementary benefits. Many of these were generated from the ever more vocal welfare rights movement that had grown up during the period. In addition, there was increasing criticism of the lack of legal aid for those appearing before tribunals in general and social security tribunals in particular. There was also much criticism of the secrecy that surrounded much of the adjudicative structure, particularly, again, in relation to supplementary benefits.

These criticisms were eventually taken on board by government and, since the publication of the Bell reports,[68] there has been introduced a series of profound changes to the system of adjudication in social security. Many of these are now well documented, so only a brief outline will be presented here.

The Creation of the Presidential Tribunal System

The Health and Social Services and Social Security Adjudications Act 1983 merged the former SBATs and National Insurance Local Tribunals into a single Social Security Appeals Tribunal (SSAT). In addition, the management of these tribunals was transferred from the Department of Health and Social Security to the President of SSATs. He became responsible for the organization of the tribunal system, through a team of full-time regional chairman, and in order to address the problems of quality of adjudication he was also given a statutory duty to provide training for tribunal chairmen and members. He is also responsible for Medical Appeal Tribunals and Vaccine Damage Tribunals. So extensive were his duties that the second President, Judge Holden, renamed his office as President of the Independent Tribunal Service (ITS). The ITS has recently been expanded by the creation of the new Disability Appeal Tribunal - which has taken over the work of the Attendance Allowance Board as well as a number of matters formerly decided by Medical Appeal Tribunals - and by the Child Support Appeal Tribunal.

The first study of the reformed system of SSATs has recently been published[69] and is in general impressed with the quality of adjudication now undertaken by those tribunals. The President also commissioned a study of Medical Appeal Tribunals, which, though identifying a number of matters still requiring attention, again demonstrated an improvement in the quality of decision taking.[70] While there always remains room for further improvements, there seems little doubt that the problems revealed in the 1970s have to a large extent disappeared.

Office of the Chief Adjudication Officer

A development of potentially even greater importance has been the establishment of the Chief Adjudication Officer, responsible for improving standards of initial adjudication in benefit offices. His appointment was also designed to enhance the sense of independence that adjudication officers in local offices were supposed to have. He produces an annual report commenting on standards of adjudication. His office, now retitled Central Adjudication Services, is also responsible for publishing the *Adjudication Officers' Guide* - a description of social security law and advice on how it should be applied. This new openness is in stark contrast to the secrecy that surrounded much social security adjudication in the 1960s and 1970s.

New Jurisdictions

Notwithstanding the two developments mentioned above, which might indicate attempts to rationalize the adjudicative structure in the area of social security, two other developments point in the other direction. Housing Benefit Review Boards were created in 1982 to hear appeals relating to housing benefit. Despite the fact that Housing Benefit is in essence a social security benefit, it is administered by local authorities. Political considerations at the time dictated that the appeal (or review) process should be internal to the local authority. Thus appeals are in fact determined by boards comprising councillors from the authority that took the initial decision. However independent they may be in practice, this arrangement does not give the appearance of independence.[71]

In addition the newly established Social Fund has brought with it a novel process of review by Social Fund Inspectors. Despite objection to the principle,[72] the evidence appears to suggest that the inspectors have in fact been dealing with reviews in a open and independent manner.[73] This certainly creates a new form of social security adjudication.

Formal Review Procedures

A further development in adjudication policy to which attention should be drawn is that, in a number of cases, those dissatisfied with initial decisions are now required to submit their case to a formal process of internal review, before their case can be referred on to a tribunal.[74]

THE EUROPEAN DIMENSION

One further issue that has not been taken into account so far arises out of what may be described as the 'European dimension'. Two particular items may be mentioned here.

The Committee of Ministers of the Council of Europe

Following a comparative survey of the protection of individuals against state administrations[75] the Committee of Ministers adopted, in 1977, resolution (77)/31 setting out five principles to guide the law and administrative practice of the governments of member states. These were, in essence, the right to be heard, access to information, assistance and representation, statement of reasons and indication of remedies.

This was followed in 1980 by Recommendation R(80)2, which dealt in more detail with the principles that should guide the exercise of discretionary powers. These included, *inter alia*, the principles that decisions be taken within a reasonable time, that reasons for decisions be given and that discretionary powers should be subject to control of legality by a court or other independent body.

Although the resolution and recommendation are not, of themselves, justiciable in the British courts, they are supposed to guide policy-making in member states. In addition, the Justice–All Souls *Review of Administrative Justice*[76] made a long list of recommendations, including one that the British Government should develop a set of Principles of Good Administration, which, it is suggested, might be based on the work done by the Council of Europe.

European Convention on Human Rights, Article 6(1)

This provides that 'In the determination of his civil rights . . . everyone is entitled to a fair and public hearing within a reasonable time by an independent and impartial tribunal established by law.' In this context there is some doubt as to how far the concept of 'civil rights' will be taken by the European Commission of Human Rights and by the European Court of Human Rights. There has been much recent litigation and it is clear that broader interpretations are now accepted than was thought likely some years ago.[77]

One commentator has recently suggested that, in the light of two cases decided by the European Court of Human Rights in 1986, at least some aspects of the British social security system could be regarded as falling within the scope of Article 6, in particular those issues relating to the administration of contributory benefits.[78] If this is correct, then the implications for aspects of social security adjudication policy would be substantial.[79]

THE EVOLUTION OF ADMINISTRATIVE JUSTICE: SOME BASIC QUESTIONS

This review of the history of social security adjudication has been undertaken not just for its own sake, but also for the light that it might throw on issues that would need to be considered should a major reform of the structure of administrative justice be undertaken in the UK. Before such a reform programme was undertaken, it would be essential that the case for and against be examined carefully. In this final section a preliminary list of the questions that would have to be addressed is presented.

Do We Need a System of Administrative Justice at All?

Logically, the first question that must be answered is whether we need a system of administrative justice at all. If the administration is running smoothly, why should it be necessary to develop additional procedures, which to many officials might be seen merely to clog up that system and inhibit efficient administration? There are probably still some who, at least secretly, share the view robustly expressed by the late Reginald Maudling: 'I can assure honourable Members I have never seen the sense of administrative law in our country because it merely means someone else taking the Government's decisions for them.'[80]

There are, of course, compelling answers to this line of argument. First, whatever the theory about what should happen, things go wrong in practice. Second, and more generally, it has become accepted that one of the fundamental principles that must apply to all public officials in the exercise of statutory powers is that they should be publicly accountable for their actions. Thus means of accountability must be created as part of the administrative structure. This will become more important as moves to create semi-independent government agencies and/or to devolve decision-taking to private bodies gathers momentum. Naturally, the appropriate mechanism of accountability will vary depending on the nature of the decision that is being called into account. (While Parliament will be the right place to call politicians to account on the main policy questions, this is not suitable for the resolution of the individual grievance.)

A third argument is also heard. It is not only important for the bureaucrat/administrator to arrive at the right decision; the process by which that decision is reached is also of importance. This must be another goal for administrative justice.

In short, administrative justice brings together the procedures needed to resolve conflict, to render officials accountable for their actions and to improve the quality of the administrative process.

The Nature of Administrative Justice

While it may be accepted that there is a need for administrative justice, the next question is what is meant by the concept of administrative justice. One of the limitations in discussions about administrative justice, until relatively recent times, is that much of the debate was based on the assumption, voiced by Lord Hewart, that the only persons who really should be implementing the law were the judges. And even if for practical reasons it became inevitable that persons other than fully fledged judges were to be involved in the taking of legal decisions, the processes by which they should take them should be seen to relate to ideal notions of justice derived from some kind of court model. Thus, in the past, discussion about administrative justice has tended to focus on appeals procedures.

Such a view tended to throw the emphasis in any analysis of administrative justice on to what happens *after* initial decisions have been taken by officials. More recently, however, consideration has begun to focus more on administrative justice in the context of initial decision-taking,[81] the essential feature of which is an examination of the nature of the decisions that have to be taken by officials and the procedures that are or should be appropriate in relation to such decisions if they are to be properly characterized as 'just'.

Thus Sainsbury argues that in an ideal sense, bureaucratic decision-taking will incorporate the attributes of 'justice' if the following characteristics are satisfied: the decision is accurate; the decision is fair. His notion of fairness incorporates four distinct elements: promptness, impartiality, participation and accountability. (Clearly this list of attributes is not the last word on the subject; some might argue that, in order to be fair, decision-takers should not simply take those decisions that have been referred to them by members of the public, but should be willing to seek out those in whose interests decisions might be taken but who have not applied for them – in the context of social security, the 'non-take-up' problem. Others might feel that a recognition of the balance between the costs of decision-taking and other costs should be made: is it right to spend large sums of money adjudicating cases of little financial value? And it may be that the notion of independence needs to be brought more clearly into the list.)

Sainsbury acknowledges that though each of his attributes may be seen to be conceptually distinct, there will be overlap in practice; more important, there will often be inconsistency in practice, and thus real-world decisions may need to be based on a compromise. For example, there will often be a tension between accuracy and promptness.

Although Sainsbury's model may need further thought and refinement, it does reflect an important point, which is that successful administration of government policy in general and social security policy in particular needs to incorporate certain standards or goals that, taken together, can try to ensure that the system is perceived as administratively just. Administrative decision-taking needs to be tested against this or some other similar set of criteria.

Even if the idea that concepts of administrative justice should also apply to initial-level decision-takers is accepted, it does raise profound practical issues. While there are some indications that when it comes to asking officials to undertake *reviews* of initial decisions it may be somewhat realistic to regard them as working independently, there are obvious difficulties in giving operational effect to the idea at the initial decision-taking level itself; the recent study of social security adjudication by Baldwin *et al.*[82] illustrates very clearly that individual officers are not actually able to operate independently, primarily because of pressure of work and lack of training.[83]

What Are the Objectives of the Administrative Justice System?

We need to ask next what the detailed objectives of an administrative justice system are. The most important consideration must surely be that the system should deliver good-quality decisions, and an efficient service for those who wish to challenge disputed decisions. This implies that there must be easy access to the system by potential users of the system; that there should be adequate independent advice services; and that there should be representation in cases that need representation.

A secondary consideration must be that the system is efficient in that resources are not wasted on processes that could be used for the direct assistance of the needy or in other ways carrying out the proper functions of government. Certainly in this sense the Franks criteria of speed and cheapness remain as desirable today as they did when they were first articulated.

A third objective is that whatever structure is chosen, those who operate it do have the specialist training and expertise to deliver a specialist service. Even if a reformed structure allowed personnel to be used more flexibly, public credibility would demand that those sitting in judgment should know what they are talking about.

A more profound question is whether the system of administrative justice should also *imply* certain standards of social justice, against which the fairness or otherwise of substantive rules can be tested. There is clearly increased interest in the influence that instruments such as the European Convention on Human Rights or the Treaty of Rome may have on social legislation; if citizens who are persistent can get issues raised in the forums associated with those documents, should it not equally be possible for them to raise questions directly within the administrative justice system itself?[84]

Finally, and more controversially, the question should be raised as to how far a system of administrative justice, while asserting its independence, should be able to go. Is there a point beyond which it should not be allowed to go, so as not to disrupt unnecessarily the work of government departments?

How Far Is Complexity a Problem?

With these general considerations in mind, we turn to the question of complexity. There is no doubt that the present system of social security adjudication is complex. Despite a number of moves to rationalize procedures and standards, particularly during the 1980s, the adjudication of disputes still involves a great variety of decisions being taken by individual officials within the Department (now Benefits Agency), some at local level, others centralized, with yet others being determined within the Department of Employment. When they are functioning as Adjudication Officers, their standards are monitored by the Office of the Chief Adjudication Officer (now Central Adjudication Services); but in other situations, where they act for the Secretary of State, managerial controls remain hidden. There is a complex system for the adjudication of medical matters, involving individual doctors, Medical Boards, Medical Appeal Tribunals and now Disability Appeal Tribunals. In some situations where appeals are lodged, there is triggered an *informal* process of review; in an increasing number of situations, there is now a *formal* review stage, which must be completed before a case can proceed to a tribunal. Some Secretary of State decisions may be appealed to an inquiry; in other cases there is no right of appeal at all. Some further appeals go to the specialist Social Security Commissioners; a few go direct to the High Court. Given that this is the 'system' in but one area of governmental activity, it would be easy to argue for a system that is more simply structured.

Complexity is not, however, *necessarily* a bad thing. At least three advantages can be identified. First, a complex structure may simply reflect the fact that in a particular area of social administration there is a complex range of issues to be dealt with. The obvious example in the social security arena is adjudication on medical matters. It is surely sensible to have such matters dealt with by people who are not necessarily needed for dealing with more general questions of entitlement to benefit.

Second, the existence of a range of adjudicative structures may give confidence to the public that matters are being dealt with by experts. If, for example, the Social Security Appeal Tribunal dealt with all medical matters, all disability appeal matters, all vaccine damage cases, all child support matters or (in the future) housing benefit matters, would this increase public confidence in the tribunal system? Separate structures for such adjudication can be argued to be, on balance, a positive rather than a negative feature.

Third, it may be very desirable to experiment with new models of adjudication, and not assume that the existing system is the only sensible way of doing things. For example, is it necessarily the case that the tribunal model that currently predominates is necessarily the best one? Where experiments are initiated, such as with the development of formal internal review procedures in social security, this will add to the complexity of the structure, but may not be a wholly bad idea from the point of view of developing ideas about administrative justice.[85]

These arguments in favour of complexity should not, however lead to the conclusion that existing arrangements are completely satisfactory. In the context of social security, Housing Benefit reviews should clearly be brought into mainstream social security adjudication.[86] The Secretary of State's adjudicative powers should not be left outside either, particularly as a range of Secretary of State decisions are not subject to appeal at all but really should be.

A system of administrative justice that was conceived of more 'in the round' could lead to a transformation in modes of work. For example, instead of chairmen being appointed to a single tribunal, they could be allowed a kind of 'career progression' whereby after a few years in one tribunal, they might be asked to move to another. There could be a more rational use of buildings for tribunal purposes; instead of large numbers of locations being hired for the purpose of individual tribunals, for example, there might be created 'Tribunal centres', analogous to the buildings used for the criminal or civil courts, in which a variety of tribunals could operate. There could be savings on rental charges and on administrative and personnel costs as a result. Certainly members of the public might be able to find their way to such tribunal buildings more easily than is presently sometimes the case.

Who Should Be Responsible for Developing Proposals for Change?

One obvious lesson from the developments over the past eighty years in relation to social security administrative justice is that developments have been driven, in the main, by civil servants working within the departments responsible for the programmes against which decisions are to be challenged. The structures that have been developed have therefore been heavily influenced by political expedience, rather than principle. Although recent developments have shown a willingness to assert the importance of independence, there will always be a tension, where adjudication policy is created in the same department that administers the system to be appealed against, between those responsible for adjudication policy and other policy-makers in the department who will not want to make life difficult for themselves. Although the British tradition of 'fair play' in public administration should not be discounted with too cynical a laugh, and while the record of the Department of Social Security in developing new models of administrative justice, and generally opening up decision-taking processes to public scrutiny, is in many ways exemplary, there must be limits to departmental even-handedness.

This raises the question of principle as to whether the policy on administrative justice should be driven wholly by the department whose decisions are being challenged. The only centralizing influence at the present time is the Council on Tribunals, which, though it has had some success in advocating more uniform practices, has also had some notable failures.

The obvious central authority for establishing both standards and the procedures of administrative justice would be the Lord Chancellor's Department - or any Ministry of Justice that might replace it. But without adequate resources, questions would arise as to whether a single monolithic department would in fact be able to develop a sufficiently flexible and imaginative structure that satisfies the fundamental objectives of the system, in particular the delivery of a system of specialized justice to the individual. Will they be able to recruit the kinds of people necessary to undertake the tasks asked of them? Perhaps what is needed is a partnership between the 'sponsoring' departments and the Lord Chancellor's Department to get the balance of independence and efficiency correct.

Where Will Pressure for Change Come From?

At the outset of this chapter, it was implied that at present the Lord Chancellor's Department is probably too busy working on other changes to the civil and criminal justice systems to be particularly bothered with broader questions of administrative justice. However, there are signs that this may change. The Department already has a number of tribunals under its control and is in the process of adding others to its administrative portfolio - in particular the General Commissioners of Income Tax from April 1994. It is likely that at some stage a critical mass will develop that will result in the department wishing to take a more structured approach to the system as a whole. In addition, as was also noted, influential voices in high places may increasingly be heard.

There will remain external political pressures. The political context has changed fundamentally over the past twenty years with the rise in the welfare rights movement and a variety of other consumer voices. It is easy to be cynical about the significance of the Citizen's Charter, but a Minister determined to make a reality of this idea could prove an important voice in the development of ideas on administrative justice. The European dimension is also potentially of great significance. Further, the changing nature of the British welfare state from one in which decisions are taken largely by officials of the state to one in which increasingly private bodies act as agents for the state will add to the necessity to call current arrangements into question.

Thus pressure is likely to remain and, indeed, grow. The success of recent reforms in the specific context of social security is likely to add strength to calls for more general reform.

What Models of Administrative Justice Might Be Adopted?

Lord Woolf has proposed that the best way forward for administrative justice is to create an Administrative Division of the High Court. At first glance this may seem a rather reactionary suggestion, harking back to the demands of Lord Chief Justice Hewart. However, it is likely that such expressions of opinion have been driven more by a perception that administrative justice is still not taken seriously enough and that a closer relationship between the structure of administrative justice and the courts would give enhanced status to the judges who operate within the tribunal system.

While it may be true that there is a lack of status associated with tribunals (which may, however, have more to do with the perceptions of the legal profession, who do not on the whole practice there, rather than any inherent lack of confidence in tribunals on the part of the public), it would be very undesirable in my view to rush into an assumption that the only or the best way forward for a reformed system of administrative justice would be based in the courts. Such a view would prevent discussion of alternatives, such as the role of ombudsmen, or other models of complaints procedure that, from the public's point of view, might be more desirable. There is also a necessity for a more general discussion about the contribution of more informal processes in our legal system. (Indeed it is arguable that the courts have as much to learn from tribunals as the other way round.)

From a purely practical point of view it has to be said that the present government is hardly likely to rush to the adoption of a court-based structure for administrative justice, if only because, by keeping tribunals separate, calls for the extension of legal aid to them can more easily be resisted. The issue of the lack of status is likely to have to be addressed in other ways.

CONCLUSION

Reforming the structure of administrative justice will be a daunting task, which will be undertaken only if the political will and determination is in place to achieve it. As this chapter indicates, it is far easier to ask questions than answer them. There will be great temptation to keep on muddling through with piecemeal additions and reforms, just as has occurred in the context of social security over the past eighty years. However, while the temptation may be there, it is important for those concerned about these issues to ensure that they are debated fully, and to consider whether a more ordered approach to the evolution of administrative justice is now needed. This chapter is offered as a contribution to that debate.

NOTES

1. See e.g. H. Woolf, *Protection of the Public: A New Challenge* (1990), Chapter 3. Lord Slynn has also argued for a new approach to the structure of administrative justice.

2. See, on Australia, M. Partington, The reform of public law in Britain: theoretical problems and practical considerations, in P. McAuslan and J. F. McEldowney (eds), *Law Legitimacy and*

the Constitution (1985); Justice-All Souls, *Administrative Justice: Some Necessary Reforms* (Oxford, 1988), especially Chapter 9; on developments in New Zealand, see S. H. Legomsky, *Specialized Justice* (Oxford, 1990).

3. See T. G. Ison, *The Administrative Appeals Tribunal of Australia*, Report prepared for the Law Reform Commission of Canada (1989).

4. This was announced in their 26th Annual Report for 1991, para 2.9 (HC 280, 1991–2).

5. The sections that follow are adapted from my research report, *The Secretary of State's Powers of Adjudication in Social Security Law*, published in 1991. The full report is available as a working paper from the School for Advanced Urban Studies at the University of Bristol, Rodney Lodge, Grange Road, Bristol BS8 4EA. Full references and footnotes are to be found there.

6. SR & O 1922, No. 2001.

7. Details of the procedures are taken from Appendix III of the Evidence of the Ministry of Health to the Donoughmore Committee. See below.

8. Thus it can be seen that in these contexts, the role of the Umpire was very circumscribed, certainly by comparison with the jurisdiction of the Social Security Commissioners in the present day. They could not deal with cases referred to the Court of Referees. See Explanatory Memorandum on Part II of the National Insurance Act (Cd 5991, 1911), p. 4. Cf. HC Debs, 7 November 1911, cols 1751–7.

9. Thus the attempt to give civil servants some kind of special status in relation to decision-taking was one of the earliest features of the modern social security system: for further detail, and a critique of the problems this causes, see J. Baldwin, N. Wikeley and R. Young, *Judging Social Security* (Oxford, 1992), especially Chapters 2 and 3.

10. See *Report on National Unemployment Insurance to July 1923*, by T. W. Phillips (HMSO, 1923), para. 169 and Appendix V.

11. These details are from *First Report of the Proceedings of the Board of Trade under Part II of the National Insurance Act 1911* (Cd 6965, 1913), at para. 36.

12. A full account of these procedures is found in *First Report of the Proceedings of the Board of Trade under Part II of the National Insurance Act 1911* (Cd 6965, 1913), at paras 34–9. It should also be noted that, as originally provided, the proceedings of the Court of Referees were to be held in private: see HC Debs, 7 November 1911, cols 1757–8.

13. 7 November 1911, col. 1753, *per* Mr Buxton, President of the Board of Trade. The argument against, from Mr Baird, stressed the delay that would be likely to result from a further right of appeal.

14. *Ibid.*

15. Cd 6965 (1913).

16. *Ibid.*, para. 190, p. 32.

17. *Ibid.*, para. 193, p. 33.

18. They were appointed by the Treasury, not the Minister of Health; see 1911 Act, s. 57. At least one of them had to be a qualified medical practitioner.

19. The possible conflicts that might arise with Commissioners if they had to hear, in effect, appeals from their original decisions were discussed in Parliamentary questions: Tuesday 2 July 1912 (reprinted in vol. 8, *Questions and Answers in the House of Commons relating to National Insurance Act*, 1913), cols 349–50.

20. National Insurance Act 1911, s. 66. The provisions as finally passed were rather different from those outlined in a Memorandum on the National Insurance Bill as passed by the House of Commons, insofar as it relates to National Health Insurance (Cd 5995, 1911). This provides further evidence of the uncertainty felt by the original draftsmen and policy-makers about the appropriate means for adjudicating disputes under the Act. Section 66, originally clause 49, was debated in detail in the House of Commons, on 9 November 1911 (HC Debs, cols 1923–34). PRO File PIN 4/4 has a file on the first appeals regulations made under s. 67 of the 1911 Act.

21. For procedures of the Commissioners see the regulations; also C. Zeffert, *Procedure in Disputes, Complaints, Inquiries etc. under Parts I and III of the National Insurance Act 1911* (1913). There are indications that, notwithstanding their title and apparent independence from Ministers, they were not intended to act independently: see the exchange between Mr Fred Hall and Mr Lloyd George in the House of Commons on 29 January 1913, the latter stating that it was essential for the Commissioners to act under the oversight of Ministers since it was the Ministers who

were responsible to Parliament for the expenditure of money voted to the Department by Parliament. Formally, however, they did not lose their jurisdiction until the National Health Insurance Act 1924 abolished them and made the Minister responsible for insurability questions, thus bringing them into line with Unemployment Insurance; see DHSS, *Report on a Study of the Secretary of State's Adjudicational Function* (unpublished typescript, 1955, Appendix A).

22. For details see PRO file CAB/24/95/325; see also CAB 37/106/46 and PIN 3/8.

23. See PRO file PIN 3/8, Memorandum on the Unemployment Insurance Bill 1920, at p. 34.

24. *Ibid.*, p. 35. It was anticipated that there would in practice be very few appeals to the courts. A single judge would be nominated for the purpose by the Lord Chancellor, a system found to work satisfactorily in the case of appeals from munitions tribunals; *ibid.*, p. 37.

25. See PRO file PIN 29/283 for early examples. The *Report on National Unemployment Insurance to July 1923* by T. W. Phillips (1923) stated that up to July 1923 the Minister had given 262 formal decisions; para. 178, p. 75.

26. These are available in typescript only and are stored in the archive library of the DSS Social Security library, Room 07/15 Adelphi, 1–11 John Adam Street, London WC2N 6HT. They are not accessible to the general public. The *Report* by T. W. Phillips (above) stated that the Judge appointed to hear appeals was Mr Justice Roche. He had taken decisions (to July 1923) in 68 cases, the bulk of them referred to him by the Minister.

27. All this information is from the *Report* by T. W. Phillips cited above, at p. 75.

28. *Ibid.*

29. See PRO file PIN 4/91. The relevant section is Appendix III of the evidence.

30. SR & O 1924, No. 1337.

31. The evidence showed that in 1927, out of 110 formal decisions made for questions arising in England, there were hearings in only 13 cases; in 1928 the figures were, respectively 206 and 50; and in 1929 (up to 30 November) 163 and 52.

32. See section 18(1). See the report of the Donoughmore Committee on Ministers' Powers, p. 88. For further information on this, see PRO File, PIN 4/133.

33. He dealt with some 19,000 cases in 1929, and 20,000 in 1930; PRO file, PIN 6/8.

34. Cmd 4185 (1932), para. 492.

35. *Final Report of the Royal Commission in Unemployment Benefit* (Cmd 4185, 1932), para. 486.

36. *Op. cit.*, para. 508. The reactions of the Ministry of Labour to the Report are to be found in PRO file PIN 6/68.

37. This argument actually raises the extremely difficult question of where the boundary between adjudication and administration actually lies: for a discussion see Partington, *op. cit.*, note 5, Chapter 1.

38. Information from PRO file PIN 4/92, document 1. The memorandum is not actually dated but was presumably written in 1929, at the start of the Committee's work. It may be noted that there is no mention here of the principles of openness or independence.

39. *Report of the Committee on Ministers' Powers* (Cmd 4060, 1932).

40. *Ibid.*, pp. 74–5.

41. *Ibid.*

42. *Ibid.*, p. 78. The Committee noted 'we do not wish to imply that the principle . . . is in fact violated in any existing statutes . . . An interesting way in which Parliament has observed the principle will be found in old age pension legislation: under Sections 7 and 8 of the Old Age Pensions Act 1908, the Minister of Health is the central pension authority for determining appeals, although the Commissioners of Customs and Excise, who are responsible to the Treasury, i.e. in practice to the Chancellor of the Exchequer, are the Department responsible for the administration of pensions.'

43. *Ibid.*, p. 80.

44. *Ibid.*, p. 87.

45. *Ibid.*, p. 89.

46. *Ibid.*, p. 93.

47. *Ibid.*, p. 96. The example they then give was of the powers given to the Insurance Commissioner in ss. 66 and 67 of the National Insurance Act 1911.

48. PATs fall into two categories: the first deals with questions of entitlement and comprises

a lawyer chairman, a medical member and a member from the armed forces, usually retired; the second handles questions of assessment of disability and comprises two doctors (one of whom is chairman) and an ex-serviceman or officer.

49. Pension Appeal Tribunals (England and Wales) Rules 1980, SI 1980 No. 1120; for comment see A. Ogus and E. Barendt, *The Law of Social Security* (3rd edn, 1988), pp. 589–90.

50. *Social Insurance and Allied Services* (Cmd 6404, 1942), para. 395.

51. *Social Insurance* (Cmd 6550, 1944).

52. *Summary of the Main Provisions of the National Insurance Scheme* (Cmd 6729, 1946), paras 48 and 49.

53. HL Debs, 8 July 1946 (Committee stage).

54. HC 144 (1947–8).

55. Probably as a background document for the Ministry's evidence to be submitted to the Franks inquiry.

56. *Committee on Administrative Tribunals and Inquiries: Memoranda submitted by Government Departments*, vol. 1 (1956). Judicial decisions of the Minister were described in Memorandum No. 2; this also contained a schedule setting out a list of questions assigned to the Ministers together with a copy of notes prepared for those assigned to hold inquiries. Memorandum No. 4 dealt with decisions taken on Family Allowances, where the Minister took initial decisions with an appeal to a referee. Memorandum No. 6 dealt with appeals and references under pre-1946 legislation (the Widows', Orphans' and Old Age Contributory Pensions Acts 1936 and 1937) which were preserved under transitional arrangements together with their adjudicative structure, which also involved the determination of claims by the Minister, with a right of appeal to a referee.

57. Cmnd 218 (1957).

58. *Ibid.*, Chapter 14, para. 171, p. 39.

59. *Ibid.*, para. 184, p. 42. This recommendation was brought into effect in the National Insurance Act 1959.

60. *Ibid.*, para. 242, p. 55.

61. *Ibid.*, para. 269, p. 59.

62. *Ibid.*, para. 271, p. 60.

63. *Ibid.*, para. 270.

64. *Ibid.*, para. 277, p. 61.

65. *Ibid.*, para. 343, p. 73.

66. *Ibid.*, para. 352, p. 76.

67. *Ibid.*, para. 354.

68. K. Bell, 'National Insurance local tribunals, (1973) 3 *Journal of Social Policy* no. 4; (1974) 4, no. 1; *Research Study on Supplementary Benefits Appeal Tribunals* (HMSO, 1975).

69. See J. Baldwin *et al.*, *op. cit.* note 9. See also J. C. Potter, Social Security Appeal Tribunals: a research report (1992) *Anglo-American Law Review* 341, and the report by H. and Y. Genn, *The Effectiveness of Representation at Tribunals* (Lord Chancellor's Department, 1989).

70. R. Sainsbury, *Survey and Report into the Working of the Medical Appeal Tribunals* (1992).

71. For a detailed study see R. Sainsbury and T. Eardley, *Housing Benefit Reviews* (University of York Social Policy Research Unit, 1991).

72. See, e.g., Council on Tribunals, *Social Security – Abolition of Independent Appeals under the Proposed Social Fund* (Cmnd 9722, 1986).

73. See G. Dalley and R. Berthoud, *Challenging Discretion* (Policy Studies Institute, 1992).

74. This had long happened informally. Indeed, many appeals never reach a formal hearing because the initial decision is superseded having been internally reviewed: see J. Baldwin *et al.*, *op. cit.* note 9 especially Chapter 3. The formal review stage is not a feature of Housing Benefit, Disability Benefits and (proposed) child support cases. The idea of an informal means of resolving disputes without the expense of a formal hearing is also seen in the so-called 'dissatisfaction' procedure for dealing with certain matters relating to contributions – see M. Partington, *op. cit.* note 5, Annex. For sharp criticism of this development, however, see R. Sainsbury, Internal reviews and the weakening of Social Security claimants' appeal rights (unpublished conference paper).

75. *An Analytical Survey of the Rights of the Individual in the Administrative Procedure and His Remedies against the Administration* (Strasbourg, 1975).

76. *Op. cit.*, note 2, pp. 8–12.

77. See, for notes on this jurisprudence, pieces by C. Warbrick in the *Yearbook of European Law*, 1985, 1986 and 1987; I am indebted to Mr Warbrick, of Durham University, for drawing these to my attention.

78. A. W. Bradley, Social security and the right to a fair hearing: the Strasbourg perspective [1987] PL 3.

79. It is also understood that consideration is being given to the creation of an additional provision in the European Convention on Human Rights which might have the effect of doing for administrative law what Article 6 has already done for civil rights.

80. Official Report, Standing Committee B, 25 May 1971, col. 1508, quoted by G. Ganz, The allocation of decision-making functions [1972] PL 307.

81. See J. L. Mashaw, *Bureaucratic Justice: Managing Social Security Disability Claims* (New Haven, CT, 1983); R. Sainsbury, Deciding social security claims: a study in the theory and practice of administrative justice (unpublished PhD thesis, University of Edinburgh, 1988).

82. Note 9.

83. The authors did find signs of independence in the context of decision-taking on Unemployment Benefit, where pressures of work were not so intense.

84. Of course, in the context of social security, EC issues can already be determined by Tribunals or Commissioners.

85. This is not to suggest that such moves are by definition desirable. One of the major developments in administrative justice that has been thrown up in recent times is that of the formal internal review. How can this work in a way that gives the public confidence that their case has been fully considered? A major advantage of the tribunal system is that it does afford the appellant the opportunity to sit down with someone and discuss his or her case. Many appellants who lose their appeals none the less appreciate the chance to air fully their sense of grievance. See R. Sainsbury, *op. cit.*, note 74.

86. R. Sainsbury and T. Eardley, *op. cit.*, note 71.

A Bibliography of the Writings of Paul O'Higgins

BOOKS

A Bibliography of Periodical Literature Relating to Irish Law (Belfast, 1966).
First Supplement (Belfast, 1975).
Second Supplement (Belfast, 1983).

(With B. A. Hepple) *Public Employee Trade Unionism in the United Kingdom: The Legal Framework* (Ann Arbor, 1971).

(With B. A. Hepple) *Individual Employment Law* (London, Sweet & Maxwell, 1971).

(With B. A. Hepple) *Employment Law* (Sweet & Maxwell, 1976) (second edition of above; third edition, 1979; fourth edition, 1981).

Censorship in Britain (London, Nelson, 1972).

(With B. A. Hepple and J. Neeson) *A Bibliography of British and Irish Labour Law* (London, Mansell, 1975).

Workers' Rights (London, Hutchinson, 1976).

Cases and Materials on Civil Liberties (Sweet & Maxwell, 1980).

(With B. A. Hepple, J. Hepple and P. Sterling) *Labour Law in Great Britain and Ireland to 1978* (Sweet & Maxwell, 1981).

Discrimination in Employment in Northern Ireland (Belfast, Labour Relations Agency and University of Ulster, 1984).

(With A. D. Dubbins and John Gennard) *Fairness at Work - Evenhanded Industrial Relations: a discussion paper* (Bedford, National Graphical Association, 1986).

A Bibliography of Irish Trials and Other Legal Proceedings (Abingdon, Professional Books, 1986). (Awarded the Joseph L. Andrews Bibliographical Award by the American Association of Law Libraries, 1987.)

(With M. Partington) *A Bibliography of the Literature on British and Irish Social Security Law* (Mansell, 1986).

Draft Labour Code for the Kingdom of Lesotho (Maseru, Department of Labour, 1989). Revised edn, International Labour Office, 1990.

(Now published as Labour Code Order, 1992; text in *Lesotho Government Gazette Extraordinary*, vol. 37, no. 118, 12 November 1992.)

BOOKS EDITED BY PAUL O'HIGGINS

Joint general editor (with B. A. Hepple) *Encyclopaedia of Labour Relations Law* (3 vols, Sweet & Maxwell, 1972–91).

Advisory editor (with B. A. Hepple and Lord Wedderburn of Charlton), *Labour Relations Statutes and Materials* (Sweet & Maxwell, 1979; second edition, 1983).

Advisory editor (with B. A. Hepple and Lord Wedderburn of Charlton), *Labour Relations Statutes and Materials 1980/81* (Sweet & Maxwell, 1981).

Consulting editor, *Employment Law Manual* (Sweet & Maxwell, 1988).

Joint editor (with J. F. McEldowney), *Essays in Irish Legal History* (Dublin, Irish Academic Press, 1989).

Consulting editor, *Sweet & Maxwell's Employment Law Manual*, 1989–.

Consultant editor, *Sweet & Maxwell's Encyclopaedia of Employment Law*, 1992–.

Editor (with J. F. McEldowney), *The Common Law Tradition: Essays in Irish Legal History* (Irish Academic Press, 1990).

Editor (with J. Hayes), *Lessons from Northern Ireland* (Belfast, SLS Publications, 1990).

MEMBERSHIP OF EDITORIAL BOARDS

Member of the Editorial Committee and Book Review Editor, *Industrial Law Journal*, 1972–.

Member of Advisory Editorial Committee, *Managerial Law*, 1975–.

Member Editorial Advisory Board, *Northern Ireland Legal Quarterly*, 1977–.

Joint General Editor, Mansell Series of Studies in Labour and Social Law, 1978–.

Member, Editorial Board, *Human Rights Review*, 1979–82.

General Editor, *Law at Work* Series (14 volumes published by Sweet & Maxwell, 1980–1).

Member, Editorial Board, *Irish Current Law Statutes Annotated* (Sweet & Maxwell), 1984–.
Member, Editorial Board, *King's College Law Journal*, 1990–.
Member, Editorial Board, *Bibliography of Nineteenth Century Legal Literature* (Avero Publications and Chadwyck-Healey), 1991–.

CONTRIBUTIONS TO BOOKS

Das Eherecht der Republik Irland, in F. Leske and W. Loewenfeld (eds), *Rechtsverfolgung im internationalen Verkehr* (Berlin, 1963), pp. 547–60.
Encyclopaedia Americana (current edition), article on The penal and judicial system of Northern Ireland.
Annual Survey of Commonwealth Law, 1965 (London, 1966), Labour law, pp. 584–619.
Ibid., 1966 (London, 1967), pp. 597–642.
Ibid., 1967 (London, 1968), pp. 607–41.
Ibid., 1968 (London, 1969), pp. 668–710 (with B. A. Hepple).
Ibid., 1969 (London, 1970), pp. 476–512 (with B. A. Hepple).
Ibid., 1970 (London, 1971), pp. 288–318 (with B. A. Hepple).
Ibid., 1971 (London, 1972), pp. 655–86 (with B. A. Hepple).
Ibid., 1972 (London, 1973), pp. 369–400 (with B. A. Hepple).
Ibid., 1973 (London, 1974), pp. 487–534 (with B. A. Hepple and P. T. Wallington).
Ibid., 1974 (London, 1975), pp. 468–507 (with B. A. Hepple and P. T. Wallington).
Ibid., 1975 (London, 1976), pp. 547–76 (with B. A. Hepple and P. T. Wallington).
Ibid., 1976 (London, 1977), pp. 435–60 (with P. Elias and B. Napier).
Ibid., 1977 (London, 1978), pp. 507–34 (with P. Elias and B. Napier).
Industrial legislation and Factory legislation, Chapters 9 and 10 in *The Origins of the Social Services* (London, New Society, 1968).
The Treaty of Limerick, 1691, in C. W. Alexandrowicz (ed.), *Grotian Society Papers 1968: Studies in the Law of Nations* (The Hague, 1970), pp. 212–32.
The adequacy of administrative structures in British social security and The efficacy of social security, in *European Institute of Social Security Yearbook 1970* (Louvain, 1971), pp. 567–69 and 63–75 respectively.

Collective bargaining in Britain, in T. Mayer-Maly (ed.), *Kollektivvertrage in Europa – Conventions collectives de travail* (Munich and Salzburg, 1972), pp. 232–74.

The Schools Council/Nuffield Humanities Project: *People and Work* (London, 1971) included, among materials used, the article Dead or injured at work.

International Encyclopaedia of Comparative Law, vol. I (Hamburg, 1973): article on Republic of Ireland.

Contributing editor (labour law), *Encyclopaedia of Personnel Management* (ed. D. Torrington, London, 1974).

The right to strike – some international reflections, in J. Carby-Hall (ed.), *Studies in Labour Law* (London, 1976), pp. 110–18.

Contributor to K. Simmons (ed.), *Encyclopaedia of European Community Law* (London, 1973, 1974).

Picketing, in E. Coker and G. Stuttard (ed.), *Industrial Studies: The Bargaining Context* (London, 1977).

Problems of teaching labour law, in *New Resources in Industrial Relations Teaching* (collected papers of the Department of Education and Science/Society of Industrial of Industrial Tutors Workshop, Lancaster, July 1978).

Discrimination in employment, in Sir John Wood (ed.), *Encyclopaedia of Northern Ireland Labour Law and Practice* (Belfast, Labour Relations Agency, 1983), vol. 2.

Foreword to P. R. Macmillan, *Censorship and Public Morality* (Gower Press, 1983), pp. iii–v.

Commission of the European Communities, *The Contract of Employment in the Law of the Member States of the European Communities* (Brussels, Commission of the European Communities, 1977. Labour Law Series No. 1). (Contributed UK material.)

Britain and international labour standards, in Roy Lewis (ed.), *Labour Law in Britain* (Oxford, Basil Blackwell, 1986), Chapter 20.

The disciplinary function of social security law in British practice, in *Liber Amicorum, Professor Dr J. M. G. Veldkamp* (Deventer, Kluwer, 1986).

Labour law in recession: the British experience, in *Schetsen voor Bakels* (Deventer, Kluwer, 1987), pp. 179–83.

Irish extradition law and practice, reprinted in M. Forde, *Extradition Law in Ireland* (Dublin, Round Hall Press, 1988) pp. 229–60.

Border control of people in the European Community in 1993. *Report of Select Committee on the European Communities 1992; Border Control of People*, (1989), pp. 176–7.

The European Social Charter, in R. Blackburn and J. Taylor (eds),

Human Rights for the 1990s: Legal, Political and Ethical Issues (Mansell, 1990), pp. 121–30.

(With J. F. McEldowney), The common law tradition in Irish legal history, in McEldowney and O'Higgins, *The Common Law Tradition* (Irish Academic Press, 1990), pp. 13–26.

(With J. F. McEldowney), Irish legal history and the nineteenth century, in McEldowney and O'Higgins, *The Common Law Tradition* (Irish Academic Press, 1990) pp. 203–30.

Actes du Colloque européen: Quel Avenir pour l'Europe Sociale: 1991 et Après? Organisé par le Centre d'Études Sociologiques du Droit Social International et Comparé de l'Université Libre de Bruxelles (Brussels, Editions CIACO, 1992), pp. 73–9.

PUBLISHED CONTRIBUTIONS TO CONFERENCES, ADDRESSES, ETC.

Proceedings, International Society for Labour Law and Social Legislation, 6th Congress, Stockholm, August 1966: Report on the UK machinery for the maintenance of the value of social security benefits as affected by changes in the cost of living.

Conventions collectives et puissance publique en droit anglais, to be found in *Journée d'Études Juridiques Jean Dabin* (Louvain, November 1969).

Proceedings, International Society for Labour Law and Social Legislation, 7th Congress, Warsaw, September 1970: Report on Disqualification for social security benefits in the UK.

Ibid., 8th Congress, Selve di Fesano (Brindisi), September 1974: Report (with B. A. Hepple) on Rights and functions of trade unions and their representatives at enterprise level.

Trade Disputes and the Law (Dublin, Society of Young Solicitors, Lecture no. 52, 1971).

The Industrial Relations Bill in Britain – Its Implications (Dublin, Irish Congress of Trade Unions, 1971).

Address on The law and safety at work in the context of the Offices, Shops and Railway Premises Act 1963, to be found in *Institute of Shops Acts Administration: Report of the Proceedings at the 25th Annual Conference. Folkestone, 28–30 September 1971*, pp. 15–19.

Industrial relations and the law – problems of legal intervention, to be found on pp. 247–63 in *Proceedings of a Seminar: Problems and*

Prospects of Socio-Legal Research, Nuffield College, Oxford, June–July 1971 (Oxford, 1972).

The Responsibility of the Employer for the Acts of His Employees, Proceedings of the Third Colloquy on European Law, Julius-Maximilianus University of Würzburg, 4 and 5 October 1972 (Council of Europe, Strasbourg), pp. 21–4, 60–1, 74–5, 81–2, 94–5.

Fourth Countess Markievicz Memorial Lecture, November 1979, Dublin. Published as *Irish Labour Law: Sword or Shield?* (Dublin Irish Association for Industrial Relations, 1981).

Southall, 23 April 1979: The Report of the Unofficial Committee of Inquiry (Chairman, Professor Michael Dummett, FBA, Wykeham Professor of Philosophy and Logic, University of Oxford) National Council for Civil Liberties, 1980: *Death of Blair Peach: Supplementary Report of the Unofficial Committee of Inquiry* (NCCL, 1980).

ARTICLES, ETC.

Americal Journal of Legal History

A select bibliography of Irish legal history, 4 (1960), pp. 173–80.

A select bibliography of Irish legal history - part 2, 8 (1964), pp. 261–3.

A select bibliography of Irish legal history - part 3, 13 (1969), pp. 233–40.

Annuaire de l'Association des Auditeurs et Anciens Auditeurs de l'Académie de Droit International de La Haye

The study of international law in Ireland, 29 (1959), pp. 68–73.

British Yearbook of International Law

Irish extradition law and practice, 34 (1958), pp. 274–311.

Unlawful seizure and irregular extradition, 36 (1960), pp. 279–320.

Bulletin of the Industrial Law Society

(With B. A. Hepple) Bibliography of periodical literature - 1, no. 8 (1970), pp. 16–17.

(With B. A. Hepple) Bibliography of periodical literature - 2, no. 10 (1971), pp. 13–14.

Adjudication of social security claims, no. 10 (1971), pp. 16–17.

(With B. A. Hepple) Bibliography of periodical literature - 3, no. 11 (1971), pp. 11–12.

Cambridge Law Journal

The Lawless case, 20 (1962), pp. 234–51.

Disguised extradition: extradition or deportation, 21 (1963), pp. 10–13.

Flaw in procedure fatal to claim, 21 (1963), pp. 172–3.

Death in police custody, 22 (1964), pp. 9–12.

Contracts of Employment Act, 1963, 22 (1964), pp. 220–3.

Complaints against the police, 23 (1965), pp. 53–6.

Redundancy Payments Act, 1965, 23 (1965), pp. 222–4.

Trade Disputes Act, 1965, 24 (1966), pp. 34–5.

Collective agreement - breach, 24 (1966), pp. 31–4.

When is an employee not an employee?, 25 (1967), pp. 27–30.

Legal meaning of 'notice to strike', 25 (1967), pp. 186–8.

Legal effect of strike notice, 26 (1968), pp. 223–7.

Report on the lump, 26 (1968), pp. 230–2.

Extradition - offence of a political character - terrorism, 32 (1973), pp. 181–3.

Cambridge Opinion

Reflections on periodicals dealing with international affairs, no. 44 (1966), p. 32.

The right to strike, no. 45 (1966), pp. 18–21.

The Conveyancer and Property Lawyer

(With B. A. Hepple) Drafting employment terms, 36 (1972), pp. 77–88.

Criminal Law Review

Voluntary deportation, 1963, pp. 680–6.

The reform of British extradition law, 1963, pp. 805–10.

Recent practice under the Fugitive Offenders Act, 1965, pp. 133–46.

The Challenor Report - I, 1965, pp. 633–5.

Rhodesian crisis - criminal liabilities, 1966, pp. 5–16 (with B. A. Hepple and C. C. Turpin).

Dublin University Law Review

William Sampson (1764–1836), 2 (1970), pp. 45–52.

Gazette of the Incorporated Law Society of Ireland

The Bourke extradition case, 65 (1971), pp. 5–6.

Haldane Society Bulletin

Political strikes, January 1974, pp. 9–11.

Human Rights Review

Numerous notes, 1979–1981.

The closed shop and the European Convention, 6 (1981), pp. 22–7.

The Independent

Time to establish an international Court to try alleged terrorists, 1 December 1988.

Index on Censorship

The Irish television sackings, 2 (1973), pp. 21–14.

Indian Yearbook of International Affairs

History of British extradition law and practice, 13 (part 2), pp. 79–115.

Industrial Design

Time to invest in factory safety, no. 249 (1969), pp. 52–3.

Industrial Law Journal

Literature on the Industrial Relations Act, 1 (1972), pp. 55–60.

(With B. A. Hepple and J. Neeson) Bibliography of periodical literature on British and Irish labour law (no. 4), 1 (1972), pp. 122–4.

(With B. A. Hepple and J. Neeson) Bibliography of periodical literature on British and Irish labour law (no. 5), 2 (1973), pp. 62–4.

(With B. A. Hepple and J. Neeson) Bibliography of periodical literature on British and Irish labour law (no. 6), 2 (1973), pp. 123–4.

Strike notices; another approach, 2 (1973), pp. 152–7.

Constructive dismissal and unfair dismissal, 2 (1973), pp. 238–9.

Bibliography of periodical literature on British and Irish labour law published in 1979 and 1980, 11 (1982), pp. 43–68.

Bibliography of periodical literature on British and Irish labour law published in 1981, 11 (1982), pp. 202–12; 12 (1983), pp. 52–65.

Bibliography of periodical literature on British and Irish labour law published in 1982, 12 (1983), pp. 187–95.

Bibliography of periodical literature on British and Irish labour law published in 1983, 13 (1984), pp. 185–91.

Bibliography of periodical literature on British and Irish labour law published in 1984, 14 (1985), pp. 233–42.

Recently published books: 1 (on labour law), 15 (1986), pp. 214–18.

Bibliography of British and Irish labour law published in 1985, 16 (1987), pp. 74–6, 138–44.
Recently published books: 2, 16 (1987), pp. 69–73.
Recently published books: 3, 17 (1988), pp. 63–72.
Bibliography of periodical literature on British and Irish labour law published in 1987 and 1988, 18 (1989), pp. 262–72.
Recently published books: 4, 18 (1989), pp. 182–92.
Recently published books: 5, 19 (1990), pp. 260–8.

Industrial Relations Review and Report
Legally enforceable agreements, no. 12 (1971), pp. 3–6.
Strikes and the Industrial Relations Act, no. 29 (1972), pp. 3–6.

Industrial Society
Donovan Commission - alterations in the law, 50 (September 1968), pp. 7–9, 25.
The Industrial Relations Bill - what will it achieve?, 53 (January 1971), pp. 7–10.
'Acting in contemplation . . .', 61 (November/December 1979), pp. 13, 20.

International and Comparative Law Quarterly
De Demko v *Secretary of State for Home Affairs*, 8 (1959), pp. 412–13.
R v *Governor of Brixton Prison, ex parte Minervini*, 8 (1959), pp. 413–16 (case note).
The Irish Maritime Jurisdiction Act, 1959, 9 (1960), pp. 325–34.
Re Shuter, 9 (1960), pp. 141–4 (case note).
IRC v *Collco Dealings Ltd*, 9 (1960), pp. 139–40 (case note).
Extradition within the Commonwealth, 9 (1960), pp. 486–91.
European Convention on Extradition, 9 (1960), pp. 491–4.
Extradition - a postscript to *Re Caborn-Waterfield*, 10 (1961), pp. 339–44 (case note).
The Enaharo case, 12 (1963), pp. 1364–78.
The Irish Extradition Act, 1965, 15 (1966), pp. 369–94.

International Law Reports
Reports on Irish cases.

Irish Jurist
English law and the Irish question, 1 (1966), pp. 59–65.

Irish Times
How the practice of extradition has arisen, 29 March 1984.
Time for an international court, 2 December 1988.

Journal of the Chartered Building Societies Institute
The Employment Act 1982, 37 (April 1983), pp. 70–1.

Law Journal
Anglo-Irish extradition, 116 (1965), pp. 69–70.

Law Librarian
Legal printing in Ireland in the eighteenth century, (December, 1986).

The Listener
When is a worker not a worker?, 27 April 1967, p. 549.

Modern Law Review
Blasphemy in Irish law, 23 (1960), pp. 151–66.
Wright v *FitzGerald* revisited, 25 (1962), pp. 413–22.
Disguised extradition: the *Soblen* case, 27 (1964), pp. 521–39.
(With M. T. Partington) Industrial conflict: judicial attitudes, 32 (1969), pp. 53–8.
The Northern Ireland Act 1972, 35 (1972), pp. 295–8.

New Community
Review article on international migration law, 2 (1973), pp. 217–18.

New Society
Deportation and extradition, 26 February 1965.
Industrial legislation, 28 March 1968.
Factory legislation, 4 April 1968.
Dead or injured at work, 28 November 1968.

Northern Ireland Legal Quarterly
William Ridgeway (1765–1817) - law reporter, 18 (1967), pp. 208–22.
Arthur Browne (1756–1805): an Irish civilian, 20 (1969), pp. 255–73.

Petroleum Legislation
Petroleum legislation of the Republic of Ireland.

Rights
The closed shop, 4 (5) (1980), pp. 2–3.

State Service
Civil servants and the Bill, (1971), pp. 144–5, 152.

Topics

The Employment Act 1982, 8 (1983), pp. 9–11.
Statutory sick pay, 10 (1983), pp. 12–13.

Yearbook of European Institute of Social Security

European social policy at the crossroads: British and European social policy, (1992), pp. 97–110.

Book Reviews

Several hundred, mainly in the following periodicals: *Cambridge Law Journal*, *Cambridge Review*, *Industrial Law Journal*, *International and Comparative Law Quarterly* and *Journal of the Royal Asiatic Society*.

Index